FROM
TRASH
TO
TREASURE

From Trash to Treasure
By Judith Miller

First published in Great Britain in 2012 by Miller's, a division of Mitchell Beazley,
imprints of Octopus Publishing Group Ltd, Endeavour House,
189 Shaftesbury Avenue, London, WC2H 8JY.
www.octopusbooks.co.uk

An Hachette UK company
www.hachette.co.uk

Miller's is a registered trademark of Octopus Publishing Group Ltd.
www.millersguides.com

Copyright © Octopus Publishing Group Ltd 2012

ISBN 978 1 84533 711 7

A CIP record for this book is available from the British Library

Printed and bound in China

BBC Antiques Roadshow Contributors Marc Allum, John Bly, Adam Schoon

Text Contributors Marc Allum, Anna Southgate
Restoration Consultants Anna Barcock, Steve Luker,
Vicki Smallwood, John Wainwright
Specially commissioned photography Graham Rae

Publisher Alison Starling
Head of Editorial Tracey Smith
Project Editor Julie Brooke
Design Tracy Killick Art Direction and Design; Ali Scrivens, TJ Graphics
Copy Editor Carolyn Madden
Editorial Assistant Katy Armstrong
Indexer Hilary Bird
Art Director Jonathan Christie
Production Caroline Alberti
Photograph of Judith Miller by Chris Terry

Jacket images
Front: (left to right in rows)
A Gallé nest of four walnut and marquetry tables, see
page 35; A rare large Yuan Dynasty mid-14thC Chinese
blue and white double gourd vase, see page 97; A
Steiff centre seam bear, see page 213; A Wedgwood
'Sheringham' candlestick, see page 119; A limited
edition Swatch wristwatch, see page 210; A Dinky
Automatic Morris Mini-Minor, see page 210; A red
Bakelite telephone, see page 146.

Back: (left to right in rows)
Repairing torn leather, see page 32; An early Meissen
teapot, see page 78; A 1940s telephone cable handbag,
£60-80; An anglepoise lamp, see page 56.

Page 3: vase, see page 17; perfume bottle, see page 184.

FROM
TRASH
TO
TREASURE

Don't throw stuff out –
fix it, give it a makeover,
or sell it and make money

JUDITH MILLER

CONTENTS

How to use this book

The information on each page will help you to identify when your treasures were made, the materials used to make them and their value. You will also find out how to care for them.

Good, better, best compares three examples to show you how to value similar objects.

The images are examples of pieces you may find at home.

Would you believe it? Surprising facts about treasure you may find in your home.

The colours of the sidebars show which chapter you are in.

The captions explain the value of the items.

List of materials and equipment you will need.

Easy-to-follow steps show you how to renovate items in your home to increase their appeal and potential value.

Before and after photographs show the results.

Photographs show the most common examples to look for to help with identification and valuing.

Fact box gives additional information.

Foreword

I bought my first antique when I was a student at Edinburgh University in the 1970s. I was fascinated by the blue-and-white plates I picked up in junk shops for a few old pennies. I became intrigued by where they were made, by whom and when and whether they could be worth more than I had paid. It was immediately obvious that 'china' covered very different materials. And so I became ensnared by the captivating world of antiques and collectables.

Many of us have accumulated treasures from different sources. We may have started collecting when we inherited certain objects, we may have been given gifts or even found objects in an attic when buying a property. These 'things' may have been hidden away in the back of a cupboard, in a garage or at the back of a drawer. The inspiration for this book came from the number of questions I get asked about how to value such treasures, how to do basic repairs and then what to do with them if there is no one in the family interested in inheriting them or when we need to down size or just de-clutter.

Antiques go in and out of fashion. Many Victorian objects, particularly 'brown furniture' and floral tea sets, are difficult to shift at the moment and probably should remain in the attic, whereas there is a strong demand for Mid-century Modern objects. That 1960s Whitefriars vase that you've always hated could sell very well in a Decorative Arts sale, and the Christian Dior necklace which was once regarded as 'of no commercial value' could now sell on eBay for several hundreds of pounds. Also should you have any early Chinese ceramics or jade, particularly Imperial wares, now could be the time to sell, with Chinese buyers competing with each other to buy the most interesting examples. Later examples of Chinese art may be worth holding onto.

This book will open your eyes to the possibilities of inspecting your treasures and finding out what they are really worth. Read this before you take anything to the charity shop, car boot sale or the church jumble. You could be sitting on a fortune!

Judith Miller.

▲ **Whitefriars vase**
Kingfisher Drunken Bricklayer vase by Geoffrey Baxter for Whitefriars. 33cm (13in) high. **£1,000-1,500**

▼ **Plastic radio**
A Fada Streamliner Model 1000 Bullet radio, with Butterscotch Catalin case and knobs. 1940 26cm (10¼in) wide **£300-400**

◀ **Chinese Kangxi period 'Soldier' vase**
Painted with a central band of dragons. 36in (92cm) high **£150,000-250,000**

HOW DO I IDENTIFY MY TREASURES?
Using the P.L.A.C.A.R.D. test to assess value

Despite what you might imagine from watching antiques programmes on television, many beloved heirlooms are worth little to people outside the family. So how can you assess what you own and bring your hidden treasures to light?

It is always interesting to find out where people have discovered their 'treasures'. The Ming canister vase used as a stick stand, the Biba dress in the dressing-up box, the 18th-century treen goblet used to keep fish food – the most unloved object can be worth money. It is also surprising what is worth very little and should be despatched to a jumble sale.

Always look at an object carefully. Would it benefit from restoration or even a simple clean? Could some research make it more saleable online? Does someone in the family know about its history – possibly giving it some provenance?

How to find valuable objects

Unappreciated presents frequently end up in the back of a cupboard, only to resurface when the great-aunt or old friend is coming for tea. As we show in this book, some unfashionable objects from the past are now in vogue again. For example, there is tremendous interest in all the 'retro' and vintage objects from the Mid-century Modern period after World War II. Many of the streamlined, modern, brightly coloured objects that were beloved by the young housewives of the time are again finding a ready market with the young. Unfortunately, there

P.L.A.C.A.R.D.

Most valuers say that putting a value on an antique or collectable is a combination of years of experience and gut instinct. That is not much help to the rest of us. In fact, there are various things you must consider and I have

devised this simple acronym to help you: P.L.A.C.A.R.D. – Provenance, Location, Age, Condition, Attractiveness, Rarity and Desirability. Use a combination of these factors to help you to identify the treasures in your home.

▲ **PROVENANCE**
This is an immensely important factor, especially for rock and pop, royal and sporting memorabilia. This autographed and inscribed copy of Tim Graham's *Diana, HRH Princess of Wales* is signed 'To Mandy with love from Diana' and dated. It sold, with a photograph of Mandy meeting the Princess and a letter relating to its provenance, for **£320**. Without this cast-iron provenance the book is worth less than 10p.

◄ **LOCATION**
If you want to sell an item linked to a town, the best price may be had there. Scottish or Irish silver tends to get better prices in Edinburgh and Dublin. This is also true of Tunbridgeware. This hand-painted sewing compendium, modelled as a Brighton Pavilion dome, made around 1825 and 23cm (9in) high, sold in Tunbridge Wells for **£6,000**.

▲ **AGE**
Age is significant when combined with rarity or desirability. Much ancient Chinese pottery is worth less than 18th-century pieces. Roman glass has little appeal, unless large and a rare shape. On a good day this *c.*100 AD Roman flask, 17cm (6.5in) high, is worth **£100-150**.

are also areas that remain completely out of fashion, such as most Victoriana and 'brown furniture'.

You may be amazed at what you can find in your attics or cellars. On one occasion a gentleman arrived on the BBC's Antiques Roadshow with a large silver bowl which was blackened with age and had squirrel droppings in it from being stored in the attic. Imagine his delight when he was told that it was made by the legendary English silversmith Paul Storr in 1808 and was worth between £20,000-30,000. Or the lady who had bought a pot plant in an old dirty vase. She carefully re-potted the plant and stuck the vase in the garage. She was truly shocked to find that it was a 'Poissons' vase by the great French glassmaker René Lalique. It had been made in 1921, is popular with collectors today and worth £20,000.

If you have an object that no one in the family wants, find out exactly what it is and what's it worth using the P.L.A.C.A.R.D. test below. Then you may want to take it to your local auction house, sell it online or drop it in to a charity shop. But that is the exciting part.

Would you believe it?

This Chinese vase was found on top of a wardrobe in a bungalow in Pinner, Middlesex, in 2011. It was commissioned for the Qianlong Emperor (1736-1795), probably for the summer palace or the Forbidden City, from the legendary kilns at Jingdezhen in Jiangxi province. It went into a sale at Bainbridge's in Ruislip, Middlesex, along with house clearance objects, including washing machines. The hammer dropped at £43 million (£51.6 million including buyer's premium). During the Second Opium War in 1860, objects looted from the palaces were sold for very little to British and French sailors, who had no idea of their worth. Some may still lurk, unappreciated, at the back of a cupboard. Have a look in yours!

▶ **Unexpected treasure**
A 40.5cm (16in) high reticulated double-walled vase, or *yang cai*, with famille rose decoration worth in excess of **£50 million**.

▲ **CONDITION**
Condition can have a dramatic effect on value. This inlaid cylinder bureau, which is 111cm (43¾in) wide, was made by Frenchman François Linke in 1910 and would usually sell for a considerable sum. But its extraordinary condition means it is worth **£150,000** or more. An auction house would catalogue it as immaculate.

▲ **ATTRACTIVENESS**
An object considered by many to be beautiful will tend to fetch more. This Goldscheider figure of a woman walking a borzoi is stylish and epitomises the elegance of the Art Deco period. At 43cm (17in) high, it would sell for **£1,500-2,000** – double the price of a less appealing female figure.

▲ **RARITY**
This is a prime value factor. Collectors want what others don't have. Apple-shaped teapots are scarce. It is Scottish silver, by a known maker, Colin MacKenzie of Edinburgh, with an early date, 1721, and only one other example is known: in the National Museum of Scotland. 581g (20½oz) 15cm (6in) high **£10,000-15,000**.

▲ **DESIRABILITY**
The most important factor of all. An object can satisfy all the other criteria but if no one wants it, it will be worth little. *The Riding Crop* is regarded as one of the best works by one of the greatest sculptors, Austrian Bruno Zach. It was made in the early 1930s, 84cm (33in) high, and it is a must for any collector. **£100,000-150,000**.

HOW DO I DATE MY TREASURES?
18th-century style

Understanding the style of the objects in your home can help you to date them. In the early 18th century, fashionable objects were handmade for the wealthy, initially in the ornate Rococo style. By the 1750s, its flamboyant shells and scrolls had been replaced by the more restrained lines of Neoclassicism.

The 17th century was dominated by the heavy Baroque style, which featured carving, gilding and floral marquetry. It lingered into the 18th century, but tastes were changing. Palladianism, briefly popular during the reign of George I (1714-1727), was bold and austere, noted for its classical motifs and rigid symmetry. It was derived from the writings and engravings of the 16th-century Italian architect, Andrea Palladio, and was influenced by the symmetry and perspective of the classical architecture of Ancient Greece and Rome.

Back to nature

By 1715, a lighter style had begun to emerge in France. Known as 'Rococo', it was influenced by nature and was popular in Britain by around 1735. The term is derived from the French words *rocaille* (rockwork) and *coquillage* (shellwork) which are distinctive features of the style. It was initially confined to repeating patterns of shells and scrolls on symmetrical pieces, but soon became more extravagant and asymmetric. Chinese motifs were also fashionable and chinoiserie (a European interpretation of Oriental artworks) featured widely. Furniture

▲ **Embellished simplicity**
Before 1740, coffee pots featured little decoration, but after this date they were often embellished with chased flowerheads, fruit and scroll designs, as seen on this George II silver example by Scottish silversmith Ebenezer Oliphant.

▼ **Birth of Rococo**
This Irish George III mahogany side table typifies Rococo style. Furniture often featured cabriole legs with acanthus carving and ball-and-claw feet and was decorated with central shell motifs.

▶ **Meissen magic**
Lively modelling and a sense of movement are hallmarks of early Meissen porcelain figures. The idyllic pastoral details and allegorical subjects reflect the romance of the Rococo style. Some of the finest figures were made by the factory's German chief modeller Johann Joachim Kändler.

◀ **Extravagant decoration**
From the 18th century onwards, French clock-makers produced a wide range of clocks, many of them highly sophisticated and with ornate decoration, as featured on this Louis XV pendulum clock. Boulle marquetry, tortoiseshell, mother-of-pearl and lacquer were used to create colourful designs which were framed by extravagant gilt-bronze mounts.

▲ **Chinese influence**
This gilt salon mirror displays fashionable chinoiserie motifs such as pagodas, lattices and openwork friezes. A leading exponent of the Rococo style was English cabinet-maker Thomas Chippendale, who first published his book of furniture designs in 1754. His models were copied throughout the world.

became lighter and more curvaceous. Cabriole (S-shaped) legs finished with scrolled or ball-and-claw feet were a common feature of furniture, which was typically made of mahogany.

Having developed the first hard-paste European porcelain in 1713, the German Meissen factory continued to dominate the ceramics market in terms of quality and influence. Meissen soon adopted the emergent Rococo style. Pieces were highly embellished with repeating rock and shell patterns and scrolls. Bright, durable enamel colours (also known as *petit feu* or low-temperature colours) were used to depict realistic flowers and foliage on porcelain.

Birth of Neoclassicism

Within 20 years, the fashion for the Rococo style had waned. The excavations of the Roman cities of Herculaneum (1738) and Pompeii (1748) led to renewed interest in classical subjects and styles. Palmettes (fan-shaped palm leaves) and festoons (garlands), urns, ram's heads and stylised corn husks were used abundantly. As it had with Rococo, France led the way with the new, or 'Neoclassical', style.

The Scottish architect Robert Adam was one of many young men to embark on a 'Grand Tour' of the classical sites of Europe. On his return in 1758, he began designing furniture in a more sophisticated, delicate variation of Palladianism. Legs were slender and tapering, edges were straight and decoration was classically inspired. Meanwhile, in Staffordshire, Josiah Wedgwood pushed the boundaries of pottery manufacture.

By the 1770s, most shapes across the European decorative arts were straight and elegant, and classical decorative motifs were predominant.

▲ **Gilded restraint**
Neoclassical style brought a degree of austerity to late 18th-century design. Swirling Rococo decoration was replaced by a more restrained geometry. Gilding added a sense of opulence, as displayed on this French Louis XVI armchair.

HOW DO I DATE MY TREASURES?
Early 19th-century style

The Neoclassical style was still popular during the first half of the 19th century but it had begun to evolve. It assumed a variety of local characteristics as it was developed in countries across Europe. The most influential of these was the French Empire style. Increased mass production made it widely available.

▶ **Machine engraving**
Advances in steam-powered machinery enabled glass factories to create elegant etched and engraved designs cheaply and efficiently. This early 19th-century rummer is etched and engraved with an Irish harp and birds.

New style for an Emperor

Napoleon Bonaparte rose to power in the late 18th century and crowned himself Emperor of France in 1804. The Empire style was inspired in part by his many victories and featured numerous military motifs, such as laurel wreaths, medallions and eagles. Napoleon's Egyptian expedition of 1798 was the source of ancient Egyptian motifs, including sphinxes and scarab beetles. The fashion for the Empire style spread across continental Europe. Although the aristocracy in the German states and Austria embraced Empire style, the middle classes favoured a more relaxed form of Neoclassicism that became known as 'Biedermeier' style. This emphasised clean lines and minimal ornamentation.

In Britain, Neoclassicism evolved into the Regency style. George, Prince of Wales, ruled as Regent from 1811 until he was crowned George IV in 1820. His elaborate tastes influenced the rest of the country. Like the Empire style, Regency style favoured symmetry and classical forms, but it was lighter and more elegant than Empire. The Regency style rejected most Napoleonic motifs and embraced influences from farther afield.

Roman inspiration

In both France and Britain, furniture designers drew inspiration from ancient history and were increasingly interested in accurately replicating classical forms. Numerous chairs were modelled on the curule (a chair used by Roman officials) and many others were given X-frames or sabre (out-turned) legs. Mahogany was still the wood of choice, but improved transport links, such as the canal system and the first

◀ **Egyptian embellishments**
Design books by the French architects Charles Percier and Pierre Fontaine helped to publicise the Empire style. This early 19th-century mahogany and cherry-veneered table features gilded sphinxes and is strongly influenced by a design from a book they published in 1808.

railways, made a larger variety of richly coloured exotic woods available. Cabinet-makers used these woods to create complex marquetry (inlaid) designs.

The early 19th century saw a revolution in the glass industry. A new steam-cutting process, introduced to Britain in 1789, allowed a whole range of glass-cutting treatments that had previously been impossible. Fluting, diamond cutting and hobnail (a form of diamond cutting with stars at the centre of the diamonds) were all used to make glass sparkle in candlelight. In Bohemia (now part of the Czech Republic), glass-makers experimented with coloured glass in an attempt to replicate Roman glass discovered in the 18th century. Count von Buquoy created red marbled glass in 1803 and jet-black Hyalith glass in 1817. Frederich Egerman patented his marbled Lithyalin glass in 1827.

Contemporary porcelain was richly gilded and colourful to complement opulent Empire and Regency interiors. The supremacy of Meissen as the leading European porcelain-maker was already challenged by the French Sèvres factory. By the beginning of the 19th century, while Meissen was still pre-eminent, factories such as Berlin in Germany and Vienna in Austria were coming to the fore.

▶ **Classical grandeur**
Wedgwood employed Neoclassical-style motifs on its jasperware pottery. The decoration, designed by eminent artists such as Englishmen John Flaxman and George Stubbs, was based on illustrations of recently excavated ancient Greek and Roman artefacts.

▲ **Gilded luxury**
Sumptuous gilding was used to enhance interiors inspired by ancient Greece and Rome. Classically decorated rooms were filled with gilded furniture and accessories. This early 19th-century French clock features an Empire-style table and stool in miniature, as well as Venus – the Roman goddess of love, prosperity and military victory.

◀ **Statement of power**
In Russia, the Empire style became bolder than it had been in France. Furniture, such as this early 19th-century mahogany-veneered armchair, was generously proportioned and featured high-quality carving and gilding. Here, the front legs are in the form of lions' heads and paws – symbols of bravery, strength and power.

HOW DO I DATE MY TREASURES?
Late 19th-century style

As the century progressed, and countries such as Italy and Germany became unified, a sense of nationalism pervaded in Europe. This led to a revival of the dominant styles of the previous 500 years, including Gothic, Renaissance, Baroque and Rococo. New methods of mass production made goods more affordable and available but it also provoked the Arts and Crafts movement as a reaction against it.

Motifs from architecture

The first of these revival styles was Neo-Gothic. Motifs taken from architecture, such as pointed arches, latticework and quatrefoils, and heraldry, were used on furniture, fabrics and tablewares. Stained glass was revived for domestic use.

In France and Italy, there was a return to the Renaissance style. Oak and walnut furniture was carved with spindles and fretwork. Meissen and Sèvres produced porcelain decorated with classical figures, grotesques and scarabs. In Britain, many factories began making a form of richly glazed ceramic known as 'majolica'. Its name was based on that of maiolica, a type of tin-glazed earthenware produced in Italy from the Renaissance period.

Neo-Baroque furniture – based on 17th-century Baroque pieces – was carved with foliage and elements from classical architecture, such as pediments. Decorative techniques from that era were revived, including Boulle marquetry (inlaid bronze), marquetry (inlaid wood) and *pietra dura* (inlaid marble). The Rococo style also enjoyed a revival. The Industrial

▲ **Fine art replica**
The new middle classes showed their sophistication and love of art by decorating their homes with Renaissance-style statues. Parian porcelain figures, such as this bust of *The Bride*, after Raffaele Monti made in 1861 (the original was exhibited at the Great Exhibition), were made by the Copeland factory.

▶ **Rococo revisited**
Porcelain vases with covers, encrusted with finely modelled flowers and painted with further blooms, epitomise the extravagance of the Rococo Revival style. First made by German factories in Dresden, they were also produced by English company Coalport between 1820 and 1850, and became known as 'English Dresden'.

▲ **Colour and light**
Throughout the 19th century glass-makers were discovering new ways to colour glass. Towards the end of the century enamelled decoration was revived. These late 19th-century Bohemian glass girandoles use a combination of these techniques and are hung with cut lead crystal lustres which would have sparkled in the candlelight.

Extravagant ornamentation
Rococo Revival pieces, such as this silver candelabrum from 1875, feature larger, heavier and more sinuous forms than the 18th-century originals, with a greater profusion of ornament – typically shells, flowers and scrollwork. A putto with a horn decorates the stem.

Revolution had brought advances in veneer cutting, carving and metal casting. This enabled Rococo furniture to be produced at a fraction of what it had cost in the 18th century.

Meissen excelled at producing porcelain encrusted with floral ornament and heavily decorated with gilding and enamel.

A mix of styles

Neoclassicism, which had been popular at the beginning of the century, was revived. The driving force behind this style was the new Emperor of France, Napoleon III, who ruled from 1848 to 1870. Some pieces were direct copies of examples from the 17th and 18th centuries; others combined details from several styles, often at the expense of decorative cohesion.

New industrial techniques reduced the cost of furniture and decorative arts, enabling them to be sold far more cheaply to the growing middle classes. The Arts and Crafts movement, which emerged around 1880, rejected mass production and called for a balance between art and craftsmanship. The English writer and art critic John Ruskin and designer William Morris led the movement, which encouraged a return to the skills of medieval craftsmen. Arts and Crafts pieces were simple and functional. Ornament was sparse but included Celtic motifs, enamelling and a wide variety of new ceramic glazes.

The sinuous Art Nouveau style was also a reaction to the glut of revival styles in the late 19th century and a desire for a fresh approach. The style had spread from Paris to the major cities of Europe by 1895 and the rest of the world by 1900.

Luxury on display
In the mid-19th century the increasing wealth of the growing middle classes led to a greater emphasis on the display of luxury furnishings. This showed itself in a demand for large case furniture for libraries and other reception rooms.

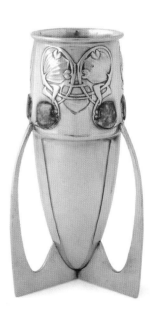

Celtic nostalgia
Liberty & Co. in Regent Street, London, has been at the forefront of design since it opened in 1875. Among the first movements it promoted was the Arts and Crafts style which Liberty popularised through its furniture, Tudric pewter and Cymric silver. This c.1900 Tudric pewter and enamel vase was designed for the store by Manxman Archibald Knox.

HOW DO I DATE MY TREASURES?
Early 20th-century style

The feminine Art Nouveau style remained popular until World War I. It was superseded by two rectilinear styles. Art Deco was influenced by the machine age, jazz and many historical styles and was the first style available to all. Modernism advocated function over decoration.

A feminine style

The term 'Art Nouveau' was derived from the *Maison de l'Art Nouveau* gallery, which opened in Paris in 1895. Influenced by nature, the style was elegant and feminine, with exotic materials, asymmetrical lines and rich colours. Plants and sensuous women were popular motifs, often metamorphosing from one to another to create *femme fleur* (half woman, half flower). The whiplash motif, based on swirling roots, is iconic.

Glass-makers, such as Frenchman Emile Gallé, produced extravagant cameo glass, furniture was carved and veneered, metalware was enamelled and set with semi-precious stones. The high level of decoration made it expensive and, with the arrival of austere times, increasingly unviable.

▲ **Sensuous women**
The female form, often semi-clad in diaphanous robes, was frequently used in Art Nouveau sculpture. This early 20th-century lamp, by French designer Raoul Larche, shows the American dancer Loie Fuller. She performed in Paris wearing sheer, veiled costumes and came to embody the Art Nouveau style.

◄ **Whiplash marquetry**
Swirling whiplash lines were used to decorate everything from furniture to metalwares. Here inlaid plant stems extend across an Art Nouveau mahogany and rosewood display cabinet made by Thos. Edwards & Sons in Newcastle-under-Lyme, Staffordshire.

Design for the masses

The Modernist movement attempted to bring affordable design to the masses. Its followers believed in the potential of machines to change the world and embraced manmade materials such as tubular steel. Designs were geometric and without ornament. Chief exponents included Swiss-born French architect Le Corbusier and German architect Walter Gropius. In 1919, Gropius opened the influential Bauhaus school in Germany.

Modernism flourished alongside what became known as 'Art Deco'. The style took its name from the *Exposition Internationale des Arts Décoratifs et Industriels Modernes* which was held in Paris in 1925. It featured strong geometric lines and stylised decoration. Manufacturers affected by the global Depression produced sleek, contoured forms that lent themselves to mass production using new, cheap materials, such as plastic, aluminium and chrome. The Art Deco style also embraced fine craftsmanship, with many furniture-makers employing exotic wood inlays. Boldly coloured, geometric patterns were created by English ceramics designer Clarice Cliff and glass-makers such as Frenchman René Lalique, whose glass often used repeated patterns.

Art Deco is often referred to as the first international style. It influenced design on every continent and drew on inspiration from around the world, including historic European styles, Egyptian motifs, contemporary avant-garde art and the machine age. Women remained popular motifs but, where they had been languorous in Art Nouveau, they were now shown dancing and participating in sports – reflecting their growing independence after World War I. Art Deco's influence was wide-ranging, affecting the design of buildings, vehicles, typography, furniture and domestic appliances.

▶ **Athletic women**
By the 1920s women were increasingly independent. They wore shorter skirts, played energetic sports and smoked in public. Sculptors celebrated this by creating daring figures wearing revealing costumes (if they wore anything at all) and performing exotic dances. This new liberation can be seen in the bronze figure *Con Brio* by Austrian Josef Lorenzl. This new feminine ideal was a marked contrast to the romantic, natural woman who had inspired the Art Nouveau movement.

◀ **Jazz Age ceramics**
Designer Clarice Cliff combined traditional subjects, such as flowers and landscapes, with bold colours and Cubist shapes to create a range of instantly recognisable ceramics called the Bizarre and Fantasque ranges. This 1930s Red Autumn square stepped vase, shape 369, bearing the combined Bizarre-Fantasque mark, was hand-painted with a stylised tree and cottage landscape.

▶ **Streamlined style**
The Jumo French Art Deco desk lamp by Brevette, *c.*1945, was made from Bakelite, one of the new plastics which helped to make the Art Deco style available to all. It was one of many streamlined homewares which celebrated machine technology.

HOW DO I DATE MY TREASURES?
Late 20th-century style

Materials that had been invented to aid the war effort were put to peacetime use by Modernist designers to create sleek, functional, affordable pieces. Postmodernism emerged in the 1980s as designers experimented with colour and symbolism.

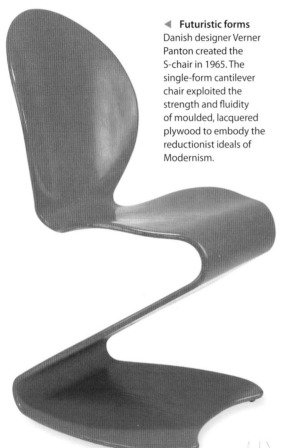

◀ **Futuristic forms**
Danish designer Verner Panton created the S-chair in 1965. The single-form cantilever chair exploited the strength and fluidity of moulded, lacquered plywood to embody the reductionist ideals of Modernism.

Post-war optimism

Many countries were still recovering from the financial cost of World War II during the early 1950s, but with economic recovery came a mood of optimism and a desire for innovative consumer goods and a 'new look'.

Designs were created with clean lines and bright colours. Many were inspired by popular culture and the latest scientific advances, such as space travel and atomic theory. Designers embraced the new materials and manufacturing techniques that had been invented during the war. Furniture design exemplified this innovation, with pieces made from bent plywood, stainless steel and aluminium. The biggest change came as a result of the availability of petroleum-based plastics. Injection moulding techniques allowed designers to create pieces in previously impossible shapes and colours. Such was the popularity of plastic that even products made from other materials, such as Holmegaard's Carnaby glass range, were designed to imitate it.

Glass designers on the Venetian island of Murano reinvented and revitalised traditional techniques, employing bolder, brighter colours than before and exaggerating the patterns. In contrast to this, Scandinavian glass factories, such as Kosta, produced organically shaped pieces in pale colours.

▶ **Feature lighting**
Danish designer Poul Henningsen aimed to create an electric light which gave the same soft glow as the petroleum lamp. He succeeded with the copper-and-steel Artichoke lamp he designed for the firm Louis Poulsen in 1957.

▶ **Plastic look**
The bright colours and bold shapes of the Pop Art movement were seen in homewares. Glass designer Per Lutken's Carnaby range for Danish firm Holmegaard in the 1960s was designed to resemble plastic.

The simple, naturalistic approach used by Scandinavian glass-makers can also be seen in the furniture created by designers such as Finnish designer Alvar Aalto. Known as 'soft' modernism, the style was strongly inspired by nature and was consequently more likely to embrace wood than metal.

The effects of recession

By the 1970s, many countries were experiencing high inflation rates and mass unemployment. By 1975, a global recession was under way and the energy crisis in America, Europe and Japan made plastic far less affordable.

Mid-century Modernism was replaced with Postmodernism. Visual impact, rather than comfort or practicality, became the guiding principle in design. In reaction to the strict forms and block colours of Modernism, designers avoided symmetry and combined clashing colours and styles. The resulting designs, epitomised by the Italian design groups Alchima and Memphis, challenged the idea of 'good design' and were rich in symbolism and humour.

Economies began to improve again in the early 1990s. Minimalism replaced the excess and mix of styles seen in Postmodernism. Simple designs in glass, brushed metals and single-colour plastic were common. The digital revolution inspired smooth and technical designs. More importantly, it enabled ideas and images to be exchanged between different countries at high speed. This allowed the creation of a truly global style.

▲ **Space Age sculptural forms**
In the 1950s post-war optimism brought a sense of fun to homewares. Inspired by the space race and new materials such as Formica, furniture took on outlandish forms.

▶ **Exploring texture**
English designer Geoffrey Baxter worked at Whitefriars and experimented with different ways to add texture to the surface of mould-blown glass. He lined moulds with tree bark, bricks, wire and nails to create designs which have come to symbolise 1960s style. Perhaps the most famous is the Drunken Bricklayer vase.

◀ **Studio abstractions**
During the 1960s and 1970s, Poole Pottery encouraged its designers to create one-off pieces with abstract designs that have come to epitomise the era. This charger, decorated by Tony Morris, features a seagull flying out to sea.

FURNITURE

While exceptional quality and rarity will always sell and a piece of high-quality 18th-century furniture will usually fetch a high price, pieces of furniture no longer have to be more than a century old to have any value. Homeowners are buying examples from the mid-20th century which sum up the sleek designs of the post-war years. At the same time, traditionalists are still looking for classic furniture so do not dismiss these pieces when considering what may be worth selling.

Hans Wegner's 'Peacock' chair was inspired by the traditional Windsor chair. Many good-quality 18th and 19th-century Windsor chairs can be worth hundreds of pounds. Wegner's chair is highly valuable in its own right as it is a classic piece by a major 20th-century Danish designer. 104cm (41in) high **£3,000-4,000**

WHAT MAKES FURNITURE VALUABLE?
The effect of age, quality and condition

Antique but unexceptional furniture struggles to sell nowadays, although high-quality pieces almost always find a buyer. But if you have the 'right' piece, and it is fit for purpose, it will have sales potential. While the price may be hundreds of pounds rather than thousands, it may be worth something nonetheless.

▲ Regency splendour
Furniture from the Regency period at the beginning of the 19th century has held its value. This good-quality mahogany sideboard epitomises the flamboyant style that prevailed from 1800 to 1830. It is 214cm (84¼in) wide and could be worth as much as **£3,500-4,500**.

One common misconception is that the older a piece of furniture is, the higher its value. This has never been true. Age is just one factor to consider when assessing a piece. Other criteria include: where it was made and by whom; what materials were used; how well constructed it is; what condition it is in; who has owned it in the past; how desirable it is today; and whether it is useful.

The style guides at the beginning and end of this book will help you with identification. Age, materials, quality and provenance all feature here (see pages 8-9). Certain periods are more fashionable with buyers than others. For example, at the moment pieces from the early 19th and mid-20th centuries realise, or even exceed, their value at auction, while generic, 'brown' furniture from the 19th and early 20th centuries – typically Victorian and Edwardian mass-produced furniture – is failing to reach estimated values. In fact, this furniture is so hard to sell that some auction houses are turning it away. Much 19th-century furniture is currently worth less than an equivalent piece of flatpack furniture. Rarity and quality dictate this to some

▲ Reliable quality
Good-quality brown furniture, such as this 132cm (52in) wide early-Victorian rosewood library table, may follow current trends and dip in price but it will never be worthless. Pieces similar to this are worth hanging on to, as their time will come again. At the height of the market it might have been worth £1,500–2,000. Today it is estimated at **£700-1,000**.

◄ All in the name
Any piece of furniture that has a maker's label or is unquestionably attributable to a specific designer is going to be more valuable than a similar piece without such provenance. This 191cm (75¼in) high Arts and Crafts mahogany, bow-fronted cabinet was made by Shapland and Petter of Barnstaple and is worth **£800-1,200**.

The Great Exhibition

Showcasing over 13,000 designs from a wide range of international exhibitors, London's Great Exhibition (1851) had more than six million visitors in just six months. Featuring the latest designs in glassware, ceramics and furniture, as well as a number of cutting-edge inventions, the fair brought industry and craftsmanship together in a way not seen before. The event was hugely influential in disseminating the styles of the day to a much wider audience and led to wide-scale mass production of imitations at affordable prices.

▲ **Bucking the trend**
Although the value of brown furniture has fallen in recent years, there are always pieces that do not follow the trend. This mid-Victorian walnut centre table, 74cm (29in) high, is similar to one made by Henry Eyles of Bath that was displayed at the Great Exhibition. This piece is attributed to him, and such provenance gives it an impressive **£34,000** price tag.

▼ **20th-century classics**
Well-known designs from the mid-20th century have been popular with young urbanites since the turn of the 21st. Must-have pieces include those by American husband and wife team, Charles and Ray Eames. This later version of their rosewood-veneered lounge chair and matching ottoman, 77cm (30½in) high, with its original label, commands a healthy **£1,500-2,000**.

▶ **Falling values**
Even some attractive pieces of furniture are failing to hold their price in the downturn. While not an exceptional piece, this mahogany tub chair is a good one which would be useful in a bedroom. The slatted sides and out-swept legs are characteristic of the Neoclassical revival during the Edwardian era. In recent years its value has fallen from £400-500 to **£150-200**.

extent but trends also have an influence and some pieces are worth keeping. Brown furniture will almost certainly become desirable once more.

How to sell

Identifying the style and age of your piece is one thing but what about its construction? Was it made by hand or machine? Is the wood solid or veneered? Are all the original decorative finishes, fixtures and fittings still intact? Look closely at these as they help to determine how much a piece is worth. Size is also an issue: a large piece is hard to sell because it is difficult to find space for it in modern homes.

"Quality is the most important factor to take into consideration when looking at antique furniture. Then consider its condition and thirdly its visual appeal."

JOHN BLY BBC *ANTIQUES ROADSHOW* SPECIALIST

▶ **Timeless simplicity**
British-made Ercol furniture is reasonably easy to come by and tends to be durable. Made using solid ash, beech or elm, it falls under the mid-20th century umbrella and may increase in value. Currently a set of six chairs similar to this will fetch **£200-300**.

TREASURE SPOTTER'S GUIDE
How do I tell an original from a reproduction?

The most popular furniture styles have been copied innumerable times, so it is likely that you will find yourself in possession of a reproduction piece. But what if yours is an original? The difference in design may not be obvious but the difference in value could be significant. How are you going to know?

The industrialisation of the second half of the 19th century meant that furniture could be made on an unprecedented scale. Suddenly it was possible to produce large numbers of tables, chairs and chests in a relatively short time and at much lower cost. At the same time the burgeoning middle classes were increasing the demand for affordable furniture. Furthermore, machines could be adapted to take on complex craftsmanship – carving, veneering and inlaying – which paved the way for a revival of many styles from bygone eras. Copies of chairs, tables, desks and chests were often faithful to the originals they sought to imitate but are now worth a fraction of the price. So how can you tell them apart?

Two pieces of furniture may look identical but there will be a number of telltale signs that establish whether or not a piece is an original. The principles apply to all furniture. Consider the overall style of the piece: are carved elements integral to the piece or applied? What shape are the legs? What materials have been used to embellish it and how? Compare various elements with the style overviews given in this book (see pages 242-251) – does the piece have the right credentials for the period it represents?

Look at the construction details

Then there is the construction of the piece. Is it made from the appropriate wood for its era? If you look at an area not intended for show, such as the underside of a chair or table, or the back of a chest, you will be able to see more clearly how the piece has been made. There may be saw marks: circular for an item made by machine and more irregular for a piece made by hand. You will also be able to

Good, Better, Best Ball-and-claw feet

Carved elements on a piece of furniture offer an instant indication of quality and this is the case with ball-and-claw feet. First seen on fine examples during the early 18th century, the ball-and-claw was the foot most associated with the elegant, sinuous cabriole leg.

Things to look for include the attention to detail in the carved elements and that matching pairs do actually match, but you should also check that the proportions are correct, as both will determine the quality of a piece as a whole.

Good
The claw follows on naturally from the end of the leg, sweeping gently over the ball. The talons are widely spaced, with just their top surfaces carved to give them a three-dimensional shape. The tips of the claws rest against the ball.

Better
The slight curve at the base of the leg imitates the stance of the bird without stylisation. The gnarled, carved claws stretch all the way to the base of the ball and are perfectly proportioned. The carving here is more detailed: the claw tips are carved in the round and the ball decorated with a textured surface.

Best
Here, there is even greater detail in the carving and a real tension in the webbing between the talons. Again, the claws are widely spaced but they stand proud of the ball at the tips, which have been carved in the round.

see how various elements have been joined together – complex cabinet-maker's joints for an early piece or screws or glue for something made industrially. It may seem obvious, but does the piece look old? Are there signs of wear and tear or restoration carried out in the past?

Finally, consider the quality of any embellishment. Slight irregularities may indicate that any veneering, gilding or carving has been carried out by hand. Generally, more luxurious and exotic materials, such as ivory and fruitwood inlay, indicate that a piece is original, as these were less likely to be used on an industrial scale.

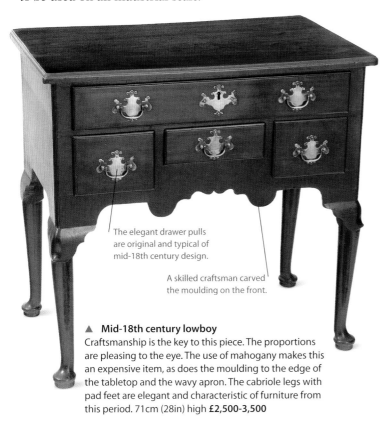

The elegant drawer pulls are original and typical of mid-18th century design.

A skilled craftsman carved the moulding on the front.

▲ **Mid-18th century lowboy**
Craftsmanship is the key to this piece. The proportions are pleasing to the eye. The use of mahogany makes this an expensive item, as does the moulding to the edge of the tabletop and the wavy apron. The cabriole legs with pad feet are elegant and characteristic of furniture from this period. 71cm (28in) high **£2,500-3,500**

The proportions are less refined, so that the upper section appears too big and heavy for the legs.

◀ **Mahogany dressing table**
Although this mid-19th century table borrows many features from its 18th-century cousin, the craftsmanship is lacking. The proportions – long and low, rather than tall and square – are less pleasing and there is not as much detail in the decorative elements. 108cm (42½in) wide **£600-800**

The carving is ostentatious and lacks the elegance of the decoration on the original.

Chippendale chairs

Georgian Chippendale chairs are among the most recognised of chair designs and were widely copied from the 19th century. Exquisitely crafted by hand, an original often has elaborate carving to the pierced back splat – itself a hallmark of the style. Though reproductions had elegant back splats, the carving may have been applied rather than integral to the piece. An early model is more likely to have stretchers between the legs and a stuffover seat.

▲ **Chippendale chair**
The finely carved ornamentation of this mid-18th century chair sets it apart from many later examples. The stretchers between the legs are in keeping with the period, offering support in the absence of corner blocks, which came later. The serpentine top rail and pierced vase back splat are key features, as is the wood – mahogany. This is one of a pair of chairs valued as high as **£4,000** for the pair. Chairs known to have come from Chippendale's workshop are rare and valuable.

▲ **Reproduction Chippendale chair**
This is a faithful 19th-century reproduction of an original Chippendale chair, made using mahogany, but lacks the quality in the carving. Where the original shown above has stretchers between square legs, this piece has elegant cabriole legs and hairy paw feet. It has a drop-in seat where the original has a stuffover version – Chippendale's preference. This is one of a set of six that is valued at **£700** for the set.

TREASURE SPOTTER'S GUIDE
What to look for in a chair

The construction, style and decoration of a chair will reveal where and when it was made. Analyse the clues to work out your chair's rarity and possible value.

The underside of a chair holds many pointers to its construction and age. The earliest chairs were held together by wooden pegs; if the components of your chair are joined by screws, pins or glue then it dates from the 19th century or later. Look for the marks made by the saw as it cut the wood: circular marks suggest a machine saw; irregular marks are likely to have been made by a hand-saw at an earlier date.

Decoration also holds vital clues. Is any carving part of the frame, or was it added afterwards? Compare the back, legs, knees and feet of the chair with examples in the reference section (see pages 248-251) for additional clues. Also consider whether the parts match each other and the style of the chair. Copies of earlier chairs, particularly those made

in the 19th century, can easily be confused with originals, so look for genuine wear to the seat, back and feet, but remember that all of these can be faked.

Changes in construction

Until the mid-17th century, chairs were often made of oak, square in form, with carved panel backs. After 1660, walnut, which was easier to carve, became the principal material. Chairs became lighter and stronger in the 18th century, following the introduction of the cabriole leg *c.*1710 and the widespread use of mahogany after 1730.

Decorative chairs were usually designed to stand against the walls of a room and were often painted, ebonised, gilded or inlaid. During the late

Chairs price line

Old does not always mean valuable
Who needs a hall chair these days? In the mid-18th century, wealthy landowners lined their halls with uncomfortable chairs to be used by tradesmen and by tenants waiting to pay their rents. This mahogany hall chair is worth **£100-150**.

A good decorator's piece
Interior designers look for style rather than history. A late 19th-century copy of a 17th-century style chair is usually worth £200-300, but the high back and carved lion masks on this French walnut upholstered armchair make the asking price **£1,500-2,000**.

One to watch for the future
Until recently, this 18th-century Chinese huanghuali side chair was worth £400-600. But the market for Chinese antiques is booming and this chair, with its marble inset back splat, may now be worth **£2,000-3,000**.

19th century, Neoclassical style became fashionable again and its chair designs were often copied, particularly painted examples by the English designer Thomas Sheraton. These later chairs tend to be more ostentatious than the originals and made from mahogany. As with chairs of any era, the more elaborate the carving, the better the quality and the more valuable the chair is likely to be.

Upholstery for comfort

Upholstery became more generous in the middle of the 18th century, when women began to entertain more. Upholstered chairs, based on French designs, were more comfortable than any that had been made previously, and were arranged in groups rather than around the edge of the room as had previously been the fashion.

The 19th century saw great changes to upholstered chairs as the growing middle classes sought increasingly comfortable seating to reflect their new-found prosperity. Deep-buttoning emphasised the curves and luxuriousness of Victorian seating. Chairs with original upholstery, even in poor condition, tend to be more valuable than ones that have been reupholstered.

What is it worth?

The more pieces in a set of chairs, the more valuable it will be, especially if the set includes a carver or – even better – two. A carver seat should be at least 5cm (2in) wider than the others in the group.

The larger a set of chairs, the higher the value of each individual chair. Use these ratios as an easy way to calculate the sales potential of a set of chairs.

- A pair of chairs is worth three times as much as a single chair.
- A set of four chairs is worth six to seven times more than a single chair.
- A set of six chairs is worth ten to 12 times more than a single chair.
- A set of eight chairs is worth over 15 times more than a single chair.

If you have an odd number of chairs in a set, it may be worth adding one more of a similar design to turn it into what is known as a harlequin set, which you will be able to sell for a greater profit than an odd number.

Mid-century Modern and designer fame
Designs by Americans Charles and Ray Eames are regarded as 20th-century classics. Copies of the fibreglass DAW armchair can be found for as little as £50, but a 1950s original, in good condition and with a walnut Eiffel Tower base, will be worth **£2,500-3,000.**

Distinctive design and known history
The Gothic Revival style is out of fashion but this oak armchair, by English designer John Pollard Seddon, was shown at the Great Exhibition in 1851. Most Gothic Revival chairs sell for £400-600, but the design and provenance boost its value to **£5,000-6,000.**

Art Deco power and a big name
The Art Deco style has been popular with collectors for years. Add a great designer and values rocket. Art Deco armchairs change hands for £300, but this 1920s mahogany example by French designer Jacques-Emile Ruhlmann is valued at **£10,000-15,000.**

REVAMPING YOUR FINDS
Re-covering a drop-in seat

Drop-in seats, used from the 17th century, consist of a pad that sits within the chair rails. On 18th-century examples, the pad rests on rebates or corner blocks. These were often replaced by rebates within the side rails and on the top of the front and back rails on 19th-century chairs, such as this one.

1 Remove the original fabric using pliers. If necessary, use woodfiller to reinforce any holes or splits, and reglue loose joints in the wooden frame.

2 Cut the fabric so that it is 5cm (2in) larger all round than the seat pad. Cut a 5mm (¼in) notch in the centre of each side. Use the pen to mark the centre point on the underside of each rail. Lay the fabric right-side down and place the frame, stuffing-side down, on top. Make sure the notches in the fabric and the marks on the frame align, that any pattern remains centred on the seat and that any stripes or checks are aligned.

3 Pull the fabric over the frame and secure with one tack in the centre of each side rail. Do not hammer the tacks all the way into the frame – just enough to hold the fabric in place. Continue tacking along the length of the back rail, placing the tacks about 3cm (1¼in) apart.

4 Rest the seat on its back rail, smooth the fabric over the seat, checking that it aligns, and tack so that the fabric is taut. Repeat with the sides. If necessary, remove the tacks, smooth the fabric and retack. When you are satisfied with the fit of the fabric, drive the tacks home.

5 To finish the corners, work the front corners first. Fold the fabric into two pleats. Secure the first pleat with a tack, then cut away the excess fabric. Fold the second pleat over the first and tack again. Repeat with the back corners.

6 Gently ease the seat pad into the chair frame. Do not use excessive force or you risk putting undue stress on the joints of the frame.

YOU WILL NEED

Pliers

Commercial woodfiller and woodworm treatment, if required

Wood glue, if required

Upholstery fabric (choose a closely woven linen or cotton, see box on opposite page)

Tape measure or ruler

Scissors

Marker pen

12mm fine tacks

Magnetised upholsterer's hammer

Swatch library

Modern interpretation of *fleur-de-lys*
The large pattern size, regular repeat and bold colours give a modern twist to the use of heraldic symbols in interior design.

Stripes follow 19th-century fashion
Striped fabrics became popular after about 1800, inspired by the campaign tents used by the Emperor Napoleon's armies.

Tartans celebrate Scottish heritage
Popular in early 19th-century interiors, the colours and design are ideal for a study or desk chair.

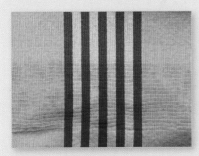

Printed or woven stripes
The striped fabrics used during the Regency and reign of George IV (1811-1830) became known as Regency stripes.

The symbol of Napoleon
Napoleon chose the bee as his emblem, partly because it was the ancient Greek symbol of order and industry.

Mix classic and contemporary
This broken stripe pattern by French designer Christian Lacroix contrasts with the classic lines of an antique chair.

Restoration tips

While the seat pad is out of the frame, clean and polish the wood. Use a wax polish containing beeswax. Silicone polishes should be avoided because the silicone will eventually penetrate the wood and adversely affect the chair's patination (the colour built up over the years).

If you suspect a serious problem with woodworm, press the blunt edge of a table knife against the wood: if the wood is soft or crumbles, the infestation is serious and should be treated with a commercial woodworm-killing fluid or by a specialist company.

When removing the original tacks, work following the grain of the wood to prevent it splitting, and out from the corners so that you do not put excessive pressure on the joints.

Check that the arms and legs will withstand daily wear and tear. The back legs may have been damaged due to sitters rocking on the legs. If the joints are loose, they should be reglued.

TREASURE SPOTTER'S GALLERY
Choosing upholstery fabrics

Choosing upholstery fabrics can be a daunting task. There are so many patterns, motifs and colours available. And then there is the question of whether to go for historical accuracy or a more contemporary look. Each period in history tends to be associated with certain patterns and colours, and choosing a fabric from a similar group will certainly be the safer option. Here is a period breakdown of some fabrics available today.

Toile de Jouy

Toile de Jouy fabrics originated in 1770, in a factory established by the German Oberkampf brothers in the French village of Jouy-en-Josas, just south of Paris. In 1810 the brothers travelled to England to find out the secret advances made in copperplate printing techniques. They managed to smuggle out the information by writing it on cotton percale fabric using an alum solution tinted with madder dye, then dipping the fabric in vinegar to render the writing invisible. Once back in France they immersed the fabric in madder dye to retrieve the concealed information.

▲ **Chantemerle by Zoffany**
A traditional *toile de Jouy* design with rural scenes and classical ruins.

▲ **Glasgow Toile by Timorous Beasties**
This modern *toile de Jouy* features blocks of flats and a tramp on a park bench.

Many manufacturers produce extensive ranges of 'documentary fabrics', as these recreations of historical designs are known, in traditional and contemporary patterns and colours.

In the 18th century, many fabrics featured naturalistic fruit and flower designs, some inspired by traditional Chinese examples. Later in the century these were in the Rococo style (see pages 10-11). *Toile de Jouy* was also popular (see box, left).

The Neoclassical style of the early 19th century (see pages 12-13) drew inspiration from the Roman empire. Motifs included laurel wreaths, trophies and shields. Designs inspired by the French ruler Napoleon Bonaparte were also popular. By the end of the 19th century naturalistic floral styles were fashionable again. So too were boteh, the paisley motif taken from Kashmiri textiles and used on shawls. The Arts and Crafts movement (see pages 14-15) saw a return to chintz patterns as well as designs created by William Morris.

In the early 20th century the Art Nouveau movement brought formalised floral patterns and whiplash motifs. The flowers and leaves were stylised during the Art Deco period, which also saw the use of geometric repeats (see pages 16-17). Later highly stylised flowers and geometric patterns celebrated modern design (see pages 18-19 and box below).

1950s fabrics by Sanderson

This is a bold collection of prints and weaves that celebrates a decade of design which transformed the boundaries of interior decoration. Mobiles was created in 1950 and printed on rayon, which at the time was a newly developed fabric and an affordable choice for a younger, design-conscious clientele.

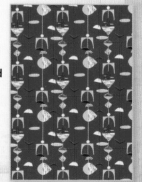

▶ **Mobiles by Sanderson**
This abstract design is by Marian Mahler.

Swatch library

18TH CENTURY	EARLY 19TH CENTURY	LATE 19TH CENTURY	20TH CENTURY

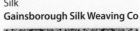

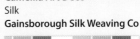

Stripe
Silk
Gainsborough Silk Weaving Co

Renaissance
Silk
Gainsborough Silk Weaving Co

Camellia Art Deco
Silk
Gainsborough Silk Weaving Co

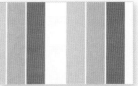

Birdbranch
Linen
Timorous Beasties

Bee Stripe
Silk
Gainsborough Silk Weaving Co

Devil Damask
Velvet
Timorous Beasties

Delphine Camille
Cotton
Harlequin

Caverley: Porcelain Garden
80% Viscose 20% Linen
Sanderson

Vintage: Pagoda River
49% Linen 38% Cotton 13%
Nylon **Sanderson**

Dandelion Clocks
94% Cotton 6% Nylon
Sanderson

Birds 'n' Bees
90% Linen 10% Nylon
Timorous Beasties

Marquee Stripe
52% Linen 36% Cotton 12%
Nylon **Laura Ashley**

Magnus Carnaby
85% Cotton 15% Silk
Watts of Westminster

Miami Fabrics: Coconut Grove
Cotton
Designers Guild

Acorn
60% Viscose 40% Cotton
Watts of Westminster

Strawberry Thief
Cotton
Morris & Co

Pompeii
Silk
Gainsborough Silk Weaving Co

Drummond
90% Wool 10% Cotton
Watts of Westminster

Arabella
Linen
Watts of Westminster

Wallace
55% Linen 33% Cotton 12%
Nylon **Laura Ashley**

RESTORING YOUR FINDS
Repairing torn leather

Old club chairs with their original leather covers are considerably more desirable than newly re-covered equivalents. Re-use the original stuffing for the arms to prevent the leather tearing when you tack it back into position. If the original leather has become rough and porous, do not re-colour it as it will absorb the dye very patchily, and the dye will almost invariably rub off on a sitter's clothing.

YOU WILL NEED

Ripping chisel

Tack-lifter

Craft knife (heavy duty)

500g heavyweight hessian

10mm or 12mm upholsterer's tacks

Magnetised upholsterer's hammer

Protective goggles and a face mask

Dust sheet

Spray adhesive for fabrics and carpets (heavy duty)

Panel pins, if required

Repairing a leather armchair

1 The front of the arm and side of the chair are finished with a leather-covered wooden facing, which is secured to the wooden chair frame with panel pins. Carefully insert the tip of a ripping chisel between the arm and the facing and, working your way around the perimeter, gently prise off the facing.

2 Using a tack-lifter, carefully prise off the tacks that secure the arm leather to the frame behind the removed facing. Then, using a heavy-duty craft knife, cut the leather from the back to the front of the chair along the line where the underside of the outer roll of the arm meets the flat side of the chair. You will also need to extend the cut for a few inches around the back of the arm and into where the leather is tucked into the side of the chair back.

3 Pull the leather cover over the top of the arm and lay it on the seat. Lift off the layer of wadding and put to one side. If the layer of horsehair or grass fibre stuffing has become uneven, re-work it as evenly as possible over the sprung base of the arm.

4 Cut a piece of hessian to size, position over the stuffing and, pulling tight as you go to compress the underlying stuffing and springs, secure to the front and back of the arm frame with upholsterer's tacks, using the upholsterer's hammer.

5 Pick up the original wadding you put aside in step 3 and reposition it over the inside and curved top of the arm, manipulating it with your fingers to make it smooth and even. No adhesive is required – it 'loose lays' in position.

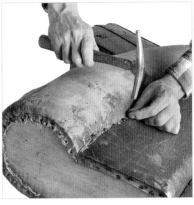

6 Cut pieces of hessian to shape, so that each overlaps the edges of the splits. Working in a well-ventilated area, wearing protective goggles and a face mask, and with a dust sheet between the seat and the pulled-back arm cover, spray adhesive around the reverse of the holes and splits and cover with hessian patches. Work on one hole or split at a time, and turn the leather over each time to the 'show' side to manipulate and tease the edges of the split to create 'near-invisible' joins over the hessian.

7 When all the splits have been repaired and the adhesive is dry, re-position the leather cover on the chair. Re-tack along the front, side and around the back of the frame, pulling very gently tight as you go. Re-fit the decorative wooden facing. Tap it down with the hammer, using the original panel pins or new ones. You can supplement the pins with spray adhesive, making sure you protect the surrounding leather with a dust sheet.

Restoration tips

For small repairs cut a piece of hessian larger than the tear and push through the hole to lie flat behind it. Spray adhesive on to an artist's brush and apply to the reverse edges of the tear, then work the edges together with your fingers over the hessian.

If pieces are missing, a professional patch repair or a complete re-cover will be necessary.

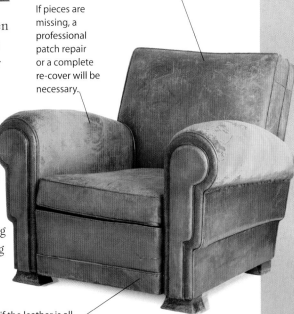

Check to see if the leather is all there, even if it is badly torn and in generally poor condition.

TREASURE SPOTTER'S GUIDE
Tables

Quality has everything to do with craftsmanship. The best cabinet-makers made furniture for wealthy households and were expected to produce high-quality work made from the finest materials. So how do you know what to look for?

▼ Skilled turning

This early-18th century gateleg table is a fine example of true craftsmanship. Not only is there a hinged design that allows the table to fold away for storage but also there is tremendous skill in the turning of eight identical oak legs. 114cm (45in) wide **£650-750**

Quality is not found in the age of a piece or in the value of the materials used; it has a huge amount to do with the workmanship that went into making it. The construction of a piece of furniture reveals a great deal about its quality. Mechanical pieces, for example, are usually among the finest available because there is considerable skill in making moving parts that function well over time. A tilting top for a table, a tambour front for a desk, or a pullout slide for a writing table all show craftsmanship.

These tables have always been great space-savers. When not in use, the table top can be placed in the upright position and stored against the wall.

The superstructure has drawers surrounding a leather writing surface, with drawers in the frieze below.

▲ Epitome of style

Known as a Carlton House writing desk (after the building for which the form was originally made), the quality of this mahogany piece lies not just in its exquisite construction and decoration but in the documentation of its design. Dated c.1790, the U-shape arrangement of the drawers was an innovation at the time and is illustrated in Sheraton's and Hepplewhite's pattern books of the period. 152cm (60in) wide **£3,500-4,500**

▲ Ingenious design

This mahogany pie-crust table is a hallmark of late-Georgian quality, the name deriving from the shaped edge to the tabletop. The ingenuity lies in the 'bird cage' mechanism at the top of the supporting column, which allows the top to tilt on its side when not in use. The mechanism, popular from 1740-1765, comprises four small pillars placed between a small square top and base. It holds the top firmly to its central support using a wooden wedge or a brass catch. 76cm (30in) diameter **£1,000-2,000**

Look at the piece as a whole

Consider whether or not your piece has been made using solid wood and, if so, which type. Over the centuries the use of oak, walnut and mahogany indicated quality. Richly veneered surfaces also signify well-made pieces, depending on the style and execution. Wherever possible, try to establish what kinds of joint have been used to assemble a piece and whether it has been hand-crafted or made by machine.

In today's age of precision manufacturing it is easy to underestimate the skills of master craftsmen who laboured over identically carved features for a piece, or the fiddly inlaying of a strip of brass, or the intricate task of setting a tabletop with a marquetry or parquetry design. Before the industrial age, these skills required years of apprenticeship. The more of this kind of superior embellishment a piece has, provided it has been executed well, the higher its quality is likely to be.

Judith's lucky find

▲ **Amazing value**
Not the most attractive piece, perhaps, it is nevertheless desirable and practical. 143cm (56½in) wide **£70**

I was thrilled when asked to pay less than £100 for this late-Georgian drop-leaf table. Made of solid oak – making the piece an absolute bargain for something of this age – it is a gift for the amateur restorer or decorator. Oak is a wood that distresses really well and can be bleached, limed or painted very successfully. Any of these methods, coupled with the rectilinear form, would modernise this piece to suit a contemporary interior.

This console table is made from exotic acajou wood and inlaid with fruit woods. It is typical of 18th-century Dutch furniture.

▲ **Skilled embellishment**
Look at the quality of any decoration – floral marquetry, carving, brass inlay – particularly when the materials used are exotic or of high value. A piece which has been skilfully made will usually have been commissioned from a known craftsman or reputable cabinet-maker and is the result of many years' experience. 71cm (28in) wide **£6,000-7,000**

▶ **Reputable craftsmen**
These walnut tables were designed by Frenchman Emile Gallé, one of the seminal craftsmen of the Art Nouveau period. His school of craftsmen at Nancy produced some of the finest furniture of the period. Made exclusively by hand, intricate, nature-inspired marquetry was a trademark feature. Many pieces are unique, adding to their value. Largest 71cm (28in) high **£11,500-12,500**

REVAMPING YOUR FINDS
French-polishing a table

French polish is a liquid polish developed during the early 19th century. It produces a smooth, mirror-like finish and enriches the colour and figuring (the natural highlights) of the wood. It is easily damaged and so is usually applied to pieces that are not subject to heavy use, such as occasional tables and pianos.

▲ **The rubbing pad creates a smooth finish**
Apply French polish with a crease-free rubbing pad (use a brush for recessed areas and mouldings). Creases will create marks which can only be removed by stripping the finish and starting again.

Types of French polish

There are five basic types of French polish, each with a different application:

- French (or 'brown') polish can be used on all but the palest of woods. Garnet polish is suited to mahogany and fine-grained oaks, where a deep, warm, red-brown tone is required.
- Button polish makes a durable finish and gives wood a brown cast with a slight orange-yellow tinge. It will enhance the colour of golden-toned hardwoods, such as walnut. It is not suitable for dark-stained woods, as it can obscure the grain.
- White polish is used to darken paler woods slightly.
- Clear (transparent) polish is mainly used on marquetry and inlay, where any darkening of the wood would spoil its appearance.

YOU WILL NEED

Wire wool grades 000 and 0000

Methylated spirits

Several squares of soft, lint-free cotton rag, about 25cm (10in) square

French polish

Two rubbing pads made from a soft, lint-free cotton rag, about 25cm (10in) square and a handful of cotton wool (see box opposite)

Airtight glass jar

Fine-grade sandpaper

Soft-bristled dusting brush

Linseed oil

Clear beeswax furniture polish

Sable-bristled artist's brush about 1cm (½in) wide

1 To remove the old polish, dip a piece of grade 000 wire wool in methylated spirits. Gently wipe across the surface, working with the grain. Change to a clean piece as it becomes clogged. Moisten a lint-free rag with methylated spirits and wipe it over the surface until no more polish can be removed.

2 Put French polish on the rubbing pad and, maintaining firm, even pressure, wipe it across the grain in straight, overlapping strokes. Sweep the pad onto and off the sides of the surface. Never stop halfway through a stroke, as this leaves marks. Store the pad in an airtight glass jar and leave the piece to dry for an hour. Repeat the process, working with the grain. Put the pad in the jar and leave the piece to dry overnight.

3 Working in the direction of the grain, lightly rub the surface with grade 000 wire wool or fine-grade sandpaper. Remove any dust with the dusting brush. Put polish on the pad and lubricate with linseed oil (see box opposite). Work in a series of overlapping circles from one side to the other, applying even pressure. Overlap rows until the surface is covered.

4 Wait two minutes. Refill and re-lubricate the pad (see box, right). Apply a coat working in a figure-of-eight from one side to the other. Alternate steps 3 and 4 until you have applied six thin coats, allowing two minutes drying between each one. Put pad in jar and leave polish to harden for at least 12 hours.

5 Lightly rub the surface with fine-grade sandpaper to remove any minor imperfections. Repeat steps 3 and 4 at least another six times. For the penultimate coat, dilute the polish as three parts polish to one part methylated spirits; for the final coat, use equal parts of each. Leave to harden for 12 hours.

6 You will now have a smooth, cloudy finish. Make a new rubbing pad, wrapping at least four squares of rag around the swab. Put methylated spirits on the pad and wipe with the grain, in long, slightly overlapping strokes. Repeat up to four times, removing the outer layer of rag each time.

French-polishing tips

To produce a satin finish, dip grade 0000 wire wool in clear beeswax polish and wipe very lightly over the surface in the direction of the grain. Wipe off any dust with a soft rag. Apply a thin coat of polish as in the caption below left.

Apply one or two coats of the French polish to any recessed areas and mouldings using a 1cm (½in) sable-bristled artist's brush.

Work somewhere dust free and dry. Any specks of dust trapped in the polish will ruin the finish. A damp atmosphere will create a cloudy finish.

▲ **Enhance the wood's figuring**
When you have finished, leave the surface for a week to fully harden. Then, either leave it as it is or apply a thin coat of clear beeswax polish using a soft, lint-free rag to apply and buff the polish. Natural burrs and shapes in the wood are emphasised by the glossy finish given by French polishing. When you finish, inspect the surface under a bright light from all angles to check that the finish is perfect.

Making a rubbing pad

- Place a rag flat on a work surface. Tease a handful of cotton wool into an egg-shaped swab and place in the middle of the rag. Fold both sides of the fabric so that it covers the swab's pointed end. Turn over the sides and end of the rag so that the swab is completely enclosed. Check no creases have formed on the underside and adjust if they have. Twist the loose fabric at the top of the pad to tighten it.
- Hold the pad in one hand, then open the fabric to expose the cotton wool. Drip French polish on to the swab until it is saturated, but not overflowing, then refold and twist the rag to enclose it. Dab the pad on a scrap of wood to bring the polish to the surface so that it is spread evenly. To lubricate the pad, rub a very thin coating of linseed oil over the surface.

Judith warns!

Applying French polish requires time and care so you must be patient. Work at a steady, even rate and be prepared to build up the finish with 12 to 20 applications of polish. If there are any flaws in the finish you will need to strip the surface and start again.

TREASURE SPOTTER'S GUIDE
Smaller furniture

When it comes to more compact items of furniture, some pieces are easier to sell than others. Commodes and chiffoniers find buyers because they are small and neat as well as offering useful storage space. Bureaux are hard to sell as they do not have space for that modern essential – the computer.

Small antique pieces score highly for a number of reasons. Besides their practicality in offering a means of storing things away, many are also visually interesting, because they were often designed and decorated to work within a specific room scheme. They appeal particularly to buyers looking for a piece of furniture to provide a focal point in a room, offering design flair and quality that contemporary pieces may lack.

Examples in good condition and/or with interesting decorative details are almost always worth more than a standard piece from the same period. Make sure fixtures and fittings are intact – a brass gallery on a chiffonier, for example – and that drawer and door handles match, even if they are not original. Stylistically, pleasing proportions are important, as is a consistent styling throughout. Neoclassical and Mid-century Modern pieces are ideal for today's minimalist interiors but buyers may also be interested in luxury pieces with decorative elements – ebonised details, brass inlay, marquetry or paintwork, for example. One technique that is worth looking out for, and which is unique to smaller furniture, is a front with *sans traverse* decoration. This means that the front has a unified decoration, regardless of the doors and drawers. First seen in Rococo pieces of the early 18th century, the fashion resurfaced later, notably during the Art Nouveau period.

Intricate Boulle marquetry has been used across the front.

The feet sit in brass sabots, or gilt-bronze 'shoes', which echo the husk decoration at the top of the legs.

▲ **Master craftsmanship**
Small pieces displaying a specific decorative technique – marquetry, fine carving or gilding – are popular at the high end of the market, especially if the technique is particularly skilled. This French, 18th-century desk, 84cm (33in) wide, features engraved brass and tortoiseshell Boulle marquetry. Sold at auction, it could fetch as much as **£8,000-10,000**.

Premium pieces

Collectors, interior designers and fashionistas often pay top prices for the more quirky pieces: an Art Deco cocktail cabinet with compartmental, mirror-lined interior; an American Folk Art painted chest, Biedermeier drawers flanked by gilt-topped, ebonised columns. The piece featured is the work of Italian designer Piero Fornasetti. One of Italy's most prolific designers of the 20th century, Fornasetti designed quirky, one-off and limited edition pieces, such as this corner cabinet. From a series of pieces decorated with black-and-white *sans traverse* architectural scenes, pieces such as this are desirable for their distinct appearance and their rarity.

◄ **Distinctive design**
This Fornasetti two-door Pompeian corner cabinet, 120cm (47in) wide, is printed with an architectural facade with unique coloration in greys and black. Not only is it a stunning piece but it is signed on back panel 'Fornasetti '87', making it worth around **£6,000-8,000**.

In working order

Pieces that have fitted interiors or working mechanisms (a fall front or pull-out slide, for example) must function well. Smooth-running drawers in a good range of sizes and working locks with keys also make a piece attractive. If the drawers stick, try rubbing a wax candle along the runners to get them moving again. A missing key or broken lock can easily be replaced by a good locksmith.

If you have a good-quality piece, or one that is particularly desirable, you may prefer to keep it as a longer-term investment. Small pieces are unlikely to go out of fashion purely because they are so useful while being relatively easy to house. Exceptional examples will almost certainly increase in value and generic pieces may also fare better with changing fashions.

▶ **Sympathetic restoration**
This versatile mahogany bureau offers plenty of storage for a relatively small piece. Dated around 1770, it is also in full working order and has a good colour. Despite this it would be difficult to find a buyer and it might be better to keep it rather than try to sell. 109cm (43in) high **£400-600**

◀ **Compact elegance**
This rosewood chiffonier combines the clean, Neoclassical lines of the Regency period with a very small footprint. The narrow depth of this piece and marble surface make it suitable for use in a hallway or living room. 125cm (49in) high **£2,500-3,000**

Good, Better, Best Chests

The standard of craftsmanship used in the decoration of furniture such as chests can make a real difference to the value.

Good

This German 120cm (47in) wide chest features walnut and rosewood marquetry and good proportions. Yet you might want to keep it in the hope that values rise. Worth around £4,000 five years ago, today it is unlikely to sell for more than **£2,000-2,500**.

Better

This late-Victorian marquetry and painted kingwood commode is of a high standard and replicates a Regency form. It is likely to command a high price when sold. At 92cm (36in) wide, its size and colouring are desirable. **£7,000-8,000**

Best

The fine perspectival marquetry makes this softwood piece unique. The craftsman, Giovanni Maffezzoli, studied under one of the master craftsmen of the early 19th century, Giuseppe Maggiolini, adding to its high value. It is 120cm (47in) wide and worth around **£35,000-40,000**.

TREASURE SPOTTER'S GALLERY
Chests

This practical piece of furniture has a rich history. From the long, low chests of the early 17th century to the multi-functional designs of the 20th century, styles have varied widely over time, yet their purpose – to provide capacious, easily accessible storage – has always been paramount in the minds of their designers. With today's small living spaces, chests score highly in a modern home, where they can double up as coffee tables.

◀ Old-style chest
The simple box with a lid dates back centuries. Here, the hinged lid, carved panelled front and use of oak are hallmarks of an early 17th-century piece. Age does not always guarantee value and this example is worth around half what it might sell for at the peak of a trend. A similar piece with a carved, raised or domed lid might hold its value better. 128cm (50in) wide **£200-300**

▲ Georgian mule chest
Combining a large storage space with three drawers, this piece lacks the elegance of a serpentine-fronted chest from the same era. Made of richly coloured elm and with its original drawer pulls, it is worth considerably less than a piece with provenance and its value has halved in the downturn. 102cm (40in) wide **£250-350**

◀ Early drawers
Drawers first appeared in the early 17th century, when a chest typically had two. Graduated drawers – the narrowest at the top and deepest at the bottom – became fashionable in the late 17th century. This *c.*1780 mahogany chest has a maker's label (Elizabeth Bell, London) which increases its value significantly. 95cm (37in) wide **£5,000-6,000**

Campaign furniture

During the 19th century, wealthy military types ordered 'knockdown' furniture to take on their travels – pieces that could be dismantled into two or more parts for transportation. They were highly practical – there was no point in elaborate decoration as it might be damaged when on the move. Surfaces were plain, with handles countersunk to avoid damage in transit. In general, campaign furniture has held its value when compared with its non-knockdown equivalents, which tend to be worth considerably less.

▲ Home from the wars
Pieces such as the mid-19th century hardwood and brass-mounted chest-of-drawers shown here are much admired today for their ingenuity, quality of construction and unembellished surfaces. 109cm (43in) wide **£2,500-3,000**

▶ Timeless desirability
There is an enduring demand for the furniture that survives from the Regency period. Quality pieces tend to be skilfully made using exotic materials – and this is reflected in the high prices they can fetch. Typical features are: a rectilinear case with tapering legs, Neoclassical decoration and mahogany wood. 102cm (40in) wide **£2,000-3,000**

◀ Mahogany Wellington chest
The tall, narrow Wellington chest is a real space-saver. Dating from around 1820, it was named in honour of the Duke of Wellington who led the campaign against Napoleon. Used to hold all manner of curiosities, a lockable stile to one side of the drawer fronts prevented them opening when being transported. In working order, this can increase the value of an already desirable piece. 126cm (49½in) high **£2,000-3,000**

▼ Defining a style
This chest is recognisably Art Deco. Characteristics that carry weight – and therefore value – are the geometric parquetry front and the knowledge that it was designed in around 1935 by Eugene Schoene for Schmieg Hungate and Kotzian, which ensures a high level of craftsmanship. 114.5cm (45in) wide **£7,000-9,000**

▲ Good design
A 1950s Thin Edge chest of drawers designed by American George Nelson for Herman Miller. The epitome of postwar 'good design', pieces such as this are minimalist. Having a named designer makes this a high-value item, but even generic pieces – rectilinear with rosewood, walnut or teak veneers and unobtrusive feet – can command prices in the mid to high hundreds. 86cm (33¾in) high **£3,000-4,000**

RESTORING YOUR FINDS
Replacing a pleated fabric door lining

During the 18th and 19th centuries, cabinet door panels were often lined with fabric. In some cases a plain fabric was employed behind a decorative brass grille, and in others – as here – the fabric was given a decorative pleated finish. Inevitably, such fabrics have been prone to damage and may require replacing.

YOU WILL NEED

Pair of pliers
Pencil or ballpoint pen
Steel ruler
Strip of thin cardboard
Cutting board
Craft knife
Lightweight upholstery fabric
Scissors
Clothes pegs (12-20)
Artist's brush
Quick-dry fabric adhesive (heavy duty)
Iron
White cotton handkerchief
Colour-matched silk or cotton thread
Curved upholsterer's needle
Panel pins (20 at most)
Magnetised upholsterer's hammer

Replace pleated fabric

1 Using a pair of pliers, either straighten or pull out the panel pins bent over the edges of the wooden door panels and secured in the door frames. Then remove the panels from the frames. (You may be able to re-use some of the pins later.)

2 If the backs of the panels (unlike these) are lined with fabric, remove this to expose the wooden reverse. Then, using a pencil or pen and ruler, mark on the reverse of the top and bottom edges of the panels the pleat divisions – these marks will be your guide when re-pleating.

Fabric selection

Whether silk or cotton, the replacement fabric should be no thicker or heavier than the original or you will be unable to form the pleats correctly. You will need a piece three times the combined width of both door panels, cut from a standard width of upholstery fabric.

3 Take the measurements for the height of a door panel and the width of a pleat, and using a pencil and ruler transfer them to a piece of cardboard. Then, working on a cutting board, and using a steel ruler and a craft knife, cut out the strip of card to form the pleat guide.

4 Cut the fabric for the first panel: three times the width of the panel, plus an extra 5cm (2in) on each side. Holding the fabric in place with a clothes peg, top and bottom, form a pleat by folding the fabric and inserting the pleat guide to form a straight edge.

5 Secure each pleat top and bottom, as you did with the first. As you work you will be able to use, by carefully positioning them, one peg (top and bottom) to secure two or more pleats. Stop when you are about halfway across the panel.

6 Reverse the panel, remove the first peg you applied, pull the top of the first pleat over the top edge and onto the reverse of the panel and, using an artist's brush, secure with fabric adhesive. Repeat for the bottom of the first pleat, then for the rest of the pleats. Having repeated steps 5-7 for the second half of the panel, secure the fabric in the same way to the sides of the panel, having cut off any excess fabric. Then repeat the technique on the second panel.

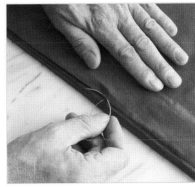

7 Place the newly pleated panels reverse side down on a flat surface and with a medium-hot iron, press the pleats to give them crisp, flattened edges. Place a clean white cotton handkerchief between the iron and the fabric to protect the latter from accidental marks or scorching, or making the fabric overly shiny.

8 Mark up and cut a piece of the fabric so that it is the height and width of one of the panels, plus 5cm (2in) extra all round. Align on the reverse of one of the panels, fold under the edges 5cm (2in) to fit the panel exactly and, using colour-matched thread, a curved needle and running stitch, secure all around the perimeter. Tie the thread with a granny knot. Repeat for the second panel.

Restoration tips

Carefully reposition one panel in the door frame.

Secure the panel either by re-bending the original panel pins over the edges of the panel using pliers or by using new pins secured to the frame prior to bending. Repeat for second panel.

REVAMPING YOUR FINDS
Repairing surface damage

You can treat deep scratches on French-polished furniture, such as this early 20th-century walnut table to improve its appearance. But bear in mind that a rare piece displaying such damage is usually considered 'honest' and tends to be more valuable.

YOU WILL NEED

Magnifying glass

French polish (see pages 36-37)

Cotton buds

White spirit

Teaspoon

Small container such as an old saucer

Small, fine-tipped artist's brush

Scalpel

Liquid metal polish

Soft, lint-free cotton rag

Tinted beeswax furniture polish

Soft cloth

Hiding deep scratches

1 Closely examine the piece, using a magnifying glass if necessary, to assess the colour of the wood. Buy a shade of French polish closest to the colour you wish to match.

2 Moisten a cotton bud with white spirit, and rub it over the scratch to remove any old layers of wax so that the new polish will adhere to the surface.

3 Leave a teaspoonful of French polish in a container exposed to the air for 10–30 minutes until it stiffens slightly. Use a fine-tipped artist's brush to apply a thin layer to the scratch. Leave to set for four hours. Build up further layers, until the last sets slightly raised from, and just overlaps, the surrounding area.

4 Leave to dry for 12 hours, or until it has hardened. Carefully position the side of a scalpel blade at slightly less than a right angle to one end of the scratch. Gently push across the surface to cut the polish flush with the surrounding area.

5 Burnish the new polish by lightly rubbing it with a cotton bud moistened with liquid metal polish. Using a rag, spread a thin layer of beeswax polish over the entire side of the piece on which the scratch lies. (For advice on different types of beeswax polish, see opposite.) Buff the wax to a shine with a soft cloth.

1

Hiding fine scratches

You can hide very fine scratches in oiled or waxed surfaces by rubbing on a little shoe polish with a lint-free rag and buffing it to a shine with a soft cloth. An alternative for waxed pieces is to use a commercial scratch remover. This works by slightly dissolving the existing layers of wax, which then re-form to produce a smooth surface. Always apply these products in accordance with the manufacturer's instructions.

The final coat of tinted beeswax polish will help to blend the repair into the surrounding area.

5

YOU WILL NEED

Wood stain(s)

Grain filler

Medium- and fine-grade sandpaper

Soft-bristled dusting brush

Fine-bristled varnishing brush

Clear or white French polish (see page 36)

Wire wool Grade 000

Wax furniture polish (tinted or clear)

White spirit

Metal container (to hold a mixture of wax and white spirit. The container must fit in the saucepan listed below.)

Saucepan

Shoe brush

Soft, lint-free cotton rags

Beeswax polishes

- Always use a wax polish containing beeswax. For a durable finish, it should also contain carnauba (palm) wax.
- Avoid polish that contains silicone, which will penetrate the wood and make it almost impossible to restore.
- Use coloured wax if you wish to darken the colour of the stained wood or create an antique finish on new wood.

Applying a wax finish

Beeswax polish is a traditional furniture finish. Its sheen is more subtle than the mirror-like finish of French polish and it is easier to apply, although successful results require strenuous efforts.

Waxing a chest

1 Remove the handles. Stain the wood if required and fill the grain of any new wood (see pages 64-65 for both of these). Working with the grain, smooth the surface with fine-grade sandpaper. Remove all dust with the dusting brush.

2 Using the varnishing brush, apply two thin coats of French polish. Allow 12 hours for each one to dry and rub with wire wool, working with the grain. Dust as before.

3 Melt equal quantities of wax polish and white spirit in a container placed in a pan of hot water to form a creamy liquid. Brush on a thin coat with the shoe brush. Allow the remaining wax to set. Lightly rub the surface in the direction of the grain with wire wool. Buff with a rag; leave for 48 hours.

4 Build up further thin coats of wax straight from the can, with a rag. Leave each coat for five minutes before buffing, and allow three to four hours between coats. Apply as many coats as are required to produce a deep shine. Replace handles.

1

4

A wax finish is easily marked by heat, alcohol and water and so it should be treated with care.

◀ It is wrong to think that the more wax you use, the deeper the resulting shine. The secret of wax polishing is to apply very thin coats of wax and buff each one as vigorously as you can – there is no substitute for hard work if you want good results.

TREASURE SPOTTER'S GUIDE
Larger furniture

Wardrobes, chests-on-chests, linen presses and tallboys are all types of large furniture. They are great for storage but can make surprisingly little money when it comes to selling. Why should that be the case and what can you do about it?

Although useful storage space is always welcome, large furniture has fallen out of fashion. The most significant reason for this is size. Before the middle of the 19th century many chests and linen presses were designed for much larger houses than the ones we tend to live in today and are now simply too large for most modern-day homes. These bulky masses would dominate a modern room, often making it feel cramped and dark. In addition to this, they are often generic and unremarkable, and fall under the 'brown' furniture umbrella that is currently struggling to realise its proper value at auction.

A difficult sale

That does not mean that the piece you have is worthless – just that it might be harder to find the right buyer. You can start by using the style guides at the back of the book to find out what you have. Is your piece desirable style-wise and in good decorative order? As with all other types of furniture, style, proportions, workmanship and the condition of a piece can have a significant impact on its value. Function is also important. Large pieces offer a wide range of storage solutions:

The flamboyant japanned Chinoiserie decoration is likely to appeal to collectors.

The workmanship is particularly fine, adding to its value.

▲ **Style over substance**
This George I tallboy is 154cm (60¾in) high, which is relatively small. Its size and (later) skilful chinoiserie decoration mean it is worth **£5,000-6,000**. With original decoration, it could make three times more.

◄ **Great space savers**
This striking Georgian mahogany linen press has a lot going for it: a huge amount of useful storage space; an understated Neoclassical elegance; fine veneered door fronts and elegant proportions. Yet, at over 2m (7ft) tall, its sheer size is off-putting and a current value reflects this. 220cm (86½in) high **£800-1,000**

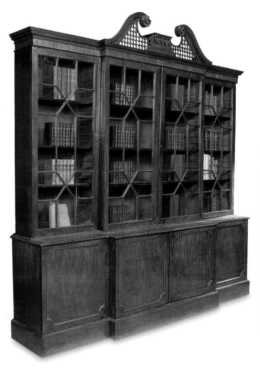

◄ **Striking storage**
This mahogany piece is big on wall space, but short on depth. Some homeowners like statement pieces such as this, which have a greater presence than modern-day equivalents – it uses no more room than simple bracket shelving, but is far more striking. This George III example 258cm (101½in) wide is valued at around **£8,000-10,000**.

some have shelved interiors or glazed display cases, others have built-in desks and drawers. It is not unusual for these items to have been altered over the years to suit changing needs or fashions. For example, a linen press would have had a shelved interior but the shelves might have been replaced with a hanging rail. Such alterations may influence value.

One benefit of many large-scale pieces, such as tallboys and chests-on-chests, is that they come in two separate sections. This may seem an odd criterion for assessing value but if you consider that two smaller sections are easier to transport in a regular vehicle (even in two trips) and to carry to an upstairs bedroom, you can see why it might appeal to buyers more than a similar single example. But if your two pieces have been altered or are a 'marriage' – were not originally made to go together – then they will be worth much less than an authentic piece.

Judith warns!

Highboys, tallboys and chests-on-chests always come as two separate sections. Over time it is not unusual for either the top or bottom to be lost or damaged and subsequently replaced. Though such marriages are often well matched, they do reduce the value of the resulting chest. Things to look for are: decorative details that appear on one section of the piece but not the other; slight variations in the colour or grain of the wood; feet that do not conform to the style and mismatched door and drawer furniture.

◄ **A poor match**
The way the top section overhangs the bottom indicates that this mid-18th century walnut chest-on-chest, 173cm (68in) high, is a marriage. As such it is worth £1,500-2,500.

▲ **Repro bulk**
Large-scale furniture tends to lack appeal in today's market. But to the right buyer a smart piece may be just what they need to bring a focal point to a room. This striking and well-made Dutch Baroque/Rococo Revival walnut cabinet-on-chest may look bulky but it is attractive and will therefore fetch a reasonable price. 190.5cm (75in) wide £1,800-2,200

◄ **Old-fashioned elegance**
This Edwardian satinwood marquetry and coromandel banded bureau bookcase has halved in value in recent years. In its favour, it is elegant and the narrow depth of the top section makes it ideal for a smaller home. But to today's buyers it is out of fashion and offers limited storage space. It is 193cm (76in) high and worth £700-1,000.

TREASURE SPOTTER'S GALLERY
20th-century furniture

Mid-century Modern furniture is all about designer credentials. This is primarily the domain of North American and Scandinavian designers who promoted an organic, 'soft' Modernism as a counter to the industrial look of the interwar years. Official re-issues of well-known designs from the original manufacturer are likely to hold their value in the long term but inexpensive copies will not.

▲ Diamond chair
Designed in 1953 by Italian-American sculptor, Harry Bertoia, the Diamond chair is a result of the experiments with new materials and sculptural forms that sum up this age. Sold by Knoll International, they were made by hand using steel rods and came with a pad cushion, which is often missing. Part of a range of seating furniture, originals are rare and this is a reproduction. **£500-600**

▲ Eames Storage Unit (ESU)
Innovative storage systems were a hallmark of the postwar years. Charles and Ray Eames designed a series of pieces that combined plywood drawers with plastic screens as well as cupboards and shelves. They were ideal for mass production and this is an original. *c.*1952 119.5cm (47in) wide **£4,000-5,000**

▲ Modernist sideboard
The sideboard made a comeback in the second half of the 20th century. Designs were typically pared back with the focus on function alone. Lacking decorative features, pieces often used of exotic veneers and new materials, such as woven or (here) lacquered panels. This is a seminal example designed by Frenchman Jean Prouvé in 1955. 92cm (36¼in) high **£3,500-4,500**

◀ Danish design
Danish innovator Verner Panton experimented with fabric-covered fibreglass forms and plastics to realise his futuristic designs. Bright colours are a hallmark of his style. This Cone chair, designed in 1956, is one of several pieces whose influence was far-reaching. This re-issue of the design is worth **£450-550.**

The influence of the big furniture company

A maker's label can significantly increase the value of a piece. Examples by firms such as Knoll International and Herman Miller in the US, and Fritz Hansen in Denmark are worth identifying. Their founders were designers in their own right who looked for raw talent or commissioned established designers to create pieces for mass production. This rosewood partner's table was designed by the co-founder of Knoll International, American Florence Knoll. 183cm (72in) wide **£3,000-4,000**

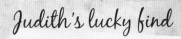

Judith's lucky find

Not that long ago, I was lucky enough to spot an Arne Jacobsen Ant chair in a skip – not the method I would use to dispose of such a classic design. Created in the 1950s, this is one of several chairs by the Danish designer that exploited the manufacturing techniques of the day. With a seat and back made from a single piece of moulded plywood, the chair was revolutionary for its time because it was relatively cheap to mass produce and yet was sturdy and light. So successful were Jacobsen's designs that they were made in large numbers and often spray-finished in a range of bright colours.

Space Age icons

The plastics revolution of the 1960s and 1970s had a profound impact on furniture design. Several designers, including Eero Aarnio, Eero Saarinen, Verner Panton, Robin Day and Luigi Colani, experimented with injection moulding. Their influence resulted in an explosion of bright-coloured, Space Age forms, including the Finnish Aarnio's Ball chair, now a celebrated 1960s design. **£2,000-3,000**

Ant chair

The beauty of the Ant chair lies partly in its simplicity. The two sections – a plywood seat and tubular steel base – have been copied many times and went on to inspire Jacobsen's Series 7 chairs. Currently, a vintage Ant chair is worth around **£100.**

Danish modern

Along with Hans Wegner and Arne Jacobsen, Finn Juhl was one of a number of Scandinavian designers who came to prominence in the 1950s. His chairs, tables and case pieces, such as this sideboard, are examples of the soft modernism he promoted. It sums up the clean, simple, organic design revolution that came to represent the era. 198cm (78in) wide **£1,500-2,500**

Scandinavian influence

Though made in Britain, Ercol furniture is a great example of the far-reaching influence of Scandinavian designers such as Hans Wegner and Arne Jacobsen. Vintage pieces have become popular as they have the simple, functional design and lack of ornament of similar Scandinavian pieces but they do not command such high prices. 112.5cm (44¼in) wide **£180-220**

TREASURE SPOTTER'S GUIDE
Mirrors

The last word in flamboyance and luxury, early mirrors were expensive to make and many of them are now extremely valuable. Most of the mirrors in ordinary homes today are likely to date from the 19th and 20th centuries.

▲ **Regency splendour**
Convex mirrors became popular during the Regency period. Carved gilt frames were fashionable, usually symmetrical in design compared with the more organic asymmetrical frames of the Rococo period. This mirror is 67cm (26¼in) wide. A piece in good condition could be worth **£1,000-1,500**.

The first mirrors were hand-held accessories but, by the 17th century, they were considered to be an important decoration in any fashionable home. Placed opposite and between windows, mirrors maximised natural daylight, while reflecting the light from candles by night. Because they were rarely handled, the frames could be made from more delicate materials than harder-working pieces of furniture. Their gesso (carved plaster) or softwood frames were elaborately carved and gilded to complement the costly glass within them. In the large rooms of 18th and 19th-century aristocratic houses, it was customary to have mirrors in matching pairs to work within a room's symmetrical design scheme.

The cost of glass

Plate glass originated in Venice with the glass-makers on the island of Murano, where it was made from the 15th century onwards. At that time it was very difficult to make large pieces of glass, so early mirrors often had a central piece within a frame of smaller pieces. Later developments – in France during the early 1700s and in Britain towards the end of that century – made larger pieces of plate glass possible, giving rise to larger, overmantel mirrors and tall, narrow pier glasses. Nevertheless, the difficulty of making large sheets of plate glass meant that mirrors continued to be expensive to buy and were rarely found outside the houses of wealthy patrons before mass production.

If you have an antique mirror, there are criteria to take into consideration when it comes to judging its value. Period

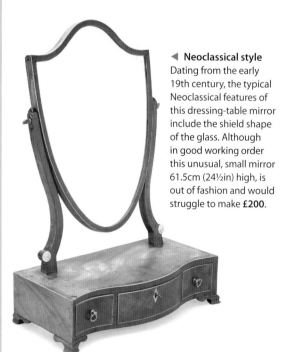

◀ **Neoclassical style**
Dating from the early 19th century, the typical Neoclassical features of this dressing-table mirror include the shield shape of the glass. Although in good working order this unusual, small mirror 61.5cm (24½in) high, is out of fashion and would struggle to make **£200**.

▶ **Chippendale style**
This late 19th-century piece is reminiscent of the Rococo-style mirrors associated with Thomas Chippendale. The frame is ornately carved and the central mirror flanked by two further mirrors. Well made and true to period, it could make as much as £600 at auction, a fraction of the price a genuine Chippendale might realise. 100cm (39½in) wide **£400-600**

Good, Better, Best *Mirrors*

As with many other pieces of furniture, the quality of a mirror will depend on the standard of the craftsmanship, the condition of the glass and the frame, and the design.

Together these affect the value and desirability of the piece. Remember that a pair of matching mirrors is likely to be worth more than twice a single example.

Good

This is a fine example of a Victorian gilt overmantel mirror. Large wall-mounted mirrors such as this are in demand for houses with restored fireplaces. The design is simple and the well-executed rope-twist borders are not overly ornate. The piece retains its original glass and the frame has been sympathetically restored. 125cm (49in) **£300-400**

Better

Dating from the late 18th/early 19th century, this Chinese export giltwood girandole mirror in the George III style is a rare example in good condition. Typical Neoclassical elements include the fluted and bead-moulded frame. Rare features, such as the lacquer panel and original candle branches, increase the value. 47cm (18¾in) wide **£3,000-4,000**

Best

This mirror epitomises the Chinese Rococo style of the early 18th century but was made in the late 19th century. The carved chinoiserie Chippendale-style giltwood frame features ornate scroll carving and is surmounted by a seated figure within a stylised pagoda. The carving is exquisite and the original glass is intact. It is 170cm (67in) wide and worth **£8,000-10,000**.

and style are naturally important but age may have an impact on value too. The earliest mirrors were expensive and so the frame-carving was probably done by a highly skilled craftsman and may be better quality than later examples. The condition and size of the glass is also significant. The earliest glass is translucent and has a more hazy appearance once silvered (the backing that makes it reflective). Early glass may have imperfections and patches where the silver is worn. Thin glass and shallow bevelling around the edge is associated with 18th-century mirrors, while 19th-century versions have thicker, precision-cut glass and bevels with sharper angles. The gilding on older pieces should be worn in places and the glass is more likely to have imperfections. Check for restoration, missing elements or replacement glass, as these may affect price. Seek the advice of an expert before having early pieces restored.

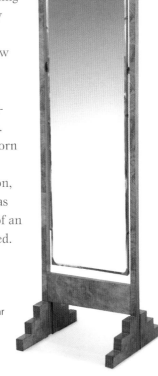

▲ **Desirable Art Nouveau**
This electroplated frame, 45.5cm (18in) high, epitomises the Art Nouveau style. It is a great example of the revival of tabletop pieces. The elaborate casting enhances its desirability. **£1,500-2,000**

▶ **Art Deco delight**
The clean lines of the Art Deco style make it a popular choice for modern homes. This 1935 Beresford & Hicks standing mirror, 153cm (60in) high, features typically geometric stepped feet. **£300-400**

RESTORING YOUR FINDS
Regilding a frame

The gilding on mirror and picture frames is often rubbed away. You can regild it yourself with gold metallic powders. The frame in the steps shown was completely regilded but you can spot-treat small areas and then blend the new into the old, as described below. If your frame is old, rare or valuable, have it repaired by a professional restorer, who will use gold leaf.

YOU WILL NEED

Soft-bristled dusting brush

Soft, lint-free cotton rags

Mild liquid soap

Lukewarm water

Terry towelling rags

Large sheet of brown craft paper

Masking tape

Wire wool grades 0 and 000

Two paint brushes 2.5-5cm (1-2in) wide

Tube of burnt sienna artist's oil paint

White spirit

Liquid gold size

Plastic goggles and face mask

Gold metallic powder to match original gilding

Saucer

Small artist's hogs'-hair brush

Soft-bristled make-up brush

Tinted furniture wax or mid- or dark-brown shoe polish

1 Dust the frame using a dusting brush. Wipe off dirt with a soft, lint-free rag dampened with a solution of soap and lukewarm water. Rinse with a rag dampened with lukewarm water. Pat dry using towelling. Do not leave water on the frame as it can soften the gesso. Cover the glass with brown paper and secure with masking tape.

2 Lightly rub the surface of the frame with grade 0 wire wool, to ensure that it accepts the oil paint. With a 2.5-5cm (1-2in) paint brush, apply two coats of burnt sienna oil paint to the frame. To make this easier, slightly thin the paint with one or two drops of white spirit. Allow each coat to dry for at least 24 hours.

Repairing damage to the frame

If there are any small holes or cracks in the frame, press premixed gesso paste (a carvable plaster) into them with the blade of an old table knife. Build up the paste until it stands slightly proud of the surface and leave it to dry for 48 hours. Using a combination of a utility knife, needle files and fine sandpaper, shape and smooth the dry repair so that it is level with, and follows the contours of, the surrounding area. If the gesso mouldings are badly damaged, seek professional help.

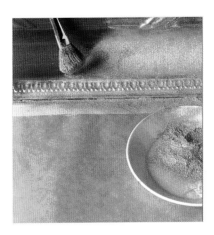  

3 Using the other paint brush, apply liquid gold size to the frame. Make sure that you cover it all. Put on goggles and a mask and decant some gold metallic powder into a saucer. Dip the hogs'-hair brush into the powder and stipple on to the size as soon as it is sticky (about half an hour after it has been applied). Work quickly and make sure that you cover the whole frame.

4 Leave the powder for a minimum of eight hours, by which time the bond between the powder and the gold size will have fully formed. Then, using a make-up brush, lightly dust off any powder that hasn't adhered to the size. If you discover bare patches where the powder hasn't adhered to the size, repeat steps 2-4 on the affected areas.

5 Make a flat pad from a piece of lint-free cotton rag. Gently rub the pad back and forth over the gilding. Some powder will come off on to the pad, so re-form it from time to time or use a new pad. If you want bright, new gilding, stop here. For an attractively worn appearance, rub fairly hard in places, so that the burnt sienna begins to show.

6 To give the new gilding an antique appearance, rub in a tinted furniture wax or shoe polish with a clean, soft, lint-free cotton rag. To give the gilding a more distressed look, apply the polish with grade 000 wire wool, which will rub away some of the gilding. Leave the wax or polish for about half an hour. Then gently buff it, using a clean, soft rag.

▲ **Restoring a vintage frame**
An antique frame, such as this one, requires traditional restoration. If your frame is of little age or value, you can use gold paint to touch up worn areas.

TREASURE SPOTTER'S GALLERY
Lamps

Oil lamps had been providing light for thousands of years in various forms until, in New Jersey in December 1879, American Thomas Edison made the first public demonstration of his light bulb. By the 1880s, his invention had revolutionised domestic lighting.

◄ Maker magic
With lamps it is important, if possible, to discover who the maker is. These blue enamelled ceramic oil lamps by Théodore Deck are signed 'THD'. Deck was a famous French 19th-century artist-potter and created his *bleu-de-Deck* glaze in 1861. His work is keenly collected. 47cm (18¾in) high **£12,000-15,000**

▲ Argand lamps
These oil lamps gave off a light equivalent to six to eight candles and were the lamp of choice until about 1850 when kerosene lamps were introduced. These gilt-brass and blue jasper-mounted Argand lamps are in the Classical Revival style. *c.*1840 35.5cm (14in) high **£1,500-2,000**

▼ Egyptian elegance
Oil lamps mirrored successive styles of the 19th century. European designers had been fascinated with all things Egyptian since Napoleon's ill-fated expedition in 1798, ending in the Battle of the Nile. This *c.*1880 bronze Egyptianesque Colza oil lamp, with a mask, would have been inspired by contemporary drawings. 35cm (14in) wide **£1,000-1,300**

► Brass oil lamp
Unless they make a period style statement, many oil lamps do not fetch much money. This late Victorian brass oil lamp, with glass chimney and etched globular shade, 61cm (24in) high, would struggle to make **£80**.

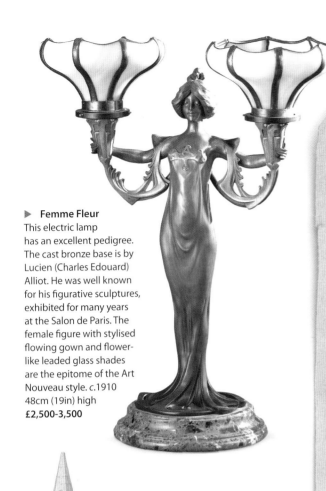

▶ **Femme Fleur**
This electric lamp has an excellent pedigree. The cast bronze base is by Lucien (Charles Edouard) Alliot. He was well known for his figurative sculptures, exhibited for many years at the Salon de Paris. The female figure with stylised flowing gown and flower-like leaded glass shades are the epitome of the Art Nouveau style. *c.*1910 48cm (19in) high **£2,500-3,500**

What is it worth?

Tiffany Studios, New York City was the first firm to capitalise on Edison's invention and produced a wide range of lamp designs from the late 1890s until its closure in 1932. The Wisteria, Dragonfly and Peony lamps are among the most recognisable and thus the most desirable designs. Prices for these can be several hundred thousand pounds.

So how much are the lamps worth?
- Lamps with blown glass or damascene shades start at about £5,000.
- Geometric-design leaded lamps start at about £7,000.
- Simple floral-design leaded lamps can cost £10,000 to £15,000 at the low end. Many sell for much more.
- A diachronic trumpet creeper leaded glass and bronze table lamp would be £200,000-300,000.
- A Poppy leaded glass and bronze floor lamp sold for more than £1,000,000.

▶ **Tiffany Poinsettia lamp**
This early 20th-century electric lamp has a leaded mottled green glass shade with deep red flowers. It is stamped 'TIFFANY STUDIOS NEW YORK 548'. It is 56cm (22in) high and is worth **£30,000-40,000**.

◀ **Beautiful complexity**
Austrian Franz Bergman was the master of the cold-painted bronze technique. This unusually large cold-painted bronze figural electrified boudoir lamp is beautifully detailed. It is formed as a mosque with a minaret, coloured glass window and a man kneeling in prayer beneath the dome. *c.*1910 74cm (29in) high **£13,000-16,000**

▶ **Cameo glass lamp**
Although Emile Gallé died in 1904, this Rhododendron table lamp designed by him was made in 1925. Glass needs to be lit and an electric lamp displays the intricate work perfectly. This 45.5cm (18in) high lamp would sell for **£140,000-160,000**.

TREASURE SPOTTER'S GALLERY
20th-century lighting

The advent of electric lighting introduced a new and exciting dimension to the home and gave rise to all manner of sculptural forms. Reflecting passing fashions, the finest examples also embraced the innovations in materials and technology of each new age.

◀ **Art Deco elegance**
Buyers will be attracted to the sculptural form of this Art Deco piece. The marbled glass shade is almost secondary to the beautifully sculpted female figure. Made c.1925 of bronze on an ebonised plinth, it exploits the lavish materials associated with the period. 60cm (24in) high **£600-800**

▲ **Bauhaus functionalism**
The work of Bauhaus designer Christian Dell, this lamp represents the functionalism of the industrial age. There are no frills – just switch on and swivel to direct the light. Pieces such as this are reduced to their simplest forms, using innovative materials such as aluminium and Bakelite. Generic imitations fetch a tenth of the price of this original Bauhaus piece. 42.5 cm (16¾in) high **£1,500-2,000**

▲ **Anglepoise inspiration**
British engineer George Cawardine's striking desk lamp, designed in 1932, captured the spirit of the industrial age, spawning numerous imitations, as it continues to do today. A versatile task light, it had spring-loaded, articulated joints, swivel action at the base and head, and could shine its light in almost any direction. 2004 re-issue 90cm (35½in) high **£400-500**

◀ **Futuristic simplicity**
The influence of a softer, postwar Modernism is evident in this Italian Arredoluce Triennale floor lamp. Pared back to a stem with three brass arms, it is lifted by the coloured enamelled shades. Function is paramount – each section can be manipulated individually. Reproductions fetch hundreds, compared with the thousands of this rare c.1955 model. 150cm (59in) high **£5,500-6,500**

▶ **Plastics revolution**
Outlandish designs from the 1960s and 1970s have much to do with innovations in plastics technology. This piece, with red cellulose balls, is the work of Danish designer, Verner Panton. Exuberant designs in good condition can command prices in the low hundreds; seminal pieces much more. 1969 44cm (17¼in) diameter **£2,500-3,500**

▼ **Sculptural forms**
These Gatto lamps, created by the prolific Italian designers the Castiglioni brothers, demonstrate how a simple wire frame can be sprayed with plastic to give a sculptural form. The light is diffuse and mellow. Pieces such as this, which epitomise the Space Age look, are in demand. 1960 30.5cm (12in) high **£800-1,000**

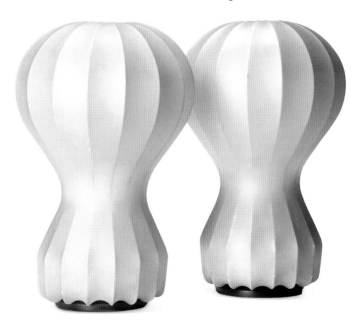

A rare find

Designed by Italian Ettore Sottsass, this quirky lamp sums up the turn-it-on-its-head attitude of Postmodernism. The movement dominated the end of the 20th century and lingers on today. The earliest designs were made as limited editions and command higher prices than later, mass-produced, wares. Many works created by Sottsass's Memphis group are worth thousands of pounds today.

▲ **Tree Tops lamp by Ettore Sottsass**
This enamelled steel and aluminium floor lamp, 180.5cm (71½in) high was often sold – and used – in pairs. The lamp is adjustable so the light can be directed as necessary. It was designed for Memphis in 1981. A pair would be worth more than twice the value of a single lamp, which is **£800-1,200**

◀ **Ron Arad's Tree Light floor lamp**
This idiosyncratic 1990s piece, by Israeli designer Ron Arad, defines the late 20th-century trend towards rough-and-ready hand-crafted items. With industrial overtones, objects were made using unusual or unexpected materials – sheet metal, cement, rubber, tubular steel. Many such creations were one-offs and can be surprisingly valuable, depending on the credentials of their makers. 150cm (59¼in) high **£1,500-2,000**

"Pieces by famous designers in styles typical of the era made using what were the latest materials are desirable today."
MARC ALLUM BBC *ANTIQUES ROADSHOW* SPECIALIST

TREASURE SPOTTER'S GUIDE
Longcase and wall clocks

Longcase or, as they are more commonly known, grandfather clocks are often treasured and passed down through generations. Many are now extremely valuable. The demand for wall clocks is lower but a good-quality design or mechanism will usually result in a high price.

The longcase clock was developed from around 1660, after it was discovered that a longer pendulum kept time more accurately. Early wall clocks, produced for taverns and public buildings from the 1720s, used the same long pendulums with a simpler mechanism and a differently shaped case. This style of clock is sometimes erroneously referred to as an 'Act of Parliament' clock, due to a tax on clocks and watches in 1797. It is popularly believed that taverns hung clocks inside the premises for their patrons, in response to the act. The pendulum-free dial clock was made from the 1750s and has become the most popular type.

The dial clock is also one of the least valuable forms of antique clock due to its relatively simple mechanism. With all clocks, the more sophisticated the mechanism, the more valuable it is likely to be. Clocks that need to be wound less often, such as those with eight-day movements, tend to be more valuable than examples that need more frequent winding. Additional features will also add interest and consequently value. These include automatons, additional dials such as moon phases, and strike/silent levers, which allow striking mechanisms to be turned off at night.

▶ **Mechanical masterpiece**
The superb mechanism, moon phase and musical chimes of this George II clock account for much of its value. The highly decorated case is attractive but several elements, including the skirting and the incongruous classical scene, are later. This is likely to lower the value, despite the fine decoration elsewhere. *c.*1740 240cm (94in) high **£12,000-18,000**

▶ **Gilt cartel clock**
Cartel clocks were made during the late 19th century and typically feature a white enamelled dial and a giltwood or gilt-bronze (ormolu) Rococo Revival case. French ormolu examples are usually more valuable but this exceptional British clock has a wonderful lightness to its asymmetric design and carving, which makes it very desirable. 82cm (32in) high **£7,000-9,000**

Judith warns!

Because so much of the value of a pre-19th century clock is located in its mechanism, it is wise to keep that mechanism in good condition. This means you should never clean it yourself. Clock mechanisms are complicated and delicate: they are easily damaged by careless cleaning. The entire movement must be disassembled, cleaned, burnished and reassembled. A professional clock-maker and restorer should be able to clean most clocks.

▼ **Victorian inlaid wall clock**
Dial clocks tend to have relatively simple mechanisms and none of the decorative splendour of cartel clocks. This wall clock, which features a mother-of-pearl inlay, is more attractive than most contemporary examples, which increases its value. An undecorated dial clock could sell for less than £100. c.1840 44cm (17½in) diameter **£450-550**

All in the name

The signature of a well-known maker, such as Thomas Tompion or Daniel Quare, indicates quality and consequently raises the value. The best examples of their work can fetch tens of thousands of pounds. A lesser-known maker based in a city known for high-quality clock-making, such as Edinburgh or London, can also add value. Rare, early clocks are desirable and often valuable, regardless of maker, particularly if they date from the 'golden age' of British clock-making c.1670-1730.

Appearance is another strong indicator to value, although the greatest prices will always go to clocks with high-quality mechanisms. Fine dials or ornate marquetry cases can push up the value of 18th-century longcase clocks, while an attractive case will account for most of the cost of 19th or 20th-century clocks. Examples in poor condition or those in need of major restoration are unlikely to fetch high sums. Unsympathetic restoration can reduce value by as much as 75 per cent.

If you have a clock that you believe may be valuable, consider consulting your local auction house. Don't get involved in expensive restoration. Most clock dealers and buyers would prefer to buy the clock unrestored.

▶ **Standard longcase**
This longcase clock would have been owned by a middle-class Victorian family. It has none of the sophistication in movement or appearance that characterises a desirable clock. Such clocks are notoriously difficult to sell because they are difficult to accommodate in modern homes. 204cm (80¼in) high **£700-900**

▶ **Atomic classic**
American George Nelson is one of the foremost names in mid-20th century furniture design. His best-known and much-loved creations, which include the atomic-inspired Ball Clock, often fetch high sums. This design is still being manufactured today and brand new examples retail at around £200. Vintage examples are desirable. 34cm (13¼in) diameter **£750-850**

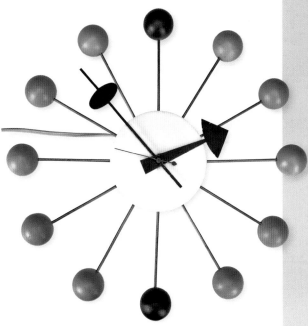

"The best prices are paid for antique clocks in original condition and in working order. Restoration can be very expensive."
JUDITH MILLER BBC *ANTIQUES ROADSHOW* SPECIALIST

TREASURE SPOTTER'S GALLERY
Lantern, bracket and carriage clocks

Small clocks, such as lantern, bracket and carriage clocks, fit easily into modern houses. Early examples with high-quality, intricate movements and attractive cases may be worth many thousands of pounds, particularly if they were made by a notable maker. Plainer or simpler clocks are unlikely to fetch high sums and can be extremely difficult to sell.

◀ **Lantern clock**
Lantern clocks were popular during the late 16th and 17th centuries and are increasingly valuable today. In 2011, an example from the 'First Period' of lantern clock-making (pre-1620) fetched £29,000. This clock has many features that are typical of late 17th-century lantern clocks, including engraving and the maker's name on the dial and decorative frets. Beware of lantern clocks that have been altered. 38cm (15in) high **£3,500-4,500**

▲ **Bracket clock**
Bracket clocks (which take their name from the wall-brackets they were originally housed on) were invented in the mid-17th century. Georgian bracket clocks were made exclusively for the rich. Consequently, they are all very good quality and are often worth thousands of pounds today. Values increase with more complicated mechanisms, elaborate cases and notable maker's names. c.1760 61cm (24in) high **£6,000-8,000**

◀ **Skeleton clock**
The skeleton clock evolved in mid-18th century France. The glass case allowed the movement to be seen and clock-makers used this to show off their skill. The most valuable have ornate frames (perhaps modelled as a cathedral), the original dome and a complex mechanism. This is a plain 19th-century example. Clock 18cm (7in) high **£700-900**

▶ **Plain carriage clock**
Many good-quality British carriage clocks (small and portable clocks with handles) fetch high sums, particularly those by notable makers such as Frodsham or McCabe. But, while the market is generally strong, plain examples with simple white enamel dials and brass cases are common and unlikely to be valuable. 18cm (7in) high **£300-400**

▲ **Revival styles**
Designers in the second half of the 19th century used mass-production techniques to revive and embellish earlier styles. Highly detailed pieces, that today look cluttered and ungainly, were common. This 19th-century clock is worth less than a tenth of an equivalent French ormolu clock from the First Empire period. 45.5cm (18in) high **£500-700**

Barometers

A barometer measures changes in atmospheric pressure. Invented by the Italian philosopher Evangelista Torricelli in 1643, it became popular during the 17th and 18th centuries and ubiquitous by the 19th century. Early stick-form barometers are rare and often valuable, particularly if by notable makers, such as English makers Daniel Quare or John Patrick. A popular style, such as Neoclassical, and quality materials add value. Prices have dropped in recent years, with all but the best examples fetching low sums. As dealers report that younger buyers are entering the market, it may be worth holding on to any standard barometers in case prices improve. Keep all barometers upright and never tip or lay them flat as this may damage the glass tubes and spill the mercury.

▶ **The wheel barometer**
These were widespread in the late 18th century and popular throughout the 19th century. This Regency example has a set of decorative inlay panels, which is likely to increase its appeal but it is by an unremarkable maker and is otherwise a standard model. 99cm (39in) high **£250-350**

▼ **Arts and Crafts enamel mantel clock**
London-based department store Liberty & Co. introduced the Celtic-inspired ranges Cymric (silver) and Tudric (pewter) ranges in 1899 and 1903. Mantel clocks were produced in both ranges and are very desirable. The most decorative examples, which might include hammered, enamelled or inset mother-of-pearl designs, can fetch tens of thousands of pounds. 23cm (9in) high **£1,200-1,800**

▲ **Clock garniture**
Clocks from the 19th century were often mass produced and many are worth just a few hundred pounds. The garniture – a set comprising a clock and two or four vases or candelabra – evolved in this period. Value is dependent on appearance with attractive examples, such as this Louis XV-style garniture, fetching the highest prices. Clock 42cm (16½in) high **£2,500-3,500**

REVIVING YOUR FINDS
Removing marks and stains

Marks and stains can adversely affect the appearance and undermine the value of furniture. Various traditional materials and techniques are available to remedy common problems.

Acids
Surfaces on which any acid has been spilled should be treated immediately.
- In a large plastic bowl, mix a solution consisting of a level teaspoon of either borax or washing soda and 500ml (18fl oz) of warm water.
- Apply the solution liberally with a sponge to the affected area.
- Rinse the area with clean, cold water and pat dry using a soft, lint-free rag.
- If the piece is French-polished and the polish has been damaged, you may be able to reconstitute the finish in the affected area by using the technique described on pages 36-37.
- On waxed or undamaged French-polished surfaces, rub the affected area with a soft, lint-free rag and tinted furniture wax. Buff with a soft cloth.

Bleaching
When a piece of furniture has been exposed to direct sunlight for many years, the colour will fade, or become 'bleached'.
- Firmly rub a little teak oil into the affected area with cotton wool. Leave it to dry naturally for about 48 hours, then repeat the application.
- After a further 48 hours, rub in a little wax furniture polish using a soft rag, and buff to a shine.

Bloom
To remove the soft, grey-white bloom (or 'blush') that can appear on waxed, lacquered or varnished surfaces, try one of the following techniques:

- Rub a little clear microcrystalline wax (available online) into the affected area with a soft rag. Leave to dry for about 20 minutes. Buff vigorously.
- Alternatively, moisten a soft rag with some oil of spike lavender (a lavender-scented liquid available from most herbalists and some chemists). Rub it well into the affected area, leave for three to four hours, then wax and polish as described above.

Candle wax
If possible, remove candle wax with a clean rag as soon as it falls on to the surface, when it is still soft. Over time, candle wax will harden. If this is the case, proceed as follows:
- Wrap crushed ice in a plastic bag and place on the wax. Leave for about five minutes so that the wax becomes brittle.
- Remove the ice-pack and carefully scrape off the wax with your fingernail or the blunt end of a lolly stick.
- Pat dry with terry towelling.
- Rub on a little furniture wax or oil with a soft rag. Buff to a shine.

Fly marks
To remove the black specks of dirt, or 'fly marks', that insects leave on the surface of furniture, try the following remedies in the sequence given:
- Brush off the marks with a hogs'-bristle brush or a stiff toothbrush.
- Carefully lift them off with a scalpel, or by gently scratching with a fingernail.
- If neither of the techniques above works, place a piece of cotton wool soaked with linseed oil on the mark, leave for about 20 minutes, then remove. You should now be able to rub off the mark with the tip of your finger wrapped in a piece of soft rag.

Candle wax
Never use metal objects to scrape off solidified wax. An old credit card can be used to scrape wax away.

Bleaching
Use an appropriately tinted wax if the area is still too light. Use clear wax if the teak oil has completely revived the colour.

Ink

Try to remove an ink spill while it is still wet using a clean, soft cloth dampened with water. If the ink has dried, and perhaps has seeped into the underlying wood, the problem is more serious. The older the stain, the harder it will be to remove. One of the remedies below should work but try them in the sequence suggested, wiping off each one with a damp rag before trying the next.

- Rub on a little white vinegar using cotton wool.
- Rub on a little neat lemon juice using cotton wool.
- Mix equal quantities of neat lemon juice and table salt, then rub on using cotton wool.
- After a successful application, immediately rinse off the solution with a little cold water and dry the area thoroughly with terry towelling, before restoring the finish.
- Re-darken the area if necessary with a little wood stain of the appropriate colour (see pages 64-65).
- Once the wood stain has dried, reseal the affected area with a thin coat of shellac (a wood varnish), and polish with furniture wax using a soft cloth.

Old ink stains

On antique desks, it is often better to leave old ink stains rather than try to remove them. Provided that they are not unsightly, they add character to the piece and are a sign of age (although such signs can be faked).

Oil and grease

Remove cooking oils, animal fats and dairy products as soon as possible by rubbing on beeswax furniture polish and buffing with a soft rag.

Remove older stains by rubbing the mark with a soft cloth slightly moistened with white spirit. Repolish the surface with furniture wax and buff to a shine.

Paint

The damage paint does depends on its type and whether it is wet or dry.

- Wipe off wet acrylic and emulsion paint with a water-dampened rag.
- Remove dry acrylic and emulsion paint by moistening a rag with methylated spirits and laying it over the area for 30 minutes. Remove the rag and scrape off the paint with your fingernail.
- Moisten a piece of cotton wool with white spirit and gently rub over the affected area in concentric circles to dissolve the old layers of polish. When you stop, the polish will re-form.
- Rub in a drop or two of teak oil using a soft rag. Leave to dry. Apply tinted furniture wax and buff to a shine.
- Remove wet oil paint using a rag moistened with white spirit. Finish by using the remedy for dry acrylic paint.
- Remove dry oil paint by brushing on a spirit-based paint stripper. Leave for no more than 30 seconds, then scrape off with a wooden spatula. Finish by using the remedy for dry acrylic paint.

Water

Use these methods to remove white rings and spots on a polished surface.

- Rub in a commercial white-ring remover with a soft cloth (following the maker's instructions). Wipe off the excess and repolish with furniture wax.
- Mix potato flour with white vinegar to form a creamy paste. Wipe it over the stain with a soft rag and leave for 12 hours. Wipe off the excess with a soft rag and repolish with furniture wax.

Burns
Furniture with heat marks, burns and scorch marks from a cigarette or a hot dish are best treated by a professional restorer. Once the underlying wood is charred there is nothing the amateur can do to rescue it.

REVIVING YOUR FINDS
Repairing surface damage

You can restore the surface of a piece of furniture by making minor repairs to the finish. But investigate carefully before replacing an original finish. You risk destroying the patina that makes a major contribution to the value of a sought-after antique. In general, you should only replace the finish on furniture which has little value or is beyond repair. Do your utmost to salvage it, even if this means employing a professional restorer.

Stripping the old finish

As these processes require specialist equipment and/or caustic chemicals, you may wish to use a professional restorer.

Industrial stripping

Some companies specialise in stripping furniture and items such as doors to the bare wood by immersing them in tanks of caustic soda. This method is quick and relatively inexpensive, but it does have drawbacks (see below). Do not use it unless you are stripping a door or a piece of rustic furniture of crude construction.

Scraping

Professional furniture restorers use a scraper to remove the finish, particularly on large, flat surfaces. It is not suitable for curved surfaces or mouldings. For these, use a liquid stripper.

Chemical stripping

Paste and liquid-gel types of stripper are available but the latter is easiest to use as it does not have to be kept moist. Always read the manufacturer's instructions before you begin, making a note of the safety precautions, and wear appropriate protective clothing including goggles, mask and gloves. Keep these substances away from animals and children.

- Apply the stripper following the manufacturer's instructions. Once the paint has been removed, rub the whole surface with a rag moistened with methylated spirits.
- When, after a few minutes, the alcohol has evaporated, use fine-grade sandpaper to lightly smooth the surface, working with the grain.
- If the stripper has removed any of the grain filler, replace where necessary (see box, below right).

Bleaching

If stripping has made the original stain uneven it will be difficult to produce an even colour if you re-stain it. Minor variations add charm and will appear less obvious once a piece has been refinished, but if it is unacceptably patchy use bleach to create an even colour.

- Dilute household bleach in a plastic bucket, in a ratio of one part bleach to six parts water.
- Using a nylon-bristled brush, apply the solution over the surface. Leave for 20 minutes. (The surface will darken.)
- Apply a second coat of bleach and leave for three to four hours. After two hours the original colour of the wood should be bleached away. If any remains apply a third coat and leave for a further three to four hours.
- Moisten a lint-free rag with water and wipe off any residue of the bleach.
- Mix a solution of 5ml (1tsp) of white vinegar to 500ml (1 pint) of water. Wipe over the surface with a lint-free rag and leave for four hours. This will neutralise any remaining bleach.
- Smooth the wood using medium, then fine-grade sandpaper, working with the grain. Re-stain and, if necessary, re-fill the grain (see box, opposite).

Methylated spirits
Pieces of furniture finished with French polish should be prepared for refinishing with methylated spirits rather than a liquid-gel stripper (see pages 36-37).

Patch repair
If you have patched in a small section of new veneer and the grain or figuring doesn't quite match the original, simulate it freehand using a fine-tipped artist's brush and slightly darker versions of the stain used to produce the colour match.

Staining wood

Wood is stained to enrich its colouring and emphasise or highlight the figuring and grain. The basic types of wood stain available to the amateur are: spirit-based, water-based and oil-based.

- Spirit-based stains are available pre-mixed in a wide range of colours from specialist suppliers (see Resources, pages 278-281). They penetrate wood deeply and produce a duller finish than water-based stains. It is not easy to achieve evenness of colour. Restrict to minor patch repairs or employ a professional restorer.
- Oil-based stains are widely available in a choice of wood colours. They provide even coloration and do not raise the grain or lift old veneers. Different shades can be mixed to produce a colour match to the wood, although they are more difficult to shade than water-based stains. Each coat takes 12-24 hours to dry.
- The water-based stains are the easiest to use. Also referred to as 'direct dyes', they produce quick-drying, clear, vivid colours that can be mixed to create a wide range of shades. They have disadvantages: they raise the grain of the wood unless you prepare it well, can lift old veneers and are absorbed at different rates and to different depths by different parts of the wood. If this happens, adjust the colour during application (see box above right).

Applying oil-based stains

- Make sure the surface is clean and dust-free. Put a generous quantity of stain on a fine-bristled varnishing brush or a pad of lint-free cotton rag.
- Start at one edge and brush or wipe in the direction of the grain, applying even pressure. Keep an edge constantly wet to prevent marks between applications.
- Leave to dry for at least six hours between coats. Leave to dry for at least 24 hours before applying the finish (see pages 36-37 and 44-45).

Applying water-based stains

- Rub a cotton rag dampened with water over the surface and leave to dry, then smooth with medium and fine-grade sandpaper, working with the grain. Remove any dust with a dusting brush.
- Dampen a pad of lint-free cotton rag with water. Pick up a generous quantity of stain and apply as for an oil-based stain. If you apply too much to one area, immediately wipe off with a clean, damp rag. If you apply too little, or it is absorbed quickly, apply more.
- As soon as you have completed the first coat, rub the surface with a fresh pad to even out the application and to remove excess stain. Leave to dry for two hours. Apply as many coats as necessary to achieve the desired colour. Let the final coat dry for eight hours.
- Apply a coat of your chosen finish – oil, wax, or clear or white French polish.

Colour-matching
In most cases, you must mix two or three different-coloured stains of the same type to create a perfect colour match. Combining medium oak (mid-brown), red mahogany (reddish-brown) and walnut (yellowish-brown) in varying proportions usually gives a satisfactory match.

Filling the grain

After stripping the original finish from a piece of furniture, you may find that the grain of the wood is filled with flecks of plaster of Paris. This was used to prevent the open grain from making the finish look pitted.

Before you re-finish the surface, seal the filled surface by wiping with a lint-free rag dampened with boiled linseed oil, then leave it to dry for 24 hours.

If you need to fill the grain of a new piece of wood, proceed as follows before staining and waxing:
- Select an oil-based grain filler that matches the colour of the wood. Thin it with white spirit until it has a thick,

creamy consistency. Adjust the colour with oil-based wood stain, but note that the filler will lighten as it dries.
- Rub the filler into the grain in a series of overlapping circles with a pad of coarse, lint-free rag (or hessian).
- Use a clean rag or a piece of hessian to wipe off the excess filler, working in the direction of the grain, before it hardens. Scrape excess filler from recesses or mouldings using a blunt wooden stick.
- Leave it to set for 24 hours. Smooth along the grain, using medium and fine-grade sandpaper, then wipe off the dust.

REVIVING YOUR FINDS
Cleaning upholstery

Upholstery in daily use will require cleaning. As well as regular vacuuming to remove dust, you may have to treat stains occasionally. The remedies for some of the most common stains are listed here. For further advice on cleaning fabrics, see pages 172-173.

Testing for colourfastness

Although professionals should always deal with antique covers, you can clean less valuable pieces, and to remove some stains. Always test the fabric first.

- Try the cleaning agent on a small area (preferably at the back). If the colour runs, call in a professional.
- If water is specified, use only distilled water (available from chemists).
- Always start with a weak solution, and work inwards in a circle to minimise the risk of leaving a ring-shaped mark.

Removing stains

You should bear in mind that the older the stain is, the harder it will be to treat.

Adhesives

- Rub in a little warm water with a cloth. If this does not work, add a few drops of acetone to the damp cloth and rub.

Alcohol (spirits)

- Remove damp alcohol with clean water. If it has dried, rub in a weak solution of warm water and wool detergent. Rinse and leave to dry.

Chewing gum

- Work egg white into the gum to soften it, then pick off as much as possible with your fingers. Sponge away the residue with a mild solution of warm distilled water and soap; rinse with distilled water.
- Alternatively, pack ice cubes around the gum to make it brittle. Pick off as much as possible. Wash as above.

Chocolate

- Gently scrape off as much as possible with a plastic spatula. Then wash with a mild solution of distilled water and soap, before rinsing.
- If this does not work, place the affected area flat over the top of a container. Mix a solution of 30g (1oz) of washing soda to every 500ml (1 pint) of warm distilled water and pour through the stain into the container. Rinse until the stain is gone, then rinse with warm distilled water.

Coffee

- If the stain is still damp, remove with a solution of 30g (1oz) of borax to 500ml (1 pint) of water.
- If the stain has dried, gently rub it with a clean rag moistened with glycerine.
- Leave it for about an hour, then rinse it with water. Finally, gently wash it with warm, soapy water before rinsing it once again. Allow to dry naturally.

Cosmetics

- Remove foundation and moisturisers with potato starch, using the dry-cleaning technique on pages 172-173.
- To remove lipstick, gently rub with warm, soapy water, then rinse. If this does not work, rub a dab of petroleum jelly into the stain, add a drop of ammonia to warm, soapy water and gently rub the stain. Rinse thoroughly. If the fabric is not colourfast, dry-clean with potato starch.
- Remove nail polish with methylated spirits. If that does not work, rub with a small quantity of undiluted acetone.

Blood
Leave well alone if it is an old stain or a valuable textile. For a relatively recent stain, sponge the affected area with a weak solution of cold distilled water and salt. Rinse thoroughly and repeat once more. If additional treatment is required, get professional help.

Candle wax
Cover the area with brown wrapping paper (matt side facing the wax) and apply a medium-hot iron. Keep replacing the paper and reapplying the iron until the worst of the wax has been drawn into the paper. Carefully remove any remaining traces of wax with a clean rag moistened with a little white spirit.

Egg

- Scrape off with a plastic spatula.
- Remove egg white with a solution of salt and water; rinse with water.
- For egg yolk, work a dilute solution of wool detergent into the stain, then rinse with clear distilled water. Repeat until stain has gone. Rinse thoroughly.

Fat and oils

Rub the stain with a clean rag moistened with a little white spirit.

Fruit juice

- On washable textiles, remove still-wet stains by placing them over the top of an open container and pouring hot water through the stain. If that proves insufficient, rub with lemon juice and rinse. Treat old stains as for chocolate, or apply warm, soapy water with a drop of ammonia in it and then rinse.
- On fabrics that cannot be washed, rub in a small quantity of glycerine. Leave for 45 minutes, then partly remove with a damp sponge. Dab with white vinegar and 'rinse' by dabbing with a slightly moistened sponge.

Ink

- Remove fountain-pen ink by dabbing with warm distilled water. Then apply a paste of salt and lemon juice and leave for 10-15 minutes before rinsing thoroughly. Repeat if necessary.
- Remove felt-tip pen ink with methylated spirits. Then wash with warm, soapy water and rinse.
- Ballpoint ink can be difficult to remove. Apply a little methylated spirits, then rinse thoroughly. If that does not work, seek professional help.

Mildew

Use a commercial mildew cleaner, following the instructions.

Milk

Wash with warm, soapy water, then rinse. You may have to add a little borax to the water if the stain is stubborn.

Tea

- If wet, rinse out with hot water. If dried, apply a solution of 1 part borax to 30 parts hot water, then rinse as above and allow to dry naturally.

Wine

- Dab immediately with cotton wool to remove as much as you can. Sprinkle potato starch, talcum powder or French chalk over the area. Knead with your fingers until it becomes tacky. Remove and repeat.
- Gently dab with cotton wool dipped in glycerine, leave for a few minutes and then sponge with warm, soapy water.
- Rinse with water by gently rubbing with wrung-out cloths. Allow to dry.

Grass
First try hand-washing with warm water mixed with wool detergent. Then try gently dabbing with a little methylated spirits. If neither of these methods works, try dabbing with a little eucalyptus oil.

Cleaning trimmings

Many pieces of upholstered furniture are embellished with trimming along the seams and edges. These decorations are collectively known as 'passementerie', and they come in a variety of forms, notably tassels, fringe and braid. Although often made of the same or a similar fabric to the top-cover material, they are sometimes worked in different fibres, including metallic silver and gold threads.

Their intricate construction can make them difficult to clean, particularly if they are tackled in situ and at the same time as the rest of the upholstery. It is a good idea to temporarily detach them from the item of furniture and clean them separately. Because they are usually secured with stitching, it is easy to unpick them with scissors or a dressmaker's seam ripper and then sew them back on later.

▲ **Upholstered side chair**
A mid 19th-century side chair, upholstered in red silk velvet and embellished with tassels on the skirt and shoulders.

CERAMICS

The market for early Chinese porcelain has risen as Chinese buyers seek to invest in their country's history. Record prices have been made and broken several times and so it is worth researching any items you own and wish to sell. Meissen's decorative figures, tablewares and other items made in the early 18th century in Germany are among the most desirable pieces of ceramic and sell for high prices. Pieces by other makers, and more recent Meissen wares, generally sell for less.

The vibrancy and modernity of the 1920s is evident in the decoration of this vase. It is likely to appeal to a large number of buyers as it was made by a very collectable manufacturer – Poole Pottery – and is in the fashionable Art Deco style. The pattern, designed by Truda Carter, and colours used vividly evoke the era when it was made. 25.5cm (10in) high **£400-600**

WHAT ARE CERAMICS?
Differentiating pottery and porcelain

The term 'ceramics' covers two areas: pottery (earthenware and stoneware) and porcelain (hard-paste and soft-paste). The most important questions to answer about a ceramic piece are: is it pottery or porcelain? Is it hard-paste or soft-paste porcelain? Value is dependent on rarity and condition.

Ancient tradition

Pottery is one of the world's oldest crafts. Since earthenware remains porous after firing, it needs to be finished with a glaze to prevent it from absorbing moisture. The glazes on early European earthenware derive from examples introduced by the Arabs when they invaded Spain in the 8th century. They developed a number of finishes using a lead glaze, to which they added oxides, among them tin – which gives an opaque, white finish – and silver, gold and copper, which give a metallic finish.

The tradition for making tin-glazed earthenware, or 'maiolica', began in Italy during the 13th century. Over the next 200 years a number of important centres emerged, particularly at Gubbio, Urbino and Faenza. It was from Italy that the fashion for maiolica spread to the rest of Europe during the 16th and 17th centuries, thanks to immigrant Italian craftsmen. It was known as 'faience' in France (the name possibly deriving from Faenza), 'fayence' in Germany, 'Delft' in the Netherlands (after the main centre of production) and 'delftware' in Britain.

At the end of the 17th century, the Staffordshire potteries discovered that salt added to the glaze resulted in a near-white, salt-glazed stoneware. The earthenware body of 18th-century pottery was often coarse and heavy in comparison with Chinese porcelain. The development of a type of earthenware known as creamware by the Staffordshire potteries in the second half of the 18th century led to the decline of tin-glazed wares.

Chinese discovery

The Chinese discovered the art of making hard-paste porcelain in the Tang Dynasty (618-906 AD). By the end of the 17th century, uncovering the secret had become a European obsession because Chinese porcelain was being exported to Europe in ever-increasing quantities.

At Meissen in Germany, Johann Friedrich Böttger and Count Ehrenfried Walther von Tschirnhaus discovered the formula for hard-paste porcelain in the early 18th century. By 1770, the secret had spread to Vienna, Strasbourg, Frankenthal and Nymphenburg. In France, Vincennes and Sèvres started

▲ **Italian maiolica charger**
This is typical of the work of the Urbino factory during the 16th century. In the 19th century, these pieces were widely copied across Europe.

▲ **Wedgwood creamware cruet set**
The introduction of creamware in the 1760s revolutionised the ceramics industry and led to the closure of many potteries in the 19th century.

▲ Yuan Dynasty plate
Early Chinese porcelain is desirable and record prices have been paid by Chinese collectors. This plate was made in the Yuan Dynasty (1260-1368).

◄ Meissen figure
This 18th-century Meissen figure by Johann Joachim Kändler shows the superiority of the hard-paste body.

► Chelsea beaker
The painting on this beaker, *c.*1748-1750, shows why Chelsea is rightly considered to be the best English soft-paste porcelain factory.

producing soft-paste porcelain in *c.*1745. Soft-paste porcelain was produced at most of the 18th-century English and Welsh factories. Only Plymouth, Bristol and Newhall used hard-paste.

The production of porcelain relied on the discovery of china clay (kaolin) and china stone (petunse). In 1745, William Cookworthy from Plymouth discovered both these in England. This was the beginning of the shortlived 18th-century English hard-paste porcelain. Soon Lund's factory at Bristol and those at Bow and Chelsea were making soft-paste porcelain using frit (a sand mixture) or soapstone in place of china stone.

What is pottery?

Pottery includes anything made from baked clay and may be made from a number of different materials. Earthenwares and stonewares can be covered in many different glazes.
- An earthenware body may be red-brown, buff, white or grey.
- The tin glaze chips easily.
- Stoneware can be thinly potted.
- Stoneware is fired at a higher temperature and does not need a glaze to make it watertight.
- The fired body can be dark grey, red, white or sand-coloured.

What is porcelain?

Porcelain is a hard, translucent white ceramic made from china clay and china stone. It makes a clear, ringing sound when struck.
- The most common distinction between pottery and porcelain is that pottery is not translucent and porcelain is. As a simple rule this has some truth, but some porcelains have little translucency.
- Porcelain is divided into hard-paste and soft-paste. The best way to tell them apart is to study damaged examples.
- Hard-paste is fired at a higher temperature than soft-paste. It is cold to the touch and any chip is flint or glass-like. It has a hard, glittery glaze fused to the paste and can become translucent during the second firing. The high kaolin content makes it more refined.
- A file will cut easily into soft-paste. It has a warmer feeling to the touch and any chips are granular. It is less stable in the kiln: figures were especially difficult to fire (English soft-paste figures do not compare with those of German factories). The glaze was soft as it tended not to fuse into the body as much as hard-paste glaze and was susceptible to pooling and crazing. Early soft-paste is prone to discoloration.
- Bone china is a porcelain recipe consisting of petunse, kaolin and dried bone, supposedly invented by Englishman Josiah Spode II *c.*1794 (after experiments at the Bow factory). From *c.*1820, it became the mainstay of the British porcelain industry.

IDENTIFYING CERAMIC DECORATION

There are four main types of decoration on ceramics: underglaze, overglaze, painted and printed. It is vital to tell the difference between hand-painted and printed decoration. Easy identification comes with practice.

Before the mid-18th century, all ceramics were decorated individually by hand, a process that in many cases required considerable artistic skill, depending on the sophistication of the imagery. The invention of transfer-printing in the mid-18th century changed that: by semi-automating the process of decoration, the cost of production was considerably reduced, making pieces affordable to the rapidly expanding middle classes.

The significance of these printing techniques lies not only in reducing the cost of ceramics to their original 18th, 19th and early 20th-century buyers, but also affects the value of those ceramics as antiques to today's buyers. There are exceptions: early, rare transfer-printed examples can fetch thousands of pounds but, as a rule-of-thumb, transfer-printed wares are worth less – often

considerably less – than their contemporary hand-painted equivalents. Of course, it is not always that simple. Particularly prevalent from the mid-19th century onwards was the practice of combining transfer-printing and hand-painting. This practice meant that the piece appeared to be hand-painted but was quicker and cheaper to produce. One characteristic of this hybrid form of decoration is regularity and uniformity (as opposed to spontaneity) in the outlines.

Also evident are the presence of brush marks or absence of hatching, or both, in the areas of colouring-in and shading. The colour is sometimes applied above the glaze. This can often be found on poorer quality services.

You must be able to tell the difference between hand-painted and transfer-printed if you wish to sell.

Hand-painted

- A hand-painted pattern is achieved by brush strokes and has a fluidity that is impossible to achieve with transfer-printing.
- Note the freedom of line in the object's outline.
- Brush work is most obvious where there is shading of colour – note particularly the irregular brush strokes in the colouring-in and shading.
- The brush tends to be less precise than an engraving.

Transfer-printed

- A printed pattern results from an etched or engraved copper plate.
- Note the hatching lines, created by the engraved lines on the copper plate to which the pattern was applied before being transferred to paper.
- They display a uniformity almost impossible to replicate by hand.
- A small break or misalignment may occur in the design where two sections of the paper transfer didn't quite meet, or were applied inaccurately.

Overglaze colour

- Known as 'enamels', these colours, painted over the glaze, are fired at low temperatures.
- Metallic compounds are combined with flux (a substance added to the ingredients to reduce the fusing temperature) and ground into a powder.
- This is mixed with oils and painted onto the surface.
- Multiple firings may be needed, which is expensive.
- Many of these early, naive Staffordshire figures are now highly desirable. Look out for unusual subjects, such as leopards, hedgehogs, zebras and squirrels.

Underglaze colour

- Finely powdered oxide is mixed with oil and applied to an unglazed surface.
- Cobalt blue is the most common colour but copper green, manganese purple, antimony yellow and iron red are often found.
- An object was only fired once which was cheaper.
- With underglaze colour it is the quality and intricacy of the painting that will determine value.
- The painting on early 18th-century Meissen wares is often exceptional, see below.

Gilding

- The surface of the ceramic is decorated with a thin layer of gold in the form of gold leaf or a fine powder. It is then fired at a low temperature.
- The gold can also be mixed with mercury to give a bright metallic finish.
- Some factories, such as Meissen and Sèvres, employed the most highly skilled gilders.
- Many gilders put their initials on the base. Research can identify the gilder, which will add to the value.

Lithographic-printed

- The key to identifying lithographically printed polychrome colour decoration lies in the areas of shading. Unlike hand-painting, shading is created by applying regularly spaced tiny dots.
- This technique was originally used on printed material, such as posters, and during the 19th century started to be applied to ceramics, allowing for greater detail in a mass-produced object.

RESTORING YOUR FINDS
Bonding simple breaks

YOU WILL NEED

Lint-free rag

Acetone

Masking tape

Two-part epoxy-resin adhesive

Cocktail stick

Cotton bud

Plastic or metal paint tray

Fine sand or modelling clay

The technique used to mend a simple break in this late 19th-century plate is not difficult to master, although it requires patience. It can also be used to repair cups, saucers and bowls.

Repair a porcelain plate

1 Clean and dry the plate. To make sure no soap or grease is left on the broken edges, wipe them with a piece of lint-free rag moistened with acetone. Cut several strips of masking tape, each 7.5cm (3in) long, and stick them to both sides of one half of the plate at right angles to the line of repair.

2 Following the manufacturer's directions, mix a small quantity of adhesive. With a cocktail stick, carefully apply adhesive to the broken edge of the untaped half. Holding the two halves firmly together, stretch the strips of tape across the joint and stick them to the other half of the repair. Wipe off excess adhesive with a moistened cotton bud.

3 When you are satisfied with the repair, stand the object in a paint tray filled with fine sand while the adhesive dries. (Small pieces can be supported on a lump of modelling clay.)

4 Let the adhesive dry thoroughly (following the manufacturer's advice on drying times). Carefully remove the object from the sand or clay, and peel off the strips of tape.

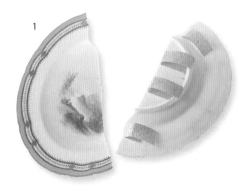

Remaking old repairs

YOU WILL NEED

Small artist's brush

Methylated spirits

Paint stripper (if required, use the water-based type with the consistency of jelly)

Scalpel (or small craft knife)

Stiff-bristled toothbrush

Warm water

Terry towelling

The adhesive used to bond an old repair often discolours with age, as it has on this late 19th-century cup. The only solution is to undo the repair and remake it using modern adhesives.

Remake a repair

1 Remove the old glue by brushing on methylated spirits to soften it. If this does not work, use paint stripper. Use a scalpel to scrape away the glue. Repeat if necessary.

2 You may be able to pry off the broken section with your fingers. If not, use the scalpel to cut through the glue.

3 Once the broken section starts to come away, carefully work it loose.

4 Clean the broken edges with a toothbrush dipped in warm water. Dry the sections thoroughly with terry towelling.

5 When you have cleaned and dried the joint thoroughly, remake the repair, following the steps on the previous page.

1
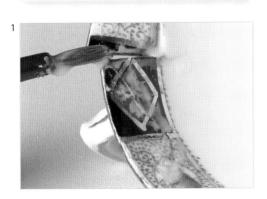

2
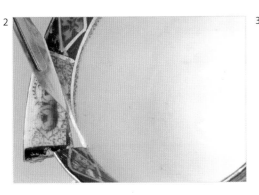

3

4
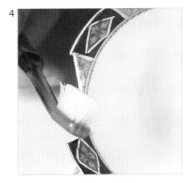

Judith warns!

Always mention any damage or repairs when selling a piece of ceramic. If you're selling online, failing to do so will lead to negative feedback and demands for a refund. It is now simple to use ultraviolet (UV) light to check for repairs. Mended breaks, cracks and even new decoration that appear to be perfect when scrutinised in daylight will fluoresce bright white under the light from a UV lamp.

5

RESTORING YOUR FINDS
Repairing chips

Chips are caused by knocks against the rims and edges of plates, bowls and saucers. Make this type of repair as soon as possible to prevent the damaged area from becoming stained or discoloured.

Repairing a chip

YOU WILL NEED

Cotton buds

Acetone

Two-part epoxy-resin adhesive

Titanium dioxide

Artist's brushes sizes 00-3

Two-part white epoxy putty

Lint-free rag

Square-ended needle file

Fine-grade silicon-carbide paper

Cold-cure lacquer

Artist's powder pigments

1 Wipe chip with a cotton bud dipped in acetone. Mix a small quantity of two-part epoxy-resin adhesive following the manufacturer's directions, adding a little titanium dioxide to counteract any yellowing. Use a small artist's brush to apply a thin layer to the chip.

2 Mix some epoxy putty, following the manufacturer's instructions. Moisten your fingers with cold water, then use to press the putty into the chip, following the contours, so it stands slightly higher than the surrounding areas. Using a rag, wipe putty from the surrounding areas.

Museum mend

A museum mend is a form of repair that does not hide the fact that the piece has been restored, but allows the owner to enjoy its beauty. It creates a perfect repair on the front of an item, with evidence of the break left on the back. This method is used by museums to respect the history of an item while showing it to the best effect.

3 Once the filler has dried use a square-ended needle file to rub the putty so that it doesn't stand out from the surrounding area. Take care not to damage the surface around the chip. Sand the putty with small pieces of silicone-carbide paper to make a smooth surface.

Repainting the pattern

If you need to repaint any pattern or motif, you can use either artist's acrylic paints, or white or clear cold-cure lacquer tinted with artist's powder pigments. Both should be applied with small artist's brushes; two or three, ranging in size from 00 to 3, should cover the largest and smallest motifs. Allow the paint or lacquer to dry thoroughly before completing step 5.

1 Touch in the ground colour of the repaired area using a thin coat of paint or glaze, working outwards from the middle using light brush strokes.

2 To blend the newly painted section into the surrounding areas, 'feather' the edges by lightly stroking the bristles over the edges of the repair.

3 Let the glaze or paint dry fully, then very lightly sand it with fine-grade silicon-carbide paper to remove any brush strokes and wear away any noticeable line between the repainted section and the surrounding area.

4 Wipe off any dust from the surface and repeat the previous stages to apply a second coat of glaze or paint, if necessary adjusting the colour. You may have to apply a third coat.

5 When you have sanded the final ground coat, brush on a single coat of clear cold-cure lacquer, feathering the edges of the repair as before. However, if you have to repaint any sections of pattern or motif, do so before applying the clear glaze.

6 To repaint part of the decoration, first create a guide by outlining the pattern with a series of faint dots made with a sharp pencil.

7 Use a fine-tipped artist's brush, ensuring you do not overload the bristles.

8 Always work on one colour of the pattern at a time.

9 Keep some thin, lint-free rags and cocktail sticks on hand, plus the appropriate solvent (water for acrylics; thinner for lacquer), so that you can immediately remove the effects of over-brushing or any accidental splashes.

4 If the background colour is white, apply a thin coat of white cold-cure lacquer with a fine-bristled artist's brush. Let it dry for at least 12 hours before proceeding to step 5. If the background colour is off-white or coloured, tint the lacquer with artist's powder pigments.

5 If you need to repaint part of a pattern do so now following the steps in the box above. When dry, brush on a coat of clear cold-cure lacquer.

There are two types of cold-cure lacquer. The clear variety is always applied as a final protective coat, while the white version can be tinted with artist's powder and used to match the original background colour of the object, or to repaint motifs and patterns.

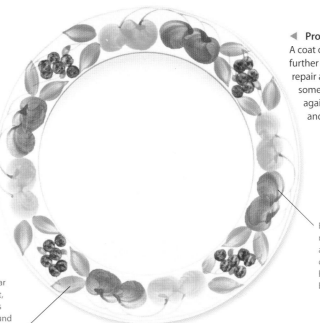

◀ **Protect your work**
A coat of lacquer will further blend in the repair and provide some protection against discoloration and wear and tear.

For the most effective result, spend time achieving a good colour match before applying the background glaze.

TREASURE SPOTTER'S GUIDE
Meissen and its imitators

The obsession with finding the secret for Chinese porcelain, or 'white gold', gripped European factories by the end of the 17th century. Augustus the Strong, Elector of Saxony, who collected Oriental wares, was so consumed by his desire to discover the formula, he set up a factory in Meissen.

▲ **Early Böttger teapot**
This early teapot shows the off-white body of Böttger porcelain. The thin, glassy glaze has a bluish tinge – typical of the 1730s and 1740s. The painted chinoiseries were popular decorative devices, as is the gilded cartouche. 13cm (5in) high **£6,000-8,000**

Meissen's hard-paste porcelain formula was developed from 1708 by German scientist Count Ehrenfried Walther von Tschirnhaus and perfected by German alchemist Johann Friedrich Böttger in 1710. From the 1720s, Meissen's output was unsurpassed for technical innovation and artistic quality, due to the skills of modeller Johann Joachim Kändler and colour-chemist and painter Johann Gregor Höroldt. Most early Meissen porcelain is of superb quality, rare and valuable.

Meissen continued to produce exceptional wares throughout the 19th century. Although valuable and keenly collected, these later pieces are typically worth less than the best 18th-century examples. Many 19th-century wares copy earlier styles and it is usually possible to distinguish them from the originals. Figures made during the early 18th century are decorated with vivid colours, such as strong red, yellow and black, and sit on simple bases in either turquoise or green. Later figures were often decorated in pastel colours. The bases of these are often highly embellished with Rococo scrolls, gilding and enamel colours. Early teapots and coffee pots usually bulge towards the foot, while later shapes tend to be top heavy. Fine painting and high-quality modelling will always add value,

▲ **Figure group by Kändler and Reinicke**
Johann Joachim Kändler and Peter Reinicke modelled and painted many porcelain figures from the 1730s. With their wonderful sense of drama, liveliness and movement, they were the envy of the other European factories. 15cm (6in) high **£4,000-6,000**

◄ **Rococo Revival figures**
From the early 1830s the Rococo style was revived. These romantic lovers were typical of the large factory productions of this period. Other subjects included shepherds and shepherdesses, allegorical figures of the seasons and the four continents. Although of wonderful quality, such pieces do not attract the values of 18th-century examples. 24.5cm (10in) high **£1,200-1,500**

▶ *Hausmaler* decoration
Hausmaler (freelance decorators) from Augsburg were among the first to decorate items outside the factory. Early pieces can still fetch good prices. This *c.*1725 bowl, 13cm (5¼in) wide, is worth **£1,000-1,200**, but a later, inferior one would be worth less than £100.

however old the piece is. All 18th and 19th-century Meissen porcelain should be sold in specialist ceramics sales, which are run by most large auction houses.

Crossed swords mark

Thanks to the success of the Meissen factory, its wares were copied by numerous Dresden factories, many of which used the crossed swords mark. Not only German factories copied the Meissen originals. At some time most factories in Europe used the mark. It is sometimes difficult to distinguish other hard-paste German factories from Meissen, but it is reasonably easy with British soft-paste factories such as Bow, Chelsea and Worcester (see pages 70-71).

Copyist or forger?

Frenchman Edmé Samson began copying designs by the major factories in the late 1830s. His factory did not set out to produce fakes and its high-quality reproductions were marked. However, Samson wares have been passed off as original as the mark can be substituted with a false one. There is a strong market for Samson pieces. The following may indicate Samson:
• The glazes were often glossy and rather glassy.
• Hard-paste porcelain was used where many of the originals were soft-paste.
• Modelling was stiff or wrong in scale.
• Heavy decoration or inaccurate colours were used.

▲ **Samson Meissen-style terriers**
A pair of late 19th-century Bolognese terriers, after Meissen. 32cm (15in) high **£600-700**

▶ **Meissen Pagoda figure**
A late 19th-century Meissen articulated Pagoda figure, after the original by Johann Joachim Kändler. Exquisitely modelled and painted, this figure is 30.5cm (12in) high and worth **£9,000-12,000**.

The modelling and elaborate decoration remain refined.

Details have been picked out in gilding, demonstrating the gilder's skill.

The palette is harsh and lacks the harmony of the Meissen original.

The form and decoration are crude compared with the Meissen example.

◀ **Dresden Nodder figure**
This late 19th-century Dresden Nodder figure, after the Meissen model, lacks the quality of the original but is still desirable. 26cm (10½in) high **£700-800**

▶ **Chelsea Meissen-style figure**
A figure of Dr Boloardo after the Commedia dell'Arte series modelled by Johann Joachim Kändler and Peter Reinicke for Meissen, *c.*1755. Even a successful factory such as Chelsea copied the Meissen figures and mark. 15cm (6in) high **£2,000-3,000**

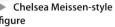

TREASURE SPOTTER'S GUIDE
Blue-and-white transfer-printed ware

The demand for transfer-printed pottery has collapsed, with some notable exceptions. The heyday for production was the early years of the 19th century when the potteries, particularly in Staffordshire, produced vast quantities of wares to satisfy the emerging middle classes' desire to possess beautiful objects for everyday use.

An extensive range of transfer-printed patterns was produced by a large number of factories – some celebrated, many unknown. The most famous example is the classic Willow pattern, which was one of the first to be produced. Thought to have been inspired by a Chinese myth, it was in fact first engraved by Thomas Minton for Thomas Turner of Caughley in 1780. For more than two centuries it has been the stock pattern of nearly every British pottery manufacturer. As such, the majority of pieces are difficult to sell – except on the internet – and you should not expect to get much money for common examples.

Factories and patterns to look for

Some of most popular factories are: Spode, Wedgwood, Minton, Davenport, Enoch Wood, Rogers and Ridgway. Many people have built collections around patterns that were copied by numerous factories. Some subjects, such as Spode's Indian Sporting series and Caramanian series, have remained popular, but still fail to fetch the prices they did a few years ago. Around 1820, views of country houses, churches, abbeys and rural scenes became very popular. Produced in vast quantities, these are in general not worth much unless the pattern is on an unusual shape, such as a footbath,

Transfer-printed price line

Good time to buy
Even though this early 19th-century blue-and-white transfer-printed pearlware baluster jug, 17.5cm (6¾in) high, is a pleasing shape, these landscape patterns do not attract buyers today in the way that they did 30 years ago. It is so undesirable, most auction houses would put it in a 'job' lot with other pieces. If you did try to sell it you would be lucky to make **£40-60**.

The bird has flown
This small Worcester sparrow beak jug, 10cm (4in) high, was made and transfer-printed in about 1770, the golden period for one of England's best porcelain factories. It is in good condition, but these pieces are out of fashion at the moment. At one time it would have made £700-800 at auction, but now it would struggle to make **£150-200** on a good day.

Rarity still sells
This Flight, Barr and Barr cylindrical mug, 11cm (4¼in) high, is printed with a view of Worcester Cathedral along from the riverside porcelain factory. The base is painted with: 'This is a Faithful Saying and Worthy of all acceptation, the Christ Jesus came into the World to Save Sinners of Whom I am Chief, 1816', making it rare and desirable. It would sell for **£700-800** in a specialist sale.

The Durham Ox

Even when standard transfer-printed wares have seen a downturn in value, interesting and rare patterns have performed very well. This Staffordshire earthenware platter is printed with The Durham Ox pattern. This famous image came from an engraving of 1802 by J. Whessel after a painting by John Boultbee of *John Day with the Durham Ox*. The series includes eight known views all with the same border of stylised flowers and was produced by an unknown maker. The famous beast was a product of intensive breeding and was prized for its 'great size and perfect shape and configuration'. It became a popular attraction. In one day in the early 1800s, Londoners paid £97 (more than £3,000 in today's money) in admission fees to see it!

▲ **Durham Ox platter**
This restored example, 53cm (20¾in) wide, from *c.*1820, is worth £900-1,200. In perfect condition it could sell for £5,000-6,000.

a Stilton bell or a four-part ice-pail. In the 1830s, views of Italy became fashionable but, again, to be valuable, these patterns need to be on rare shapes.

Probably the least desirable are the floral designs. Incredibly popular at the time, such designs tend to be the least saleable now. The earliest were produced by Wedgwood in its Botanical series, around 1810. Spode also made a number of floral patterns, as did Ridgway and Minton. One pattern that is keenly collected is the Sweet Pea pattern by the Brameld Yorkshire pottery.

The Registration of Design Act of 1842 meant that the copying of prints, paintings and other designs was prohibited. This led to a looser, more romantic style with paler colours and less pattern. The quality tended to be poor, hence such items are even more difficult to sell.

As it happens, the demand for blue-and-white ware in the US has held up better than it has here, particularly for any pieces featuring American scenes, such as John and William Ridgway's Beauties of America series.

American interest
A vast amount of English transfer-printed ware was specifically designed for export to America. This 37.5cm (14¾in) wide platter, by John and William Ridgway, Hanley, 1814-1830, is decorated with the Deaf & Dumb Asylum, Hartford Connecticut, Larsen No. 176, from Ridgway's Beauties of America series. Although not the most cheery print, it is rare and would fetch **£900-1,200.**

Must-have design
One of the most popular series with collectors is the Indian Sporting group produced by Spode around 1815, and based on prints by a Captain Thomas Williamson. They depict the killing of various animals in the jungle, in this case Shooting a Leopard. These platters are highly collectable and even in a depressed market this 51cm (20in) wide example would make **£2,000-2,500.**

Age, rarity and desirability
This black transfer-printed mug comes from what is known as the early First Period at Worcester. Printed and signed by Robert Hancock, it has a rare print of William Pitt the Elder shown in half-length portrait between Fame and Mars. Made around 1760, this 8.5cm (3½in) high mug would sell for **£3,000-3,500** because of its rarity and historical significance.

TREASURE SPOTTER'S GALLERY
Afternoon tea sets

In the 18th century, only the wealthy could afford tea so the need for tea sets was limited. Within 100 years, the cost of tea had fallen and the burgeoning middle classes all wanted ceramic tea sets. Recently, habits have changed again and tea sets are out of fashion, although some hotels now offer afternoon tea featuring Victorian tea sets – perhaps indicating a resurgence in popularity.

◀ **Staffordshire set**
Many of these transfer-printed patterns are seen as old-fashioned and fussy – and, of course, they don't go in the dishwasher! This Staffordshire Floral Vases pattern part tea set, printed with the sheet-like pattern of vases and floral border, comprising teapot with cover, footed bowl, covered sugar box and six London-shape teacups and saucers, from c.1830 is worth **£160-180**.

▶ **Fussy design**
Although undoubtedly excellent quality this Minton porcelain Rococo Revival blue-ground part tea service, from around 1840, is considered over-decorated and unusable. You get a lot of tea set for your money – a teapot, cover and stand, a sugar box and cover, a cream jug, two sandwich plates, ten teacups and nine saucers. And what would you get if you could sell it? Unbelievably, **£80-100** on a good day.

◀ **Majolica novelty**
Some styles buck the trend and majolica is still selling well. Particularly desirable are pieces with monkey handles. This George Jones part tea service, c.1875, comprising teapot and cover, sucrier and cover, milk jug and three saucers, is worth **£2,000-2,500**.

Big name, low price
Even the Wedgwood name and the fact that this *c*.1890 set was retailed by the smartest shop in London, Thomas Goode & Co., does not make this set especially desirable. It has eight cups, eight saucers, 11 tea plates, two bread and butter plates, a sugar bowl and a milk jug but would only make **£100-140**.

Childhood favourite
Designed by Mabel Lucie Attwell for Shelley in 1926, this Boo Boo tea set comprises an elf milk jug, a toadstool house teapot, and a toadstool sugar bowl. It highly collectable today. Kitsch still sells. **£450-650**

Judith warns!

The popularity of 'retro'-themed tea parties, and the accoutrements that go with them, has led to a revival in the use of cake stands. To take advantage of this, enterprising dealers have converted plates by drilling holes and fitting metal parts. To see if a stand is original, carefully unscrew the metal parts and look inside the hole. If the glaze runs inside, as here, it's original. If it doesn't, and you can see unglazed ceramic, it's a conversion.

The glaze is visible in the hole proving it is a genuine piece.

Chintz cake stand
This genuine *c*.1950 Grimwades Royal Winton Julia pattern chintz cake stand, 23cm (9in) wide, with chrome-plated handle, is worth **£55-65**.

Retro appeal
This 1930s James Kent chintz Hydrangea pattern tennis tea set has recently become much more desirable for trendy retro tea parties. Remarkably useful for a small cup of tea and a dainty cup cake, this would fetch **£90-110**.

Art Deco style
Stylish, elegant and so evocative of its time, this 1930s Shelley Art Deco tea set would do very well in any 20th-century decorative arts sale. The Vogue shaped set, printed in black and over-painted in orange with the 11792 pattern, comprises a milk jug, sugar bowl, two sandwich plates, 12 cups, saucers and tea plates. It should easily make **£2,500-3,000** and could, on the right day, make more.

TREASURE SPOTTER'S GUIDE
British Art Deco ceramics

After the deprivations of World War I, British potteries relished the clean, angular lines, modern geometric shapes and highly stylised motifs of Art Deco. The best examples were produced by Clarice Cliff – and her Bizarre and Fantasque ranges are particularly desirable.

▼ **Susie Cooper jug**
Susie Cooper ceramics have a strong collectors' following. There is great demand for the Art Deco geometric patterns with striking colours such as the Moon and Mountain pattern, designed in 1928. This jug, 12 cm (4¾in) high would sell for **£350-450.**

▶ **Carlton Ware vase**
The Stoke-on-Trent firm of Carlton Ware produced striking Art Deco pieces during the 1920s and 1930s. This Red Devil vase (pattern 3765), 18cm (7in) high was made in limited numbers from 1932-1935. It was not popular at the time, hence its rarity now. **£2,500-3,000**

Prolific potter and decorator Clarice Cliff pushed the boundaries with her dramatic Art Deco designs. Cliff designed more than 500 shapes and over 2,000 patterns. Alongside traditional shapes, she created many futuristic forms, such as cone-shaped sugar sifters and beehive-shaped honey-pots. Most of her output consisted of tableware but she did produce some novelty wares, the most collectable being figures, particularly The Age of Jazz figures and the newly fashionable wall masks.

Although overshadowed by Cliff, Susie Cooper designed an equally popular range of shapes, including Kestral, Curlew, and Wren, and patterns such as Scarlet Runner Beans, Polka Dots and Cromer. Other early, desirable ranges include abstract geometric designs, of which the pre-1939 wares are the most sought-after by collectors.

Carlton Ware enjoyed its heyday with Art Deco wares in the 1920s and 1930s. Most collectable are the factory's lustrewares, inspired by Wedgwood's highly successful Fairyland Lustre range by Daisy Makeig-Jones.

The Poole Pottery (known as Carter, Stabler & Adams from 1921) produced collectable Art Deco tablewares in the 1920s and 1930s. Desirable designs include Studland, Picotee and Everest.

Would you believe it?

After 30 years on top of a wardrobe a Clarice Cliff charger in the desirable May Avenue pattern, made around 1932, sold for £39,950 in May 2003 at Christie's in London. The pattern was produced briefly in 1932 and 1933, making it rare. Chargers are desirable as they show off the pattern so well and this, at 46cm (18in) diameter,

was a particularly large charger. Cliff's inspiration for the May Avenue design came from an oil painting by the Italian artist Modigliani and the name of the design was taken from a street near her Tunstall birthplace. This more modest version of the pattern on a 12.5cm- (5in) high vase is worth a mere £5,000-6,000.

Matt glazes and geometric forms

Wedgwood also had many successful ranges in the Art Deco period. The New Zealand Modernist architect Keith Murray designed a range of simple geometric forms, with lathe-turned decoration and semi-matt glazes often in soft grey, black basalt, green, straw and ivory-white. From 1926, the modeller and sculptor John Skeaping designed 14 stylised earthenware animals and birds for Wedgwood, which can sell for up to £500.

Doulton produced some Art Deco tableware, such as the Dubarry service, but it is the bone china figures, many by Leslie Harradine, that are the most collectable today. To be valuable, these should be overtly Art Deco, showing young ladies in informal poses, often with bathing costumes on or off.

The Shelley Pottery employed talented designers in this period. Mabel Lucie Attwell introduced a range of charming nursery wares that remain collectable. In 1930, Eric Slater introduced two Modernist forms, Vogue and Mode. These streamlined architectural shapes were suited to Shelley's fine bone china. Also popular is the Eve geometric design introduced in 1932. Many other Stoke firms produced Art Deco wares, with varying success. Myott was one of the most prolific but its wares are generally cheaper than its contemporaries.

As the demand for Art Deco wares is strong, all these pieces should be sold in a specialist 20th-century design sale.

Clarice Cliff is perhaps the most famous name in British Art Deco ceramics and her colourful designs are keenly bought by collectors. Prices range from under £50 for a Crocus pattern small tray, to the world record price of £39,950 for a rare May Avenue pattern charger. She was an excellent painter and modeller and was influenced by Art Deco and Cubism.

Good

This 13 cm (5¼in) high cone-shaped sugar sifter is a highly desirable Art Deco form. It is painted with the Crocus pattern which was Cliff's most successful design. It is not particularly rare but this example has the advantage of its collectable shape and the fact that it is a variant of the pattern. It would sell for **£300-500.**

▶ **Keith Murray vase**
Keith Murray designing for Wedgwood c.1934 produced some futuristic Modernist designs in matt colours. This large shoulder vase with horizontal banded body all in a matt blue glaze is typical. The market for these is not as strong as it was a few years ago but this 28cm (11in) high vase would still sell for **£400-500.**

Better

The high quality of painting on this rare 1930 Appliqué Lucerne vase and the fact that it is a miniature suggest that it is a tradesman's sample vase. It is painted with the whole Lucerne pattern between black and red bands. The rare pattern and size – 7.5cm (3in) high – make this worth **£2,500-3,000.**

Best

The unusual, geometric Cubist Cafe pattern on this rare 1929 vase from the Bizarre range shows the diverse range of influences on Cliff's work. It has printed factory marks to its base, is 18cm (7½in) high and, thanks to its scarcity, is worth **£10,000-15,000.**

◀ **Poole Pottery vase**
The Poole Pottery Leaping Deer pattern was a celebrated Art Deco design. Pattern 599/TZ was designed by Truda Carter and produced from 1934 to 1937. These early Poole designs are very desirable and should sell for **£800-900.** This vase measures 21cm (8¼in) high.

TREASURE SPOTTER'S GUIDE
Figurines

By the 20th century, figurines exuded a new energy and daring, giving a modern twist to a form that had been a staple of ceramic factories for 200 years. Many figurines made during the 1920s and 1930s harked back to previous eras, but those in the Art Deco style embody the emancipated women of the time.

It is interesting to note that it was not the established firms such as Meissen and Derby that were market leaders with these figures but newcomers such as Goldscheider, Lenci and Rosenthal. Inspired by women's new-found confidence, and changing social patterns, these colourful ceramics were affordable works of art. Many ceramics designers also created the bronze and ivory figures that have become synonymous with the Art Deco period.

Arguably the best exponent of this style was the Goldscheider factory. The firm was founded in 1885 by Friedrich Goldscheider in Vienna, Austria. A man with outstanding creative vision, he recognised the importance of the Orientalism movement at that time and decided to develop a particular style of Orientalist terracotta sculptures. In 1920 his sons, Walter and Marcel, became the joint owners.

Designs by the best artists
They employed the best artists, such as the Austrians Josef Lorenzl and Stefan Dakon, who reflected the advent of the Art Deco style and created a magnificent selection of colourful models capturing the flamboyance, glamour and flair of postwar Europe. Most pieces were made from a refined earthenware in sections which were assembled before being decorated. Meticulous attention to detail, with elaborate moulds and complex arrangements of elements, are hallmarks

Figurine price line

Unfashionable ladies
This Royal Doulton Autumn Breezes figure, HN1911, was created by Leslie Harradine, who designed at least one figure a month for the company for over 40 years. Thousands of this immensely popular figure, 19cm (7½in) high, were sold between 1939 and 1976. They are now unfashionable and even an example in perfect condition would struggle to sell for **£30**.

A taste for the exotic
The Bavarian firm Rosenthal depicted exotic dancers inspired by the tales of One Thousand and One Nights from 1924 until 1939. This figure was designed by Berthold Boess and is typical of the abandon of the dancers in the Art Deco period. There is a demand for these figures although this is not the most collectable factory. This piece, 24cm (9½in) high should fetch **£200-300**.

Exotic style
When assessing the value of a figurine, one has to ask 'does it encapsulate the era?' And that is exactly what this Goldscheider figure does. The new style 'bob' hairstyle and the slightly risqué butterfly costume are both strong Art Deco indicators. Goldscheider is a highly desirable company, as is the designer Josef Lorenzl. This figure, 25cm (9¾in) high, would sell for **£900-1,100**.

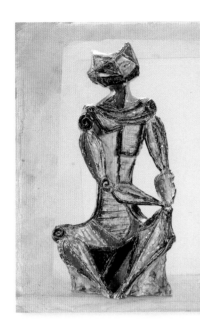

Marcello Fantoni

Marcello Fantoni was born in Florence, Italy, in 1915. He graduated from the Institute of Art at Porta Romana in 1934 as a 'maestro' of art and began working as a ceramicist. He consolidated his already established reputation between the 1950s and 1970s. His interest in Cubism, Picasso and other modern art, and his Italian heritage, led to the creation of new and unique forms that were frequently more sculptural than functional. His figures took on a distinctly modern feel as he experimented with glazes, forms and colours. Many of his pieces are now in major collections and values have risen dramatically. Collectors look for his whimsical, angular shapes, with strong colours and the typically rough texture of the glaze.

◀ **Geometric whimsy**
This Cubist figure, Satire in Love, features multi-coloured decoration.
It is 38cm (15in) high and would now be worth **£2,500-3,000.**

of Goldscheider figures. Gracefully posed dancers wearing risqué dresses were a popular subject.

From 1928, the Italian firm of Lenci (established in 1919) in Turin produced earthenware and porcelain figures, mainly of women, either nude or in stylish modern dress. These figures are more naturalistic than most French examples and are distinguished by elongated limbs and bright yellow hair. Many of Lenci's figures are strongly coloured, strike a bold pose, and wear fashionably small hats or headscarves.

Look out for figures designed by Englishman Leslie Harradine for Doulton, particularly the Bather. Other British factories that produced collectable figures at this time included Crown Devon and Shelley.

Superb condition
Lenci specialised in elegant and stylised figures. In the 1920s and 1930s, women began to enjoy athletic pursuits more publicly and this was celebrated in ceramics. Lenci is a good firm with a small production and the condition of this piece, which is 43cm (17in) high, is remarkable – down to the original wooden ski poles. Both of these factors contribute to the **£2,500-3,000** value.

Ugly but worthy
The Royal Doulton Autumn Breeze figure was very common – the secret to the value of this figure is that it is early and rare. It is One of the Forty (thieves) figures, designed by Harry Tittensor, HN501, and was produced from 1921 to 1938. It was unpopular because it lacked aesthetic appeal, and was made in small quantities. It is 18cm (7in) high and worth **£3,500- 4,000.**

Advertising quality
Rarity, condition and desirability combine to make this Shelley Girl advertising figure, 31cm (12¼in) high, valuable. Made around 1925 at the Shelley Pottery in Staffordshire, these figures of a stylish young woman were given to shops which stocked its wares to advertise Shelley as a maker of fashionable china. It is now one of the most valuable pieces of Shelley, fetching **£4,500-5,500.**

TREASURE SPOTTER'S GALLERY
Mid-20th century ceramics

Ceramic design was a conservative business in 1950s Britain. Factory-owner Roy Midwinter was among the first to realise the need for a 'new look'. On a trip to the US in 1952 he was shocked when a buyer said, 'I will shoot the next man who comes all the way over from Stoke to show me English roses'. By appointing Jessie Tait, Hugh Casson and Terence Conran as designers, he began producing wares that fed the new-found optimism of young homemakers. Others followed suit.

◄ **Terence Conran plate**
Terence Conran's design for Midwinter Saladware, inspired by the 1955 salad set designed by Piero Fornasetti in Italy, is redolent of the fun and humour of mid-1950s design. The market was tired of the utilitarian designs of the war years and young homemakers longed for stylish and inexpensive homewares. This 19.5cm (7¾in) plate would sell for **£60-80**.

"The most desirable ceramics are colourful, stylish and evocative designs which encapsulate the optimism of the postwar era."
JUDITH MILLER BBC *ANTIQUES ROADSHOW* SPECIALIST

▶ **Hugh Casson vase**
The Midwinter Pottery Cannes pattern celery vase, designed by Hugh Casson, was a 1960 re-working of the company's Riviera design of 1954. These patterns 'spoke' of the joy of holidays spent on the French Riviera – a dream to many Brits in the 1950s and 1960s. The new shapes were also revolutionary. This unusual 17.5cm (6¾in) high vase is worth **£275-325**.

▲ **Jessie Tait teapot**
Midwinter's Zambesi early morning teapot was designed by Jessie Tait in 1956. This popular hand-painted design in black and red with tribal-influenced stripes was an immediate success and widely copied by other factories. The introduction of the signature red accents has made this style a collector's classic. If you have this highly desirable teapot, 12.5cm (5in) high, it will sell for **£120-180**.

The Homemaker series

The Ridgways transfer-printed Homemaker series was designed by Enid Seeney in 1957 and was made until the early 1970s. Pieces are commonly found now as they sold in vast numbers through Woolworths. The simple forms and the characteristic abstract motifs used exemplify 1950s styling. A cup, saucer and plate are worth £30-40, rarer shapes such as teapots can sell for £200-250 and a dinner set is valued at £500. As the interest in vintage and retro homewares grows, these pieces may increase in value and may be worth holding on to – or offering to younger family members.

▶ **Quintessentially 1950s design**
Bringing 1950s style to the dinner table, this plate, 17.5cm (6¾in) diameter, sold for 2½ pence in 1960 and is now worth **£12-18**.

▶ **Hornsea jardinière**
Many of the ranges that John Clappison designed for Hornsea Pottery were so popular at the time that surviving examples are relatively common today and values are low. Rarer ranges and unusual shapes, such as this Slipware jardiniere, 25.5cm (10in) diameter, from 1963, are likely to be worth more, fetching **£60-80**.

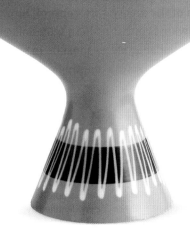

▶ **Poole Delphis vase**
The Poole Delphis range, launched in 1963, was conceived by Guy Sydenham and Robert Jefferson. Every piece is pretty much unique. Delphis is easily recognised: it is psychedelic, with vibrant colours and designs. It was not particularly popular at the time, so it is comparatively rare. This shape 84 vase was painted by Ingrid Hammond c.1972, is 23cm (9in) high, worth **£100-150** and rising.

◀ **Poole bottle vase**
The shape of this Poole Freeform large bottle vase was designed by Alfred Read and Guy Sydenham and inspired by Scandinavian studio pottery. It is particularly desirable, painted by Gwen Haskins in the harder to find PKL pattern combination of charcoal, lime and Purbeck stone, c.1955 and 39cm (15.5in) high. Due to the sophistication of the shape and the colour combination, this would sell for **£400-500**.

▶ **Arnold Machin bull**
The Wedgwood Queensware Taurus the Bull, 40.5cm (16in) long, was designed by Arnold Machin and is printed with zodiac signs. It has the date code for October 1950. The simple shape was designed to be easy for unskilled potters to make during World War II. Prices are rising fast and **£250-350** may soon be £400-500.

TREASURE SPOTTER'S GUIDE
Royal commemoratives

Historical memorabilia offers a tangible reminder of key events. The passion for collecting royal memorabilia is long established but the golden era was undoubtedly the 19th century. With mass production came affordability as most people could buy a memento of a coronation, a visit or a jubilee.

Would you believe it?

This delft portrait charger was taken to Rosebery's Auctioneers, London, by a person who had been assured it was a 19th-century copy but wanted a second opinion. They were told that it was in fact a portrait of Charles II and dated the year of his Restoration, 1660. The date, condition and sophisticated decoration place this 30.5cm (12in) diameter dish in a very elite group. In December 2011 it sold for £105,000.

Items made before the 19th century tend to be rarer and potentially more valuable than later wares. Most families own some pieces of memorabilia from the reigns of Victoria, Edward VII, George V, Edward VIII and George VI. Many of these pieces are not worth much today as they were produced cheaply, in vast quantities and have been 'kept as good' in granny's display cabinet. There is also a diminishing demand as much of the dreary 19th-century, brown-and-black, transfer-printed ware is out of fashion with collectors. Because of the quantity available, pieces must be in superb condition – rubbed gilding, poor transfers, staining or even the slightest damage render the object valueless.

▶ **Queen Anne charger**
As can be seen with the Charles II charger (see box, left), there is a strong demand from collectors for early tin-glazed earthenware dishes with blue-dash decoration around the rim. This c.1710 Queen Anne 35cm (14in) diameter example is beautifully painted, with the Queen identified by the initials 'AR'. Even though it has been restored, it is worth £6,000-7,000.

▲ **Queen Victoria's Golden Jubilee**
A great deal of transfer-printed ware was produced to commemorate every aspect of Queen Victoria's life. This Hines Bros. 23cm (9in) wide plate was made for her Golden Jubilee in 1887 and is worth £20-30.

◀ **Unpopular royals**
The Staffordshire factories produced vast number of figure groups during the 19th century. They were very keen to represent foreign royalty, as with this group of the Queen and King of Sardinia, 32.5cm (12¾in) high. These are unpopular and, even though the group is not particularly common, it is not worth much. £90-110

▶ **Queen Victoria cup**
The three sides of this Copeland Spode 1899-1900 Transvaal War subscriber's three-handled tyg or loving cup, are printed with a portrait of Queen Victoria, a vignette emblematic of 'Britannia - Tower of Justice', and details of the war. This piece also attracts militaria collectors. 14cm (5½in) high **£800-1,000**.

Limited editions by a good factory can be worth something but they should have all the documentation to show that the object is from a genuine limited edition if they are to achieve their full value. Many items are sold as from a limited edition but they are 'limited' to several hundred thousand objects. With low values it is difficult to sell these objects to a dealer and they often come under the minimum lot value demanded by an auction house. That leaves the internet or car boot sale if you want to sell – or even the charity shop. There is, however, great demand for early, rare examples.

▼ **Edward VIII**
People often think that memorabilia from the proposed coronation of Edward VIII in 1937 will be valuable, but so many items were made that they are not rare. Even though this beaker is by a good maker, Minton, and from a limited edition of 2,000, it is worth **£80-110**.

▶ **The Queen Mother**
Demand for more recent royal pieces seems to be waning. This Royal Doulton H. M. Queen Elizabeth The Queen Mother, (Doulton model number HN2882) designed by Eric J Griffiths, was produced in a limited edition of 1,500 in 1980 and is 20cm (8in) high. It is worth **£150-200**.

Good, Better, Best
Eric Ravilious mugs

Eric Ravilious (1903-1942) was a British painter, designer, book illustrator and wood engraver. He studied at the Eastbourne School of Art and at the Royal College of Art. He was already a successful artist when he was introduced to Tom Wedgwood in 1935 and worked for the firm from 1936-1940. His first design to go into production was the commemorative mug originally produced for the coronation of Edward VIII, and adapted for that of George VI in 1937. Because of wartime restrictions on the production of decorated ware, many of his designs were not made in any quantities until the 1950s. Ravilious was an official war artist and was killed in action in 1942.

Good

This is the more common colourway for the 10cm (4in) King George VI 1937 coronation mug but is still desirable and worth **£600-700**.

Better

This blue print over pink ground was not as popular at the time and so was produced in smaller numbers. It is now worth **£1,400-1,600**.

Best

And the one that everyone is looking for! The rarest of the colourways, Marina Green, is worth **£2,000-2,500**.

TREASURE SPOTTER'S GUIDE
Beswick figurines

Collections of animal figurines are out of fashion, so most Beswick figurines have dropped in value. But if you have a rare example in good condition, it may still be worth hundreds or even thousands of pounds.

Would you believe it?

▲ A rare beast
The rare Beswick Galloway bull (no.1746B) was in production from 1963 to 1969. It is 11.5cm (4½in) high and worth **£2,000-3,000**.

Beswick cattle remain popular, particularly with butchers and members of the farming community. Bulls often fetch the highest sums, but don't despair if you only have a cow or a calf as collectors often buy such figures to accompany their bulls.

As with all Beswick figurines, rarity is the key to value. Popular breeds, such as the black and white Friesian, had long production runs. This means there is a large number on the market today and even examples in mint condition tend to fetch relatively low sums – in 2009 a Friesian bull sold for less than £100.

Although they look relatively similar, the much rarer Galloway bulls are worth significantly more than their Friesian cousins. Both the black Galloway bull (no.1746A) and the fawn version (no.1746C) can be worth more than £1,000 each, but the black-and-white belted Galloway bull (no.1746B) shown above is even rarer.

Beswick Pottery began as a manufacturer of tablewares in Staffordshire, England, in 1894. It produced its first animal figurines around 1900 and by 1930 they had become a major part of the factory's output. In 1969, Beswick was sold to Royal Doulton but various pottery items, including figurines, continued to be sold under the name 'Beswick'. In 1989, production of Beswick and Doulton animals merged under the Royal Doulton mark. The name 'Beswick' was used again from 1999 until the factory closed in 2002.

Large numbers of Beswick figures have been made and sold since the early 1900s, as they appealed to a wide range of people. Prices for figurines have dropped generally, as for many people the decoration of their home has become more minimalist in style, eschewing clutter. But some rare Beswick figurines are still making high prices. Cattle, horses, dogs and cats are continually popular, as are ranges such as the Beatrix Potter characters. Limited editions can be valuable if the edition was small and there is demand today.

◀ Most common
Shire Mare was produced in 14 different colours during a long production period of 1940 to 1989. The rarest variation is gloss blue, although rocking-horse grey is also unusual and examples can be worth £400-600. The brown gloss-glazed Shire Mare, 21.5cm (8½in) high is extremely common and prices are consequently low. 1940-1989 **£30-40**

▶ Burning bright
Wild animals are not as strongly collected as horses or cattle, but they do have their fans. Rare models, such as the black satin-glazed tiger, fetch high sums. How much the rare tiger would make is not known as none have ever come up for sale. The standard tiger, 19cm (7½in) high, is worth about the same in gloss and matt glaze. 1967-1990 **£70-100**.

▶ **Easily damaged**
The fins on Beswick's fish are vulnerable to damage. This large-mouthed Black Bass (no.1266) was designed by Arthur Gredlington and produced from 1952-1968. 4.75in (12cm) long **£200-250**

▼ **CM series**
Colin Melbourne's highly stylised CM series was not popular when it was released in the 1950s, as most Beswick collectors prefer naturalistic figures. Today the range is becoming increasingly popular among fans of mid-20th century design. The Bison is one of the most valuable pieces. c.1956 28cm (11in) long **£150-250**

Variations in price

Small variations of colour, glaze type and form (such as a differently positioned tail) can have a huge effect on the price a collector is willing to pay. Matt-glazed pieces are often more valuable than glossy figures and rocking-horse grey is generally a more valuable colour than brown. Early pieces can make high prices but can be hard to identify as the Beswick backstamp and shape numbers were only used from 1934. If you have a large collection of Beswick figures that you are hoping to sell, it may be worth investing in a specialist guide to see whether you have any of the most valuable variations.

Collectors always aim to buy Beswick figurines in mint condition so any damage will reduce value dramatically. Only very rare figures will still be worth more than around £20 if they are not mint. Examine protruding areas, such as horns and hooves, carefully for damage. Unfortunately, a restored area will still be considered damaged by many collectors.

Damaged figurines should be sold either at a car boot sale or online. If you do sell over the internet, remember to use plenty of bubble wrap and newspaper when you're packing to avoid breakages. Good condition figurines can often be sold in specialist Royal Doulton and Beswick figurine sales, which are run by several auction houses, including W. & H. Peacock, Charterhouse and Tennants.

▶ **The Duchess**
Duchess, who appears in *The Tale of the Pie and the Patty-Pan*, is not one of Beatrix Potter's best-known characters – except in Beswick collecting circles. The second version of this figure, which features Duchess holding a pie, can be worth around £150, but the first version with flowers, shown here, can be worth up to ten times that amount. 1955-1967 9.5cm (3¾in) high **£1,000-1,500**

▶ **Popular budgies**
Budgerigars are popular pets and models are keenly collected. Left- and right-facing budgies are worth around the same but models with flowers on the base are worth more than plain bases. Colour affects value even more strongly – the yellow shown here is the rarest and most valuable variation. 1970-1972 18cm (7in) high **£800-1,200**

TREASURE SPOTTER'S GALLERY
Studio pottery

Studio pottery (items handmade or hand-decorated by independent potters) became popular in the 19th century and boomed during the 20th century. Complex forms, glazes or designs usually add value, with the highest prices going to work by pioneers of the movement. Studio pottery is now one of the most vibrant art forms on the market.

▶ **Bernard Leach**
Bernard Leach is considered by many to be the father of studio pottery. His work was highly influential and his St Ives Pottery was the training ground for many of Britain's best studio potters, including his wife, sons and grandsons. Pieces by these 'second generation' St Ives potters are generally less valuable than pieces by Bernard Leach himself. 20cm (8in) high **£1,500-2,000**

▼ **Shoji Hamada**
Shoji Hamada co-founded the St Ives Pottery with Bernard Leach in 1920 and worked with him until 1923. Hamada is one of the biggest names in studio pottery and many of his designs command high prices. This dish is particularly valuable as two similar pieces can be seen in a 1971 photograph of Hamada and Leach. *c.*1963 55cm (21¾in) diameter **£18,000-22,000**

▲ **Martin Brothers**
Working in a Middlesex studio from 1877, the Martin Brothers produced some of Britain's most idiosyncratic studio pottery. They have become known for their characterful bird figures but they also produced a range of other ceramics, typically decorated in range of muted colours and featuring grotesque animal faces. Martin Brothers pottery is rising rapidly in value. 32cm (12½in) high **£8,000-10,000**

▲ James Maltby

Trained under David Leach, James Maltby is known for his unique sculptural forms decorated with simple geometric motifs. This tea bowl is typical of his work, which is likely to attract collectors. Maltby is currently one of the UK's most celebrated living studio potters and prices for his work may still rise. 9.5cm (3¾in) high **£250-300**

▶ Parkinson Pottery

Pieces made at the Parkinson Pottery by Susan and Richard Parkinson have become highly collectable, particularly since they were featured in a 2004 book and exhibition. The pottery was only active for 11 years from 1952, so even standard examples of its output are hard to find. This Hand in Glove sculpture is particularly rare. 1952-1963 35cm (13¾in) high **£1,000-1,500**

▶ Aldermaston Pottery

The Aldermaston Pottery was founded by Alan Caiger-Smith in 1955 and became a training ground for a new generation of potters. Interest in its output is rising and large, attractive examples are selling for hundreds of pounds. Pieces decorated by Caiger-Smith himself, such as this plate, are likely to be among the most valuable. 28cm (11in) diameter **£400-500**

◀ Students of St Ives

This vase was made at the St Ives Pottery by Peter Bernard Hardy. Unlike other St Ives students, such as Michael Cardew and David Leach, Hardy has not become well known in his own right. This vase is also small and not especially attractive, resulting in a relatively low price. 13cm (5¼in) high **£60-80**

Would you believe it?

The Troika Pottery was founded in 1963 and soon became successful, moving from St Ives to larger premises in Newlyn in 1970. Although the shapes were slip-moulded using liquid clay, all decoration was done by hand. A matt, textured glaze became the main decorative treatment around 1974. Value is likely to be affected by the shape, size and colour of a piece, with rare examples generally being worth more. Complex geometric patterns, including figural or pictorial images, are often rare, as are shapes such as Anvil vases and plaques. The work of some decorators, particularly those who went on to become head decorators, such as Honor Curtis, can also add value. Many pieces are marked with a decorator's monogram, which should help you to identify who painted your piece. It may be worth consulting a specialist reference guide to find out more about them.

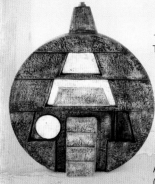

◀ Rare shape

The Wheel lamp base is one of the rarer Troika shapes, which means examples are more desirable than other shapes. Even scarcer forms, such as plaques, are still more desirable. This base was decorated with an Aztec pattern by Avril Bennett, c.1970. 37cm (14½in) high **£1,000-1,500**

TREASURE SPOTTER'S GUIDE
Chinese ceramics

China has one of the oldest ceramic traditions, dating as far back as 7000 BC. The Chinese were the first to use glazes in around 2000 BC and by 300 AD were making a refined pottery. Fine porcelain was produced by the 14th century and during the Ming Dynasty Chinese potters perfected the craft.

Age is not everything when dealing with Chinese ceramics. Many provincial pieces that precede the Ming Dynasty (1368-1644) are not particularly valuable. However, Imperial pieces have seen dramatic price rises.

Blanc-de-Chine pieces are made from a pure white porcelain with a smooth glaze and have been made since the 16th century at the Dehua kilns in the Chinese province of Fujian. The most common shapes are small figures of Ho-tai, Buddha and Guanyin, the Chinese goddess of mercy.

During the reign of the Emperor Wanli (1573-1619) the quantity of porcelain made for export increased dramatically. The main centre was still the ancient kilns at Jingdezhen in Jiangxi province. During the Transitional period (1620-1683) potters, who had lost the imperial patronage, were given more creative freedom. New shapes and decoration, combined with an improved ceramic body and glaze, were the result. The Emperor Kangxi (1662-1722) took an interest in porcelain and reorganised the kilns in 1683. What is considered to be a golden age of porcelain production followed and lasted well into the 19th century.

In general, the quality of Chinese export wares deteriorated during the 19th century at the same time as demand for them from Europe and the USA was increasing. Currently quality examples in good condition from that time are in great demand. Interestingly, porcelains from the early 20th century, predominantly from the Xuantong (1909-1911) and Republic Period (1915-1916), have seen a rapid increase in value. Many of these feature a delicacy and attention to detail most 19th-century export wares lack.

▲ **Blanc-de-Chine figure**
Collectors look for early examples of blanc-de-Chine, which tend to have a warmer, ivory tinge, while later pieces are a 'colder' white or have a slightly blue tinge. This is a 23.5cm (9¼in) high, 17th-century figure of Guandi, the god of war. **£2,500-3,000**

◄ **Armorial plates**
European merchants ordered high-quality armorial services for their wealthy clients, such as these Yongzheng period 23cm (9in) diameter plates, from c.1732, painted with the arms of Lord Ross of Halkhead and the motto 'Think On'. The pair is worth **£1,500-2,000**.

Good, Better, Best *Blue-and-white vases*

Chinese potters began to use underglaze blue decoration in the mid-14th century using cobalt from Persia. The method of painting cobalt oxide on to white porcelain is still used today. During the Ming period the blue occasionally filtered through the glaze creating a pooled effect known as 'heaped and piled'.

Good

By the 19th century, the Chinese potters had perfected the shapes and decoration on their export wares. Although this is a pleasing double-gourd vase with hand-painted prunus, it lacks the spontaneity of earlier decoration. It has the earlier four character Kangxi mark but is actually from the Daoguang period (1821-1850), it is 30.5cm (12in) high and is worth **£150-200**.

Better

During the 16th century the potters of Jindezhen (the main porcelain centre from the 14th century) began to produce fine wares for export. This vase is a good example with a continuous garden landscape figural scene depicting a nobleman, sages and various attendants. Jiajing mark and of the period, (1522-1566). 23cm (9in) high **£7,000-8,000**

Best

This rare Yuan Dynasty mid-14th century double gourd vase, 47cm (18¾in) high, has all the elements to make it desirable – early date, fine quality, rarity and Imperial provenance. It is one of the first Chinese vessels where shape and decoration matched, an idea used in later reigns. It cost 10 guineas in 1900, but is now worth more than **£3,000,000**.

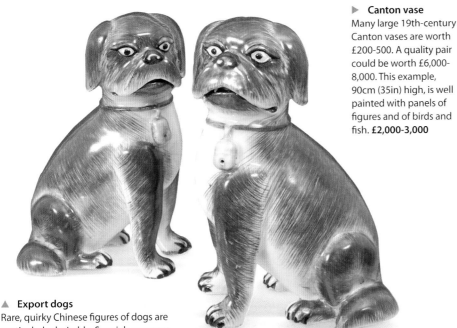

▲ **Export dogs**
Rare, quirky Chinese figures of dogs are particularly desirable. Spaniels are more common than these realistic Qianlong export pugs, 18cm (7in) high, with unclipped ears, from *c.*1760. They are worth **£18,000-20,000**.

▶ **Canton vase**
Many large 19th-century Canton vases are worth £200-500. A quality pair could be worth £6,000-8,000. This example, 90cm (35in) high, is well painted with panels of figures and of birds and fish. **£2,000-3,000**

TREASURE SPOTTER'S GALLERY
Chinese ceramic decoration

Since the 1st century AD, Chinese ceramics included funerary figures to accompany the deceased into the afterlife. Not all were as large as the terracotta army of Xian but many were realistically and crisply modelled. The potters of the Song Dynasty (960-1279 AD) made exquisite porcelain for the Imperial court and in the Yuan Dynasty (1279-1368) underglaze painting was developed. The most important decorative techniques are described here.

Judith warns!

▲ **Authenticated horse**
This large pottery model of a white horse, Tang Dynasty (618-906 AD), 48cm (19in) high, with the all-important TL test certification, would sell for **£5,000-7,000**.

When selling a Tang figure, it is essential to have a TL (thermoluminescence) certificate. The testing measures the amount of natural radiation absorbed over the lifetime of an object and from this an approximate date is obtained. This horse's age report was issued by Oxford Authentication in October 2004. Authentication reports are increasingly important, owing to the large number of fake Chinese pieces entering the market, creating a lack of public confidence in buying. False positives can occur, as a result of the deliberate insertion of genuine fragments into modern pieces (typically bases in porcelain) or artificial exposure to the same amount of radiation as a genuine piece would have absorbed over its lifetime.

▼ **Tang Dynasty funerary figure**
Many Tang Dynasty funerary figures were left unglazed, decorated with pigment or straw-coloured glaze or, as in this case, covered in a *sancai* (three-coloured) glaze. According to its TL test (see box, left), this 43cm (17in) high figure is dated to 618-906 AD and is worth **£6,000-8,000**.

▲ **Kraak porcelain bowl**
The segmented decoration on this bowl is called *Kraaksporselein* after the carracks – Portuguese ships – that transported porcelain to the west from the Wanli Dynasty to the end of the Ming. Normally thinly potted, often moulded, the design is divided into panels and motifs can include flowers, animals and masks. This 34cm (13½in) wide bowl, *c.*1640, would sell for **£4,000-5,000**.

▲ *Famille verte* **plate**
The translucent colours of the *famille verte* palette are dominated by apple green, introduced in the Kangxi period (1662-1722). Colours resemble *wucai* and the glaze can appear thin and glassy. The palette includes blue, yellow, aubergine, iron red and black. Gilding can also be used. This plate is worth **£1,000-1,200**.

◄ **Wucai vase with stand and cover**
Developed in the reign of the Emperor Jiajing (1522-1566), the *wucai* palette has five colours. Decoration is in underglaze blue as an outline or wash, with an overglaze green, iron-red, brown, yellow and black. It was less refined than the 15th-century *doucai* palette. This mid-17th century vase, 30.5cm (12in) high, is worth **£4,000-5,000**.

▶ *Famille rose* **plate**
The *famille rose* palette was developed in the early 18th century, with pink enamel colours made opaque with white. Popular motifs include landscapes, flora and fauna. From the mid-19th century the decoration was often more dense with scenes set within medallions. This 18th-century charger, 56cm (22in) in diameter, would sell for **£800-1,000**.

▲ **Export porcelain naïve cat**
By the early 19th century much export porcelain, such as this rare 23cm (9in) long lantern cover, was made to order for European merchants. Export wares are now attracting the attention of Chinese buyers and prices may rise steeply. Currently this is worth **£2,000-3,000**.

◄ **Chinese Imari platter**
Because the Japanese Imari style had been popular in Europe since the late 17th century, the Chinese devised a 'Chinese Imari' palette. This is an early 19th-century example. Later wares were densely painted. At 44cm (17½in) wide, this charger would sell for **£300-500**.

TREASURE SPOTTER'S GUIDE
Shipwreck cargoes

From the 17th century onwards, a number of the trade ships carrying goods from China to the lucrative western markets sank. Some of these cargoes have been recovered and the porcelain is now keenly collected. At the time they sank, much of the porcelain on board was little more than ballast compared to the valuable silks, spices and tea also in the hold.

Although part of the interest in shipwreck cargoes lies in the romance of something that has lain at the bottom of the sea for centuries, these pieces of porcelain can also help us date and understand more about the porcelains produced in China over the centuries. It may be possible to establish the date that the catastrophe struck the ship, whether storm, fire or striking a reef, from its porcelain cargo.

For example, a jar cover retrieved from the Hatcher Cargo, dated 1643, neatly provided the date of the sinking of the vessel in the South China Sea. The unidentified Asian vessel was salvaged by English-born, Australian-based salvage expert Captain Michael Hatcher in 1983.

Probably the most famous wreck was that of the *Geldermalsen*. By no means the most important wreck, or the earliest or the best quality porcelain, it caught the world's

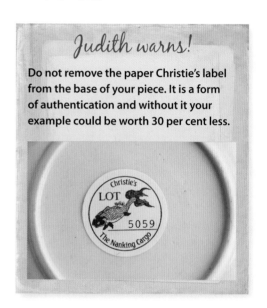

Judith warns!

Do not remove the paper Christie's label from the base of your piece. It is a form of authentication and without it your example could be worth 30 per cent less.

Shipwreck cargoes price line

Provincial wares
Although the oldest piece, dating from Yuan period (*c.*1279-1368), this provincial ware is not of great interest to collectors. It is not from a known ship, which also detracts from its desirability. It is 15cm (6in) in diameter and would sell for £60-70. Without the shell encrustation, it would be worth **£40-50.**

Growing demand
The *Tek Sing* (*True Star*) sank in 1822. More than 350,000 pieces were salvaged from it, which shows the popularity of Chinese porcelain with the growing middle classes in the west. This Magnolia pattern dish is typical of pieces from the cargo. Measuring 20cm (8in) diameter, it is worth **£200-300.**

Made in vast quantities
This *Ca Mau* plate was painted in the very productive Yongzheng period, from around 1723-1735. Such finely painted pieces were popular at the time and vast quantities came into Europe. Not as rare as some of the other wrecks, this 23cm (9in) diameter plate would sell for **£400-500.**

imagination. The wreck has been referred to as the Nanking Cargo ever since the original auction took place in 1986. The name came from the 18th century, when blue-and-white Chinese porcelain was sold as Nanking or Nankeen China.

Built in 1746, the *Geldermalsen* was one of the newest and finest of the Dutch East India trading vessels. Loaded with cargo, it was heading for Amsterdam. However disaster struck on Monday, January 3, 1752, when the ship hit a reef off Indonesia and sank. It was carrying an extremely valuable cargo of tea, silks and spices, none of which survived. The vast cargo of Chinese porcelain on board, around 150,000 pieces, as well as a collection of gold ingots, did survive. The ceramics only represented 5 per cent of the total value of the load. There is no doubt that tea had been the principal export cargo.

Wares with European appeal

By the mid-18th century, Chinese export porcelain shapes had become more standardised and patterns were designed to appeal to European taste. The middle classes were expanding, and huge services were ordered for the newly fashionable formal dinner parties. The Nanking Cargo included 171 dinner services. Every item needed for the table was produced, so the services sometimes contained between 150 and 300 pieces.

The quality of the porcelain found in shipwreck cargoes varies tremendously. Other cargoes of importance to collectors include the Hoi An Hoard, and the Ca Mau, the Vung Tau, the Diana and the Tek Sing Cargoes.

Judith warns!

For centuries, Chinese potters copied earlier work and marks out of respect. There are also fakes. This late 20th-century fake is worth £20; an original Xuande vase would be worth £20,000 or more.

The mark is too rigid to be original.

- This was slip-moulded. If correct, this shape would have been made in two or three pieces joined together.
- The cobalt blue glaze is evenly applied. An original piece would have areas of darker cobalt, known as 'the heaped and piled effect'.
- The base is too uniform. The glaze inside the foot rim does not have the pin-prick marks seen on an early vase.
- The Xuande period mark (1426-1435) is too formal to be an early example.

A notorious wreck
Much of the Nanking Cargo was decorated with landscapes in blue and white. The painting on this *c.*1752 piece is accomplished but not exceptional. Much of the value is dependent on the notoriety of this wreck. This 28.5cm (11.25in) diameter plate would sell for **£450-550**.

Unusual decoration
The *Vung Tau* sank in around 1690. Much of the cargo is unremarkable but this 33cm (13in) vase is decorated with Dutch canal houses. Ordered by rich Dutch merchants, it would have been expensive then. Now, its rarity and historical significance mean it will fetch **£1,500-2,000**.

Historical find
Of all the cargoes to come to market, the Hatcher is of the greatest historical significance. Its early date, about 1643, and high-quality decoration, shows it was intended for the Dutch upper classes. This rare and desirable vase, 37cm (14½in) high, is worth **£3,000-4,000**.

TREASURE SPOTTER'S GUIDE
Japanese ceramics

Almost all early Japanese porcelain was produced in and around the port of Arita on Kyūshū, the Japanese island that lies closest to Korea. Consequently it is collectively referred to as Arita. Early Japanese porcelain falls into three main decorative types: Arita blue-and-white, Imari and Kakiemon.

Noritake

The ceramics known as 'Noritake' grew out of a company established in Tokyo and New York by the Morimura Brothers in 1876. It is famous for the mass production of high-quality, yet affordable, dinnerware mostly aimed at the European market. Until 1921 Noritake marked export wares 'Nippon'. Backstamps after 1921 state 'Japan' or 'Made in Japan'. Millions of pieces of Noritake were brought over to the west from the 1920s to the 1940s so most pieces are worth little. But there is a growing collecting interest and some pieces are beginning to make money. Many tea services of this fine porcelain were 'kept for best' in display cabinets and never used.

▶ **Noritake vase**
This 25.5cm (10in) late 19th-century Noritake vase was worth under £10 a few years ago, now its value is **£350-400**.

The earliest Arita porcelain was crude, heavily potted, mainly decorated in blue and white, and intended for sale in Japan. By the mid-17th century, the potters were producing a more refined porcelain for the rapidly developing export market.

Initially developed in the second half of the 17th century, the Imari style matured in around 1800. There are many decorative types of Imari, including blue-and-white and Kakiemon (see pages 104-105), although we typically tend to think of the porcelain having an underglaze cobalt blue and overglaze red and gold palette. The subject matter of Imari is diverse, ranging from foliage and flowers – often the chrysanthemum – to people and landscapes. Much background decoration is styled on brocade: a rich silk textile run through with gold and silver thread. Some Imari designs, such as *Kraaksporselein*, were adopted from China but most designs were uniquely Japanese, owing to the country's rich painting tradition.

The majority of Imari wares are decorative pieces intended for display. The most common

▶ **Ko-Kutani dish**
Ceramics from the village of Kutani are generally enamelled in iron-red, green and yellow. This mid-17th century heart-shaped dish, 16cm (6¼in) wide, is decorated with tied ribbons and has a brown rim. **£2,000-3,000**

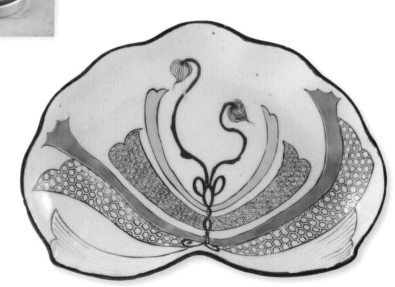

▶ **Nabeshima dish**
Nabeshima ware is arguably the most refined pre 19th-century Japanese porcelain. It was made at Ōkawachi near Arita for the sole use of the governing Nabeshima clan. It was decorated with Japanese motifs in a bold and striking way. This 19th-century Japanese Nabeshima bamboo dish, 18.5cm (7¼in) diameter, would sell for **£600-800.**

Good, Better, Best *Satsuma*

Satsuma is a fine earthenware with a cream-coloured, delicately crazed glaze decorated with overglaze enamel and gilding. It is known in Japan as 'Satsuma *nishikide*'. From the 1870s, the best Satsuma by highly skilled craftsmen was displayed at international exhibitions. This created a demand for more affordable Satsuma, much of which is quite gaudy and bears little resemblance to the best quality pieces.

Good

This late 19th-century Satsuma vase is typically heavily decorated with immortals seated in a landscape. The shape is dull and it is decorated with overcrowded designs in garish polychrome enamels and lots of gilding. By the late 19th century, factories were turning out thousands of copies of these scenes. Viewed close up it lacks the spontaneity and quality of the best Satsuma. Many of these pieces were made with plaster moulds and metal stencils. 24cm (9½in) high **£200-300**

◀ **Imari vase**
Imari porcelain was made from the late 17th century and has the distinctive palette of dark underglaze blue, with iron-red, yellow, green and gold. By the late 19th century, when this vase was made, the quality had become variable and gold became much more prominent. The panels are well painted. 47cm (18¾in) high **£900-1,200**

Better

This large Satsuma vase is by the Shijo artist Hosai, who was active from 1840-1860. It has the blue enamel Shimazu family crest, enamelled 'Dai Nippon Ijuin Satsuma Yaki'. The Shimazu were one of the wealthiest and most powerful clans of the Edo period (1615-1867). Hence the piece is intricately enamelled with blue, orange and gold chrysanthemums and floral sprays, a crosshatched border and scrolling base. 48cm (19in) high **£3,000-5,000**

Best

An early Meiji (1868-1912) Satsuma plate with a shaped and pierced rim. This was decorated by one of the most highly skilled artists and took months to paint, using a brush with a single rat's hair. It is intricately decorated with a city scene. The characters have expressive faces and look full of life. 21cm (8¼in) diameter **£12,000-16,000**

objects were high-shouldered, dome-covered jars, trumpet-shaped beaker vases and saucer dishes.

The export of Imari to Europe stopped in the mid-18th century when China began exporting to Europe again because its porcelain was much cheaper. The Europeans liked the Imari style so the Chinese potters copied both the Imari and Kakiemon styles, which became known as 'Chinese Imari'. Export of Japanese Imari increased again in the late 19th century, the Meiji era, when Japonism was all the rage in Europe.

TREASURE SPOTTER'S GALLERY
Kakiemon and its imitators

In the 17th century, Kakiemon was produced at the kilns at Arita using a distinctive palette of iron-red, sky-blue, yellow, aubergine, turquoise and black. It was named after the potter Sakaida Kakiemon who is credited with introducing enamel decoration to Japan in the 1640s. The exceptional quality of the decoration was imitated by most European porcelain factories.

Japanese Arita

This Japanese Arita vase is modelled after an archaic bronze beaker. The *nigoshide* (porcelain body) is relatively primitive and is composed of a greyish paste, covered in a thin off-white glaze. It is decorated with the thick and irregular saturated enamel colours characteristic of the earliest phase of Arita export ware, between around 1660 and 1680.

▲ **Ancient form**
This Japanese Arita vase dates from around 1680 and is 17cm (6½in) high. **£15,000-20,000**

▶ **Meissen interpretation**
From 1729, Augustus the Strong commissioned the Meissen painters to copy his Japanese Kakiemon designs on hard-paste porcelain. They created a decoration known as *Indianische Blumen* (Indian flowers). Like the Japanese, Meissen artists applied the enamels sparsely to emphasise the pure white body and glassy glaze. This milk jug and cover are painted with the Quail pattern. *c.*1730 16.5cm (6¼in) high **£2,500-3,000**

▼ **Chantilly translation**
The collection of Japanese Kakiemon porcelain also inspired the Prince de Conté to open the Chantilly factory in France in 1725. The soft-paste porcelain has a creamy tin glaze and the decoration tends to faithfully copy the Japanese originals, although with black-painted outlines. These boxes and covers are painted with beetles and flowers. *c.*1740-1750 7.5cm (3in) high **£3,500-4,500**

◀ Chelsea inspiration
Soft-paste Chelsea porcelain looks milky-white and waxy when compared to the Japanese and Meissen hard-paste. The impurity specks in the glaze, quite common on Chelsea wares, were often covered by birds and insects. This plate is painted with the Hob in the Well pattern. *c.*1752 24cm (9½in) diameter **£5,000-6,000**

▶ Derby emulated Meissen
Derby has a soft-paste creamy porcelain body that has a faintly bluish appearance. Many pieces were copied from Meissen rather than the Japanese Kakiemon originals. This barrel-shaped jug is typically painted with a bird in a branch, bamboo and scattered flowers. *c.*1760 19cm (7½in) high **£700-900**

▲ Worcester decoration
Worcester also looked to Meissen to inspire its Kakiemon wares. The green-tinged body has a greenish glaze. The designs were often combined with European decoration. Worcester continued to use Kakiemon decoration into the 1770s, after the fashion had faded elsewhere, as shown by this tea bowl and saucer, painted with the Sir Joshua Reynolds pattern. *c.*1770 12cm (4¾in) diameter **£1,200-1,500**

Would you believe it?

It is thought that the first live elephants were seen in Japan in 1408. There are brief mentions of a 'black elephant' brought to the court of the Emperor Go-Komatsu. The first documented models of Kakiemon porcelain elephants to arrive in Europe were those at the Elizabethan mansion Burghley House in Lincolnshire, inventoried in 1688.

Some antiques are worth considerable sums because they combine many of the value points discussed on pages 8-9.

- **Provenance:** If it could be proved the porcelain elephant was in Burghley House in the 17th century it would add considerable value.
- **Age:** This is an early piece of Kakiemon porcelain dating from the mid- to late 17th century.
- **Condition:** It is remarkably well preserved considering its age and the elephant's protruding trunk.
- **Rarity:** Very few Kakiemon elephants were made in the 17th century and even fewer are known to have survived.
- **Desirability:** International collectors love these early unusual pieces of Kakiemon. The demand for such a piece would be strong.

▲ Kakiemon elephant
At 20cm (8in) long, it is worth over **£200,000.**

REVIVING YOUR FINDS
Cleaning ceramics

Ceramics must be regularly dusted and cleaned to preserve their appearance, condition and value.

Dusting

All ceramics should be dusted regularly, and always before washing and removing stains. To do this, lightly flick a make-up brush across the surface. Gently work the bristles into any crevices as well.

Cleaning glazed ceramics

First inspect for signs of damage or repair. If a piece has been repaired with adhesives, is damaged, or the glaze is worn, use the technique for unglazed or partly glazed ceramics. However, if it is in good condition, proceed as follows:

- Line the bottom of a plastic basin with a sheet of foam about 2.5cm (1in) thick. Fill with hand-hot water and mix in a few drops of mild liquid soap.
- To minimise the risk of breakage, wash one piece or part at a time.
- Lower the piece into the water and gently wipe it with a soft, lint-free rag. To loosen dirt from crevices, use the bristles of a make-up brush.
- Line the bottom of a second plastic bowl with a 2.5cm (1in) thick sheet of foam and fill it with hand-hot water. Transfer the piece from the soapy water to the clean water to rinse.
- Remove it from the rinsing bowl and dry it carefully with terry towelling.

Cleaning unglazed and partly glazed ceramics

Unglazed ceramics are highly porous and can be damaged by regular or lengthy immersion in water. You may have to dip them in water to remove certain types of stain (see below), but do not use this method for general cleaning.

Washing
One inflexible rule when cleaning an antique ceramic piece is never to put it in a dishwasher. High water temperatures, turbulence and abrasive cleaning agents will damage glazes, fade colours and may even cause chips and cracks. There is no acceptable alternative to careful cleaning by hand.

- When possible, restrict surface cleaning to dusting with a make-up brush.
- Try to remove accumulations of dirt in crevices by working a little whiting (calcium carbonate powder) into them with the tip of a make-up brush. Then brush out using another brush.
- For stubborn dirt, wipe the surface with cotton wool moistened with lukewarm water. Work lukewarm water into the crevices with a brush. Then, using terry towelling, pat the piece completely dry as quickly as possible.
- If the piece is still dirty, add a little mild liquid soap to the water before applying. Immediately rinse the item several times using cotton wool moistened with clean, lukewarm water. Finish by patting the surface completely dry with terry towelling.

Removing stains from glazed ceramics

Before you attempt to treat the stains listed below, always inspect the glaze for damage. If the glaze is worn or chipped, do not immerse the piece in any liquid. Instead, apply the appropriate fluid sparingly on a moistened cotton bud.

Removing grease from glazed ceramics

To remove stubborn greasy marks try one or more of the following methods:

- Gently rub the area with a soft, lint-free rag moistened with mild liquid soap. Then repeat the general washing technique described above.
- If soap fails to remove the mark, moisten a cotton bud with either white spirit or methylated spirits and lightly rub it over the mark.
- If either of these methods fails, rub with a cotton bud moistened with acetone.

- After successful removal, wash with liquid soap, as described above, and pat dry with a soft, lint-free rag. Lightly buff the surface with a soft, dry, lint-free cloth.

Tea and coffee stains

- Pour clean, lukewarm water into the pot and let it stand for about an hour before emptying the pot.
- Mix a solution consisting of 55g (2oz) of borax to 500ml (18fl oz) of lukewarm water and pour it into the pot. Let the solution stand for an hour, occasionally stirring it and brushing it against the inside of the pot with a soft-bristled brush. Pour away the solution.
- Mix a solution of one part household bleach to three parts lukewarm water, and pour it into the pot. Let it stand for an hour. During this time stir it occasionally with a brush.
- Pour away the solution and rinse five times under running cold water. Dry thoroughly with terry towelling.

Metallic stains

Copper and iron rivets or staples were once used to repair breaks in glazed ceramics. Over time they can stain the surrounding area.

- Rub off copper stains with a cotton bud moistened with ammonia.
- Rub off rust stains with a cotton bud moistened with a rust remover designed for use on ceramics. Rinse the treated area with distilled water immediately.

Removing stains from unglazed pottery

Stains on rare and valuable pieces of pottery should be treated by a professional restorer but you can remove stains from lesser pieces yourself. The treatments require you to immerse the piece in water. Because of the porosity of unglazed pieces and the damage that can result from absorption of water, do this as infrequently as possible.

Unidentifiable stains

To remove most stains from unglazed pottery, even if you are not sure of their origin, try the following method:

- Immerse the piece in clean lukewarm water for one to two hours.
- Position the piece so that cotton wool dampened with a solution of one part household bleach to three parts lukewarm water can be pressed on to the stain. If the stains are on more than one side of the piece, treat them in turn.
- Wrap a plastic bag around the object to keep the cotton wool moist and leave for three or four hours.
- Remove the bag and cotton wool and rinse thoroughly with clean water.
- Repeat the procedure, soaking the piece in water before you apply fresh cotton wool, until the stain has gone.

Limescale

A thin white layer of limescale (calcium carbonate) often builds up on the inside of unglazed ceramic pots and bowls used to display houseplants. To remove it, seek professional help.

Salts

Powdery white salts can accumulate on unglazed pottery and earthenware as a result of exposure to moisture. If the piece is rare or valuable, or its surface is fragile, seek help from a professional restorer. If the piece is sound, try the following:

- Place the object in a plastic basin and pour in distilled water. Do not completely cover it: leave about 2.5cm (1in) of the top exposed to the air.
- Let the piece stand for 24 hours, then change the water. Repeat this procedure at least three or four times.
- To test if all the salts have been removed, remove a teaspoonful of the distilled water and hold it over a flame until the water has evaporated. If there is any residue of salts in the spoon, repeat the soaking technique and test again until no salts are left.

Glazed ceramics
The glaze on many pre 19th-century pieces is unstable. Leave the removal of stains from such pieces to a professional restorer.

GLASS

Inherently fragile yet strong, and able to catch the light like no other material, glass is a magical substance. In general, glass made before the 20th century has fallen out of fashion unless it is of exceptionally high quality. But pieces made since 1900 – particularly sculptural forms made in Italy, Scandinavia and the UK in the mid-20th century – are popular with collectors and have risen in value accordingly.

Stylish and brightly coloured, glass produced during the 1950s and 1960s on the Venetian island of Murano is highly desirable today. Many techniques are associated with this period of design, but multi-layered cased glass known as *sommerso* is particularly notable. This *sommerso* bowl by Seguso Vetri D'Arte is desirable due to its multiple layers and striking form. *c.*1950 29cm (11½in) high **£1,000-1,500**

WHAT MAKES GLASS VALUABLE?
Modern can be more valuable than ancient

The discovery that a simple mixture of sand (silica) and sodium carbonate could make glass is attributed to the Mesopotamians 5,000 years ago. We still depend on this formula today, exploring its versatility and beauty in countless ways.

▶ **Roman glass phial**
A Roman glass unguent phial from around the 2nd century AD. Note the iridescent finish caused by burial and the reaction of oxides in the glass and earth. This is a difficult finish to fake and rarely attempted on pieces such as this small and relatively low value phial. 11cm (4½in) high
£150-250

Age is not an accurate barometer of value when assessing glass. A colourful 1950s Murano vase might be worth more than a 2nd century AD Roman glass phial. The assumption that a roughly made piece must be old, or that glass full of bubbles is an antique, isn't necessarily true either.

The art of making fine glass was mastered many centuries ago and it is such a versatile medium that over many millennia it has been fashioned into a diverse selection of articles. Differentiating between valuable pieces of 1930s Murano glass, an 1880 Bohemian overlay vase or a 1790s English Beilby enamelled drinking glass could make the difference between selling an items for a few hundred pounds or tens of thousands.

Over the centuries, the basic recipe for making glass has been refined. The addition of lime transformed humble water-soluble soda glass into the more durable soda-lime glass that accounts for most of our everyday glass objects. The use of potash and lead oxide were pioneered by leading glass-makers such as Englishman George Ravenscroft in the late 1600s. The term 'lead crystal' dates from this period. It denoted a higher quality glass with an enigmatic sparkle, prevalent in old glassware

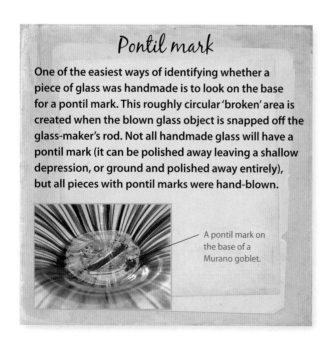

Pontil mark

One of the easiest ways of identifying whether a piece of glass was handmade is to look on the base for a pontil mark. This roughly circular 'broken' area is created when the blown glass object is snapped off the glass-maker's rod. Not all handmade glass will have a pontil mark (it can be polished away leaving a shallow depression, or ground and polished away entirely), but all pieces with pontil marks were hand-blown.

A pontil mark on the base of a Murano goblet.

◀ **Punch bowl**
A French Baccarat cranberry glass punch bowl. It has a flared rim and the body is decorated with etched and gilt flowering ivy. It is on a gilt-bronze stand with four naturalistic feet in the form of oak branches, leaves and acorns. 23cm (9in) high.
£1,500-2,000

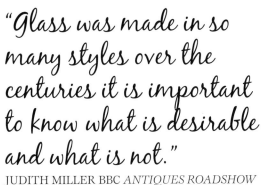

"Glass was made in so many styles over the centuries it is important to know what is desirable and what is not."

JUDITH MILLER BBC *ANTIQUES ROADSHOW* SPECIALIST

The applied black glass detail is typical.

◄ **Rare Murano bird**
A rare Primavera bird designed by Italian Ercole Barovier *c.*1929 and made by Vetreria Artistica Barovier & Co. Barovier discovered the technique while experimenting with chemicals, but the recipe is now lost. Only four are known to exist. This striking design, 30.5cm (12in) high, was avant-garde for the period. One example was sold by Christie's of London for **£70,000.**

Primavera glass has a cobweb-like internal crazed effect.

▲ **Bohemian goblet**
A currently unfashionable but handsome mid-19th century Bohemian ruby overlay glass goblet or vase. It's important to differentiate between 'cased' or 'flashed' glass and 'stained' glass. Cased or flashed glass has a coloured layer of glass that has been cut through. Similar but cheaper to make, stained glass is coloured with copper salts and silver nitrate to produce a similar effect. 29cm (11½in) high **£600-800**

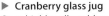
▶ **Cranberry glass jug**
Once highly collectable and avidly bought by Japanese collectors, the demand for cranberry glass has diminished in recent years. This example dates from around 1880 and has a clear applied handle and collar on a crackle effect body. 25.5cm (10in) high **£200-300**

made for the table. People still refer to their best glass as 'crystal'.

It is worth looking to see if you have any 18th- or 19th-century glasses lurking in the back of a cupboard. Often surviving as single entities, they sit unused for lack of matching companions or perhaps they simply don't hold much liquid. Ale glasses from the 18th century are a case in point; usually conical with perhaps a spiral or 'wrythen' body, their small measure is an historical testament to the strength of 18th-century brews. Typical examples sell from around £30-80, more for a less common design or one with an engraved pattern.

The art of cutting, engraving and polishing glass is another important aspect. Machine-made glass must never be discounted. Depression glass is popular in the United States; 19th-century British pressed glass manufacturers, such as Sowerby and John Derbyshire, are collected, although they are unpopular at the moment. There are even collectors of Pyrex, who can pay up to £15 for a 1950s lemonade jug with six glasses.

The best place to sell art glass from any era and rare drinking glasses is at auction. Pieces from the 20th century will do best in a dedicated 20th-century design sale. Or try specialist dealers or sell online.

IDENTIFYING HOW GLASS WAS MADE

Before you can work out the value of a piece of glass, you need to know how it was made. Most techniques have been practised for centuries, although they have been reinvented to suit changing tastes. In general, the more complicated and time-consuming the process was, the more valuable the object is likely to be.

Enamel

- Enamelled glass typically refers to glass that has been decorated with a mixture of metallic oxides and ground glass suspended in an oil base.
- The piece is then fired to fuse the decoration to the base. Some pieces are cold painted with enamel without a second firing and therefore damage easily.

Colour in batch

- Coloured glass is produced by adding chemicals or powdered enamel to the molten glass, or 'batch'.
- The tone or depth of colour varies with the amount of colourant used or the thickness of the glass. Blue is simple to produce and is often inexpensive; red and orange are more difficult and often more valuable.

Manipulation

- Patterns can be created by applying 'trails' of molten glass to the surface of a larger piece of glass while it is still hot. These can be left as simple lines or marvered (rolled) into the surface and then tooled and combed, as below.
- Surface manipulation was a popular technique during the Art Nouveau period.

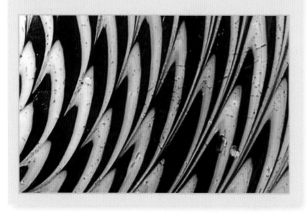

Cased

- Cased glass comprises two or more layers of differently coloured glass. A coloured core covered with colourless glass is the most basic form.
- Murano's *sommerso* (submerged) glass is one of the best-known examples of casing in multiple colours.
- Motifs, such as air bubbles, can be trapped between the layers. This may increase the value of a design.

Cameo

- When a piece of glass has been cased in one or more layers of differently coloured glass, the top layers may be partly cut away to reveal the glass underneath, creating a pattern or figurative design.
- The best glass-makers, such as French designer Emile Gallé, used up to five layers of glass. The more layers used, the more valuable a piece of glass is likely to be.
- The best pieces of cameo glass are hand-cut. Acid-etching can also be used to create cameo designs, although such pieces are typically of lower quality.

Moulded

- Some mass-produced glass objects are made by blowing glass into metal or wooden moulds by hand or by machine.
- Patterned and textured surfaces can be made easily by creating a raised pattern inside the mould.
- The same design can be used many times and much mass-produced glass is made in this way.
- Mould-blown glass is often inexpensive but pieces by designers such as René Lalique can fetch thousands of pounds.

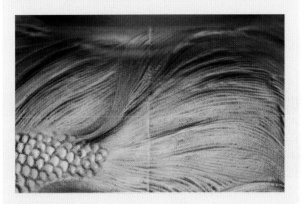

Pressed

- Pressed glass, created by manually or mechanically pressing or injecting glass into textured moulds, is often used to create a similar effect to hand-cut lead crystal, at a much lower cost.
- It is commonly used for mass-produced glassware.
- The raised areas of the designs typically feel rounded and less sharp than hand-cut examples. The 'cutting' may also be shallower than on genuine cut glass.
- You may be able to see lines remaining from the mould on the finished piece.

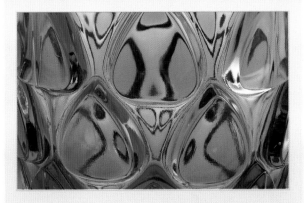

Iridescent

- Popular from the 19th century, iridescent glass was used widely for Art Nouveau-style pieces.
- The shimmering, rainbow-like surface is typically created by exposing glass to metal-oxide fumes or by spraying or painting it with metal oxides such as tin or iron chloride and heating it.
- The best examples, by manufacturers such as the American maker Tiffany and the Austrian company Loetz, can be worth high sums. Carnival glass, however, is far less valuable.

TREASURE SPOTTER'S GUIDE
Victorian glass

The 19th century was a richly innovative period for developments in glass manufacturing. Mass-production techniques, pioneered by entrepreneurs and industrialists, provided new middle-class homes with all manner of objects.

Judith warns!

▶ **Old or new?**
A modern Murano Cristallo glass goblet made in traditional form. *c.*2000 20cm (8in) high **£30-50**

Glass-makers frequently use historical models as reference for new production. Fashions change and revisiting styles is common throughout history. The techniques for making glass by hand have changed little over several hundred years and many of the tools are similar. For this reason, it can be difficult for beginners to differentiate between old and new. The Venetian island of Murano has been producing glass since the 13th century. Dealers, collectors and auctioneers alike are often confused by patterns that have been made for long periods of time. This goblet is similar to finely made Venetian 16th and 17th-century Cristallo glassware but it is a modern revival style. Techniques may have changed little but period pieces often have deterioration problems that are impossible to fake. Detecting 19th-century copies can be a lot more difficult. This is something that affects many areas of the market, particularly where the addition of engraving on a plain period glass can seriously enhance the value. Jacobite glasses often exemplify this.

Many products of the Victorian era have been carelessly disposed of. The 1950s fashion for de-cluttering reduced many 19th-century houses to characterless shells with countless objects sadly destined for the dump or the attic. Interest in glass was largely characterised by older academic collectors who specialised in 18th-century glassware; trendy 20th-century collectors were disparaging about the 'tat' of the Victorian period. Fortunately, people gradually realised the importance of this legacy and the skill of both the art glass-makers and innovative industrial producers has resulted in a far greater appreciation.

Innovation was never stagnant but many epochs, such as Regency glass, are well defined. Experimentation seems to increase around 1820 and the explosion of British coloured glass flooded the market with new forms and finishes. On the Continent, too, fabulous forms and decorative techniques found their way to other markets; Bohemian confections were characterised by their heavy lozenge-cut, beautifully decorated,

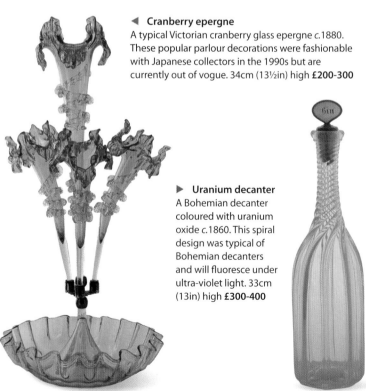

◀ **Cranberry epergne**
A typical Victorian cranberry glass epergne *c.*1880. These popular parlour decorations were fashionable with Japanese collectors in the 1990s but are currently out of vogue. 34cm (13½in) high **£200-300**

▶ **Uranium decanter**
A Bohemian decanter coloured with uranium oxide *c.*1860. This spiral design was typical of Bohemian decanters and will fluoresce under ultra-violet light. 33cm (13in) high **£300-400**

▶ Bohemian vase
A northern Bohemian vase, c.1870, lavishly decorated in typical style with enamelled designs on a milk-glass base and opulently gilded. 21.5cm (8½in) high **£600-700**

The bold enamelled colours are enhanced with gilding.

Enamelling became a Bohemian speciality from the mid-16th century.

cased and enamelled decoration. Interestingly, cut 'crystal' remained a mainstay of the British glass industry but millions of pieces of coloured glass were also manufactured as it, too, was in great demand from the burgeoning middle classes.

Knowledge of manufacturing methods is crucial when valuing Victorian glass and many individual pieces employ several techniques. It was not uncommon for Bohemian glass to be blown in iron and bronze moulds and decoration to be added later. British glass-makers often worked from drawings. Many pieces display national characteristics: French vases often have disproportionate necks; German mass-produced glass often resembles its British counterparts, because it was exported specifically to satisfy English taste.

Collectors specialise

Some collectors specialise in different genres including commemorative pressed glass and 'Vaseline' or uranium glass. Its distinctive green and yellow hues were caused by the addition of uranium oxide; true pieces fluoresce under ultra-violet light and colours vary from translucent to solid custard colours. The term 'vaseline' stems from a coloration similar in appearance to petroleum jelly. Despite the scare stories, few pieces register higher than background radiation. Items such as epergnes, vases, light shades, pressed decorative objects and Depression glass are often seen in these colours. Values vary but the big statement pieces such as epergnes can still make several hundred pounds whereas a small posy holder may be just £30-40. If you want to sell you will find youself at the mercy of current collecting trends. Your local auction house may sell higher value pieces. Otherwise, try approaching a dealer or sell your pieces online.

▲ Cranberry vase
A white-and-cranberry glass vase c.1880, made by the factory of the famous English glass-maker Thomas Webb, which was later famed for the superb cased glass cameo work of craftsmen such as J.T. Fereday. Thomas Webb and Sons was founded in 1837. This vase is typical of the factory's Satin glass production. 19.5cm (7¾in) high **£180-220**

▶ Cut-glass bowl
A cut-glass footed bowl, c.1820-1830. Typical of the period, this type of glass fulfilled the fashion for highly decorative cutting which refracted candlelight. Many such bowls were made by Irish glasshouses. Beware later revival pieces that are often difficult to tell from an original. 12.5cm (5in) high **£200-250**

TREASURE SPOTTER'S GUIDE
French 20th-century glass

The colourful art glass pieces made in the early 20th century by French designers, including Emile Gallé and René Lalique, can be worth many thousands. But beware of the many copies and imitations of their work, which do not show the same high standards of craftsmanship.

▲ **Cameo glass vase with bellflowers by Emile Gallé**
Cutting back the glass layers was a highly skilled job. The more layers, the more valuable the vase. This cameo glass vase, c.1900, has one overlay cut back; a vase with five layers could be worth more than £20,000. 17cm (6½in) high **£800-1,200**

Cameo glass consists of two or more layers of etched, coloured glass. The technique, which was first used in Roman times, involves coating a molten mass of glass – known as a 'gather' – with one or more layers of a different coloured glass. Once solidified, the layers are cut away to create a pattern in relief.

The masters of cameo glass

Emile Gallé's early cameo vases are masterpieces of precision cutting. From about 1899, he began the commercial production of cameo glass, making use of wheel etching. Production became more streamlined after his death in 1904 and the pieces made after this date are marked 'Gallé*'.

Inspired by the Gallé pieces shown at the Paris Exhibition of 1889, the Daum Frères factory began to produce its own art glass. Many others followed suit, including Schneider, Müller Frères and De Vez. By the 1920s, Daum Frères was pioneering the new Art Deco style – for which it became famous.

An exceptional piece of Gallé will have more than one layer of glass – he typically used up to five. The surface should be raised and the complex design will have subtle tones of colour that have been achieved by only partially removing some layers.

▲ **Pâte-de-verre dish by Amalric Walter**
Rare items, such as this pâte-de-verre dish from c.1925, are often overlooked due to their small size. But all pâte-de-verre in good condition is worth a considerable sum. 17cm (6½in) wide **£10,000-15,000**

◀ **Acid-etched Art Deco bowl by Daum Frères**
The stylised leaf-and-berry pattern of this 1920s bowl was created by deep and precise acid-etching. This, and its geometric design, will attract Art Deco buyers. 32cm (12½in) diameter **£3,000-4,000**

Traditional pâte-de-verre

Other designers used traditional techniques to create limited-edition pieces. Among these was Frenchman Amalric Walter who used pâte-de-verre, where a mould is filled with glass paste and heated until it has fused, to make naturalistic designs.

Pressed glass copies

René Lalique made his name at the turn of the 20th century, producing Art Nouveau jewellery. By the mid-1920s, he had built three factories producing decorative pressed glass, which was often made by pouring molten glass into a mould.

Lalique used clear glass that might be frosted, stained with colour (shades of blue, amber, green, red or black), or opalescent. His work was so widely copied – by Etling and Sabino among others – that it is vital to check for authenticity. Most items bear an impressed or etched mark. If the piece is marked 'R. Lalique France' it is most likely pre-1945. (The 'R' was dropped after his death). Acid marks were used after 1945 and, since 1980, engraved marks include ®. These marks may have been faked, making an expert opinion essential.

Judith warns!

Research is key when trying to identify Lalique glass. The Czech factory that made this Bacchantes vase in the 1930s set out to defraud the buyer by copying a Lalique design and using the mark 'R. Lalique France'. I have seen many of these fakes at antiques fairs. If you see one and the price looks too good to be true, it probably is a fake!

▲ **Czech fake**
Lalique never used malachite glass, nor produced this size or exact design. The mark on the base of this 1930s vase makes it a fake rather than a copy. 15cm (6in) high **£60-80**

Crisp moulding is highlighted by a stain applied to the surface of the glass – both signs of quality craftsmanship

The moulded detail is not as crisp as on a genuine Lalique.

▲ **Lalique Bacchantes vase**
This genuine Lalique vase, c.1927, is moulded with athletic women in realistic poses. It has a sepia patina. 25.5cm (10in) high **£2,000-3,000**

◀ **Czech copy**
This 1930s art glass vase is referred to as a copy of Lalique's work because it is not pretending to be genuine. It was simply inspired by his work. 15cm (6in) high **£60-80**

TREASURE SPOTTER'S GUIDE
British 20th-century glass

For many collectors, it is all about predicting the next 'big thing'. Despite the quality of production and diverse range of British design talent, the 20th-century glass market has ebbed and flowed with fluctuations in the economy and changes in fashion. Knowing the market is essential if you hope to profit.

Many devoted collectors promote the skills of British glass-makers and designers from the 20th century and their work has emphasised the growing importance of this area in the last few decades. This has led to a burgeoning, but fluctuating, market over the last 30 years. A knowledge of styles and production techniques can help you with some of the distinctive features that are particular to many of these designers.

Eminent British glass manufacturers of the early 20th-century period, particularly the 1920s and 1930s, include Monart, Thomas Webb and Stevens & Williams. Before World War II, designers such as Keith Murray and Clyne Farquharson exemplify the historic and technical ability of the industry.

Postwar, Geoffrey Baxter was one of the leading designers. He worked for Whitefriars Glass between 1954 and 1980. Founded in 1834 as James Powell & Sons, the company already had an historic legacy making glass for luminaries such as William Morris. Its reputation was on a par with many internationally renowned companies. In the 1920s and 1930s, it embraced Modernism and pushed the boundaries of design. After the war, few companies could compete with the flood of imports from Scandinavia but Baxter's diverse repertoire, ranging from cut glass through to a revolutionary Textured range in 1967, made Whitefriars competitive. The Banjo and Drunken Bricklayer vases from this range are perhaps his most famous designs.

Most factories in Stourbridge – the heart of the British glass-making region – continued to make more traditional, expensive cut lead-glass but it is the innovators of the period that fuel the current largely

◀ **Dartington Greek Key vase**
A Dartington Midnight colour Greek Key vase by chief designer Frank Thrower, pattern no.FT58. Flame and Cobalt examples command around double the price of the Kingfisher and Midnight examples. 24.5cm (9¾in) high **£60-80**

◀ **Chance Brothers vase**
A Chance Brothers transfer-printed handkerchief vase, similar in design to the famous Venini *fazzoletto* vases (see pages 120-121). These come in many different sizes and colours and are decorated with gingham and polka dot patterns. They are popular with collectors today, helping to maintain their value. 18cm (7in) high **£70-80**

◀ **Monart vase**
This Monart vase was made at Moncrieff's North British Glass Works in Perth, Scotland, a brand and style developed by Salvador Ysart, a master glass-maker from Spain. Production began in the early 1920s. Salvador's oldest son, Paul Ysart, became one of the superlative paperweight makers of the 20th century. 24.5cm (9¾in) high **£300-400**

Would you believe it?

Whitefriars glass has been susceptible to economic pressures and changing fashions. Prices have fallen for mid-range examples but have tended to hold for statement pieces in rare colours such as the Meadow Green Banjo vase. These innovative cased glass pieces were designed in 1967 by Geoffrey Baxter as part of the Textured range. They were made using cheaper soda glass in moulds textured with all sorts of unusual materials, including bark, bricks and wire. The use of innovative 'Pop' colours, such as Tangerine and Kingfisher, furthered their appeal to young buyers.

▲ **Cinnamon**
A Banjo vase in Cinnamon has a lower value than the rare Meadow Green colour. 32cm (12½in) high **£400-600**

▲ **Meadow Green**
A superb Whitefriars Meadow Green Banjo vase, pattern no. 9681. 32cm (12½in) high **£1,500-2,000**

fashion-led increase in demand for postwar designs. Uncluttered interiors favour 'stand alone' pieces such as those of Baxter. Frank Thrower's extensive range of designs for Dartington are also keenly collected. His popular Greek Key vase came in several colours and is one of more than 500 designs executed for Dartington.

Scandinavian influence

The Scandinavian-influenced designs of Ronald Stennett-Wilson have also risen in value; the desirable range of Sheringham candlesticks created in 1967 epitomises the glass-maker's economic and stylish ideals. It was designed for his company King's Lynn Glass which was bought-out by the Wedgwood Group in 1969. The candlesticks were made with one, two, three, five, seven and nine discs – the greater the number of discs the higher the value today. The seven and nine-ring versions are rare as they were the hardest to make and have often been damaged because they are unstable.

Makers to watch include the 'utilitarian' productions of companies such as Chance Brothers whose mass-produced, transfer-printed pieces from the 1960s and 1970s, such as Fiestaware and their Venini-like Gingham Posy or Handkerchief vases, have become collectable.

The more valuable pieces of 20th-century glass tend to do well at dedicated 20th-century design auctions and online, or you can try selling them to a specialist dealer.

◄ **Powell & Sons decanter**
A Powell & Sons/Whitefriars amber glass decanter c.1930, possibly designed by Harry Powell, grandson of the founder. He was renowned for his experimental and scientific approach, achieving previously unobtainable colours and heat-resistant glass, which had many industrial applications. 25.5cm (10in) high **£60-80**

► **Sheringham candlestick**
Values are dictated by the number of discs on the stem and the colour of the glass. Amethyst is most rare, followed by green, blue and topaz, with clear being the least desirable. Consequently, a nine-disc amethyst candlestick can be worth £3,000, while a clear one-disc example just £15. 15cm (6in) high **£35-40**

TREASURE SPOTTER'S GUIDE
Murano glass

The period of optimism following World War II inspired designers on the Venetian island of Murano to reinvent traditional glass-making techniques. The designs they produced were often high quality and vibrantly coloured. Today, the best examples by top glassworks are worth thousands of pounds.

▶ Ancient techniques revisited
In the 1950s and 1960s Fratelli Toso was one of the Murano factories that began reviving many ancient techniques. This 32cm (12½in) high Gran Redentore vase by Ermanno Toso consists of a clear glass body covered with multi-coloured murrines (slices of multi-coloured glass rod). It is a complex and time-consuming technique and this is reflected in its value. *c.*1960 **£20,000-30,000**

In the 13th century, Venice's thriving glass-making industry was forced to move to the nearby island of Murano to protect the city from the threat of fire. From the 15th to the 17th century, Murano glass was unsurpassed in quality and quantity. To protect it, members of the glass-making guild were forbidden to divulge their knowledge to outsiders or even to travel.

The invention of lead crystal, which could be easily cut and shaped, allowed glass-makers in other countries to excel in the 18th and 19th centuries. Murano became less and less important and by the early 20th century the island's output was largely confined to reproductions of its popular historical styles.

In the 1950s Murano underwent a design revolution that put it back at the forefront of glass design. Artists, architects and sculptors from outside the island were invited to work on Murano for the first time in its history. Historical techniques, such as lampworking (pieces made from glass rods or tubes), the use of coloured glass canes, mosaics, tesserae (mosaic glass

Murano glass price line

Tourist appeal
A cheerful souvenir of a holiday in Venice, this 15cm (6in) high clown figure lacks the sophistication of design associated with the best Murano glass. Its place of origin means there is a market for it and the thousands of similar figures produced for the tourist trade. An individual clown may be worth **£15-20**, but a collector will pay more for a pair.

Bright colours are valuable
This 1960 vase, 28.5cm (11¼in) high, is typical of the pure colours and clean-lined forms of Flavio Poli's *sommerso* designs for Seguso Vetri d'Arte. It would be worth more than its **£300-500** price if it featured more coloured layers, and if the glass was more vibrantly coloured. The best examples of Poli's work can fetch thousands of pounds.

Recent investment
Despite its relatively recent date, 1998, this 25.5cm (10in) high vase designed by Vittorio Ferro and made by the Vetreria Fratelli Pagnin glassworks, will attract keen interest from collectors. The high value – **£700-900** – is due to the strong design, striking colour combination and the name of this noted glass designer.

shapes) and casing, became popular. The new generation of designers used them to create stylish designs in dramatic colour combinations, decorated with stripes, patchworks, swirls and abstract designs. Today, many of these can be worth large sums.

The value of the factory and the designer

Value is primarily based on the names of the glassworks and designer. The leading companies are: Venini & C.; Seguso Vetri D'Arte; Barovier & Toso; A.V.E.M.; Cenedese; Salviati & Co.; Aureliano Toso; and Vetreria Vistosi. A signature or label from any of these is likely to increase value. Pieces that are unattributed and unsigned can fetch under £100. Smaller factories copied successful designs and these are worth a fraction of the originals.

The most valuable pieces of Murano glass are the work of designers who were influential from the 1950s to the 1970s, such as Paolo Venini, Fulvio Bianconi, Flavio Poli, Ercole Barovier and Dino Martens. The most celebrated ranges from these designers, such as Bianconi's Pezzato range, or those that are rare today, are likely to be desirable. Pieces by designers who became known after the 1970s, such as Pino Signoretto, Vittorio Ferro, Laura Diaz de Santillana and particularly Dale Chihuly (an American who was awarded a Fulbright Fellowship, which he used to work at Murano), may also be valuable.

Damage or flaws, such as bubbles (unless intended), will always decrease desirability and value. To achieve the best prices, postwar Murano glass should be sold in specialist 20th-century design sales. Such sales are run by many auction houses.

Handkerchief vase

The Fazzoletto, or handkerchief, vase was designed by Paolo Venini and Fulvio Bianconi in *c.*1948. It has since become an icon of Muranese design and has been widely copied, notably by Chance in the UK. Large, well-decorated and signed Venini examples can fetch many times the value of plain examples. However, copies by other factories are worth very little.

▲ **Inspirational form**
A Fazzoletto vase made by Fulvio Bianconi for Venini & C. The mark on the base states that it was made by 'Venini Murano ITALIA'. *c.*1950 15cm (6in) high **£2,000-3,000**

Watch the birdie
Not all Murano figurines fetch low prices. This is part of a series of five geometrically shaped bird sculptures designed by Alessandro Pianon for Vistosi in 1961. Revolutionary in their day, these remain appealing to collectors due to their whimsical appearance and high quality. 20cm (8in) high **£1,500-2,500**

Revolutionary design
Dino Martens is one of the most important and desirable names in mid-century Murano glass. Pieces from his Oriente series for Aureliano Toso are particularly highly prized due to their striking design and the sophisticated range of techniques needed to produce the effect. This vase from *c.*1952 is 33cm (13in) high and worth **£4,000-6,000**.

Popular patchwork
Fulvio Bianconi's Pezzato (patchwork) vases for Venini are arguably the best-known examples of Murano glass. This vase from 1951 in the Paris colourway, 23cm (9in) high, is the most commonly found and is worth **£6,500-7,500**. Other rarer variations, including Americano (green, aubergine, colourless and yellow), may be worth more.

TREASURE SPOTTER'S GUIDE
Scandinavian 20th-century glass

Over the past few decades, mid-20th century Scandinavian glass has become increasingly collectable and valuable. Brightly coloured, mould-blown pieces are still fetching low sums because so many were produced, but the best handmade pieces by known designers can be worth thousands of pounds.

▶ **Palet range**
Plastic was so popular in the 1950s and 1960s that many products that were not made of plastic imitated the look. Designed by Danish artist Michael Bang, Holmegaard's Palet range featured a range of bright colours and modern shapes. Larger or more complicated shapes are likely to be more valuable. 1968-1976 16cm (6¼in) high **£200-300**

During the 1930s, Scandinavian designers strove to produce glass that had a handcrafted quality despite being mass produced and affordable. The success of this initiative led to a boom in glass design, production and export, which, in turn, led to Scandinavian style becoming increasingly influential. Across the world the organically shaped, thick-walled, clear-cased pieces created in Scandinavia were imitated and adapted by a host of factories and designers.

Typical 1950s Scandinavian designs feature curving forms, asymmetric styles and cool colours. Designers in the 1960s were influenced by Pop Art and turned to geometric and cylindrical mould-blown shapes in bright colours. This gradually gave way to the textured forms of the 1970s.

The popularity of the Mid-century Modern style and the high status of Scandinavian glass means that most glass from this period is desirable. However, mass-produced pieces are common and are consequently unlikely to fetch high values, despite demand. Unique hand-blown pieces are almost always worth more than mould-blown examples, particularly if the techniques used are complex.

▲ **Apple vase**
Swedish artist Ingeborg Lundin's Apple vase for Orrefors has been called 'the world's best-known piece of 1950s glass' – and examples are highly sought-after today. The apple form is appealing and shows Lundin's sense of humour, while the varied thickness in the free-blown body shows the skill of the glass blower. 38cm (15in) high **£3,000-4,000**

▶ **Fish Graal vase**
The complex Graal and Ariel techniques were used by Orrefors to produce beautiful, desirable, three-dimensional designs. Fish Graal vases, which were made between 1937 and 1988, are popular with collectors. Earlier examples tend to be more complex and consequently fetch higher prices. This vase 20cm (8in) high dates from around 1950. **£600-800**

► Engraved design
Tapio Wirkkala's engraved glass helped bring Finnish factory, Iittala, to the forefront of Scandinavian design in the late 1940s and 1950s. Wirkkala had trained as a wood carver and used cut lines on glass, as carvers used wood grain, to highlight the form and give additional surface interest. 10cm (4in) high **£100-120**

Look at the piece as a whole

The key criteria for assessing value are designer and maker. Several factories were at the forefront of production during the 1950s to 1970s, including Orrefors, Kosta Boda, Holmegaard and Riihimäen Lasi Oy. They have dedicated groups of collectors and good glass from these factories is desirable. Value will increase for the work of a designer who defined or influenced the movement, such as Tapio Wirkkala, Sven Palmqvist, Vicke Lindstrand, Tamara Aladin, Nanny Still and Simon Gate.

Examine the base, as engraved marks can help with identification and dating. Not all pieces are signed but those that are tend to be worth more. If the lettering or signature is hard to read, try placing a piece of black paper or fabric inside the item and examining the signature again with a magnifying glass.

Values for examples by lesser factories, designers or ranges, such as John Orwar Lake for Ekenas, Strömbergshyttan and Eric Höglund for Boda, are currently low but may rise. Consider holding on to them in case they do.

◄ Mould-blown vase
This Riihimäen Lasi Oy vase is a typical example of a 1960s Scandinavian mould-blown vase, large numbers of which are on the market today. Mould-blown vases are more valuable if they were designed by a notable designer, such as Tamara Aladin or Nanny Still. 25.5cm (10in) high **£20-30**

Good, Better, Best
Orrefors Ariel

Orrefors' Ariel technique was supposedly invented by accident in 1937. As with Graal, Ariel involves casing a layer of clear glass with a layer of coloured glass, creating a design on the coloured glass and re-casing it with colourless glass. Unlike Graal, in which the design is made by engraving or etching, Ariel designs are formed by sandblasting, which makes channels or holes that trap air. These air bubbles then form an integral part of the design.

Good

In general, bowls are not as desirable as vases. This piece was designed and signed by Edvin Öhrström, the designer who is most closely associated with the Ariel range, which might make it more desirable, but it features a fairly simplistic pattern in an unappealing colourway. 18.5cm (7¼in) diameter **£450-650**

Better

Ingeborg Lundin adopted the Ariel range after Öhrström left Orrefors in 1957. This vase is typical of her designs, which often feature geometric patterns against coloured backgrounds. Rarer Ariel designs by Lundin, such as her Face vases featuring heads in profile, will fetch more. c.1968 16cm (6¼in) high **£1,200-1,800**

Best

This early figural design by Öhrström is much more appealing than most geometric Ariel designs. It would also have been more difficult to make and is far rarer than either of the other designs shown. In 1988, an exceptionally rare and fine Ariel No.125 by Öhrström fetched almost £100,000. 17cm (6½in) high **£4,000-5,000**

TREASURE SPOTTER'S GUIDE
Paperweights

The small glass paperweight holding down your papers could be worth a large sum of money. Complex designs produced in France during the mid-19th century are generally worth the most, but more recent designs by British – and particularly Scottish – makers can sell for hundreds of pounds.

▲ Baccarat carpet-ground paperweight
These feature many types of cane and those by a major maker, such as Baccarat, are valuable. This paperweight is 7.5cm (3in) in diameter. With so many canes in such a small dome, a skilled glass-maker was required, adding to its desirability. 1848 **£4,500-5,500**

The first paperweights were made in 1843 on the Venetian island of Murano. Many featured patterns made of tiny sections of glass canes known as millefiori (Italian for 'thousand flowers'), a decorative technique that epitomises paperweight design. Italian paperweights are rare today and can be worth great sums. One of the most notable makers, Pietro Bigaglia, signed many of his weights with a 'signature cane' containing a 'PB' monogram, making them easier to identify. Large and complex examples of his work can be worth over £5,000.

The 'golden age' of the paperweight, from late 1845 until the mid-1850s, was inspired by French designers. They created elaborate millefiori designs and introduced weights containing lampworked flowers or fruit. Paperweights from this period are often the most valuable, especially those by one of the three major French factories: Baccarat (est. 1764); Clichy (1837-1885); and St Louis (est. 1767). Some weights include 'signature canes' – Baccarat used the

▶ Lamp-worked fruit
Paperweights featuring lamp-worked flowers or fruits on swirling white canes were made at the French factory of St Louis. The more examples there are of different fruits or flowers within the weight, the more valuable it is likely to be. 1848 7cm (2¾in) diameter **£600-800**

St Louis weights use lead glass and feature a high dome.

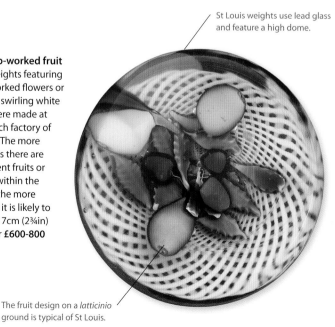

The fruit design on a *latticinio* ground is typical of St Louis.

▲ Scottish heritage
Paul Ysart designed some of Britain's finest paperweights for Monart. This Scottish paperweight, featuring a well-structured millefiori design, is unattributed. A similar design, bearing Paul Ysart's signature 'PY' cane, might be worth twice as much. *c.*1970 7.5cm (3in) diameter **£180-220**

▲ Whitefriars candle cane
Geoffrey Baxter's paperweights for Whitefriars are fairly traditional in style, meaning they do not appeal to the same collectors as his Scandinavian-influenced vases, which fetch high prices. Values are generally low. *c.*1970 7.5cm (3in) diameter **£70-80**

letter 'B' and Clichy used a 'C' or a trademark cane called the 'Clichy rose'. If a weight is not marked, and many are not, the maker can still be identified from the shape, colours or patterns used.

Complexity enhances value

Generally, the more complex a paperweight is, the more it will be worth. Well-structured patterns took skilled glass-workers a long time to make and are highly valued. 'Scramble' weights, with a random selection of different canes melted together in an unstructured pattern, are less desirable. The type of cane used can also affect value. Baccarat is known for its technically demanding silhouette canes, featuring animal profiles, made up of thin rods compacted together. These canes (known as 'Gridel' canes) can increase a weight's value.

The mid-20th century onwards saw a second 'golden age'. Values are usually less than £500, unless a design is rare. Notable Scottish firms include Monart (particularly work by Paul Ysart) and Caithness. Collectable English makers include Wedgwood and Isle of Wight Studio Glass. Most 20th-century makers signed their work on the base or include a 'signature cane' in the design. As with 19th-century examples, more complex weights are worth more but value is also driven by other factors. Limited editions, particularly those with cross-market interest, such as Whitefriars' Royal Jubilee designs, are highly desirable.

Good, Better, Best
Clichy paperweights

The company that would become Cristallerie de Clichy was founded in 1837 and moved to Clichy, then a suburb of Paris, two years later. The paperweights it produced from the mid-1840s to the late 1850s are now highly desirable. Many believe the colours of Clichy weights are richer than those of rivals Baccarat and St Louis. Even Clichy 'scramble' weights can be worth over £200, but more complex designs fetch thousands of pounds.

Good

Although the set-up for this paperweight is simple and does not form a pattern, the millefiori are skilfully spaced. A variety of canes have been used and the colours are harmonious, resulting in an appealing and attractive design. *c.*1845 7.5cm (3in) diameter **£600-1,000**

Better

This design is known as a 'barber pole' or 'candy cane' design, due to the blue and white spiral pattern canes. This example was produced by an expert glass-maker, as it is well organised. This increases its value, as does the presence of three examples of the desirable Clichy rose cane. *c.*1850 7cm (2¾in) diameter **£2,000-3,000**

Best

Honeycomb paperweights by Clichy are extremely rare and this usually adds value. As with Baccarat carpet-ground paperweights, the density of canes is desirable. This example is attractive, as it features three even rows of honeycomb millefiori in vivid colours. *c.*1850 7.5cm (3in) diameter **£7,000-10,000**

REVIVING YOUR FINDS
Cleaning glass

Clean your antique glassware to restore its original shine and beauty. The procedures to follow are reasonably safe and straightforward, but it is important that you stick to the simple precautions explained below.

Clear and coloured glass

Never wash antique glassware in a dishwasher. To avoid breakages, handwash one piece at a time, using the following method.

- Line a plastic basin with three or four layers of thick terry towelling.
- Fill the basin with warm water and mix in some washing-up liquid. If the glass is particularly dirty or greasy, add a few drops of ammonia.
- Wearing rubber gloves, immerse the glass and wash it by hand. You will find a soft-bristled toothbrush is ideal for cleaning crevices and engraved areas. Remove stubborn dirt by dipping the toothbrush in a little methylated spirits.
- Rinse the glass under lukewarm water, then dry as described below.

> **Cleaning**
> Never use methylated spirits on the inside of decanters or containers used for liquids that you may want to drink.

Stained glass

Old and valuable stained glass that has deteriorated badly should be entrusted to a professional restorer.

- Gently clean lesser pieces with a soft-bristled scrubbing brush, warm water, washing-up liquid and a few drops of ammonia (as described above), then rinse and dry (as described right).

Enamelled and gilt glass

- Wipe away dirt with a soft chamois leather moistened with methylated spirits. Then buff with a dry chamois.

Mirrors

Even if the silver backing of an antique mirror has deteriorated badly, you should never attempt to repair it, because any such restoration will always substantially devalue the piece. Three traditional methods are used to clean the fronts of mirrors and all are effective. Whichever you choose, make sure that you don't allow any moisture to creep behind the glass, which will cause further deterioration of the silvering.

- Wipe with a lint-free linen cloth moistened with methylated spirits.
- Immerse a lint-free linen cloth in a bowl of lukewarm water to which you have added a few drops of ammonia. Wring out the cloth until it is moist, then wipe the surface of the glass.
- Lightly moisten a lint-free rag with paraffin and wipe the glass. Although this method works well, it leaves a smell of paraffin in the air for some time afterwards.

Drying glass

Prolonged exposure to moisture or dampness will produce either a dull white cloudiness or iridescence (a rainbow-like effect) on the surface of glass. In some cases general cleaning (see above) will eliminate the problem, but failing that you must employ a more radical treatment (see Removing stains, opposite).

It is far better to prevent the problem than to have to cure it. You can do this by always drying glass thoroughly with a soft, lint-free cloth after cleaning, and by always storing or displaying it in well-ventilated, damp-free surroundings. The best way to dry all glass is as follows:

- Wipe it gently with either a chamois

leather or a soft, lint-free linen cloth. You should not use a cotton or woollen cloth as these can deposit small flecks of material that will spoil the appearance of the glass.

- If you can't pass a cloth through the narrow neck of a vessel such as a decanter, try directing a hair-drier, on a low or medium heat setting, into the opening for two or three minutes. Take care not to overheat the glass or you risk cracking it.

Removing stains

There are two basic causes of stains on glassware: exposure to moisture or dampness, and exposure to alcohol.

- The iridescence and cloudiness caused by moisture and dampness can sometimes be removed during general cleaning and drying (see opposite). But you will probably have to consult a professional restorer to remove the grey-white limescale (calcium carbonate) deposits that can also form on glass during prolonged exposure to moisture and dampness.
- Alcoholic drinks, in particular red wine, port and sherry, will leave a residue that forms dark stains on the surface of the glass. The insides of decanters are particularly prone to this.
- Various remedies are outlined below, although you should note that stains that have been left untreated for a considerable length of time often prove impossible to remove completely.

Iridescence and cloudiness

To remove or reduce iridescence and cloudiness, proceed as follows:

- Soak the glassware in distilled water for up to seven days, changing the water every day.
- At the end of this period, remove any remaining cloudiness with a soft-bristled brush. If this proves only partly successful, try the remedy for removing alcohol stains.

Alcohol

Virtually all alcohol stains the inside of decanters. If the first remedy is unsuccessful, try the next, and so on.

- Pour white vinegar into the decanter to a depth of 2.5cm (1in). Add 5ml (1tsp) of mild scouring powder. Fill with warm distilled water. Insert stopper, shake carefully, holding both the stopper and the decanter, and leave for 24 hours. Pour off the solution, rinse with warm water, dry with a hair-drier.
- Pour white vinegar into the decanter until it is a quarter full. Add 10ml (2tsp) of table salt. Insert the stopper and shake the decanter. Leave for 24 hours, empty, rinse and dry as before.
- Put a handful of crushed eggshell, warm distilled water and a few drops of ammonia into the decanter. Shake vigorously, leave for 24 hours. Empty, rinse and dry as before.
- Fill the decanter with lemon juice, water and 10ml (2tsp) of salt. Shake, leave, empty, rinse and dry as before.
- Put a handful of sand into the decanter. Add water and shake for a few minutes. Empty, rinse and dry as before.

Removing limescale
To remove or reduce grey-white deposits of limescale (calcium carbonate) fill the vessel with a solution of white vinegar and warm water and leave overnight. Pour away and wash as normal. If this is not successful contact a professional.

Freeing a glass stopper

Glass stoppers often become stuck in the neck of decanters and claret jugs, particularly if they were replaced when the neck was still wet with alcohol. You should never attempt to wrench, twist or tap out a stopper: you risk breaking the neck of the decanter. Instead, pour a small amount of olive oil around the stopper. Leave the vessel to stand for a few hours, while the oil gradually seeps between the stopper and the neck. It should be easy to remove the stopper. Then wash off all traces of the olive oil, using the method for cleaning clear and coloured glass.

◀ A 19th-century cut glass decanter. 25.5cm (10in) high £100-150

SILVER and METALWARE

Style and the name of the maker or designer are vital when valuing examples of silver and metalware. But the intrinsic value of the precious metal is also an important factor with silver and gold items. For items made from base metals, the skill of the maker has a larger part to play in determining value. Knowing what the object is made from, when it was made, and by whom are crucial factors.

Although they are not made of precious metal, bronze figures can fetch extremely high sums. Value is typically dependent on the name of the sculptor, the style and appearance of the object. This patinated bronze Art Deco figure on a marble base, by Austrian sculptor Josef Lorenzl, evokes the Jazz Age of the 1920s and 1930s. 47cm (18½in) high **£800–1,200**

WHAT MAKES SILVER VALUABLE?
Weight, maker and craftsmanship are factors

The value of a piece of silver, or any other metal, depends both on its weight and value as a raw material, and on its desirability as a designed object. In recent years the value of silver has increased substantially and so, if you own some, now could be the time to sell.

Georg Jensen

Danish silversmith Georg Jensen is perennially popular with collectors. The son of a blacksmith, Jensen trained as a sculptor and opened his workshop in Copenhagen in 1904.

His artistic designs were popular at home and abroad – in 1915 he exhibited at the San Francisco Panama-Pacific International Exposition. Not only did his work gain several gold medals but the newspaper magnate William Randolph Hearst purchased almost the entire stock on display and Jensen's enduring international reputation was assured.

When he died in 1935, the *New York Herald* declared him to be 'the greatest silversmith of the last 300 years'. A number of designers have worked for the company including Henning Koppel and Johan Rohde, making tablewares, decorative items and jewellery.

▲ **Georg Jensen sterling silver compote**
The flared bowl is raised on a support with a typically organic motif, on an oval base. The piece is signed on the base. 394g (13oz) 13cm (5¼in) high **£1,200-1,800**

Whether a silver item is worth more than its weight will depend on a combination of factors, the most important of which is the maker. Silver by members of the Bateman family, top makers including Paul Storr or Paul de Lamerie, or retailed by companies such as Garrard & Co will almost always fetch higher prices than similar pieces by lesser names.

The next thing to take into consideration is date – early pieces will usually be worth more than their later equivalent. Ornate 'statement pieces' such as Rococo Revival candlesticks are holding their value among buyers as are small, highly decorative items. Sets of silver cutlery often fail to sell for more than their value as a metal as they cannot be cleaned in a dishwasher and are seen as impractical. Early silver spoons are collected and can be valuable – a spoon made in London in around 1500 may sell for £25,000 but a 19th-century caddy spoon for under £100.

The importance of hallmarks

For a piece of silver to realise its best price, it should not be damaged or have been altered in any way. British silver will also need a full set of hallmarks (see pages 262-263). With most antiques, pieces made in London will be worth more than those made in the provinces. But the mark of a rare assay office such as Newcastle, or any of the Irish offices, will increase the value of a piece of silver substantially.

Hallmarks provide a useful guide to dating a piece of silver. As a basic rule, the marks should follow the shape of the piece: arranged in a circle on a round-based piece and in a row on a square-based one. Each piece of a multi-part item – such as a tea kettle with a lid and a stand – should have its own set of marks. All legitimate repairs must be separately marked. New marks on a lid, spout or handle indicate a repair, which reduces the value of the piece. Also check for a patched-on hallmark. Marks were sometimes taken from a spoon, watch-case or small object and added to a more substantial piece to avoid duty. Patination can be a helpful guide in distinguishing between the two areas when this has happened. Or look for 'junction lines' that will show up on a tarnished piece when you breathe on it. A piece of British silver without a hallmark is not necessarily a fake: very small pieces were not always marked.

A coat of arms, known as an armorial, initial or dedication which has been re-engraved, erased or replaced will lower the price. If this has happened it is likely some silver will have been removed, making the metal thinner.

Damage to the joints at handles, spouts and feet as well as the rim will also decrease value. Also look at the patina – the colour that builds up on silver over time due to oxidation, age and handling. Any breaks in patination suggest a repair or alteration that will lower the value. Poor patination may also mean that your piece is plated rather than solid silver (see pages 132-133). Also, do not be tempted to clean an old piece of silver you wish to sell – as a general rule dealers and collectors prefer to buy pieces with patina.

If you have silver you are interested in selling, find out its weight and look online for the current price per gram. Then check the hallmarks in a specialist guidebook. This will tell you the age and the maker. If you want to sell, contact a specialist dealer or your local auction house.

▲ **Victorian monteith**
These large bowls were filled with cold water and used to chill glasses. This example was made in 1896. 2,665g (94oz) 31cm (12¼in) diameter **£4,500-5,500**

Identifying how silver was decorated

Engraving
A pattern is scratched or incised into the surface. It will not show on the reverse. Modern engraving is usually carried out by machine rather than by hand.

Bright-cut engraving
Shallow, faceted cuts made at an angle create a sparkling effect. It was popular from the late 18th to the early 19th centuries. Any wear will reduce the value.

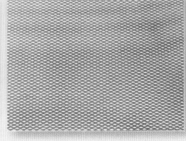

Engine turning
A form of machine engraving to create a uniform pattern. It was introduced in the late 18th century and is found typically on small items such as snuff boxes and pens.

Cut-card
Shapes cut from a metal sheet are attached using heat; may be decorated with engraving or other techniques. Strapwork is a similar method.

Repoussé
A combination of embossed and chased decoration. Embossing creates a raised pattern that can be seen from both sides. Chasing adds finer and lower-relief details.

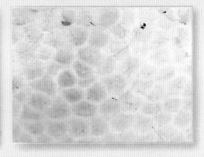

Hammered
A dappled patchwork of irregular dents on the surface. It is also known as 'martele' or 'planishing' and was used in the late 19th-century Arts and Crafts tradition.

TREASURE SPOTTER'S GUIDE
Silver and silverplate tablewares

Until the end of the 19th century, silver tablewares were a luxury reserved for the very wealthy. Then the development of new manufacturing techniques allowed silver items to be made at prices the growing middle classes could afford.

The fashion for complete silver dinner services began in late 17th-century France, where royal and aristocratic families showed off their wealth and status with silver services decorated with their coat of arms. These services often comprised 200 pieces, including tureens, centrepieces, plates, dishes, drinking vessels, casters, cruets, mustard pots and salt cellars. The desire to emulate this extravagant dining style spread across Europe.

Pieces found in average homes today are likely to date from the early 18th century onwards and most from the 19th and early 20th centuries, when the Victorian love of extravagant display was fed

◀ **Condiment set**
A Victorian silver condiment frame and bottles made in 1877 by Edward Barnard & Sons, London, 28cm (11in) high. It is fitted with cut-glass condiment bottles, three with matching silver covers, and a mustard spoon. **£600-800**

Silver plate

The demand for a less expensive substitute for solid silver was met by silver plate and, later, electroplating.

Plated silver from the 18th century is known as Old Sheffield plate. The process was developed by Sheffield cutler Thomas Bolsover in 1742. A sheet of copper was fused to a thin sheet of silver (or fused in a sandwich between two sheets of silver). Items were then constructed from this sheet. Old Sheffield plate was made in Sheffield and Birmingham as well as Russia, France and Austria. It was used until the 1840s when cheaper electroplating became common.

Electroplating is said to have been developed by cousins Henry and George Elkington in the 1830s. A piece of base metal was placed in a tank of molten silver and an electric current used to bind them.

A piece of silver plate will be less valuable than a similar solid silver piece because of the intrinsic value of the metal. Old Sheffield plate is more valuable than electroplate because there is more demand from collectors, although this depends on the design.

• A piece of Old Sheffield plate will have joins or seams between the sections and may have rolled edges. Worn plate may appear pinkish as the copper shows through.

• Electroplated items tend to be brighter in colour as they are covered with a layer of pure silver. Designs may be more intricate as the base metal could be cast in a mould rather than made from a flat sheet.

• It is unlikely that any 18th-century plated silver retains its original plating. The metal was gradually removed during cleaning and would have been re-plated.

◀ **Old Sheffield plate candelabra**
The Birmingham industrialist Matthew Boulton was renowned for his high-quality goods. His factory made this three-light candelabra. *c.*1815 45cm (17¾in) high **£1,000-1,500**

◀ **Electroplated candelabra**
Items made from electroplate may have more detailed decoration because they can be moulded before plating. 51cm (20in) high **£600-800**

by domestic silverwares made on an industrial scale and at a price many could afford. The invention of silver plate (see box, opposite) lowered the cost and increased the availability of these wares.

Today's less formal dining and demand for tablewares that are easy to care for means that silver pieces are more likely to be used as ornaments.

Condition and weight

When selling, condition is a vital factor. To fetch the best price there must be original decoration, no damage or alteration and a full set of marks. Many casters are pierced which makes them prone to damage; again this reduces value and desirability.

Values for most tablewares today are determined by the weight of the silver as well as the style and condition of the piece (see pages 130-131). Much of the silverware that was mass manufactured at the end of the 19th and beginning of the 20th centuries was not of a high standard and so earlier pieces – and later pieces made by the best craftsmen – are generally worth more. The importance of the weight of the metal is amplified when considering later, mass-produced pieces which are likely to have been made using less of the precious metal than earlier examples or those made for wealthy clients. If you are looking to sell, it is worth remembering that having a set or pair of dishes and tureens will be worth more than each item individually.

The legs feature lion's head capitals and lion's paw feet.

The serpentine oval base has bold scroll handles and is engraved with armorials.

▲ **George II tureen and cover**
Paul de Lamerie was possibly the greatest silversmith in 18th-century England. His name and the quality of this tureen, made in 1747-1748, assure its value. It is 37cm (14½in) wide and weighs 3,288g (116oz). **£50,000-60,000**

Judith warns!

The mark 'Sheffield Plate' – without the word 'Old' – means that you have a piece of silver that was plated in Sheffield, but it could have been made yesterday.

The other common mark on silver plate is E.P.N.S. A few years ago, while on a trip to an American antiques fair, a lady came up to me to say how delighted she was with the antique silver biscuit box her husband had bought her while on a business trip to London. It was marked E.P.N.S. which she proudly told me stood for 'English Pure Natural Silver'. I didn't have the heart to tell her it was really 'Electroplated Nickel Silver'.

▲ **Electroplated sauceboats**
This pair of sauceboats are in the style of the mid-18th century but probably date from the late 19th century. An original pair in solid silver could be worth five times as much. 19cm (7½in) long **£60-80**

▶ **George I silver caster**
Casters became common from the late 17th century. They were used for sugar and pepper. This one, by Samuel Weldon, London 1721, is 12.5cm (5in) high, 3oz (85g). **£350-450**

◀ **George III silver salt**
From the 18th century, salts were often made in pairs or sets. A pair of these 7.5cm (3in) wide salts by William Skeen, London, 1772, would be worth **£400-500**.

▶ **Silver-plated spoon warmer**
Englishman Christopher Dresser is considered to be one of the first modern, industrial designers. He designed this spoon warmer in around 1880 and it was manufactured by Hukin and Heath in Birmingham. 14.5cm (5¾in) high **£1,500-2,000**

TREASURE SPOTTER'S GUIDE
Candlesticks and candelabra

Once only used by the wealthy, candlesticks and candelabra have become the hallmark of special occasions and romance. With the trend towards home entertaining on the increase, this could be a good time to sell.

▲ **Generic style**
A pair of early George III brass candlesticks with shaped and welled square bases and knopped stems. Generic pairs of candlesticks such as this are worth considerably less than silver examples because brass has a lower intrinsic value than silver. 18.5cm (7¼in) high **£150-200**

Almost always made in pairs or sets, the earliest surviving domestic candlesticks date from around 1650. At that time wealthy patrons used candlesticks made from solid silver – usually cast in two or three sections that were soldered together. The less wealthy used simple brass or pewter candlesticks. Most candlesticks on the market today date from the 18th century onwards.

From around 1800, technological developments in silver candlestick-making saw a fundamental change in the way they were made. Instead of being cast from solid silver, they were made using rolled and stamped sheet silver. The result was a much lighter item, the base of which was 'loaded' with wood, pitch or plaster of Paris to give it greater stability. This method of production speeded up the manufacturing process significantly, allowing for a high number of candlesticks to be made at a lower cost.

Candelabra were also made in pairs or sets. The earliest pieces had just two or three arms, while later examples may have as many as seven.

Chandelier appeal

There is no denying that a chandelier makes an impressive focal point. Currently fashionable, such pieces are a hit with people wanting to bring a high-gloss sparkle to a room. Late 19th- and early 20th-century examples, such as this one, appeal because they are usually quite easy to fit for use with electricity. Specialists in restoration and cleaning can also find antique replacement parts, such as glass and crystal drops, should you find any missing.

▲ **Statement piece**
This 99cm (39in) high chandelier has ornate out-scrolling branches with crystal drops and is worth around £2,000-2,500.

▲ **Exceptionally high value**
Dating from the same period as the brass candlesticks, these three are worth 20 times as much. Cast from solid silver, they are stamped 'George Ashworth & Co., Sheffield', a reputable 18th-century silversmith. Their elegant forms with simple Neoclassical styling add to their desirability. 30.5cm (12in) high **£2,500-3,500**

The twisting branches are typical of Rococo style which was used by silversmiths to demonstrate the plasticity of the silver.

The extravagant tastes of the 19th century saw the number of sockets increase from two or three in the 1770s to seven, as here.

▲ A rare find

This pair of silver Rococo Revival candelabra is by the Austrian silversmith J. C. Klinkosch, who made pieces of the highest quality for Viennese nobility. The elaborate floral decoration, with acanthus leaves and rocailles, and sculpted putti, characterises the style. Extremely rare, 73.5cm (29in) high and weighing 16.5kg (36lb 6oz), they are worth **£40,000-50,000.**

▼ Neoclassical Revival

The Neoclassical style resulted in countless column candlesticks emerging in the late 18th century, and the style was revived towards the end of the 19th century. This 28cm (11in) high, loaded silver-plated pair with stop-fluted columns, Corinthian capitals and square stepped bases is typical of pieces produced by William Hutton & Sons of London and Sheffield. The pair is worth **£500-800.**

Clues in the decoration

The stems and bases of the candlesticks and candelabra that survive today are often profusely decorated in the style of their time – reeded columns with Corinthian capitals for a Georgian piece, swirling tendrils of wild flowers for an Art Nouveau example – and many have become highly desirable. Of particular interest to collectors are early solid Rococo and Neoclassical pieces, which are rare, but also pieces made at the turn of the 20th century, such as Arts and Crafts examples made for Liberty & Co. or pieces originating from the Wiener Werkstätte in Vienna, Austria.

When using the style guides at the back of the book to identify your candlesticks, first look to see if they a have vertical seam – the best indication of a loaded, rather than solid, piece. Loaded candlesticks are worth less than solid silver examples, simply because far less metal is used in the process. The stamp of a renowned silversmith from any era can significantly increase the value of a piece. Don't be tempted to split a pair: the value of a lone piece can be as little as a quarter the value of two that match.

For further information about lighting see pages 54-57.

▶ Stamped factory marks

It is always worth taking a close look at any maker's stamps as well as hallmarks. These 1910 silver-plated candlesticks were made by the German firm Württembergische Metallwaren Fabrik (WMF), one of the leading manufacturers of Art Nouveau designs. Such a stamp makes this pair worth several times more than a similar generic pair. 28cm (11in) high **£800-1,200**

TREASURE SPOTTER'S GALLERY
Silver novelties

Throughout history, wealthy households used all manner of small silver items as part of their daily lives. While the necessity for knife rests, pocket nutmeg graters and stamp boxes may have all but disappeared, they attract dedicated collectors which means there is a ready – and sometimes high-paying – market for them. Condition, maker and design all influence value. If you have some you wish to sell, contact your local auction house or a specialist silver dealer.

The image of the cathedral is well defined, evidence that it is of higher quality than similar boxes by some other makers.

The box contained a sponge soaked in perfume that could be inhaled as necessary. The sponge was held in place by a pierced grille.

▲ **Vinaigrette**
In the 18th and 19th centuries, wealthy people masked unpleasant odours by sniffing at their vinaigrettes. Examples from the 19th century tend to be larger and more elaborate. Particularly valuable are castle-top vinaigrettes by the Birmingham maker Nathaniel Mills. These are decorated with views of landmarks such as this one of Gloucester Cathedral made in 1844. 44g (1½oz) 4.5cm (1¾in) wide **£4,000-5,000**

▲ **Wine label**
Until 1860, when wine merchants were required to label bottles before they were sold, ceramic, parchment and then silver labels were used to identify the contents of wine bottles. Around 1,500 different wines and spirit labels have been recorded, made in a wide variety of shapes and sizes. Common examples may fetch £50, with rare names and styles fetching £500 or more. This ornate George III label from around 1817 is decorated with a border of fruiting vines, a shell and scrolls. **£250-350**

▶ **Stirrup cup**
Before a morning in the saddle, huntsmen shared a warming alcoholic drink from a stirrup cup. These were passed around while on horseback. They often feature a fox's head, making this boar's head, 12cm (4¾in) high, made in London c.1856, unusual. 510g (18oz) **£2,500-3,500**

▶ **Pepperette**

In the 19th century, tableware was made in an array of shapes and sizes. Collectors will pay a premium for salts (salt holders), mustard pots, sugar sifters and pepperettes (pepper holders) in novelty shapes. This Victorian frog pepperette, 11.5cm (4½in) high, was made by London silversmith James Barclay Hennell in 1881. 170g (6oz) **£4,000-5,000**

▶ **Card case**

The use of calling cards began in the early 19th century and a complicated etiquette built up around them. The earliest examples of card case were made from silver, but later carved wood, ivory, tortoiseshell and mother-of-pearl were also used. The most valuable examples today tend to be castle tops (see vinaigrette). In general, the more attractive the decoration the more desirable the box will be. Repoussé decoration, such as that on this late 19th century Dutch card case, was common. **£350-450**

Omar Ramsden

The work of Omar Ramsden has become highly desirable in recent years. He produced high-quality re-interpretations of Tudor and Celtic silver, metalwork and jewellery, often featuring hand-hammered finishes, enamels and applied decoration. Ramsden operated a small workshop from 1898-1919 in partnership with Alwyn Carr, and went on to register his own mark in 1919. His workshops produced a large volume of ecclesiastical, civic and corporate work in the Art Nouveau and Art and Crafts styles. He produced numerous presentation pieces and private commissions. His works often have the engraved inscription '*Omar Ramsden Me Fecit*': 'Omar Ramsden made me'.

◀ **Vesta case**

The first matches were extremely volatile and required a metal box, known as a vesta case, to keep them – and the user – safe. The introduction of the safety match in around 1830 meant that matches could be carried in the pocket, and so small vesta cases began to be made, with production peaking in the 1870s. Plain, common examples are worth as little as £20 but novelty cases, such as this Victorian silver vesta case modelled as Mr. Punch's dog Toby, 6cm (2½in) high, are worth far more. **£800-1,200**

▲ **Omar Ramsden caddy spoon**

Caddy spoons were used to measure tea leaves from the caddy to the teapot. This spoon, by Omar Ramsden and Alwyn Charles Ellison Carr, has a planished finish and central red enamelled panel, with marks for London 1906. 8cm (3¼in) long 25g (1oz) **£1,200-1,800**

▶ **Cigarette case**

Good-quality sporting-themed items will usually find a willing and generous buyer when offered for sale. This 1920s Austrian silver and enamel combination cigarette and vesta case, 7.5cm (3in) wide, shows the jockey Digby Blackburn on horseback – knowing the name of the subject increases its desirability and it would make **£600-800**. Any damage to the enamel will lower the value considerably.

TREASURE SPOTTER'S GUIDE
Bronze sculpture

Figures and sculptures designed for people's homes encapsulate the spirit of the time. Bronze sculptures by well-known artists can be especially valuable but damage or over-enthusiastic cleaning can reduce their value considerably.

The invention of the pantograph in 1830 triggered a boom in demand for domestic sculpture. This enabled foundries to create scaled-down versions of monumental sculpture for display in the home. As a result, the growing middle classes, who wanted to display their wealth and taste, were able to buy sculptures to decorate their drawing rooms. Many foundries created series of affordable replica statues, which can be worth anything from £2,000 to £25,000 or more today depending on their size, the artist and condition. Victorian taste included Classical reproductions, romantic figures such as cherubs and work by many artists of the day. Also fashionable were animalier bronzes – cast-bronze, limited-edition naturalistic sculptures of animals including horses,

▶ **Bergman cold-painted pheasant**
One of the most successful producers was Franz Bergman who created cold-painted bronze figures at his foundry in Vienna. He depicted everything from dogs and pheasants to exotic dancers. Values range from a few hundred pounds for a small dog to £15,000 for a large-scale boudoir lamp. This early 20th century pheasant is 26cm (10½in) high and worth **£1,500-2,000.**

dogs and mythological beasts. The work of Parisian artists such as Antoine-Louis Barye and Pierre-Jules Mêne can be worth considerable sums. Animalier sculptures were often cast at the foundry of Ferdinand Barbedienne and his mark – as well as that of the sculptor – can be found on many pieces.

A new eroticism

These sculpture styles remained popular into the early 20th century. However, the arrival of the Art Nouveau movement brought a new eroticism to sculpture. Bronze figures depicted semi-clad women

◀ **Classical figure of Mercury**
The Victorian taste for classical subjects was fed by reproductions of ancient Roman statues, such as this late 19th century depiction of Mercury seated on a tree stump, or modern interpretations of them. These figures are often referred to as being 'after the Antique'. 64cm (25¼in) high **£2,000-2,500**

The sculpting of the muscles encapsulates the animal's power.

◀ **Antoine-Louis Barye panther**
The French animalier sculptor Antoine-Louis Barye created lifelike depictions of wild animals, often capturing their prey. This sculpture of a panther pouncing on a civet cat from around 1870 is signed. 32cm (12½in) high **£10,000-12,000**

emerging from flowers or pools of water. French sculptor Raoul Larche, inspired by American dancer Loie Fuller, showed her draped in fabric. These rare masterpieces, with a gilt finish, can fetch anything from £5,000 to £30,000. Bronze figures by lesser artists can be worth between £500 and £2,000.

In the 1920s and 1930s, domestic sculpture reached its zenith with Art Deco figures by Demêtre Chiparus, Ferdinand Preiss, Josef Lorenzl and Pierre Le Faguays, among others. They depicted women in athletic poses, playing sports or dancing in revealing, exotic costumes.

Size is not necessarily an indicator of value. A small, exquisite piece should be worth more than a large, mediocre one. Condition is vital. Damage and worn patination decrease value considerably. Figures have been copied or faked, so an expert opinion is vital. The best pieces should be sold at a specialist decorative arts auction; damaged figures, or those made from spelter, online.

◄ **Ernest-Louis Barrias figure**
Most Art Nouveau sculpture was designed for an elite clientele, used expensive materials and often featured provocative subject matter. This gilt and patinated bronze figure of *Nature Revealing Herself To Science* is signed by French sculptor Ernest-Louis Barrias, and bears the foundry mark for Susse Frères. 24cm (9½in) high **£8,000-12,000**

Good, Better, Best Art Deco figures

The most valuable Art Deco sculptures – now and then – were made from chryselephantine, a mixture of bronze and ivory. The bronze might be painted or patinated to enhance the design. Cheap copies were made from spelter (a bronze substitute) and other base metals.

High-quality pieces sat on impressive marble or onyx bases and were signed by the artist. Sculptures were also incorporated into mantel clocks and table lamps. Watch out for fakes and copies – these are worth a fraction of the value of genuine pieces.

Good

Spelter lamp
Spelter figures enabled the less wealthy to own a piece of the fashionable Art Deco style. The majority do not display the elegance and energy of equivalent bronze or chryselephantine figures. While demure for an Art Deco figure, this girl holding an ivorine ball is well modelled. 50cm (19¾in) wide **£300-500**

Better

Female dancer
Exotic dancers wearing revealing costumes are the epitome of Art Deco figures. Less glamorous examples, as well as depictions of children, fetch lower prices. This is the case with the work of Pierre le Faguays (who also signed his work Fayral). This figure has symmetry and is elegant. 52cm (20½in) high **£10,000-15,000**

Best

Chiparus figure group
Chryselephantine figures by Demêtre Chiparus and Ferdinand Preiss are masterpieces of Art Deco design. Chiparus' *Bal Costume* was designed in the 1920s and was inspired by a Ballet Russes production of *Petrouchka*, in which Nijinsky wore a similar outfit to the male figure. 49cm (19¼in) high **£25,000-35,000**

TREASURE SPOTTER'S GUIDE
Stainless steel

Vast quantities of stainless steel tableware were produced from the 1950s to the 1970s and – thanks to its durability – much survives today. Because of this, only the best examples by known designers fetch reasonable sums and could still rise in value if demand from collectors increases.

▲ **Old Hall Alveston tea set**
According to the Old Hall Collector's club, the Alveston tea set, designed by Robert Welch, is Old Hall's most collectable design. The set is unofficially known as 'Aladdin's lamp' due to the shape of the teapot. *c.*1962
£150-250

Stainless steel was developed in the early 20th century by English metallurgist Harry Brearley, who added chromium to mild steel to stop it rusting. In 1928, ten years after the new material had first been used to make cutlery, the wife of William Wiggin of J&J Wiggin in Bloxwich, Staffordshire, asked him to make a stainless steel toast rack. The resultant range of functional domestic items, including teapots, milk jugs and, of course, toast racks, was exhibited at the 1934 Ideal Home Exhibition in London under the name 'Old Hall'. It was a success and inspired many other companies to produce stainless steel household goods.

Sleek look back in fashion

The clean lines and minimal surface decoration that characterises much of the period's stainless steel tableware are now back in fashion, which means these objects are becoming collectable. Good condition is crucial. Mint condition, boxed examples are unusual and so attract the highest values – often up to 50 per cent more than damaged examples.

Unfortunately, prices are still generally low as most stainless steel objects were produced in large numbers and the resilience of the material means that many have survived. Values are higher for designs created by well-known names. Many of the best stainless steel designers are known for their related work in silver and gold, meaning that mass-produced stainless steel objects are seen as a good way of buying into the look.

▲ **Candlesticks by Robert Welch**
Robert Welch's pair of triple candlesticks for Old Hall are among the most desirable stainless steel designs. These candlesticks may still rise in value due to the innovative design and popular name. Make sure the wooden feet are present as prices drop if these are missing. 23cm (9in) high **£100-150 pair**

▶ **Toast rack**
The Campden toast rack was one of three designs to win Robert Welch and Old Hall a Design Centre Award. It was made with two or six sections. Due to its popularity, it is not rare and values are low. 18.5cm (7¼in) long
under £20

◄ Pride cutlery
David Mellor's elegant and distinctive Pride cutlery is still being manufactured today in both silver-plate and stainless steel. Vintage sets, such as this ivorene-handled selection, can be found in good condition but values are not high. Knife 21cm (8¼in) long
£50-60 per place setting

Old Hall appointed silversmith Robert Welch as design consultant in 1955. Welch's Scandinavian-influenced designs, which won him three Design Council Awards, helped establish Old Hall as a market leader in British metal. Notable ranges include Campden (1957), Oriana (1960) and Alveston (1964). Viner's of Sheffield made attractive modern designs by Gerald Benney, a leading silversmith and royal-warrant holder, and silversmith Stuart Devlin (see box). David Mellor's influential cutlery ranges, such as Pride (1951), Embassy (1963) and Thrift (1965), are desirable today, as are pieces from the 1960s Cylinda-Line, by Arne Jacobsen for Danish company, Stelton.

Not all pieces from the ranges mentioned are valuable and even the best pieces are often worth under £100. However, these designs are currently of interest to collectors and may increase in value if you hold on to them.

Stuart Devlin

In the early 1970s, Viner's commissioned Australian-born British silversmith and metalworker Stuart Devlin to design a range of stainless steel tableware. Devlin produced nine objects, including several goblets, all of which featured shiny stainless steel and textured gold-plated areas which mimicked his precious metal designs. A limited number of his designs for Viner's were also produced in solid silver but these are very rare today. The range was phased out in 1979.

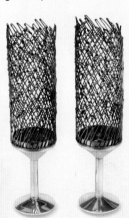

▲ Textured candlesticks
These silver-gilt candlesticks are typical of Stuart Devlin's designs, both in their contrast of plain silver and textured gold and also in their extravagance and almost Space Age appearance. Candlesticks, candelabra and drinking goblets are among the most widely collected Devlin designs. 1971 27cm (10¾in) high **£1,200-1,800**

◄ Chelsea Steel
The striking artwork on this boxed set of Chelsea Steel knives and forks adds significantly to their value. Cutlery should always be sold as a set to achieve the highest prices. If you are missing pieces, it may be worth completing it by buying individual items that show the same level of wear. 26.5cm (10½in) wide **£30-50**

► Cylinda-Line coffee pot
Dane Arne Jacobsen is well known for his softly rounded furniture designs, such as the Swan chair (1957-1958). His stainless steel Cylinda-Line designs for Stelton are less known but their connection to such a popular Mid-century Modern designer means they may yet attract interest and rise in value. 1967 20cm (8in) high **£50-80**

TREASURE SPOTTER'S GUIDE
Chinese and Japanese cloisonné

In recent years the desirability of China's metalware has risen, although not as far or as fast as the values of Chinese ceramics and jade. As a result Chinese cloisonné has been selling well, although you might want to hold on to Japanese examples until that country's economy improves.

The smooth, glassy finish was achieved by repeated firing and polishing.

Ruyi-shaped feet symbolised good wishes or fortune.

▲ **Qianlong quality**
Although it is relatively small, this Qianlong brushpot features highly detailed and appealing decoration of squirrels playing among grapevines. This pattern, popular during the late Qing dynasty, symbolises longevity. Larger or more complicated examples from the Qianlong period can fetch significantly more.
15.5cm (6¼in) high **£10,000-15,000**

Cloisonné is a French word but the decorative enamelling technique it describes originated in the Byzantine Empire and has been most famously used by Oriental and Russian artists. The technique involves applying soft glass pastes to a metal base within fields or 'cloisons', which are formed by soldering or gluing wire to the metal's surface. When the piece is fired, the enamel melts and fuses to the metal. It is then polished into a flat surface. Chinese artists have been using this technique since the 14th century and it reached Japan in the 17th century. Significant numbers of objects began to be exported to Europe in the 19th century.

Imperial pieces

Interest and prices for Chinese cloisonné have increased dramatically in the past decade, driven by a thriving Chinese economy. Some of the most intricate (and consequently most desirable) Chinese cloisonné was made during the Qianlong period (1735-1795). At this time, many craftsmen were encouraged by patronage of the emperor. Pieces that were made specifically for the Imperial palaces will be marked and will always command a premium. Most Chinese cloisonné is marked with a four or six-character symbol that will allow you to date it. Consult the reference guide at the back of this book for help.

Cleaning cloisonné

Cloisonné can be cleaned at home, but inspect the enamels with a magnifying glass before you begin. If they are loose, have them secured by a professional restorer, as lost enamels will damage value considerably. If they are secure, you can use a soft-bristled artist's brush to gently work a solution of liquid soap and lukewarm distilled water over the surface. Rinse in clean water before removing any spots of grease with an artist's brush moistened with white spirit. For more on cleaning metals see pages 144-145.

◄ **Rare shapes**
The charming and unusual form of these early 19th-century, 19.5cm (7¾in) long, Chinese cloisonné bird boxes accounts for much of their high value. The design is well considered, as the wings act as a cover for each box and the cloisons are used to represent individual feathers.
£6,000-7,000

◄ Nothing special
The basic design, brash colours and brassy-toned metal of this Chinese cloisonné dish are all indicators of poor quality. It's likely that, like many other similar pieces, it was produced for the tourist trade. Such pieces are unlikely ever to fetch high sums. 21cm (8¼in) diameter **£25-35**

▲ Dramatic design
Bronze *gu* vessels (wine containers of this form) have been made in China from the 18th century BC. This 28cm (11in) high vase was made in the late 19th century, but the traditional shape and decoration are likely to make this piece appealing to buyers, despite its later date. **£1,800-2,200**

The Japanese economy is still relatively depressed in comparison to the Chinese, meaning that prices for Japanese artworks remain significantly lower. While the best quality pieces are worth thousands of pounds, in most cases it may be worth holding on to your Japanese treasures until demand for them improves.

Japanese cloisonné is often more sombrely coloured than Chinese cloisonné. From the mid-19th century, Japanese artists aimed to remove the copper wires, creating a more delicate design. The golden age of Japanese cloisonné enamels is held to be 1890-1910 and pieces from this era are likely to fetch the highest prices, particularly if they are by a notable workshop. Names likely to add value to a piece include: Namikawa Yasuyuki, Namikawa Sosuke, Ando Jubei, Hayashi Kodenji and Hattori Tadasaburo.

Both Chinese and Japanese cloisonné should be sold at auction in a specialist Asian art sale. Given the increased popularity of Asian art, such sales are now run by many auction houses, including the main London rooms, Woolley & Wallis in Salisbury and Lyon & Turnbull in Edinburgh. Be aware that any damage, such as knocks, dents or bruises, will significantly decrease the value of a cloisonné object and is impossible to reverse.

► Ando workshop
A large number of pieces of varying quality have been produced since the Ando workshop, which is still in operation today, was established in Nagoya, Japan, in 1881. While the best Ando pieces can fetch thousands of pounds, more standard pieces such as this vase decorated with flowers, 28cm (11in) high, are worth **£150-250**.

► Decorative effect
This charger is relatively recent and is not marked with the name of any of the most important Japanese cloisonné workshops. However, it is extremely large and the cloisonné decoration is intricate. This 25in (63.5cm) diameter piece would look very striking mounted on a wall, which explains its value. **£200-300**

REVIVING YOUR FINDS
Cleaning metalware

Most metalware is affected by various forms of tarnishing and discoloration. If a piece contains more than one metal (or another material), you may have to isolate and treat each one in turn to protect areas from inappropriate cleaning agents.

Patination
Whatever metal you are treating, work slowly and carefully. It is easy to overdo cleaning and remove desirable patination rather than just surface tarnish and dirt. This is particularly important if you use an electric drill and lambswool buffing mop to polish robust base metals, such as iron and steel, rather than polishing them by hand with a cloth.

Brass
- Treat minimal tarnish with brass polish and a soft, lint-free rag.
- For obstinate marks, mix paraffin with jeweller's rouge to form a thick paste and apply with a rag. Adding two drops of ammonia may help.
- For heavier tarnish, mix 15ml (1 tbsp) each of salt and vinegar with 300ml (10fl oz) hot water. Gently apply with fine-grade wire wool. Wash with warm, soapy water, rinse and dry.
- Protect and polish with brass polish or microcrystalline wax. Protect door furniture with a layer of clear lacquer.

Bronze
Treat bronze with caution and never use abrasive powders. A considerable part of its value lies in the subtle patination that accumulates over the years.
- Dust with a soft-bristled brush and clean recesses with a soft-bristled toothbrush moistened with white spirit.
- If it was originally polished, use a thin coat of microcrystalline wax (available online).

Copper
Clean copper using any of the methods recommended for brass or the chemical dip for cleaning silver described opposite.
- Remove small spots of blue-green verdigris (a copper-carbonate deposit) by using cotton wool to wipe on a paste made from white vinegar and salt, then rinse with water and dry.
- To treat more extensive verdigris, mix a solution of 15ml of lemon juice to 600ml (1 pint) of warm distilled water, and sponge over the piece. Rinse with a weak solution of warm, soapy water, and then with clean water. Finally, dry it. Protect with a thin coat of microcrystalline wax.

Iron and steel
Cast and wrought iron, and steel are prone to rusting. Treat it when it first appears with a commercial rust remover, or by wiping with a brush soaked in paraffin. In both cases, rinse with white spirit, before drying thoroughly with towelling. Protect by heating it (with a hair-drier) and applying a coat of microcrystalline wax.
- If the metal is pitted, brush off and treat as described above. Never grind down the pitting, you will destroy the value.
- Cast-iron fittings such as fire surrounds can be shot-blasted to remove rust and paint. Then wipe on microcrystalline wax and polish with an electric drill and a lambswool buffing mop.
- Use paint stripper to remove paint.

Lead
The bluish-grey green patina that develops on old pieces is easily destroyed.
- Limit cleaning to brushing the surface with a stiff-bristled artist's brush.
- Mould growth, which is common on garden ornaments, should be allowed to dry out naturally indoors first.

Using an electrochemical dip

- Work in a well-ventilated area and wear rubber gloves. Line a plastic bowl with aluminium foil and place the piece of silver in it.
- In a plastic bucket, mix 140g (5oz) of washing soda with 600ml (1 pint) of very hot water. Carefully pour over the silver until it is immersed. It will bubble violently.
- If the piece is solid silver, or silver plate in good condition leave for one to two minutes. Leave silver plate that has eroded for 20 seconds.
- Using a pair of wooden tongs, remove the piece from the dip. If the tarnishing has not disappeared, dip again. Rinse with hot water.
- Remove the rubber gloves and wash, rinse and dry the piece then buff to a shine with a soft cloth or a chamois leather.

▲ **Silver cleaning tip**
If the piece has a handle, you can use dowelling instead of tongs. Don't use your hands to remove the silver: rubber gloves don't guarantee protection from washing soda, and the interaction of the chemical and the rubber will mark the silver.

Pewter

The patination on pewter, which adds to its value, is easily destroyed by abrasive cleaning agents and overwashing.

- Limit cleaning to dusting down with a soft-bristled brush and gently rubbing over the surface with a clean chamois.
- Old pewter is subject to contamination by salts that form spots. These should be treated by a professional.

Silver

- Wash silverware after use in hot, soapy water, wiping it with a soft cloth and scrubbing recesses with a soft toothbrush. Rinse with clean, hot water and then dry immediately with a soft cloth. If the silver is not tarnished, buff with a clean, dry, soft cloth; if it is, polish the piece as described below.
- Most items of tarnished silver and silver plate can be successfully cleaned and polished by hand, using a soft cloth and a proprietary silver cleaner.
- Once the tarnishing has been removed, wash, rinse and dry as described above. Buff the surface to a deep shine with a clean, soft cloth or a chamois.
- Use a fine-bristled artist's brush to buff any recessed areas.

- For light tarnishing, use an impregnated silver cloth. More serious tarnishing will require a liquid or paste. If it is very bad, use an electrochemical dip (see the box above). Less abrasive than manual cleaning, it won't remove a thin layer of silver every time it is used. This makes it suitable for cleaning worn silver plate, provided that you don't immerse the piece for too long.
- Proprietary silver cleaners have a mild abrasive action which remove a minute layer of silver each time they are used. For this reason, use the gentlest possible buffing and polishing action when treating silver items – especially silver plate – with a cleaning agent.

Removing stains from silver

If used regularly, silver coffee pots and teapots tend to become stained inside.

- To remove staining, mix 5ml (1 tsp) of borax with 600ml (1 pint) of hot water. Fill the pot with the solution and let it stand for about two hours. Swirl the mixture around the pot with a soft-bristled artist's brush then pour out and wash the inside with warm, soapy water. Rinse with clean, warm water and dry using a soft cloth.

Coins and medals
The patination that builds up on coins and medals is highly prized by collectors and can contribute substantially to their value. For this reason, you should entrust treatment for corrosion, and even general cleaning, to a professional.

Tarnishing
Because silver and silver plate are vulnerable to tarnishing, always wear white cotton gloves to handle silver or when cleaning it by hand.

HOUSEHOLD OBJECTS

The items people lived with and used every day offer fascinating insights into the past. In some cases they also have surprisingly high values when you consider that they were designed to be practical rather than decorative. A colourful telephone, a pieceof advertising memorabilia or an old wooden box may turn out to be an unexpected treasure if you know what to look for.

The Series 300 telephone is a celebrated design and examples are highly sought after. Most of those on the market today are black, so red Series 300 phones can command high prices if in good condition. Green examples are even more desirable. Beware of fakes or reproduction models – uneven mouldings may give copies away. **£1,000-1,500**

WHAT MAKES HOMEWARES VALUABLE?
The importance of aesthetic appeal

Many of the items that your parents may have once used every day are unlikely to be valuable. But collectors appreciate the aesthetic appeal and the historical and personal significance of vintage home and kitchenware, and are willing to pay for the right piece.

All the objects in this section could potentially be found in your attic or on your mantelpiece. Although a general dealer may not be interested in such homely pieces, they will appeal to collectors in that area. If selling, it is often best to list household items on an online auction site, such as eBay, where they can find the right collector and the highest price. Good items of scrimshaw are the exception and should be sold at auction.

Treasures in your home

The more attractive an item is, the higher its value is likely to be. In many cases, aesthetic appeal is located directly in the quality of the material. Collectors look for treen objects with attractive grains and original patina; un-dented and gleaming copper saucepans; and pewter with silvery-grey patination.

Quality of craftsmanship is important when assessing many of the oldest household objects, such as 18th-century treen bowls and scrimshaw powder horns from the 19th century. These individual and unusual items appeal to a

▲ **Novelty value**
Snuffboxes in novelty forms, such as this shoe, are popular with collectors and likely to fetch reasonable sums. This shoe is appealingly shaped and has good patina, but it would have fetched more if the form had been more complex. 11.5cm (4½in) long **£800-1000**

Judith warns!

Guinness is such a popular brand that fakes, particularly of its famous toucans, are common. Reproductions of figurines and lamp bases, originally made by Carlton Ware, are often crudely modelled and decorated, which makes them relatively easy to distinguish from the originals. Fakes are likely to have smudged colours on the beak, rather than graduated colours, and cream, rather than white, necks. Tails are usually completely black, rather than highlighted in orange and red, and the pint is likely to have a dirty white head, whereas originals feature a creamy tone. Check the base, as many fakes have Carlton's marks applied over, rather than under, the glaze.

▲ **Advertising symbol**
The Guinness toucan was introduced in 1935 and is synonymous with the brand. As a consequence good-condition figures are likely to fetch high values. Lamps and other variations on the figure can be worth more – it may be worth consulting a specialist guide.
£250-350

collector not only because they are old and often finely made, but also because they show signs of being made and used by people in the past. A good story or a way to connect an object to a person, such as a name or date carved into piece of scrimshaw, is likely to raise value and interest.

Style is another strong indicator to value, particularly with newer items such as advertising and plastic. Collectors of advertising collect by brand or time period. The early to mid-20th century is extremely popular. High prices are likely to be paid for examples in the Art Deco style or pieces that are typical of the 1950s and 1960s. Except for the very best examples, Art Nouveau is currently out of vogue.

Decoration not function

In general, value is determined by a piece's condition, rarity, age and, most importantly, desirability. For many items of antique homeware, such as butter pats, milk churns and base-metal coffee pots and teapots, desirability (and consequently value) is low. Most of these cannot be used today and so their appeal is largely decorative and confined to a small number of collectors.

▲ **Uncommon plastic**
This miniature Bakelite quaich (a two-handed drinking cup or bowl) is marked 'MADE IN SCOTLAND'. This makes it rare as very little Bakelite was manufactured in Scotland. Unfortunately the value of this piece is still low, due to its undesirable brown colour.
11cm (4¼in) long **£8-12**

▶ **The value of a set**
This set of Victorian copper fire tools is complete and is likely to be worth more than the sum of the individual parts, if separated. The tools are also attractively shaped and the shovel features additional pierced detail, which adds to the value.
Shovel 66cm (26in) long **£350-450** the set

▲ **Handmade for the home**
During the 19th century, many rural families kept at least one cow and made their own butter and cheese. These spoons, which are handmade, would have been used to work the butter. They have a naïve charm but the crude form is unlikely to appeal to many collectors.
Larger 23cm (9in) long **£20-30 each**

▶ **Souvenir biscuit tin**
From the 1890s, biscuit tin shapes became more inventive, with some featuring moving parts. Elaborate tins, including this W. & R. Jacobs & Co. coach from 1937, were designed to be kept. They were often used as toys or storage and few are in such good condition. 23cm (9in) wide **£100-150**

TREASURE SPOTTER'S GUIDE
Copper, brass and pewter

Today many copper, brass and pewter items are obsolete because people are no longer using these objects. However, because they add visual warmth and charm to a home, attractive pieces in good condition still appeal to collectors.

◄ **Bed warmer**
Before central heating became common, it was essential to have a warming pan, filled with hot water or embers, to heat bed sheets. Copper examples are ubiquitous today but brass warming pans, like this early 18th-century example, are relatively rare and slightly more valuable. 110.5cm (43½in) long **£100-150**

Copper and brass objects became common in the home during the 17th and 18th centuries and these early pieces are the most desirable for buyers today. Items from the 19th and the early 20th centuries are typically not as valuable. Many people keep their brass and copper highly polished, which removes patina. Unlike silver, most brass and copper objects were unmarked until the Companies Act of 1862. This can make dating difficult, but not impossible, if you know what you're looking for. For example, brass candlesticks were not cast as one piece until the 18th century. Previously they had been cast as two parts and soldered together, so it is worth checking hollow examples for evidence of seams, which might indicate an early

► **Dessert mould**
Jelly moulds were popular during the 19th century. Pottery examples were made but copper moulds are often the most valuable, particularly complex designs. Reproductions may be distinguished by their lighter weight. This plain late 19th century example is 18cm (7in) wide. **£100-200**

Is it copper, brass or pewter?

- Copper can be easily shaped or hammered. Its resistance to corrosion makes it suitable for jewellery and its conductivity of heat to cooking vessels.
- Brass (an alloy of copper and zinc) was used for household wares as it is highly durable and resistant to tarnishing.
- Pewter (an alloy of tin and lead) is soft, malleable and ideal for casting. As it is durable and inexpensive, it was used for domestic wares until the 19th century.

◄ **Pewter plate**
British pewter plates and chargers were hammered in the booge (the area between the well and the rim) to strengthen them after casting. Modern reproductions may be missing these marks and they may feel thin, brittle and soapy to touch. This is a plain, 18th-century example. 38cm (15in) diameter **£70-90**

▲ **Trivet**
Trivets were used as stands for cooking pots by an open fire. They have little practical use today, but decorative examples like this 19th century brass trivet are likely to fetch more than plain designs. 21.5cm (8½in) wide **£30-40**

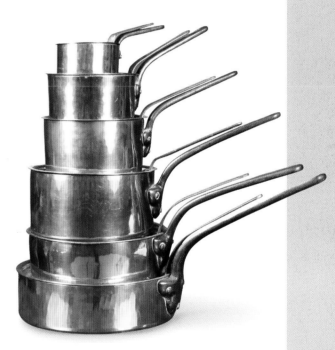

▶ **Pugin sacring bell**
The English architect and designer Augutus W. N. Pugin created furniture for the Houses of Parliament, among other commissions. This 29cm (11½in) high bell would have been used in Mass and Pugin's name adds to the value. **£1,000-1,500**

date. An early 18th-century brass candlestick might be valued at £200, while a similar-shaped Victorian example may be worth less than £50.

The appeal of pewter

Many pewter objects are likely to be older than copper and brass examples. The metal declined in popularity during the 18th century and by the 19th century only tavern mugs were being made in large numbers. Much early pewter was melted down and re-cast into more fashionable styles, making good condition pewter from before the 17th century rare. There are, however, relatively few collectors, so values tend to be modest.

Fortunately, not all base metalware is selling for low sums. During the Arts and Crafts movement of the late 19th and early 20th centuries, several craftsmen abandoned mass production and returned to handcrafting copper, brass and pewter objects. Some of the best pieces were produced by the Newlyn School, the Keswick School and Liberty & Co. – which produced its 'Tudric' range of pewter wares in 1903. As with most Arts and Crafts objects, the hand-worked metalware took time and skill to make. These pieces were costly at the time, so relatively few were sold, and they should continue to fetch good prices due to their rarity and quality.

Unfortunately, the market for standard pewter, copper and brass objects is unlikely to improve. The best prices may be achieved on eBay or at a car-boot sale.

▲ **Copper saucepans**
Copper saucepans should not be used as there is a risk of poisoning if the protective linings are not in perfect condition. This is a nice set of lidded saucepans but value is still comparatively low as few people are interested in saucepans as purely decorative pieces. **£200-250**

◀ **Arts and Crafts copper bowl**
The Newlyn Industrial Class was founded in Cornwall in 1890 to bring work to a coastal village that had previously depended on fishing for survival. Many designers, including the creator of this bowl, looked to the sea for decorative inspiration. Typical wares include vases, candlesticks and jugs, which were mainly stamped 'Newlyn'. 29cm (11½in) diameter **£700-900**

151

TREASURE SPOTTER'S GALLERY
Treen and Tunbridgeware

Since medieval times, wood has been turned to make practical items for the home. Some objects were purely functional but many were also decorative. Today, these can fetch high sums. While condition and patination are important, pieces with high-quality turned and carved decoration, and those bearing dates, names or mottoes, command the highest prices. Collectors refer to them as 'treen', which means 'from the tree'. If you think you have a good example, contact an auction house or a specialist dealer.

Judith warns!

Tunbridgeware, or other wooden boxes or furniture with inlaid decoration, must be treated with care to maintain their value. Modern central heating dries the air which in turn dries out the moisture in wood and the glues used to hold any decoration, causing inlays and veneers to lift and separate from the base wood. Examples with damaged inlay are worth considerably less than those in good, original condition. While the inlay can be repaired it is costly and a repaired piece will not be as valuable as a perfect example. If you have an inlaid or veneered item you wish to keep, turn down the heating or invest in a humidifier. For more information on caring for wooden objects see pages 62-65.

▲ **Tunbridgeware box**
Tunbridgeware – a form of wood mosaic – was used to decorate souvenirs from the town of Tunbridge Wells in Kent in the 18th and 19th centuries. This box is decorated with a view of Bayham Abbey. Early and extravagant boxes can be worth £2,000 or more. 26cm (10½in) wide **£350-450**

◀ **Pestle and mortar**
These sets are highly collectable. Even the damages and splits in this example do not detract from its value because they are signs of authenticity. A clue as to the date of this English example lies in the wood: *lignum vitae*, a tightly grained and resilient wood which was widely used in the mid-18th century. 26cm (10½in) high **£300-500**

▶ **Fruitwood goblet**
Turning wood on a lathe to create a symmetrical shape, such as this late 18th-century English goblet, was a skill learnt by journeymen – craftsmen who travelled from town to town to work for different employers. Despite being cracked and having stapled repairs, the quality of this piece helps it to retain its value. 18cm (7in) high **£300-500**

◀ **Scandinavian tankard**
Tankards such as this late 18th-century example were communal drinking vessels. A series of pegs inside mark off equal measures of drink – drinkers would consume a 'peg' and then pass the tankard on. Scandinavian examples, of horn, pewter or ceramic, were usually made in traditional shapes. Wooden tankards had a similar status to those made from precious metals. 20cm (8in) high **£400-500**

Miniature globe

Pocket globes were used from the 18th century onwards to teach children, as an *aide mémoire*, or educational entertainment for adults. They were made of pasteboard, wood or ivory and housed in a wooden case, the inside of which usually depicted the celestial sphere. An early example in good condition might fetch upwards of £2,000-3,000.

◄ **Pocket globe**
This is a 19th-century globe in a *lignum vitae* case with a finial. 10cm (4in) high **£1,000-1,500**

◄ **Polychrome domed casket**
Painted chests and boxes were common in Scandinavia and central Europe, especially in the mid-18th century. They were often made to commemorate an event such as a marriage or a birth. Most were made by rural craftsmen and then painted by amateur or itinerant decorators. The paint disguised and protected poor quality wood. Examples made in America, and painted by named artists, can be worth tens of thousands of pounds. This casket was made in the early 19th century, in Scandinavia, and has later adaptations. 50cm (19¾in) wide **£300-500**

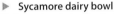

► **Sycamore dairy bowl**
Daily use has helped to build up a rich patina on this 19th-century bowl. As a practical object the decoration is limited to incised line banding around the rim. 38cm (15in) diameter **£180-220**

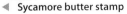

◄ **Sycamore butter stamp**
From the 17th century, farmers, dairies and households which made their own butter often decorated it using wooden stamps. These stamps could be decorated with traditional geometric designs, animals, initials or heraldic symbols. Today, pieces with high-quality or unusual carving command the highest prices. This is a relatively common example from the West Country and dates from the 19th century. 14cm (5½in) long **£40-60**

TREASURE SPOTTER'S GUIDE
Scrimshaw

Scrimshaw received a boost in popularity in the 1960s as US President John F. Kennedy was a collector. Today buyers will pay large sums for unusual or personal examples, particularly if they are dated. However, in general, the proliferation of fakes has depressed the market.

▲ **Stay busk**
Stay busks were worn at the front of women's corsets in order to flatten the stomach. Most scrimshaw was purely decorative but this early 19th-century item was intended for use. It also features unusual polychrome decoration and an inscription from the carver to his sister. 35cm (13¾in) long **£700-900**

◀ **Patriotic tooth**
Scrimshaw was made by sailors of many nationalities, including British and Australian, but today it is largely viewed as an American art form and examples from the States are likely to fetch the highest prices. The patriotic imagery of Lady Liberty with an eagle and a flag on this 19th-century piece is particularly appealing. 18cm (7in) high **£5,500-6,500**

▼ **Whalebone cane**
This 19th century whalebone cane features a marine ivory pommel and is decorated with scrimshaw designs and inlaid mother-of-pearl, abalone and tortoiseshell. The sophistication of the design is highly unusual and desirable. Scrimshaw canes are also extremely rare. 95cm (37½in) long **£6,500-7,500**

Scrimshaw is a type of carving most commonly found on bone or ivory. The process involved extracting and preparing the raw material, such as teeth from sperm whales, and then smoothing it to provide a flat background for a design pricked out with a needle. The dots were joined using ink, soot or tar, to create an image. Coloured pigments were rarely used and authentic scrimshaw with coloured designs is rare and popular today.

Most of the images are of ships and whaling scenes, as most scrimshanders were bored young men on whaling voyages. These might last several years and feature periods of idleness. For this reason, hobbies, such as scrimshawing, making wool-work pictures and ships in bottles, were more common aboard whaling ships than any other 19th-century vessels. Scrimshaw featuring other images is less common and can be more valuable, particularly if the imagery is patriotic.

The skill of the carver
As scrimshaw was so widely practised, the skill of carving varies. The most intricate examples were probably carved by veteran whalers, who had honed their skills over several voyages. High-quality craftsmanship is not always the best indicator to value. Less skilled carvings, particularly personal ones, can be more charming and this can raise the value.

'A genuinely old example of a large tooth with an attractive design will appeal to collectors – especially if it includes a date or the name of a ship.'
ADAM SCHOON, BBC *ANTIQUES ROADSHOW* SPECIALIST

▶ Vegetable canteen
This 19th-century canteen was carved from a root vegetable. The intrinsic value of the material is less attractive to collectors, which accounts for the lower price, despite the profusion of well-drawn detail. 12.5cm (5in) diameter **£300-400**

Examples carved with dates are rare and likely to be sought after. Inscribed dates do not necessarily indicate when the specimen was carved, as they may commemorate an earlier event, but they do allow a rough estimate of the date of carving, which is of interest to collectors. Carved names that link pieces to the original makers or owners will also increase value. Condition also strongly influences value. If you have a piece of scrimshaw, keep it dry and away from direct, bright sunlight. The pigments used to highlight the decoration are likely to fade in water and the ivory itself could crack or swell.

Under the Convention on International Trade in Endangered Species (CITIES) the trade in ivory 'worked' after 1947 is banned. Knowing the date a piece was made is therefore essential if you wish to sell.

Judith warns!

Much fake scrimshaw is made out of resin, rather than tooth. Such fakes are typically heavier than originals, have a milkier, shinier finish and lack the natural veining of the tooth. Ivorene (see page 157) fakes are known. If the amount of detail (such as dates, names and hearts) seems too good to be true, it probably is. Another indicator that an example is a fake is the level of wear and distress – genuine scrimshaw is usually treated carefully.

◀ Modern fake
Resin is obviously a less valuable material than whale bone. Modern fakes also have none of the history or personal significance that attracts collectors to good examples of scrimshaw. The value of this example is consequently low. 12cm (4¾in) high **£60-80**

▲ Scottish horn
This mid 19th-century cow horn is profusely decorated with names and dates around its base. That the horn depicts Glasgow may attract Scottish buyers, particularly if they recognise the buildings shown. The tiered design is nicely balanced and well executed. 33cm (13in) long **£800-1,200**

The post-shipwreck scene of a sailor kneeling in prayer beside the body of another is highly unusual. This adds to its appeal to collectors.

The design was drawn well, with a sense of movement and proportion.

◀ Pair of teeth
The fact that these two teeth appear to have been carved by the same artist and have come from the same animal adds to the value of this early 19th-century pair. Taller 18cm (7in) high **£1,000-1,500**

155

TREASURE SPOTTER'S GALLERY
Plastics

The first truly synthetic plastic was created in 1907 by Belgian chemist Dr Leo Baekeland, who named his invention Bakelite. It was marketed as 'the material of a thousand uses' and was used for a wide variety of functional and decorative objects. Today values are often low, though telephones, radios, brightly coloured objects and Art Deco pieces can fetch high prices.

◄ **Plastic telephone**
This 1960s telephone by the Reliance Telephone Company lacks the celebrated Art Deco styling of the Series 300 telephone (see page 146). Red Series 300 phones in good condition can be worth £1,000-1,500 as they are rarer than black ones. Green examples are even more desirable. Beware of fakes or reproduction models – uneven mouldings may give copies away. This telephone, 12.5cm (5in) wide is valued at **£40-60**.

▲ **Bakelite brooch**
Simple Bakelite brooches are often worth less than £50, but values can rise for designs that are strongly Art Deco (as here). This late 1920s brooch also has a high level of detail, including brass and painted detail and a textured 'fur stole'. It also depicts the famous singer and dancer, Josephine Baker, which adds interest. 7.5cm (3in) high **£75-95**

Caring for plastics

All plastics are prone to deterioration. This can range from discoloration or crazing to blistering or crumbling. Many plastics are easily scratched and become very brittle with age.

• Never store or display them near direct light or heat. This is particularly important in relation to Celluloid, which is flammable.

• Prolonged immersion in water or exposure to high moisture levels can also damage them.

• Use a standard, commercial metal polish (such as Brasso) to clean Bakelite. Apply a small dab to a cotton pad and rub on in a circular motion. Leave to dry until cloudy, then buff to a sheen with a soft pad.

▲ **Bandalasta tea set**
Bandalasta, the moulded and marbled plastic used for this tea set, was devised by chemist Edmund Rossiter in 1924 for a company that later became known as BEATL. This red and black marbling is the most desirable colour and, along with the Art Deco styling, accounts for much of the high value of this 1930s set. Teapot 17cm (6½in) wide **£250-350**

▲ Innovative ink stand

This 1940s ink stand is attractively formed and the pale green is an unusual colour for early plastic. Unfortunately, rarity does not always result in high values. Aside from collectors of fountain pens, few buyers are interested in ink stands today, so interest and consequently values are low. 17cm (6½in) wide **£50-80**

◄ Bakelite ashtray

As well as being muted and arguably boring, brown is the most common colour of Bakelite. Bright and cheerful colours, such as red, green and orange, will almost always be worth more. The undesirable colour and the shape of this 1920s ashtray is unattractive, resulting in a low value. 6cm (2½in) high **£2-5**

Judith warns!

It's important to know what your treasures are made of before you can value them. Plastic became common from the 1930s and has since been used to manufacture inexpensive replicas and fakes of bone and ivory pieces. Values for plastic copies are mostly low. Ivory and bone look and feel similar, but ivory is rarer and is considered a finer material.

Ivory
Ivory is patterned with a strong grain of parallel lines running down the length of the tooth or tusk. If you look at the base of an ivory figure, or a cross-section of the tooth, the lines should form V-shapes or circles.

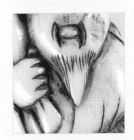

Bone
As well as a strong grain, bones have canals that carried nutrients. Look for signs of dark material clinging to them. In well-bleached pieces, the canals can be hard to see, but they will show up if you move the piece back and forth under a light.

Plastic (ivorene)
Plastic will warm in your hand, while ivory and bone will not. Edges may be rounded and obviously moulded. If you are still unsure about your object and you are brave enough, you can insert a hot pin into the base. The pin will enter a plastic object but not ivory or bone.

▲ Fada radio

Vintage radios are extremely desirable. A classic form, popular maker, such as Fada, and a colourful case will all add value. The lapis lazuli blue of this Fada radio is not only attractive, but is also rare, which enhances the value. The company's Bullet radios (rounded at one end) are also in demand, particularly in the white, blue and red All American colourway. 1939 23cm (9in) wide **£1,500-2,000**

▶ Plastic compact

Powder compacts are typically worth low sums, though values can increase with precious metals, interest from buyers of other collectable items (early plastics in this case), and attractive and skilful designs. The stylised ivorene scene of two dancers lacks quality and this is likely to deter buyers. **£20-30**

TREASURE SPOTTER'S GUIDE
Advertising and promotional items

Vintage advertising is highly desirable and can fetch large sums. Items from well-known brands, such as Coca-Cola, and those with buyers in more than one collecting area, such as railway advertising, are often the most valuable. More obscure pieces can be worth money if they are attractive and in good condition.

Advertising became more organised as an industry in the mid-19th century. Since this time a wide variety of items, including posters, fliers, display boards, tins, signs and ashtrays, have been produced with the intention of selling a product. The first half of the 20th century was a particularly vibrant period for advertising, as more and more companies vied with each other to create innovative ways to catch consumers' eyes. Pieces from this period are now highly in demand, particularly if they are typical of popular styles, such as Art Deco and 1950s kitsch.

Today's collectors value advertising pieces for their connection to beloved brands, decorative appeal and historical significance. Of these, brand is the most important and a popular brand is the most obvious indicator that an item may be valuable. Guinness and Coca-Cola are the two biggest names in advertising memorabilia but many other brands also have their own collecting base. Food and drink-related advertising and packaging is consistently popular and the recent restrictions on smoking brought an increased interest in tobacco advertising.

▲ **Michelin Man ashtray**
Bibendum (the symbol of the Michelin Tyre Company) was created in 1898. The fact that he is still used on advertising today is a tribute to his popularity and effectiveness. This Bakelite ashtray is relatively early and shows the him to good effect on a contrasting black base. 12.5cm (5in) high **£80-120**

▼ **Biscuit tin with a secret**
Recent tins with simple shapes are unlikely to fetch high prices, no matter how attractive the artwork. This 1980s example features several lewd images added to the design by a disgruntled employee, so it was quickly withdrawn and re-issued. Such a story might appeal to some collectors but will put others off. 20cm (8in) high **£25-30**

◀ **Babycham glass**
The bright colours and kitsch appearance of the Babycham deer are typical of the 1950s, a highly desirable period of vintage advertising. Following the brand's relaunch in 1996, Babycham memorabilia is increasing in value but most pieces were produced in such large quantities that prices are still relatively low. 10.5cm (4¼in) high **£5-8**

▶ **Dubonnet figure**
Dubonnet is a sweet wine-based aperitif popular with the Queen. The brand is known, but does not have a wide collecting market. Much of the value of this rare Beswick figure group is as a result of interest from collectors of dog memorabilia and Beswick figures by Arthur Greddington. 1963-67 30.5cm (12in) high **£200-300**

Items with diverse appeal

Tobacco advertising is also a good example of a field that attracts more than one group of collectors. The memorabilia has a strong collecting base of its own, so smoking advertising also appeals to collectors of pipes and lighters. This can raise value, as can the image of a celebrity on a piece of memorabilia.

Eye-catching, visually appealing designs will usually be desirable. The form of the object can also affect value. Lithographed tin signs, which are easily displayed, have a strong collecting base and are often more valuable than small items from the same period. Tins also attract collectors but are often worth low sums as so many survive in good condition.

Mint condition items are preferred and can fetch many times the value of worn equivalents. But beware items that are too clean, show no signs of wear and are brightly coloured. Many pieces have been faked or reproduced and are worth low sums. Repainting or repairs will also reduce value. The best place to sell is online.

▶ **Cigarette sign**
In general, the more colours used on a lithographic sign, the more desirable it is likely to be. Most of the value of this Woodbine sign comes from its association with the high-profile brand and competing interest from smokers, although the strong typography is also striking. 91.5cm (36in) high **£120-180**

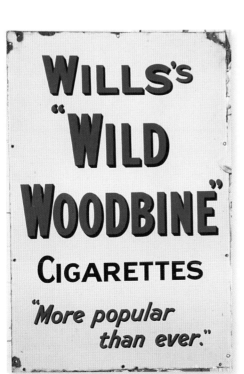

Judith warns!

Valuable, early pieces of Coca-Cola memorabilia are often reproduced or faked. Fortunately knowledge of Coke's changing designs can often help to date and authenticate pieces, as many fakes are not accurate. Further confusion arises as some companies who produced Coke advertising in the early 20th century used outdated logos. Pieces by such companies may seem to be earlier than they are but they are not actually fakes. Compare your piece to authenticated originals in reference books and look for differences in the detail. If you can't find an authenticated example of your piece in a reference book, you may have what is known as a 'fantasy'. Such pieces were never released by Coke and have been subsequently invented by forgers.

The illustration has an Art Nouveau feel to it. The tray is an early example and is in good condition.

▲ **Early Coca-Cola tray**
Early trays are some of the most desirable pieces of Coke memorabilia. Frequent contact with coins is likely to have damaged most tin tip trays, so the good condition of this example, which only features minor chipping to the rim, ensures it will command a premium. 1913 15cm (6in) wide **£500-600**

CLOTHES and TEXTILES

For many years, vintage fashion had a limited market of dedicated followers who collected – and often wore – clothes from previous decades. Recently, more people have started to wear vintage fashions as a reaction to the trend for cheap, 'throwaway' clothes and a desire to show individuality. Furnishing textiles, such as rugs and samplers, have been collected for many years too, and understanding how to identify signs of quality will help you date and value them.

Clothing from the 1950s is highly popular with vintage fashion collectors. Although it is not typical of the period, this brightly coloured jacket is in excellent condition and likely to appeal to someone looking to add a quirky touch to an outfit. A summer dress or circular skirt from the same decade may fetch two or three times its value. **£40-60**

WHAT MAKES TEXTILES VALUABLE?
Age and condition are key

People first created textiles during the late Stone Age, 40,000 years ago. Many of the pieces made since have decayed or faded. As a consequence, textiles made before the 1800s in good condition can be worth thousands of pounds. Attractive and well-made pieces that can be easily displayed command the highest prices.

The embroidery was skillfully executed.

The cushions are in excellent condition and the fact they are a matching pair adds to their desirability.

▶ Queen Anne cushions
Age is important when assessing the value of pre-20th century textiles. Pieces from the 16th and 17th century can be worth thousands of pounds, while early 18th-century textiles, such as these cushions, can be significantly more valuable than later textiles. *c.*1705 Larger 48cm (19in) wide **£5,500-6,500**

▼ Patchwork quilt
While American quilts are hotly collected and often sell for thousands of dollars at American auction houses, there is no similar market for European quilts. Regency quilts with complex patterns can fetch high sums, but most British quilts, including this early 20th-century patchwork example, are worth relatively little. 231cm (91in) long **£50-70**

Before the 20th century, needlework such as samplers were one of the primary means of displaying a girl's skills. Although large quantities were produced, many textiles from the 18th century and earlier have not survived in good condition. Those pieces can be valuable. In general, 19th-century textiles are less desirable than earlier pieces. This is not simply because they lack age but because, as a rule, quality declined during the 19th century. Many Victorian samplers are worth less than £100. Late 19th- or early 20th-century woven or embroidered textiles by design reformers such as William Morris are often more valuable than early 19th century pieces, although exceptional early 19th-century examples can fetch higher prices.

Quality of design is important when valuing textiles. Those that embody the style of the period are often highly prized – this is particularly true of 20th-century textiles. The 1950s and 1960s are currently popular and prints by definitive designers such as Lucienne Day or Emilio Pucci sell well. With earlier pieces, the best prices generally go to lively designs. Skilful embroidery can add value, but naïve compositions are appealing and can sell for more than technically proficient pieces.

Good, Better, Best Samplers

The earliest samplers were a practical record of stitches and designs, rather than decorative items. By the 18th century, the sampler was part of a young girl's education.

Valuable samplers show a variety of motifs and stitches and feature details such as houses and animals, the embroiderer's name and a date.

Good

This design is typical of 19th-century samplers. It features a religious verse and the embroiderer's house as the central image. It is more desirable than many similar pieces due to its well-balanced design, fine stitching, lack of fading.
51cm (20in) high **£1,000-1,500**

Better

Although it is faded, this late 18th-century sampler is valuable due to its age and naïvety. Rather than a religious verse it features the young needleworker's record of selling it to a named relative, though the money 'will soon be spent'.
48cm (19in) high **£2,000-3,000**

Best

Samplers depicting current events are extremely rare. The image of a kneeling slave used on this William IV sampler, dated 1831, is from a design by Josiah Wedgwood, who was an important member of the Society for the Abolition of the Slave Trade.
38cm (15in) diameter **£6,000-8,000**

Quilts and lace lose value

The type of object can also affect value. Haute couture fashion, rugs and tapestries are some of the most valuable textiles, as they were expensive objects when they were produced. Conversely, British quilts are often worth less than £100 as there are many on the market and few interested buyers. Similarly, lace, which was once so rare that it was regarded as a status symbol, is now often worth little, although museum-quality 17th and 18th-century pieces and large 19th-century lace dress flounces can command high prices.

If you have an intricate or early textile or an example of haute couture fashion, it should ideally be sold in a specialist auction such as those held by Kerry Taylor Auctions and Christie's South Kensington. Most general auction houses accept good examples of 19th-century and earlier textiles. Other items, particularly 20th-century pieces, could be sold online. Good condition is generally essential if a textile is to achieve the highest price possible. Wear and damage decrease value.

◄ **Fashion for vintage**
The fashions of the 1930s and 1940s have become popular in the past few years, thanks to celebrities such as Kate Moss who based some of her range for Top Shop on vintage designs, and Pearl Lowe, who produced several lines of 1940s-style dresses for high street chain Peacock's. Original pieces from the era in good condition can fetch hundreds of pounds.
107cm (42¼in) long
£100-150

TREASURE SPOTTER'S GUIDE
Rugs and carpets

Rugs and carpets have been woven for centuries in countries around the world to make warm and decorative floor, wall and furniture coverings. The most valuable tend to be early, high-quality examples.

▲ **Heriz carpet**
Carpets have been made in the town of Heriz in north-west Persia (now Iran) since the 19th century. They are typically made of wool on cotton, although some were made of silk. The designs have an overall repeat pattern or a central medallion. Older rugs may include ivory, terracotta and pale blue, but stronger colours – such as those on this 1920s carpet – were popular in the 20th century. 344cm (135in) long **£3,000-4,000**

The fashion for decorating middle-class homes with Persian rugs exploded in the 1870s as more homes could afford such luxurious furnishings. Rug makers in cities such as Kashan, Heriz, Tabriz and Tehran in Persia (now Iran) fed this increased demand, with rugs decorated with traditional designs. They were packed with floral motifs, arabesques and palmettes in curvilinear designs which often featured a central medallion. The rugs were made from brightly coloured threads – tinted with natural dyes – often with ivory highlights. Rural and tribal weavers in areas including Afshar and Khamesh made smaller rugs with geometric patterns.

Persian designs influenced those made by rural and nomadic tribes in Turkey and the Caucasus (an area between Turkey and the Caspian Sea). They favoured bold geometric designs.

Prayer rugs were made across the Middle East but the areas best known for their manufacture are Dagestan in the Caucasus and Ghiordes in Turkey. Tree-of-life motifs are common and designs are always directional: the mihrah (arch pointing to Mecca) shows the direction in which to kneel and pray.

Most Chinese carpets were made in the north-west cities of Beijing and Ningxia. They generally have a single-colour field (background) with sparse floral motifs scattered across it.

◀ **Ziegler carpet**
Ziegler was a British/Swiss carpet-making firm, established c.1885 in Sultanabad, in north-west Persia (now Iran) which made high-quality carpets designed for wealthy European clients. They typically feature large-scale motifs in a vine lattice combined with an overall repeat pattern within large borders. The main field is frequently terracotta or ivory- coloured, with pale or dark blue borders. They are among the most finely woven and tend to use lustrous fine-quality wool. This 19th-century example is 570cm (224in) long. **£40,000-50,000**

British rugs and carpets

Moquette or pileless carpets were made in Axminster in Devon, from the mid-18th century until 1835, when the factory was moved to Wilton in Wiltshire. There has been a carpet factory at Wilton since *c.*1740. At first it used a moquette weave, but switched to knotted carpets and mechanised the process in the 19th century. At Wilton, 'Axminster' mechanically woven carpets continue to be made today. The decline in handmade carpet manufacture was halted briefly by William Morris and the Arts and Crafts movement in the late 19th century. Morris and his business partner John Henry Deale set up a workshop in Hammersmith, London, where carpets inspired by traditional Turkish designs were hand-knotted.

▶ **William Morris design**
A 20th century 368cm (145in) long room-size rug based on a design by William Morris, with a floral pattern in amber and dark plum on a black field. **£400-600**

▲ **Kazak prayer rug**
Armenian (southern Caucasus) Kazak rugs are known for being of exceptional quality and feature bright geometric designs of reds, blues and ivory. Made from the 18th century and still in production today, they may also include stylised floral and animal forms. The pile tends to be long. This early rug, 146cm (57½in) long, dates from around 1890. **£3,500-4,500**

How to value

Depending on condition, the older the rug the greater its value will be. 'Antique' rugs – those over 100 years old – generally command the highest prices; 'old' rugs – those over 50 years old – sell for less. Fine silk rugs from Persia (now Iran) and Turkey tend to be the most valuable. Quality wool rugs from Persia and the Caucasus also command good prices. When working out the desirability of a rug, the attributes to consider include condition, the richness of the design, the harmony of colour and the fineness of the design. A handmade rug will often be more valuable than one that was made on a machine. If handmade, you will see rows of knots at the base of the tufts when you part the pile. There are many different types and patterns of rug and carpet and only a small selection are shown here. Take yours to your local auction house or specialist dealer if you wish to sell.

▶ **Chinese carpet**
The Chinese have made carpets for more than 2,000 years. They are typically woven in a harmonious mix of geometric and curvilinear designs. Patterns on older examples may be taken from porcelain decoration or use religious symbols. This 20th century example is 420cm (165in) long.
£2,000-3,000

▲ **Aubusson carpet**
This French factory began producing carpets in *c.*1743 but most of those seen today date from the 19th century onwards. Carpets from the mid-19th century feature strong colours and intricate designs. These shades became softer later in the century. This carpet, from the reign of Napoleon III (1852-1870), is 364cm (143¼in) long and worth **£2,000-3,000**.

RESTORING YOUR FINDS
Making a bolster from a kelim

A kelim rug that has suffered irreversible damage, such as a large hole or a bad stain, can be recycled to make a bolster. Insert a tube of sand into the bolster and it becomes a draught excluder – the sand adds weight and keeps it tight against the door, keeping heat in and cold air at bay. You can also use rectangles of kelim to make cushion covers.

YOU WILL NEED

Bolster cushion pad

Tape measure

Pattern paper (or newspaper)

Pencil and felt-tip pen

Long glass-headed pins

Kelim

Sturdy scissors

Rubber-based fabric adhesive

Circular template or saucer

Wool needle

Embroidery wool

Thimble and/or pliers

Calico for sand tube (12cm [5in] x length of bolster)

Sewing needle or machine

Sewing thread

Funnel

Dry sand

Making a bolster

1 Measure the length and circumference of a ready-made bolster cushion pad, and transfer these measurements to a sheet of pattern paper (or newspaper), adding an extra 2.5cm (1in) to the circumference as a seam allowance. (Note that the circular ends of the bolster are prepared in steps 3 and 4.) Pin the pattern on to an undamaged section of the kelim, and cut out.

2 Using a rubber-based fabric adhesive, spread a thin layer of glue along the reverse side of the edges of the section of kelim you cut out in step 1, and allow to dry. This will help to prevent the fibres fraying when the kelim bolster is in use.

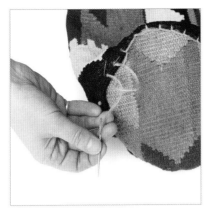

3 Measure the diameter of the bolster ends, adding 2.5cm (1in) as a seam allowance. Use a plate or saucer whose diameter roughly matches this combined measurement as a template. Then transfer the outline to pattern paper or newspaper, and cut out. As in step 1, use the pattern to cut out two circular end covers from the kelim and, as in step 2, seal the reverse of the cut edges with glue.

4 Pin the circular kelim bolster ends to the barrel body of the bolster. Then sew, removing the pins as you work around the perimeter, with a looping blanket stitch and a double-thickness of suitably coloured embroidery wool, as shown. You will need to use either pliers or wear a protective thimble to help pull the needle and thread through the thick kelim weave.

5 To make the tube of sand, cut out a piece of calico the length of the bolster cushion and 12cm (5in) wide. Fold the calico in half lengthways, and machine-stitch together the long edge and one end. Hold the calico tube to hang vertically and, placing a funnel in the open end, pour in sand to fill up to 5cm (2in) below the open top. Then machine-stitch the tube to seal it.

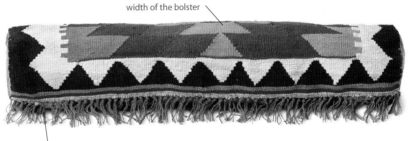

Try to keep any pattern centred over the finshed width of the bolster

When cutting out a large piece of the original kelim to make the central tube of the bolster, as in step 1, it's always worth trying to use a tasselled edge, if there is one, as it is, it makes a pleasing decorative addition.

6 Place the tubular sand weight made in step 5 into the bottom of the open bolster cover. Then insert the bolster cushion on top of it. Pin together along the length of the seam, and then close using a blanket stitch, as in step 4.

Making additional cushions

If you have kelim left over you can make a square or rectangular cushion in a similar way. Cut a rectangle of kelim to the same dimensions as your cushion pad, adding 2.5cm (1in) to the length and width to act as a seam allowance (you will have one folded edge and three stitched seams). Seal the edges with glue and fold the kelim fabric in half. Blanket stitch along two of the edges. Insert the cushion pad and stitch the opening closed.

TREASURE SPOTTER'S GUIDE
Vintage fashion

Vintage clothes can be divided into three categories: historic, couture and high street. The first two are rarer and more valuable than the third – but old clothes at the back of the wardrobe can still fetch unexpected sums.

For a few people, that old dress or jacket in the back of the wardrobe or in a dressing-up box may turn out to be a Victorian day dress or Georgian waistcoat preserved as a family heirloom. Apart from such items, the most valuable vintage clothes are usually either excellent examples of fashions from the 1920s onwards, or eye-catching pieces by designers such as Chanel or Dior. There is also a thriving market for wearable clothes from recent years, but prices for these pieces are nowhere near as high.

In general, the clothes worn by us, our parents and grandparents tend to be from department and high-street stores and their value as vintage pieces depends on the maker, quality and condition. Flapper dresses from the 1920s are popular as party dresses today but they need to be in good condition – with their beading and embroidery intact. Greater prices are paid for examples with extravagant beading or printed with geometric Art Deco designs. Also wearable – and saleable – are 1930s bias-cut satin dresses that have all the elegance of a Hollywood movie. These, and elegant 1940s tea dresses, can sell for £150 or more.

After the restrictions of World War II, Christian Dior's 'New Look' of 1947 fuelled the demand for elegant clothes. His extravagant creations reflected the new optimism and created a revolution that influenced fashion into the 1950s. It is estimated that a New Look skirt needed 23-46 metres (25-50 yards) of fabric in contrast to a war-time Utility

Vintage clothing price line

Fabulous 1950s
Ball gowns from the 1950s make ideal – and unique – party dresses. This jade green halterneck dress in a jacquard fabric and with a bow at the bust is stiffened with a calico petticoat and a hooped petticoat for a typical 1950s silhouette. 121cm (47¾in) long **£100-150**

Charleston style
The dresses worn by Flapper girls in the 1920s are evocative of the age of the Charleston. This dress is decorated with sequins and beads. A more complex design would increase the value substantially, but if many of the beads were missing it would be worth a fraction of its **£250-300** price tag.

Evening coat
The flimsy evening dresses of the 1920s required a warm cover-up. An opera coat – an elegant evening coat that was worn over an evening dress – still makes a wearable jacket for a special occasion. This pink velvet and beaded coat is a great colour and has an intricate beaded decoration. **£400-500**

skirt, which by law could use no more than three yards. Dresses from the late 1940s and the 1950s have been popular for many years, thanks to the femininity and defined silhouette of the designs. Those in floral fabrics can fetch £80 or more. A Christian Dior dress from the same era could be worth £600, but generally sells for much more.

The value of a couture label

From the 1960s onwards the more valuable vintage clothes are couture pieces. While a mini-dress from a high-street boutique may sell for £40, one by Mary Quant could be worth £80, and a rare Yves Saint Laurent African Collection mini-dress sold for £13,000 in 2007.

When looking for clothes with label-appeal one of the big names in vintage fashion is Biba. Founded by Polish-born Barbara Hulanicki and her husband Stephen Fitz-Simon, its first store opened in Kensington, London, in 1966. The property crash of 1974 resulted in the collapse of the Biba empire, although it has recently been revived.

The best place to sell historic and couture garments is at a specialist auction house such as Kerry Taylor Auctions or Christie's South Kensington. A vintage clothes dealer may buy other high-fashion items, or you can sell them online or at a car-boot sale. Recent high-street pieces, and those that do not truly represent the fashions of their time, can be sold at a car-boot sale, or given to a charity shop. Before you give away a piece of clothing in poor condition check the buttons – there may be profit in a set of say, Art Deco or 1950s buttons.

Judith warns!

When selling clothing it is important to remember that presentation is all. It should be clean and pressed. More recent clothing may have a washing care label but check that it is sturdy enough to withstand a modern washing machine. Check for stains. Perspiration marks are some of the most common and stubborn to remove but you can try these traditional remedies:

- Gently dab with cotton wool moistened with a solution of 1 part white vinegar to 15 parts warm distilled water. Rinse.
- If this is ineffective, dab with cotton wool moistened with a solution of ammonia (15 per cent volume). Rinse.

For advice on other stains see pages 172-173.

Aesthetic style
In the late 19th and early 20th centuries, the Liberty & Co. store in London promoted the Aesthetic Movement. It sold loose clothes inspired by ancient cultures. This black-and-gold damask evening mantle, made in around 1915, has knotted tassels at the sleeve openings. **£600-700**

Symbolic design
The decoration on Imperial Chinese robes was symbolic of the status of the wearer. This late 19th-century semi-formal robe is embroidered with figures in roundels and willow trees. Chinese buyers are starting to buy textiles such as this and values are rising. The value of this robe is **£800-1,000**.

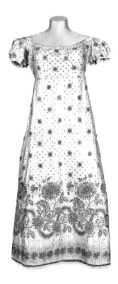

Empire-line ornament
The rarity of well-preserved clothing dating from before the 20th century is reflected in the value of this ivory silk ball gown. Made between 1810 and 1820, it is richly embroidered with a deep border of sunflowers, further embellished with sequins and worth **£3,000-4,000**.

TREASURE SPOTTER'S GALLERY
Vintage fashion

Dresses – from the everyday to the special occasion purchase – encapsulate the fashions of their era. Good-quality and designer dresses will usually be worth more than high-street examples.

◀ **Summer special**
With or without a stiffened petticoat, 1950s dresses are a perennial favourite with vintage fashion buyers and quality examples generally fetch a reasonable sum. This floral frock has a draped neckline and contrasting red lining. It could be worth twice as much if it had been made by a company such as Horrocks – the British ready-to-wear label renowned for its high-quality clothes and use of fabric designs by British artists such as Eduardo Paolozzi and Graham Sutherland. Size 10/12 **£50-80**

◀ **Cotton dress and bolero**
The floral fabric and full skirt are a feminine touch associated with 1950s fashion, which tended to be frivolous when compared with the clothes of the war years. Under the jacket the dress has a halterneck top, which is also typical of the period. 114cm (45in) long **£80-100**

▲ **Biba brilliance**
Biba's clothes were designed to supply fashionable clothes to teenage girls. The British store was a runaway success in the 1960s and 1970s and nostalgia for its designs mean they change hands for far more money on the vintage market today than they cost when new. This early 1970s cotton midi-dress is decorated with ladybirds and is worth **£150-200**.

Caring for vintage clothing

- To prevent fading, never store textiles in direct sunlight.
- If possible, store in the dark at a temperature of around 12°C and a relative humidity of around 55 per cent. Avoid damp surroundings, which encourage mould.
- Never fold or crease delicate textiles. Roll large textiles, right side out, around a cardboard tube covered with acid-free tissue paper. Cover with a clean dust sheet. Roll small textiles around pads or tubes of acid-free tissue paper.
- Never store textiles in or under plastic bags or sheets, which encourage mould. Calico bags will protect them from dust.
- Regularly dust cupboards and other storage areas and insert mothballs. Make sure that the mothballs do not come into direct contact with the surface of the textiles.
- Store period costumes flat. Pad out the shoulders, sleeves, and any unavoidable folds with acid-free tissue paper. Insert slivers of tissue paper between the material and any metal buttons. Remove any jewellery.
- Dresses made from synthetic polymerics, such as nylon and other vinyls, pose particular problems because of the way in which plastics age: some harden, others become granular and sticky, most give off low levels of corrosive fumes. To minimise deterioration, you should store in a well-ventilated space, at 50 per cent humidity and 18°C. Pad them out with acid-free tissue paper, so that they don't harden to the wrong shape, and don't store them with any other textiles, as the fumes can damage their threads and fibres.

▼ **Fashion favourite**
The exuberant prints designed by Italian Emilio Pucci were popular as soon as they were introduced in 1962. They have been copied many times but genuine Pucci fabrics feature Emilio's name discretely repeated in a small signature all over the design. This 1970s silk jersey dress is typical of the tight-fitting shapes for which the company is known. Size 8 **£250-300**

◄ **French couture**
The shirtwaist dress which had been a staple of 1950s fashion, made a comeback in the 1970s. This Yves Saint Laurent silk organza harlequin print shirtwaist dress shows the soft, draped effect that was fashionable at the time and also features the archetypal full sleeves, calf-length full skirt and belted waist. Size 34 **£550-650**

▲ **Sculptural silhouette**
In the late 1950s and early 1960s Spanish-born, Paris-based Cristobal Balenciaga designed bold clothing using stiff fabrics inspired by historic fashions. This hot pink and fuchsia matelassé cocktail ensemble shows his skill as a tailor; the dress is inspired by the early 19th-century Empire line, and the jacket by Japanese kimonos. A rare piece from a couture designer such as this, bust 92cm (36in), is worth **£2,000-2,500**.

▲ **Romantic design**
Ossie Clark was one of the most influential English fashion designers of the 1960s. He is known for his use of flowing chiffon and moss crêpe to give a flamboyant, romantic and floaty feel to his dresses, which is backed up by the use of printed patterns of stylised natural motifs designed by his wife Celia Birtwell. This late 1960s Floating Daisies dress, bust 92cm (36in), is worth **£500-600**.

REVIVING YOUR FINDS
Cleaning textiles

Dusty or dirty textiles can usually be hand-washed (but never machine-washed) or dry-cleaned. Tapestries, most silks and other pieces that are particularly valuable or fragile should be entrusted only to a specialist dry cleaner.

Testing colours

To check whether you should wash or dry-clean a piece, test for colourfastness.

- Dab a small, unobtrusive area (preferably the back) with cotton wool moistened with warm, soapy water. Use a soap for hand-washing wool.
- Leave for five minutes, then press white blotting paper to the area. If the paper remains unmarked, the area is colourfast. If it absorbs colour or dye, the fabric should be dry-cleaned with potato starch (see box).
- If there is more than one colour, test each one.

Hand-washing small textiles

- Remove dust as described in dry-cleaning fabrics (box). If the textile is frayed, put nylon mesh on clean white towelling and place the textile flat on top. Dab with a clean, damp sponge. If the piece is sound, place on mesh and immerse in a bowl of cold water.

- If using the bowl, drain the water and replace with hand-hot, soapy water. Use a mild wool detergent. Dab with a sponge, and keep replacing the water until no more dirt appears. If using towelling, dab with a sponge moistened with the soapy solution. Rinse by dabbing: use a wet sponge in the tray, or a moist sponge on the towelling.
- Gently remove the textile and pin it flat with brass pins, on a table covered with plastic or towelling. Dry using a hair-drier on a low heat or by gently dabbing with clean white towel or white blotting paper. Then allow it to air-dry.

Hand-washing large textiles

- Fill a bath with cold water to a depth that fully covers the textile.
- Place the textile flat on a piece of nylon mesh and lower it into the bath.
- Work the water into the fabric with your fingers, then soak for 10 minutes.
- Drain the water, then refill the bath with cold water. Immerse the piece for 10 minutes. Drain water.
- Remove the textile and mesh, drain and refill the bath with hand-hot water.
- Mix in a wool hand-washing detergent. Re-submerge the textile on the mesh and gently knead it in the soapy water.

Decorative trimmings
If you are testing a textile with decorative trimming and the main body of the textile is colourfast but the trimming is not, unstitch the latter before washing the main part. The trimming should be dry-cleaned then reattached.

Dry-cleaning fabrics

- Place the textile on a sheet of plastic and cover it with a piece of nylon mesh. Pass the nozzle of a vacuum cleaner 2.5-5cm (1-2in) above the surface to remove any dust.
- Lay the textile on the mesh. Heat dry potato starch in a saucepan until hand-hot. Cover the textile with flour to a depth of about 2.5cm (1in), and work into the textile with the back of a spoon. Leave for 10 minutes, during which time the starch will absorb the dirt, then brush it off.
- Repeat, using fresh starch each time, as many times as necessary, until all the dirt has been removed.

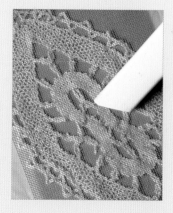

- Remove the textile and mesh again, and drain off the water. Refill with clean, hand-hot water, re-submerge, and rinse (again kneading with your fingertips).
- Rinse the piece with fresh hand-hot water at least twice more.
- Remove the textile, drain off the water and slide onto a clean, flat surface.
- Dab off the excess water with clean white towelling. Allow to dry naturally or use a hair-drier on a low heat.

Rugs

To maximise the life of rugs and carpets clean them regularly and deal with any stains as soon as possible. Apart from dusting it regularly, never attempt to clean a rare or valuable rug or carpet yourself. Instead, you should take it to a specialist cleaner.

Dusting a small, sturdy rug

- Rugs should be dusted regularly, and always before cleaning.
- Hang outdoors on a clothesline. Choose a dry, windless day and hang with as much as possible of the back exposed.
- Beat vigorously across the back with an old-fashioned carpet beater.
- Once the dust has stopped rising, pull the rug over the line and attach it near to the other end, and beat as before.
- Attach a curtain and upholstery cleaning accessory to a vacuum cleaner. Vacuum the back, using a light suction setting for finer rugs and medium suction for coarser ones.
- Vacuum the front of the rug. With flat-woven rugs, work up and down the length of the rug. With knotted-pile rugs, always work in the direction of the pile so you do not loosen threads.

Dusting a large or fragile rug

- If a rug is too fragile to be beaten vigorously, or too large to be hung from a clothesline, clean it flat on the floor.
- Put sheets of brown paper on the floor, and place the rug pile side down on top.

- If the rug is fairly sturdy, beat it vigorously with a carpet beater. If it is fragile, beat it very gently. Every now and then, give the rug a shake to help dislodge the dirt.
- Lift the rug and dispose of the paper.
- Carefully vacuum the back of the rug. Use the lightest possible suction on fragile rugs. Use a mid-strength suction on sturdier ones.
- Turn the rug over. If it is flat-woven, work up and down its length with the vacuum cleaner. If it has pile, work in the direction of the pile.

Washing a rug

You can wash an antique rug or carpet with a good-quality carpet shampoo. However, if the piece is rare, valuable, fragile or made of silk, take it to a cleaner specialising in antique rugs.

Washing on a tabletop or floor

- Dilute some carpet shampoo with warm water using the ratio and to the volume recommended by in the manufacturer's instructions.
- Tackling no more than a quarter of a square metre (a square yard) at a time, gently work the solution into the fibres with a large, soft-bristled scrubbing brush. With a pile carpet, first gently brush against the direction of the pile, then with the pile.
- Rinse off the shampoo by gently dabbing the carpet with pieces of white cotton rag dampened with lukewarm water. Work against any pile and then with it.
- Repeat this dabbing process, changing the rag and water when necessary until all the shampoo has been removed. Then move onto an adjacent, slightly overlapping area. Repeat until you have covered the entire surface of the rug.
- Clean fringes, Kelim ends and side cords in the same way.
- Leave the rug to dry flat on the work surface or floor.

Pressing fragile textiles
Lay the textile flat on white blotting paper or acid-free tissue paper and put this on a sheet of hardboard (smooth side up). Put another sheet of blotting or tissue paper on the textile, and another sheet of hardboard (smooth side down) on top of that. Apply pressure with heavy weights and leave for an hour.

Ironing fragile textiles
If the textile is sound and fairly strong, use a domestic iron, with its temperature at one setting below that recommended for the fabric. Never iron or press dirty or stained textiles, as this will further fix the discoloration.

HANDBAGS, SHOES and ACCESSORIES

The trend for vintage fashion means that many accessories are enjoying a revival. There is a market for vintage shoes, handbags, sunglasses, perfume bottles and even lighters and fountain pens. Although condition is important, the style and visual appeal of an item are vital too. A designer label will add value, so it is a good idea to research the names to look for.

This American daisy motif handbag is marked Source-Bag, New York. Postwar optimism brought a playfulness to 1950s handbags and collectors will part with considerable sums of money to own one today. The brass frame, black plastic handle and beaded fabric flowers of this bag are in excellent condition – adding to its desirability. 26cm (10½in) high excluding handle **£150-200**

WHAT MAKES FASHION VALUABLE?
The appeal of vintage accessories

As more and more people buy into the vintage trend, distinctive and well-made fashion accessories have increased in value. The greatest prices are likely to be paid for pieces made by couture houses, but stylish items from other makers can be surprisingly valuable too.

Scarves

When the scarf became part of the look of the 1950s, many retailers started mass producing new designs in bright colours and busy patterns. With 1950s style back in fashion thanks to television shows such as *Mad Men*, this is a good time to sell your vintage scarves. The most valuable examples are likely to be the work of notable brand names, such as Hermès or Pucci, but even designs by unknown makers can be worth reasonable sums if they are brightly coloured and feature motifs that are typical of the era. Fashionable ladies, dogs or foreign places are all very 1950s. As most people buy to wear, all scarves should be in good condition to attract the highest sums.

If you are planning to sell, bear in mind that while some collectors buy shoes and accessories to record developments in fashion or because they like the work of a particular designer, most people buy to wear. For many, wearing a vintage accessory is an easy way to add an individual touch to a modern outfit and there is a young and enthusiastic market for pieces such as handbags (see pages 178-179), scarves, shoes and ties.

Because vintage accessories are usually bought to be worn, condition and appearance are extremely important when assessing value. A striking design will usually attract buyers, particularly if it is typical of a popular era of fashion, such as the 1950s or 1960s. Good prices are paid for vintage spectacles in the 1950s 'cat's eye' style and pairs with the circular frames

▶ **Geek chic**
Vintage eyewear, such as these 1930s-1940s tortoiseshell plastic spectacles, can be surprisingly valuable, especially if they echo current trends. Most buyers will want to fit prescription lenses so price is not usually affected if lenses are cracked or even missing. 13.5cm (5¼in) wide **£70-100**

▲ **Valuable scarf**
Hermès is an important name in fashion, having created the desirable Kelly and Birkin bags (shown right). The company is also known for its scarves. Equestrian themes, such as the late 20th-century Eperon pattern shown here, are typical and often command the highest prices on the vintage market. 90cm (35in) wide **£150-200**

◀ **Birkin bag**
The Hermès Birkin bag is one of the world's most exclusive and desirable handbags. To buy one new costs between £3,000 and £30,000 or more and until recently there was a waiting list of six years. The demand for this classic bag means they generally fetch high prices on the secondary market. This blue Brighton crocodile bag dates from 2008. 35.5cm (14in) wide **£20,000-25,000**

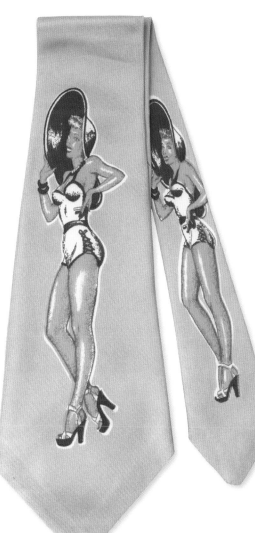

◄ **Saucy sells**
Hand-painted ties produced during the 1940s and 1950s can fetch large sums today if well-executed and typical of the period. As with many collecting areas, erotic or nude themes are highly popular. In this case, the price of this 1950s tie is increased by the 'sauciness' of the showgirl depicted. 9.5cm (3¾in) wide **£120-180**

popularised by John Lennon in the 1960s. Accessories from the 1970s and 1980s are less valuable but are growing in popularity and can fetch relatively good prices, particularly if they evoke the disco period.

Even the name of lesser-known makers can add value to an accessory if they have a desirable address, such as Fifth Avenue, New York, or Bond Street, London. These locations indicate that an item was originally expensive and is likely to be fairly rare and of exceptional quality. In general, the better and more typical of the era the design, the more valuable an item will be, so a quirky chrome lighter, or one associated with a celebrity, could be worth as much as a gold equivalent.

Fashion accessories by famous and desirable manufacturers or designers, such as Dior, Chanel, Hermès and Gucci, can attract much interest and may be worth selling with a specialist auction house, such as Kerry Taylor Auctions or Christie's South Kensington. The most visually appealing or typical pieces from these makers often fetch thousands of pounds. Pieces by lesser and unknown makers are worth anything from a few pennies to £200. Some general auction houses have fashion and textiles sales. Otherwise, search the internet for specialist dealers in the relevant field or sell online.

◄ **Cheap and cheerful**
These 1950s Bobby Pins are quirky, in mint condition and feature hand-painted designs. Due to their small size and the inexpensive materials used, they are only worth a low sum. Card 12cm (4¾in) high **£10-15**

▲ **1920s style**
Cloche hats have come to symbolise the 1920s and good vintage examples are extremely popular today. This straw hat is attractive but it is quite small so it will fit fewer people. Consequently, its value is lower than it might otherwise have been. 18cm (7in) high **£25-35**

TREASURE SPOTTER'S GUIDE
Handbags

Vintage handbags have become a popular fashion accessory and are collectable, which is good news if you have one to sell. Top prices are paid for quirky examples and bags in excellent condition that epitomise the style of their era.

Handbags from the 20th century illustrate the changing fashions and attitudes of each decade. The exuberance of the Art Deco movement can be seen in leather, beaded and Bakelite handbags from the 1920s and 1930s. Examples with geometric Art Deco designs on them can be worth £200 or more. Many were designed to be held tucked under the arm or to co-ordinate with a particular outfit.

During World War II most bags were homemade as materials were directed to the war effort. Rationing continued after the war but handbag designers soon began to create exciting designs, which were a welcome relief from the austerity of the war years. Colourful leathers and patterned fabrics were used, while the first novelty bags were made, some shaped as champagne buckets or birdcages. These bags can be worth in excess of £1,500 but a simple leather bag only £200-250.

A sense of frivolity took hold in the 1950s when designers began to employ the new plastics which had been developed for the war. For many women in the emerging middle classes, leather and fabric bags were too expensive. The Lucite bag, a plastic box-bag made from a tough plastic which had been developed in the 1930s, came in myriad colours and designs. Although handmade, these Lucite bags were affordable and their fun colours and shapes were testimony to postwar optimism. Bright colours, with pearlised patterns or carved details, or those with fitted interiors are the most desirable today. By the end of the 1950s, the availability of cheap, mass-produced bags caused the Lucite craze to die out. Now, however, these masterpieces of 1950s design are appreciated and collected as classics of their time. Examples in good condition typically fetch £100-£200, with many worth £500 or more.

Handbags price line

Art Deco chic
Collectors of classic Art Deco designs look for bright or strongly contrasting colours and geometric patterns. Consequently, this 1930s beige Corde handbag would not fetch a top price, despite its Bakelite clasp. It is marked 'Made in England' and measures 21cm (8¼in) high. **£50-80**

Novelty value
In the 1950s and 1960s embellished baskets were decorated with fantasy scenes. This 31cm (12¼in) wide wickerwork bag was made in Hong Kong. The front shows a felt mermaid and dolphin and natural shells. A more feminine design would command more than this **£100-150** price tag.

Classic style
A black leather handbag will usually be popular with collectors. Many consider them to be better made than modern bags – adding to their desirability. This 1950s Bellestone bag is 24cm (9½in) wide. If it had been made by a designer such as Hermès it could be worth 10 times its value. **£200-250**

Other novelties include frog- or elephant-shaped bags made from woven wicker, baskets decorated with fabric flowers or poodles and mini picnic baskets with miniature tennis courts on the lid. These can be worth between £100 and £300 or more depending on the condition and design.

Designer arrivals

The 1950s also saw the arrival of several 'designer' bags which are still made today, including Hermès' Kelly bag, named after the American actress Grace Kelly, the classic quilted Chanel shoulder bag known as the 2.55 and Gucci bags with bamboo handles. A Chanel 2.55 will sell for around £1,000 (about the price of a new bag) and a Kelly for up to £6,000 depending on the colour, leather and condition.

Mass-produced tapestry and other fabric evening bags from the 1950s onwards are generally worth £5-20, depending on condition and design. Extravagant beaded bags from the 1930s onwards generally fetch £30-100, but can make much more.

Handbags from the 1960s reflect the obsessions of the times: Space Age metal disks, hippy raffia and beads and novelty wooden bags such as those made by Enid Collins. These can be worth £50-80.

There is a thriving market for vintage bags from the 1970s onwards but – with the exception of designer names – few sell for more than £20-50.

Judith's lucky find

Thanks to my Scottish roots I'm always keen to buy a piece of tartan. I found this handbag at The Atlantique City Antiques and Collectors Fair in Atlantic City, USA. I immediately realised it was reversible – a 1950s trick that gave you two bags for the price of one. I paid $25 for it ten years ago. Today it would be worth £80-100 but I could never part with it.

▲ **Transforming tartan**
A 1950s rare, reversible woven plaid bag with black trim and interior, unsigned, with vinyl glove-holder strap. 37cm (14½in) wide **£80-100**

A specialist auction house, such as Kerry Taylor Auctions or Christie's South Kensington, is the best place to sell high-end and designer bags. Vintage fashion dealers may take good-quality bags, but other vintage and second-hand bags are best sold online, at a car boot sale or given to a charity shop.

Exquisite beadwork
Good-quality 1940s beaded purses fetch around £50 but extravagant bags such as this beaded floral example with an enamel clasp will sell for far more. Check the silk linings of these bags for damage. This example, marked 'Bag by Josef', was made in France and is 24cm (9½in) wide. **£250-300**

Lucite box-bag
Collectors prize Lucite bags in bright colours or with a fitted interior as they both tend to be rarer. Plainer black and brown examples generally fetch half the price. This turquoise example by Charles Khan has a carved clear Lucite lid and faceted handle. 20cm (8in) wide **£800-1,000**

Pooch purse
The poodle was a popular motif in the 1950s and is desired by fans of Fifties memorabilia and dog collectables today. This beaded poodle was made in Belgium for American manufacturer Walborg. It is 34cm (13½in) wide, and was also made with black beads. Its rarity means it is worth **£1,200-1,500**.

TREASURE SPOTTER'S GALLERY
Shoes

Shoes are one of the best-loved fashion accessories. But for a pair of old shoes to be valuable – whether they are Victorian buttoned boots or 1970s platforms – they must be in excellent condition and typical of the style of their era. Excessive wear or other damage will decrease their worth, but a very decorative pair, or a designer name, will increase it. Try selling them at a specialist auction, to a specialist dealer, or online.

▲ **Victorian wedding finery**
These cream satin shoes, with a Louis heel and embellished with pearl beads, were fashionable in the late 19th century, when it was just acceptable for a lady's feet and ankles to be on show. They are lined with leather, which may have helped them to stay in excellent condition. **£200-300**

▲ **Charleston style**
In the 1920s and 1930s, Flapper girls danced the night away in elegant buttoned shoes. By this time shoes were being mass produced, making the latest styles available to more people. These gold- and blue-patterned brocade evening shoes, with gold leather trim and paste decoration, are marked 'Babers of Oxford Street'. **£200-300**

◀ **Fifties frivolity**
After the restrictions and rationing of the 1940s, the 1950s saw a new sense of fun in fashion that attracts collectors today. The uppers and straps of these 1950s slingbacks are made from clear flexible Perspex – a revolutionary new material at the time. They also have diamanté detail on the toes and heels and are marked 'Mackay Starr New York'. **£120-180**

◀ **Early stilettoes**
The stiletto heel was developed in the 1950s, although by whom is subject for debate: French designers Charles Jordan, Roger Vivier and Italian Salvatore Ferragamo are all given credit for it. Whoever it was, it was a success and soon spread worldwide. These 1950s black suede court shoes, the toes decorated with red velvet ribbon bows, are marked 'Michelé Fifth Avenue Paris custom made'. **£150-200**

▶ **Wearable history**
Shoes from the 1960s and later are considered to be more wearable than earlier examples. They may also echo current trends, making them attractive to buyers of current as well as vintage fashion. These 1970s mustard snakeskin-effect leather and clear plastic court shoes are marked 'J Renee'. **£50-100**

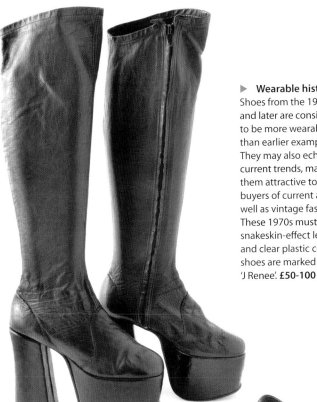

▲ **Seventies boots**
The platform soles which have come to define 1970s footwear originated in 1930s and 1940s Florence. There, designer Salvatore Ferragamo experimented with wedges made from cork, crocheted plastic and raffia to create stylish shoes at a time when leather and other traditional materials were hard to come by. If these knee-length black leather boots bore the iconic Biba label they would be worth £300 or more. Unlabelled, they are valued at **£60-80**.

◀ **Designer value drops**
Contemporary designer shoes rarely retain their value as they are generally considered to be second-hand rather than vintage once they have been taken out of their box. These Gucci satin peep-toe stiletto pumps, with the company's signature 'horse bit' detail on the toe, would have cost £500 or more when new. Today they are worth **£80-120**.

Notorious fashion favourite

While, as a general rule, recent fashions are often not worth even half their original price once they have been worn, there are exceptions. When supermodel Naomi Campbell fell over on the catwalk while wearing a pair of Vivienne Westwood super-elevated court shoes, they found a place in fashion history. The shoes are typical of Westwood's subversion of traditional British style – a platform sole added to a Scottish dancing shoe known as a 'gillie'. This style of shoe has featured in several of her collections and has become an emblem of 1990s style. If you have a similar pair – or a version of another notable fashion design – it may be worth holding on to.

▲ **Shoe style**
Although not the same as the pair worn by Naomi Campbell – which are now in London's Victoria & Albert Museum – these patent red leather 1990s shoes are worth **£1,000-1,500**.

TREASURE SPOTTER'S GALLERY
Compacts

Powder compacts became an essential accessory for women from the late 1920s. The golden era of design lasted until the 1960s, although cosmetics companies such as Christian Dior have recently started to make collectable compacts. The use of top-quality materials with attractive design will usually add value. Examples from the 1920s and 1930s are desirable and can be worth hundreds of pounds.

Stratton compacts

By the early 1930s, the British firm Stratton was producing around half of all of the compacts made for the UK cosmetics industry. The company's self-opening lid was introduced in 1948 and featured in Stratton's Compact-in-Hand mark, used between c.1950 and c.1970. As millions of Stratton compacts were made before the company was sold in 1997, most examples are unlikely to be worth great sums, particularly if they are a common shape such as the Rondette. Rarer shapes include the early Stratnoid (circular and stamped with its name), the Thinette (circular with a shallow well) and the Pontoon (rectangular with purse-snap closure). The most valuable Strattons are likely to be made from precious metals or feature Art Deco designs.

▲ **Style is valued**
The manufacturer of this compact is unknown, although it is likely to have been a German factory. While this compact lacks a well-known brand name, it is desirable due to its striking Art Deco design and early date. c.1935 8.5cm (3½in) diameter **£200-300**

▲ **Common example**
The romantic scene in pale, feminine colours and the indented edges of this compact are both typical of Stratton designs. This 1960s compact is in good condition but is unlikely to appeal to collectors due to its late date and the large numbers of similar compacts on the market. c.1960 9cm (3½in) wide **£20-30**

▶ **Bakelite beauty**
Compacts made from early plastics, such as Bakelite, can be surprisingly valuable. Early plastics were brittle and so metal was used for the hinges and thumb-catches. The Art Deco design adds to the value of this piece. c.1930 8cm (3¼in) wide **£150-200**

▶ Novelty value
The British firm Pygmalion produced some of the best and most desirable novelty compacts, including this Sonata piano compact and a range of globe-shaped compacts. In general, an amusing or charming form will add value. Other top manufacturers of novelty compacts include Kigu, Henriette and Volupté. *c.*1954 9cm (3½in) wide **£120-150**

▲ Cross-market interest
Collectors of advertising and the 1938 Disney film are likely to be interested in this *Snow White* printed card compact. This example is in extremely good condition given its age and the material used. Any damage would make it less appealing to buyers. 1938 9cm (3½in) diameter **£20-30**

▶ Two of a kind
A matching set will usually be more valuable than the sum of its parts, particularly in the original case. From the 1920s, when it became fashionable for women to smoke in public, compacts were made with matching cigarette lighters. This Ronson silver and enamel set is marked Birmingham. 1948 14cm (5½in) wide **£250-350**

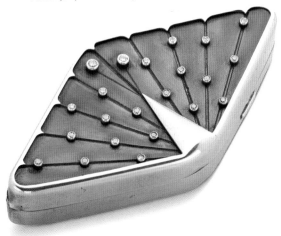

▼ Worth its weight
Fine materials and craftsmanship are crucial to the value of accessories. This lozenge-shaped compact was designed by contemporary American silversmith Michael Brophy. It is the most valuable compact shown as it is made from silver and set with diamonds. 7.5cm (3in) wide **£800-1,000**

▲ All that glitters
The House of Fabergé has produced some of the world's most exquisite *objets d'art*. The name has been sold several times and from 1964 until 1989 was owned by the company which made Elizabeth Arden cosmetics and Brut aftershave. This mass-produced gold-plated compact dates from that era. *c.*1975 6cm (2½in) high **£25-35**

TREASURE SPOTTER'S GUIDE
Perfume bottles

The half-used perfume bottle sitting on your dressing table may hold a sweet-smelling profit. A huge variety of perfume bottles, especially those from the 19th and 20th centuries, are popular with collectors.

A rare 'umbrella' stopper echoes the V-shaped neck.

Until the 20th century, most perfume bottles were bought empty from bottle-makers and filled with perfume purchased separately. Bottles dating from the mid-19th century are often highly decorative. Embossed silver, cut glass and ceramic bottles encrusted with flowers were fashionable and fetch between £50 and £1,000 today. Double-ended perfume bottles or those with a vinaigrette (a separate container for smelling salts) in the base can be worth from £100 to £500. Cameo glass bottles made by Stourbridge factories such as Stevens & Williams and Thomas Webb & Sons fetch £1,000-2,000 or more.

The first commercial bottles

In the late 19th century, perfumers realised the commercial potential of commissioning bottles: these pieces have a strong collecting base today. Bottles made in the early 20th century for famous perfumers, including Coty and Guerlain, or leading fashion houses, such as Chanel and Dior, can fetch the highest prices, particularly for limited edition and other rare pieces.

Bottles made in large numbers may be worth less but an unopened bottle or one in its original packaging will often be worth more. Bottles of Schiaparelli's signature scent, Shocking, can be worth from £100 to £1,000 depending on whether the bottle is unopened and in a special edition box. Bottles of L'Aimant by Coty fetch from £20 to £200. If you think you have a bottle that will appeal to collectors check its condition – a chip will lower the value of most examples, as will a replaced or missing stopper.

Examples by famous glass-makers such as Baccarat, Depinoix and Daum are widely collected. Lalique bottles can

▲ **Engraved Bohemian glass**
In the 19th century and earlier, glass-makers created extravagant bottles, which customers filled with their own perfume. In Bohemia many factories specialised in flashed glass, a form of casing (see page 114) and then engraving the glass. 22.5cm (8½in) high c.1870 **£650-850**

▶ **Webb cameo glass**
A Webb cameo glass perfume bottle, decorated with vines and a butterfly. It has a silver top marked 'Gorham Sterling'. These slender vessels, dating from c.1890, often feature hinged silver lids – if the hinge is broken or damaged the bottle will be less valuable. 26cm (10.5in) long **£1,500-2,000**

Good, Better, Best *Shocking by Elsa Schiaparelli*

Italian-born French fashion designer Elsa Schiaparelli commissioned imaginative and witty bottles and packaging for her signature scent – Shocking. The bottle was inspired by the silhouette of Mae West, for whom the designer created costumes. Unable to travel to Paris for fittings, the actress sent a plaster statue of herself posing as the Venus de Milo. The result is one of the most collectable commercial perfume bottles ever made. It was designed in 1936 by the artist Eleonore Fini. Schiaparelli also created what may be the most valuable collectable perfume bottle – Le Roi de Soleil. Designed by her friend Salvador Dali, and made by the glass-maker Baccarat, an example would fetch £8,000 or more at auction.

Good

Miniature bottle
This miniature 1930s bottle is unopened. The dressmaker's dummy form has a tape measure around the neck and a bunch of bows at its head, all sitting under a plastic dome. It combines Surrealism with fashion. 5cm (2in) high **£250-350**

Better

Christmas packaging
Schiaparelli designed Christmas packaging. This Shock-in-the-Box from around 1938 consists of a glass bottle in an animated box. It is small and the box has some wear but its rarity means it would be prized by a collector. 3.75cm (1½in) high **£400-600**

Best

Special edition
For Christmas 1940, Schiaparelli created Shocking Scamp, a miniature glass bottle of her signature scent in an enamelled metal fencer brooch, seen here on its original metal stand. 14cm (5½in) high **£1,000-£1,500**

fetch between £400 and £40,000, depending on rarity, age and design. Also collectable are Art Deco bottles by Czech firms such as Hoffman and un-named glass-makers which appeal to both perfume bottle and Art Deco collectors.

Valuable bottles, such as those by Lalique and Baccarat, are best sold through an auction house which organises 20th-century design sales. For commercial bottles it is worth contacting a dealer – those specialising in vintage fashion often also deal in perfume bottles – or try selling online.

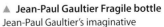

▲ **Jean-Paul Gaultier Fragile bottle**
Jean-Paul Gaultier's imaginative perfume packaging is collectable. He chose a snowdome bottle and packing crate box for his 1999 fragrance Fragile. Many of his other bottles are based on the male or female torso. Bottle 2.75in (7cm) high **£20-25**

▶ **Art Deco design**
During the 1920s and 1930s, vast numbers of cut- and etched-glass perfume bottles were exported from Czechoslovakia as part of dressing table sets. Often designed with spectacular stoppers – such as the dancing female figure on this example – they are highly collectable. 15.5cm (6.25in) high **£600-800**

TREASURE SPOTTER'S GUIDE
Lighters

Over the past few decades, smoking memorabilia has become highly desirable because we have become less sensitive to it. Attractive, well-made pieces such as cigarette lighters are often extremely valuable. Look for the name 'Dunhill' on your treasures, as it signifies quality and could indicate a high price.

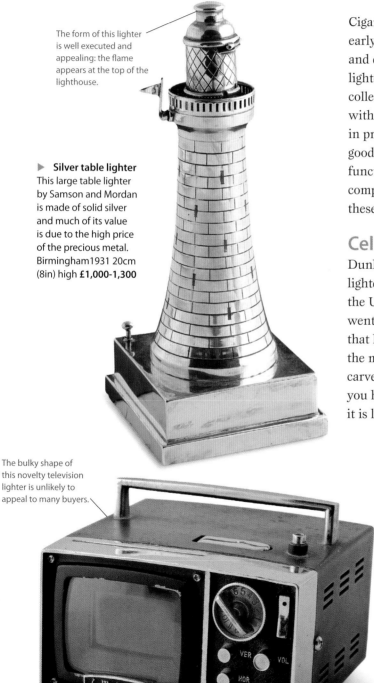

The form of this lighter is well executed and appealing: the flame appears at the top of the lighthouse.

▶ **Silver table lighter**
This large table lighter by Samson and Mordan is made of solid silver and much of its value is due to the high price of the precious metal. Birmingham 1931 20cm (8in) high **£1,000-1,300**

Cigarette smoking was extremely fashionable in the early 20th century, as it was thought to be glamorous and even good for your health. The portable petrol-lighter was developed in response to this. Today's collecting market focuses around the petrol-lighter, with high prices being paid for lighters that are cased in precious metals, made by a major maker and in good working condition. Lighters with unusual functions, such as built-in watches or powder compacts, are favoured by collectors, especially if these functions are concealed in an ingenious way.

Celebrated lighter

Dunhill, which is known as the 'Rolls-Royce of lighters', introduced one of its best-known products, the Unique petrol-lighter, in 1923. The company went on to manufacture a wide range of designs that have become some of the most desirable on the market, including the hand-painted and hand-carved Lucite-cased Aquarium and Aviary ranges. If you have a Dunhill petrol-lighter in good condition, it is likely to be valuable and you should contact

The bulky shape of this novelty television lighter is unlikely to appeal to many buyers.

▶ **Zippo lighters**
There is a strong collecting base for Zippo lighters, partly because most examples remain affordable. Generally, a stainless steel or chrome-plated lighter will sell for £30-50. High prices are usually paid for Zippos connected to a well-known brand, with a military connection, or silver lighters such as this one. 1960 5.5cm (2¼in) high **£80-100**

◀ **Novelty lighter**
Table lighters are generally not as desirable as portable lighters. Amusing or attractive forms can be worth relatively high sums, particularly in precious metals. This example by Swank is 10cm (4in) wide **£40-60**

Good, Better, Best
Dunhill lighters

Alfred Dunhill inherited his father's London-based saddlery business in 1893 and soon began to develop a line of automobile accessories under the slogan 'Everything But The Motor'. In 1919, Dunhill hired Willey Greenwood and Frederick Wise to design a lighter for the range. The prototype was created from an old mustard can and featured a horizontal flint, which allowed the smoker to operate it with one hand. Dunhill went on to produce what are considered to be the foremost in cigarette lighters. Most pre-1950s Dunhill lighters are particularly valuable.

Good

This classic Dunhill Unique design, introduced in 1923, is consistently popular with collectors, particularly in precious metals. The engine-turned design on this solid gold example adds interest but, in general, the lighter is fairly standard and there is little to set it apart from other Dunhill Uniques. 5.5cm (2¼in) high **£350-450**

Better

Dunhill watch lighters are rare and desirable, particularly in precious metals. This model is known as the Sports, as the vented chimney protects the flame from the wind during outdoor pursuits. This feature is desirable to collectors today. 1928 5.5cm (2¼in) high **£1,500-2,500**

Best

Dunhill's hand-carved and hand-painted Lucite lighters are extremely valuable. Aviary lighters are less common than Aquarium lighters and this 1950s example, 7cm (2¾in) high, is particularly rare as it features a bird of prey and is the miniature size, rather than the more common full size. Only the badly worn plating on the metal decreases its value. Undamaged it is worth **£5,000**. With the original box its value is **£10,000-15,000**.

◀ **Dunhill Rollagas**
Dunhill's petrol-filled Rollalite lighter was superseded by the gas-filled Rollagas (shown here). The designs are similar but equivalent Rollagas lighters are worth less than half the value of equivalent Rollalite models, due to their later date. This lighter dates from the 1970s. 5.5cm (2¼in) high **£60-80**

your local auction house. Dunhill marked many of the parts of its most complex designs with matching serial numbers – check that these are consistent, because mismatched parts will lower value. Having the original box will increase the value substantially.

Gas-lighters took over in the 1950s and were produced by companies such as Thorens in Switzerland and Ronson and Zippo in America. They typically fetch lower sums than equivalent petrol-lighters, although some precious metal examples can be worth more than £100.

With all lighters, value increases with the quality of the materials, condition and eye-appeal. Check for wear, dents and splits as well as missing or replaced parts, which all make a lighter less desirable. Precious metal examples are fashionable and usually valuable, as are high-quality lacquerwork models. Lighters with coverings such as shagreen and leather are less desirable but often worth more than plain lighters.

Novelty-shaped lighters are highly collectable, particularly humorous forms and shapes that appeal to buyers not necessarily interested in smoking memorabilia (for example, racing collectors may be interested in a lighter shaped like a race horse). Without a good name and high quality materials, values will still be relatively low.

◀ **Elisorm Auto-Tank**
Elisorm is not a well-known name in lighter manufacture but this does not account for the low value of this 1950s solid gold Auto-Tank lighter. Personalisation will always reduce desirability whatever the item. Most buyers will not have the initials 'JP', therefore interest and value drops. 3.75cm (1½in) high **£35-45**

TREASURE SPOTTER'S GUIDE
Fountain pens

While many vintage fountain pens are worth less than £30, the best and rarest examples can fetch high sums. As with many collecting fields, the maker is the most important indicator to value. Early pens from the big names – Parker, Waterman, Montblanc and Dunhill – fetch the highest prices.

◄ **Waterman's quality**
This pen, by a good maker (Waterman's), is in very good condition and even has its original box, which will generally raise prices. Unfortunately, as it was made after the 'golden age' and is in a relatively common colourway, it is not very desirable, generating a low price. *c.*1946 **£30-50**

► **Conway Stewart**
Pens by this British maker, such as this 1930s Cracked Ice, are desirable because of the plastics used. Reverse Cracked Ice (silver with black veins) can fetch 25 per cent more. **£120-180**

Fountain pens became available in large numbers in the late 19th century after Lewis Edson Waterman and George S. Parker separately patented reliable ink-feed systems. During the late 1910s to the 1930s, now known as the 'golden age' of the fountain pen, a wide range of different ink-filling mechanisms and barrel shapes, colours and sizes was introduced. Pens produced during this period are the most desirable today. As these pens are rare and expensive, interest in pens produced between the 1930s and 1970s is increasing.

How to spot value

Modern limited edition pens are typically not valuable, unless kept with their original box and paperwork. Fountain pens from the late 19th century attract interest but, as most were black, they are not as appealing or desirable as examples from the early to mid-20th century. In general, visual impact and an attractive design are good indicators to value. Unusual, brightly coloured celluloids or pens with lacquerwork designs or gold-plated overlays are desirable.

Would you believe it?

The intricately decorated maki-e lacquer pens produced by Namiki and retailed by Dunhill during the 1920s and 1930s are miniature works of art. Simpler designs are often worth a few hundred pounds, but the best Namiki lacquer pens can fetch extremely high sums. In 2000, a Dunhill Namiki No.50 Giant, decorated with a dragon by Iijima Genroku, sold for a world-record price of £183,000.

▼ **Dunhill Namiki**
The high quality and three-dimensional lacquerwork on this pen covers most of its body, which is desirable. It would have been worth more if the design had been more complicated or featured the signature of a known artist. 12.5cm (5in) long **£2,000-2,500**

▶ **Parker Duofold**
The iconic Big Red Parker Duofold was one of the first brightly coloured pens in a market where most were black. Vintage examples are worth around £120-180 today. Other colour variations were introduced in 1927. The 1928 Mandarin Yellow shown here is the rarest and most valuable colour. **£500-700**

Most collectors focus on the biggest brands, such as Parker, Waterman's and Montblanc. Well-known models, such as the Parker's Duofold or 51, are often the most keenly collected. Over the past few years, smaller brands, such as De La Rue (Onoto), have risen in desirability and value, although pens from such companies are still likely to command lower figures than equivalent pens from premier pen manufacturers.

After brand, rarity and quality determine value. Size is also a consideration, as many pen collectors are men and favour larger pens that fit their hands. All pens should be in good working order as many collectors intend to use them. Perished ink sacs can be replaced by a restorer but cracks, burn marks or scratches on plastic pens and dents or splits on metal pens cannot be restored. Pens with this sort of damage will be worth much less than mint condition examples. Replaced nibs will also decrease value.

Although the market for vintage fountain pens has declined recently, the internet has broadened the market since, unlike other larger or more delicate collectables, pens are easy to ship. If you have a vintage fountain pen, consult a specialist reference guide to find out what you have before listing it on an auction site, such as eBay.

◀ **Montblanc limited edition**
In 1993 Agatha Christie was the second design in Montblanc's collectable Writer's Edition series. Easily identified by its snake-shaped clip, it was produced on a variety of different pens and pen sets, with differing edition sizes. This pen, which has a silver-gilt clip with sapphire eyes, is the most valuable single piece in this design. **£300-500**

Good, Better, Best
Parker 51

The Parker 51 is one of the world's best-loved vintage fountain pens. The revolutionary design, which features a nib covered with a plastic hood, dates from 1939, the 51st anniversary of the Parker pen company. Numerous model variations were subsequently produced and millions of 51s were sold during the pen's main production lifetime, 1941 to 1978. Most standard models are worth under £30 but rare examples can be worth much higher sums.

Good

Barrel colour can affect value. Black, burgundy and grey are the most common, followed by teal. Forest green and particularly plum (shown here), which was only produced in the USA for two years, are rarer and more valuable. This pen is also in good condition, which increases its desirability. 1949 **£100-150**

Better

Parker initially used the Vacumatic system, which can be identified by its internal plunger, before switching to the simpler Aerometric system, which is generally less desirable than the Vacumatic. The aluminium ends on this Vacumatic example indicate that it was made in the 51's first year of manufacture, which makes it particularly rare and valuable. **£180-200**

Best

The Parker 51 Red Band used a new button-filling system, which was soon revealed to have design problems and withdrawn. This example of the rare model is in mint condition and was owned by Merle Heskett, who first brought the Red Band to the attention of collectors in 2001. 1946-47 **£500-700**

JEWELLERY and WATCHES

The design, craftsmanship and name of the maker all dictate the value of a piece of jewellery made from precious materials. The market price of the raw materials should also be taken into account. Costume jewellery – pieces made from base metals and paste – have increased in price as the number of people who prize them for their aesthetic appeal grows. The desirability of a wristwatch depends on maker, quality and style. Examples by companies such as Rolex usually fetch high prices.

American designer Kenneth J. Lane is known for his jewellery inspired by historical styles. His bib necklaces are some of the most eye-catching examples of costume jewellery on the market. As the value of much costume jewellery is based on style, design and quality, good condition examples of Lane's bibs can fetch hundreds of pounds. *c.*1970 43cm (17in) diameter **£800-1,000**

WHAT MAKES JEWELLERY VALUABLE?
Precious stones and design can be crucial

The value of an item of precious jewellery is partially determined by its intrinsic elements. Costume jewellery is usually made from base materials – often designed to resemble precious ones – and its value depends on the style and maker. But the value of many pieces may be sentimental rather than financial.

◀ **Georgian style**
Some Georgian jewellery may not realise the same price as a similar Art Deco piece. This pendant, *c*.1760, features a large amethyst and hangs on a metre-long solid gold chain. The intricate wirework around the setting of the stone and textured chain links suggest high-quality craftsmanship. Chain 98cm (38½in) long **£2,000-2,500**

▶ **Brilliant diamond**
The large brilliant-cut diamond (2.02cts) mounted on this early 20th-century Scottish ring accounts for most of its high value. The understated setting shows the stone to best advantage. **£4,500-5,500**

Precious jewellery made for the wealthy can fetch high sums because such pieces were made by the best craftsmen from the finest materials. However the value of costume jewellery depends entirely on the maker, quality and design.

Although materials have a huge impact on value, other factors can also have an effect. One of the most important is the style of a piece of jewellery – an attractive or novel design will always have buyers competing to own it. In general, early 20th-century precious jewellery is more popular than 19th-century pieces. Art Deco jewellery – precious or costume – is particularly desirable as the style is popular and still looks modern today.

Prices increase with a top maker such as Chanel for costume jewellery, or Cartier for precious. Buyers look for a desirable form, ingenious design, craftsmanship and good provenance and condition.

There is a market for 18th and 19th-century costume jewellery, made from materials such as paste, seed-pearls, jet, bone, copper, cut steel and pinchbeck (a metal alloy with the appearance of gold). But the main market is for 20th-century pieces (see pages 196-199).

▼ **Striking design**
Art Deco design often featured Egyptian motifs, such as scarabs. The clean, geometric lines and rich enamelling add to the quality and appeal of this 1920s brooch. 3.75cm (1½in) wide **£300-400**

▲ Major maker
The name of a superior maker significantly enhances value as, in general, it guarantees good design, fine materials and excellent craftsmanship. This 1950s necklace by Van Cleef & Arpels, made from gold set with diamonds, emeralds and rubies, has it all. Panel 6cm (2½in) wide **£12,000-14,000**

Quality materials

There are three main precious metals used for precious jewellery: platinum is the rarest and most valuable; most quality gold jewellery is 21 carat, 18 carat or 14 carat; silver is the least valuable, although all metal prices have risen.

Gemstones add value, depending on their carat weight, colour, brilliance and cut. They must be assessed by a professional jeweller. If you sell at an auction house, a specialist will verify the stones. Damage, repairs and replacements decrease value.

Certain types of jewellery are more valuable than others. Late 20th-century silver jewellery by Georg Jensen (see page 130), earrings, especially chandelier forms, and cufflinks have recently seen a revival in interest. Complete parures (a matching set) are rare and fetch more than the separate items.

If you wish to sell, look for marks on your items which may help to identify them (see pages 268-269); precious metals are usually hallmarked, while costume pieces may bear a maker's mark. Most jewellers and auction houses sell precious jewellery but try a specialist dealer for costume jewellery, or sell it online.

Good, Better, Best Cameos

Cameos were often used during the 19th and 20th centuries as the focal point of a piece of jewellery. Mythological subjects were popular during the early 19th century, with the profile portraits most people now associate with cameos coming into vogue in the latter half of the century. Many were carved from shells.

Good

Good-quality cameos, such as this late 19th-century shell cameo brooch, have crisp, well-defined carving and no sharp edges. The design is also appealing and the level of detail on areas such as the goddess's hair and the eagle's feathers is good. The overall piece, in an engraved gold frame, is in good condition. 6cm (2½in) long **£500-700**

Better

The Three Graces (mythological givers of charm and beauty) depicted in this c.1900 shell cameo, are a consistently popular motif and the carving is far finer on this example than the carving on the previous cameo. Furthermore, as it is more challenging to carve, a depiction of three figures is far more unusual than a single figure and adds aesthetic interest. 16.4g (0.6oz) **£1,200-1,800**

Best

Agate is an ideal material for cameos as it is made up of differently coloured layers. This property has been employed for the lace collar here – by varying the thickness of the top layer the lower colour shows through. The frame adds to the value of the late 19th-century piece, as it is made of seed pearls and rose-cut diamonds. 3cm (1¼in) diameter **£2,500-3,500**

RESTORING YOUR FINDS
Repairing brooches

Most brooches are secured by a metal pin, which is hinged on one side and anchored on the other within a clasp – usually a hook or cylinder. These are subject to wear, but can be easily repaired, although if the brooch is valuable it's best to seek professional help.

YOU WILL NEED

Flat-nose pliers
Taper-nose pliers
Needle-nose pliers

▲ **Cut steel and ruby paste brooch**
This late 18th-century brooch is fastened with a cylinder clasp.

▲ **Diamanté star brooch**
A safety catch secures the clasp on this brooch that dates from the 1930s.

▲ **Victorian 'love knot' brooch**
This 19th-century brass and ruby paste brooch has a simple hook closure.

Adjusting a bowed pin
Grip the pin just in front of the hinge with flat-nose pliers (to isolate the hinge from undue pressure) and, with taper-nose pliers gripping the middle of the pin, gently bend it either up or down to straighten.

Re-straightening a pin
Sometimes a pin bends right at the end where it enters the clasp or hook. Even bends of well over 45 degrees can be straightened by gently squeezing the end flat again in the jaws of a pair of flat- or taper-nose pliers.

Repairing hinges
If the metal flanges that form the sides of a hinge have become flattened or distorted, and disengaged from the pin, straighten and re-engage them by gently squeezing between the jaws of taper- or flat-nose pliers.

Adjusting a hook
If an open hook snaps off, have it re-soldered by a professional repairer. If it's become crushed or distorted, so the pin won't sit in the opening, very gently bend it back into shape with a pair of needle-nose pliers.

Restringing a necklace

Wear and age can cause the stringing on a necklace or bracelet to break. If the beads are loose, put them in sequence before restringing. If the original stringing is frayed but the necklace is intact, cut the clasp free, and slide or cut off the beads one at a time, as you restring, to keep them in sequence.

YOU WILL NEED

Small pair of scissors

Silk thread four times the length of the necklace and no less than half the diameter of the bead holes

Cutting board

A sharp knife

White PVA adhesive

French wire 1-2cm (½-1in)

Pair of tweezers or small taper-nose pliers

Restringing a necklace

1 Cut a length of silk thread four times the length of the necklace. Fold it in half, place the two cut ends on a cutting board, and with the edge of a sharp knife scrape to thin them.

2 Roll one end between your finger and thumb. Smooth on little PVA adhesive and allow to set to create a 'needle'. Cut 1cm (½ in) of French wire and thread the silk 'needle' through it.

3 Insert needle through one side of clasp and, with French wire looped through it, pull thread through and join ends with PVA to form a new needle. When dry, thread first bead. Make knot on other side of bead and pull tight with fingers and pliers. Repeat.

4 Before final bead, pull 'needle' apart. Insert one thread through last bead, 1cm (½ in) of French wire, the other side of the clasp, and back on itself through last bead. Pull tight. Double-knot threads together and apply PVA. When dry trim excess thread.

▲ **Protecting the necklace**
French wire, also known as bullion or gimp, is a flexible, hollow coil of fine wire which will protect the thread by preventing it wearing and fraying on the clasp when the necklace is worn. The wire should slide easily, but not loosely, on the silk thread. The knots between the beads will prevent them falling off if the thread breaks.

195

TREASURE SPOTTER'S GUIDE
Costume jewellery

Until about ten years ago, costume jewellery – that is pieces generally made from glass and base metal – was seen as cheap trinkets. But as people have come to appreciate the designs of costume jewellery its desirability and value have soared.

The materials used to create costume jewellery generally have no intrinsic value and so it is the quality of the design, the workmanship and the name of the designer which tend to dictate value.

Non-precious jewellery has been made for centuries, from ancient Egyptian glass beads to 18th-century cut-steel bracelets. It was designed to enhance the fashions of the day without the expense of the precious materials used in other pieces. But the 20th century saw the democratisation of jewellery thanks to a Parisian couturier, the 1929 Wall Street Crash and the growth of Hollywood. It is these pieces that can fetch high prices today.

The French influence came from Coco Chanel. The first person to make wearing costume jewellery acceptable in fashionable society, it's rare to see a photograph of her without her faux pearls and heavy cuffs. Together with Italian-born French couturier Elsa Schiaparelli and American Miriam Haskell, Chanel transformed costume jewellery from tawdry to tasteful. All three created high-end pieces that sell for between £100 and £4,000 depending on the age, rarity and complexity of the design.

Many precious jewellers who lost their jobs after the Wall Street Crash found work at costume jewellery companies. For example, the designer Alfred Philippe went from Van Cleef & Arpels to Trifari. Meanwhile, women who could no longer afford new clothes – let alone precious gems – bought the latest costume jewels to brighten up their wardrobes. In Hollywood, the movies brought orders and fame to Joseff of Hollywood and Hobé among others.

Costume jewellery price line

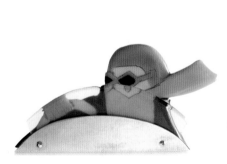

Eighties classic
Butler & Wilson's early jewellery tended to be inspired by the Art Deco designs they saw at antique fairs. Classic designs from the 1980s by the British duo – including their famous lizard and articulated dancing couple brooches – feature masses of sparkling diamanté. Early and unusual pieces such as this 1980s, 7cm (2¾in) wide, Amy Johnson plastic and chrome pin are increasingly collected and values are likely to rise in the future. **£100-150**

Two-in-one
In the 1940s American company Corocraft (or Coro) was the largest costume jewellery manufacturer in the world. The company created the Duette – two small brooches which can be worn separately or assembled on a frame to create one large one. The 1940s 7.5cm (3in) long Quivering Camellias Duette is one of the most desirable. The diamanté and enamelled flowers are mounted on springs that tremble as the wearer moves. **£200-300**

Flower power
Stanley Hagler worked briefly for Miriam Haskell and her influence can be seen in the extravagant, intricate, three-dimensional, hand-wired pieces he created from the 1950s to the 1980s. Hagler's work is increasingly collectable – particularly matching necklaces and earrings – and values have risen so now could be the time to sell a brooch such as this 1980s floral and foliate pin which is 12.5cm (5in) wide. **£250-300**

▲ **Christian Dior brooch**
A Dior pin in gold-tone metal with irregularly shaped glass stones. 1962 7cm (2¾in) long **£200-250**

Jewellery for all

By the 1950s, costume jewellery was being mass produced to suit all budgets for department stores, boutiques and couture houses, by companies such as Trifari and Corocraft. Such jewellery is widely collected today and values depend on the quality of the materials used and the design. Prices range from a few pounds for a pair of earrings sold in stores such as Woolworths, to £500 or more for a brooch sold in a department store.

The 1980s saw a renewed enthusiasm for costume jewellery which brought success to makers including Butler & Wilson in the UK and Kenneth Jay Lane in the US. Both continue to produce jewellery today. Their earlier work is becoming increasingly collectable and may be worth hanging on to as values continue to rise.

If you have a piece to sell, the first step is to look to see if it is marked with the maker's name. Marks often changed over time so this may help you to date it as well. However, many makers left their work unsigned or used paper labels which were discarded. Unmarked pieces are generally less valuable then marked ones unless they are exceptionally well designed. Unless you have a very old or rare piece the best place to sell is online or to a specialist dealer.

Hollywood hero
Eugene Joseff, founder of Joseff of Hollywood, made jewellery for the movies and created a matt 'Russian gold' that did not create a glare under the studio lights. He rented rather than sold his jewels to the studios, and then sold them through up-market department stores. This rare 1940s, 6cm (2½in) diameter, Moon God with Ruff pin, with clear rhinestone eye tremblers, has maintained its value. **£900-1,200**

Wartime restrictions
In the run up to, and during, World War II, restrictions on materials meant that American jewellery manufacturers began to use silver rather than base metals for their designs. Trifari began making 'jelly bellies' – animal brooches and earrings with a large clear or coloured Lucite ball for the body. These are in demand from collectors today and values are high. This 1930s silver, enamel and diamanté jelly belly poodle, 5cm (2in) high, is worth **£1,500-2,000.**

Fashion favourite
Much of the jewellery designed by Coco Chanel was inspired by Byzantine mosaics and the cultures of India, Persia and Egypt. Typical pieces include strings of faux pearls, gilt Maltese cross brooches, necklaces set with poured glass stones and enamelled cuffs. Pieces created in this style and dating from the 1980s and 1990s tend to be more affordable. This rare 1930s Chanel poured glass peacock pin is 14cm (5½in) long and currently valued at **£2,000-3,000.**

TREASURE SPOTTER'S GALLERY
Costume jewellery settings

Understanding the settings and stones used by 20th-century costume jewellery designers helps you to identify, date and value their work. As a general rule, the more time and skill required to make a piece, the more valuable it is likely to be.

▶ Pavé setting and poured glass

Early pieces by French company Chanel often featured pavé-set diamanté stones: small stones set close together like paving stones. These may be combined with poured glass and high-quality faux pearls. This stylised flower pin is a typically complex Chanel design from the 1920s. 10cm (4in) high **£2,000-3,000**

▲ Invisible setting

Frenchman Alfred Philippe, chief designer at Trifari from 1930 until 1968, had previously worked for precious jeweller Van Cleef & Arpels. He used the invisible-setting technique pioneered there for costume pieces. The result is tiny stones set so close together they appear to be one, larger, carved stone. This 1950s poinsettia pin is considered to be a masterpiece of costume jewellery design. 7cm (2¾in) wide **£1,500-2,000**

▼ Prong setting

This claw-like setting is common in costume and precious jewellery. The metal prongs on these earrings by American firm Weiss hold the faceted stones securely but unobtrusively. The earrings are marked 'Weiss' and date from the 1950s. 3.75cm (1½in) long **£60-80**

◀ ▼ Hand-wired setting

Beads and stones are hand-wired on to a filigree backing to create a three-dimensional finish. American designer Miriam Haskell, who created this necklace in the 1960s, is noted for combining this technique with high-quality art glass and faux pearls. 56cm (22in) long **£300-500**

Back view

Judith's lucky find

While working in the USA, I happened to see a thrift store (charity shop) next to the dealer I was visiting. I went in, not expecting to find anything that would tempt me to carry it as I travelled from state to state. However, displayed in the glass cabinet by the till, a pair of earrings caught my eye. When I asked to see them, I saw the words 'Christian Dior' etched on their backs. The shop obviously had no idea how valuable these were as they were marked at $5. To salve my conscience, I gave the saleswoman $40 and walked out knowing that my find was an extremely lucky one. The moral of this story is that it is vital to do your homework before giving something away – you may be parting with more than you think!

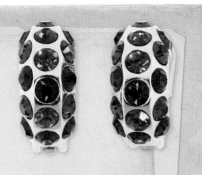

▲ Mark of a master
A pair of Christian Dior earrings, made from gold-tone metal and set with ruby and emerald rhinestones. Marked 'Christian Dior 1958'. 3.75cm (1½in) long **£60-80**

▲ Glued setting
Using glue to hold flat-backed stones and beads in place ensures that the setting does not interfere with the design but usually denotes poor quality and low value. It was used to great effect on affordable ranges. This mid-1950s brooch and earrings, by American manufacturer Art, features carved, translucent Lucite flowers highlighted with rhinestones. 5cm (2in) long **£40-60**

▲ Fantasy stones
Rather than mimic natural stones, many costume jewellery designers commissioned fantasy glass crystals which bore no relation to 'real' jewellery. In the 1950s, Italian-born French fashion designer Elsa Schiaparelli used fantasy pastes such as the blue stones – known as aurora borealis – in these earrings. The technique used to create the stones was developed by Austrian firm Swarovski in conjunction with Christian Dior. 3.75cm (1½in) long **£300-500**

▶ Multi-faceted stones
The more facets, or cut surfaces, a stone has, the better it reflects the light and the more it sparkles. High-quality costume jewellery, such as these 1958 earrings by French designer Christian Dior, features stones with a variety of cuts. Here, they are enhanced by a discreet setting. 3.5cm (1½in) long **£200-300**

"The better the materials and more attractive the design, the more valuable the jewellery."
JUDITH MILLER BBC *ANTIQUES ROADSHOW* SPECIALIST

199

TREASURE SPOTTER'S GUIDE
Watches

The modern wristwatch evolved from the pocket watch in the late 19th and early 20th centuries. Value is dependent on a host of factors, but comes down to quality and style. Wristwatches from big names, such as Rolex and Patek Philippe, will usually fetch high prices.

Production of pocket watches boomed as a result of the Industrial Revolution of the late 18th and early 19th centuries. Most pocket watches are open-faced, but the hunter (solid flip-open cover) and the half-hunter (flip-open cover with a central aperture for viewing the dial) were also made.

As so many were produced, plain silver or gold-plated pocket watches that are either unmarked or by a prolific maker, such as the Swiss firm Waltham or Elgin in the US, are usually worth less than £100. Look for hallmarks inside the case as these indicate a precious metal, which will increase the value of the watch, as will enamel and other decorative features. Such watches can be entered into general or jewellery sales at many auction houses. Valuable

pocket watches are likely to have extra mechanical features including a secondary, moon-phase dial, a chronograph, calendar or a repeating mechanism. The highest prices are reserved for pieces by notable makers such as Swiss company Patek Philippe, whose watches can be worth £10,000 or more.

Wristwatches

Wristwatches achieved widespread popularity following World War I because they were much more practical than pocket watches. Early designs from this period were often strongly influenced by the style of the traditional pocket watch and are often valuable today as they represent an important stage of evolution in wristwatch design.

Watches price line

No longer wearable or valuable
Most vintage watches are bought to be worn. Unfortunately few people today wear pocket watches and there are many watches similar to this example on the market. Values are consequently low, despite this example being cased in silver. 1884 **£70-100**

Quality and classic styling
The watches made by Swiss manufacturer Omega in the 1950s and 1960s offer classic styling with consistent, accurate movements. The company's notable ranges are the Constellation and Seamaster. This example features a 17-jewel movement, stainless steel case and silvered dials. **£250-350**

LED display retains novelty appeal
Increasing numbers of young collectors are interested in the look and technology of the 1970s. The Omega Digital Time Computer was a prestigious LED display digital watch in the mid-1970s. It also has a unique way of setting the time – with a magnet – making it more unusual. c.1975 **£2,000-3,000**

As with pocket watches, in general, the more complex a wristwatch movement is, the more valuable it will be. Ladies' gem-set watches have the added value of the gems and are regarded by auction houses, dealers and collectors as items of jewellery.

With all wristwatches, a good-quality brand will attract more interest and higher values. Look out for names such as Rolex, Omega, Patek Philippe, Audemars Piguet, Vacheron & Constantin and Jaeger-LeCoultre. Rare models or notable designs, such as the Omega Seamaster, are likely to fetch the highest prices. Enter watches from these makers in specialist watch sales held at most leading auction houses. Watches from lower-end manufacturers can also be entered in these sales but fetch a higher price when sold online.

Condition and value

To achieve maximum value, wristwatches should always be in working order, with the case in good condition. Remember that a clean dial may indicate that a watch has been well looked after or that the dial has been replaced – the latter would impact adversely on value. If in doubt, consult an expert. An unworn strap may be a replacement that reduces the value of the watch.

Would you believe it?

The Swatch watch was sold by the million in the 1980s and 1990s, marketed as a casual, disposable accessory. Today, some early or designer models are worth hundreds of pounds. Check for examples such as this, Swatch's first special edition. Designed by Swiss partners Marlyse Schmid and Bernard Muller after a poster by Keith Haring, it commemorates the First Breakdance World Championship and only 9,999 were made. In mint condition, with instructions and box, it is worth £500-600. Without these, with a worn strap or scratched case, the value will be at least 50 per cent less. The most valuable Swatch on the secondary market is the Omega, valued at £1,055.

Space Age design for electric watch
The Ventura, produced by American watch manufacturer Hamilton, was one of the first electric (battery-powered) watches. The striking and unusual design emphasises the latest technology and taps into the Space Age craze inspired by the space race of the 1950s and 1960s. c.1960 **£3,000-4,000**

Precious metal and great workmanship
Swiss manufacturer LeCoultre was founded in 1833 and became Jaeger-LeCoultre in 1937. This gold-cased watch, decorated with Father Time and putti (a form of cherub or cupid), is an example of the high-quality workmanship for which the company is known. c.1880 **£3,500-4,500**

Classic design
The Cartier Tank (designed by the French company in 1917) was named after and inspired by the tanks used in World War I. It is one of the world's most famous and important wristwatch designs, which means that many collectors will seek to own an example. c.1935 **£30,000-40,000**

TREASURE SPOTTER'S GUIDE
Rolex watches

Renowned for innovation and design, Rolex is the world's largest luxury watch brand and there is keen interest in almost all models on the secondary market, particularly for the Submariner and Daytona.

Although Rolex, established in Switzerland 1905, had previously produced wind-up wristwatches, the company became more highly regarded with the development of its first automatic watch in 1934, the silent and waterproof Bubble Back. Subsequently, Rolex has developed several major watch innovations, which helped its reputation as the name in luxury watches. It is one of the few watch manufacturers that produces its own movements, which enhances the quality of its watches.

Rolex watches are undoubtedly well made, but much of their market value today comes from the company's brand recognition. During the 1980s, Rolex became a household name, associated with the rich, powerful and high achieving. It is a desire to buy into this image that drives prices up in many cases.

Categories to look for
Rolex watches can be divided into sport and non-sport categories – both of which are desirable to collectors. The main sport models to look out for are the Submariner, Daytona, GMT-Master, Explorer and Explorer II. In the non-sport category, the

The protective case is clearly influenced by the hunter pocket watch.

The luminous hands were designed to make it easier for troops to see the time in the dark.

▲ **Pocket watch heritage**
This early silver, water-resistant Rolex, probably designed for military use, represents an important evolution in watch design. It is also a rare model from an important brand, which makes it very attractive to collectors. 1916-1917 **£2,500-3,500**

▶ **Long-running success**
The Rolex Bubble Back is an important design in the company's history. The watch had a long production run, which gives collectors plenty of models to choose from. The excellent condition of this watch, reference no.3131, and its gold case increase its value. 1942-1945 **£1,500-2,500**

▶ **Precious metal**
Cellini, Rolex's line of dressy watches, is less collectable than the Oyster Perpetual line. This 1970s watch is not a particularly well-known model, but it is cased in 18ct gold and it is a left-handed design, which increases interest. **£4,000-5,000**

key models are the Day-Date and the Datejust. Within these brandings, rare and unusual models, such as the 1972 military-issue Submariner, are likely to make the highest prices, as are watches that have been worn by celebrities. Complicated and interesting watches, particularly those that were not widely sold, such as the Milgauss – a watch designed to be unaffected by high magnetic fields – are also often worth high sums.

Rolex holds records of all its watches and dial types, so a watch's case, number and model reference can be checked. If you have a good Rolex to sell, you should enter it into a specialist watch sale at a leading auction house or contact Antiquorum Auctioneers, wristwatch specialists.

Good, Better, Best
Rolex Submariner

Diving became a popular sport during the 1950s, leading Rolex to design a watch that would accurately measure time underwater at high pressure. The first Submariner was launched in 1954 and was pressure tested to 100 metres (330 feet). Due to the high-quality workmanship and ground-breaking design, almost all Rolex Oyster Submariners are highly desirable to watch collectors.

Good

This model, reference 14060, was introduced in 1989 and remained in production for ten years. By this time the Submariner had gone through most of its radical upgrades – this model is similar to new Submariners being produced today, which makes it less collectable than other model numbers. 1989-1999 **£2,500-3,000**

Better

Sean Connery wore an early Submariner in the first four Bond films, causing models 6538 and 6536 (also known as 5508) to be referred to as 'James Bond watches' by collectors. Roger Moore also wore a Submariner in the 1973 film *Live and Let Die*. This film connection makes an already collectable watch even more desirable. 1957 **£5,000-7,000**

Best

Rarity will usually increase value in a popular market. This official military issue model was ordered by the Royal Navy in *c*.1972. It includes features unique to this small series, such as a diamond-tip second hand. The back is engraved with an arrow, indicating the watch was made for the military – a popular collecting area in itself. **£80,000-100,000**

The push pieces (to stop and start the chronograph) are screwed down. This is a change from early 1960s models.

The subsidiary dials have the plainer-style printed numbers. Earlier models have different typeface and block markers.

▲ **Rarer than precious metal**
Initially a slow seller, the Rolex Cosmograph Daytona chronograph became highly popular after Paul Newman wore an 'exotic dial' Daytona on the cover of an Italian magazine in 1986. Stainless steel Daytonas are rarer and consequently more collectable than precious metal examples. 1984 **£30,000-40,000**

REVIVING YOUR FINDS
Cleaning jewellery

As jewellery is usually made from a combination of materials, it is important to prevent cleaning agents that are suitable for one material from damaging another. In some cases, you will need to mask an area with tape, while others require a small brush or tiny pieces of rag, chamois leather or cotton wool.

- Examine the setting of the stones before you begin, using either a magnifying glass or a jeweller's eyeglass.
- A piece that has a claw setting (see pages 198-199) can usually be cleaned without loosening a stone.
- If the piece has a pavé or invisible setting (see pages 198-199), make sure no liquid seeps behind the stone, as this can loosen the glue or cement that holds it in place. With a closed setting, carry out only a very careful surface cleaning with a cotton bud moistened with the specified cleaning agent. Alternatively, try using a dry-cleaning agent.
- Dry-clean strung necklaces, because silk or cotton thread should not be dampened. If you are in any doubt, consult an expert before proceeding.

Agate
- Remove dirt and grease by dabbing with cotton wool dampened with warm, soapy water.
- To clean stubborn dirt, gently rub in the soapy water with a toothbrush. Then dab off with clean cold water before drying with a soft towel.
- Clean agate has a slightly waxy lustre, so don't try to achieve a shine by vigorous buffing with a soft cloth.

Amber
- Clean by gently rubbing with a cotton bud dipped in warm, soapy water. Dry at once with a soft cloth.
- To revive the sheen, apply almond or olive oil with a cotton bud, wipe off the excess and buff with a chamois leather.

Aquamarine
- Clean with lukewarm, soapy water and a cotton rag. Rinse with clean water. Dry and buff with a cloth. Never use hot water, which may crack the stone.

Cameos and intaglios
- Remove dirt with warm, soapy water, cotton buds and a make-up brush. Rinse with a cotton bud dipped in clean water and dab dry with terry towelling.

Carnelian
- Use the method for cleaning agate.

Coral
- Clean with cotton buds or a small artist's brush dipped in warm, soapy water. Rinse with the cotton buds or a brush and clean water. Dry with a cotton rag. Never soak coral in water.

Diamond and artificial diamond
- Wash in warm, soapy water, rinse with clean cold water and dry thoroughly.
- Clean an artificial diamond with an artist's brush dipped in methylated spirits. Blow on the stone to evaporate the excess alcohol as quickly as possible. Never wash artificial diamonds as they may be glued and dislodged when wet.

Emerald
- Clean with a small artist's brush dipped in methylated spirits. Gently buff to a shine using a chamois leather.

Enamel
- Always have enamel cleaned by a professional as it is easily damaged.

Amber
Never allow amber to come into contact with methylated spirits, white spirit, toilet water, hair spray or perfume, as they will permanently dull it. Never soak amber in water, because this gives it a cloudy look that is almost impossible to remove.

Metal
For advice on cleaning metals including brass, bronze, copper and silver, see pages 144-145.

Gold

- Buff with a dry chamois to remove dirt. Clean recessed areas and chains with a stiff-bristled artist's brush.
- Wash with warm, soapy water then rub with a clean, soft cloth or brush. Rinse with cold water and dry with terry towelling.

Horn and ivory

- Wipe with cotton wool dipped in warm, soapy water. Then rinse with cotton wool dipped in clean water and dry with a soft towel.
- Polish by gently rubbing almond oil into the surface with a soft cloth.

Jade

- Wipe with cotton wool dipped in warm, soapy water containing two drops of ammonia. Rinse with a cloth moistened with clean water, dry with a soft cloth and buff with a chamois. Use an artist's brush to clean crevices.
- For stubborn dirt, dip the brush in methylated spirits or white spirit.

Jet

- To clean, rub with soft, fresh bread.

Mother-of-pearl

- Wipe with a soft cloth moistened with milk. Dry and buff with a soft cloth.

Onyx

- Use the method for cleaning agate.

Opal

- Use the method for cleaning pearl.

Pearl

- Clean real pearls by placing them in a glass jar with a handful of potato flour. Shake the jar for three minutes, then leave for 24 hours. Repeat. Shake again, remove the pearls, and dust them with a soft brush.
- Wipe artificial pearls with a chamois moistened with water.

Platinum

- To remove discoloration, add olive oil or methylated spirits to jeweller's rouge to make a paste with the consistency of double cream. Rub it on to the metal with a clean soft rag, wipe off and buff with a second rag.

Ruby

- Wipe with cotton buds dipped in warm, soapy water, rinse with clean water and dry with a soft cloth. Rub with a chamois moistened with alcohol.

Sapphire

- Use the method for cleaning rubies.

Tortoiseshell

- Wash with a cloth and warm, soapy water. Rinse with clean water and dry with a cloth. Moisten a cloth with almond oil, add a little microcrystalline wax and rub in. Buff with a cloth.
- To remove scratches, mix methylated spirits and crocus powder to form a paste. Rub on with a chamois. Wipe the paste off with a cloth and buff with a dry chamois.

Turquoise

- Use the method for cleaning agate.

Horn and ivory
Both horn and ivory tend to become brittle with age, and exposure to excessive temperatures and immersion in water can split or warp them. After cleaning and drying, rub a little almond oil over the surface with a cotton bud, leave for two minutes, then wipe off.

Storing jewellery

Always store pieces of jewellery separately, in the compartments of a jewellery box or separate boxes lined with acid-free cotton. Wrap each piece individually in acid-free tissue paper. Keep the box or boxes out of direct sunlight, away from other powerful sources of heat, such as radiators, and in a well-ventilated, low-humidity atmosphere.

◀ **Protect chains or other strung necklaces**
During storage you should wrap them in acid-free tissue paper.

TOYS, DOLLS and TEDDIES

The playthings we remember from childhood hold a special place in our hearts, but in general the more playworn they are, the less valuable they are likely to be. Teddy bears and dolls by the great makers of the late 19th and early 20th centuries, such as Steiff, Jumeau and Bru, will usually fetch high sums even if worn, as will any exceptionally rare toy. As a rule, more modern toys should be in perfect condition – known as 'mint and boxed' in the collecting world – if they are to fetch high sums.

British company Chiltern introduced the 'Ting-a-Ling' as part of a series of musical bears. Identified by a large head and feet, and widely spaced ears, he produces a charming musical tinkling sound when moved. Chiltern is known for its high-quality bears and this example, which dates from the years after World War II, is in excellent condition. 30.5cm (12in) high **£350-450**

WHAT MAKES A TOY VALUABLE?
Rarity and nostalgia boost prices

The toy market is driven by nostalgia, as many collectors seek to be reunited with familiar toys from their childhood. Condition and rarity are crucial factors, as is an association with the major names in toy-making, such as Steiff and Jumeau for teddy bears and dolls, or series of films such as Star Wars and James Bond for figures and cars.

Many factors determine the value of a toy but the most important is rarity. It is worth researching the market because it is full of surprises. For example, brightly coloured teddy bears are often rarer and more valuable than their gold-coloured equivalents. Often the most desirable vintage toys were unpopular objects in popular ranges when new. Few children wanted an action figure of the Star Wars character Yak Face in 1977 – now he's worth £1,000, five times as much as a popular character such as Han Solo.

Condition is also extremely important – a damaged or uncarded (with no packaging) Yak Face is worth substantially less than £1,000. In general, mint condition toys from before the 1980s are rare and fetch the highest prices. Some wear as a result of play is accepted on items such as teddy bears, but any damage normally decreases value. Boxed items and those with original makers' labels or tags are the most collectable. Boxes should be in excellent condition to command the highest prices.

Would you believe it?

The space race of the 1950s and 1960s inflamed the public imagination. Manufacturers in Japan responded by mass producing space-themed toys, which are rocketing in value today. Rare, large and early robots by well-known makers are likely to be worth the most, particularly if they have complex mechanisms. Look for toys by Alps (which printed its name in full), Masudaya (marked 'TM') and Yonezawa (marked 'Y' in a flower). Excellent condition will increase value substantially.

▲ **Unique design**
Reminiscent of *Forbidden Planet's* famous Robby, this robot toy by quality maker Alps has a unique design and transfers. The rubber hands are prone to perishing but this example is still in good condition. It also still has its box, which features an amusing and appealing graphic – all of which adds value. 1958 25.5cm (10in) high **£1,500-2,500**

◀ **Classic puppet**
Prices range for Pelham Puppets range from £10 for new and common puppets to £1,500 for rare puppets such as Wolf, King, Crow, Frog and 1960s Thunderbirds characters. This witch is not rare but she is a well-loved character in good condition with original box.
1963 33cm (13in) high **£80-120**

◀ **Look for brand names**
Advertising vehicles with well-known brand names are a significant part of the die-cast collecting market and rare examples can be valuable. This van is popular with collectors of Corgi toys for obvious reasons and tends to be one of the most valuable pieces in the Bedford range. 1960-1962 8.5cm (3½in) long **£350-450**

▲ Search for a set
Lead figures enjoyed a golden age between 1893 (when William Britain introduced his 'hollow-casting' method) and the 1950s (when they were replaced by cheaper, safer plastics). Most Britains boxed sets will command more than £100 in good condition. Rare sets might fetch up to £2,000. *c.*1950 **£120-180**

▲ Character collectables
The popularity of cheaper German dolls forced French doll-makers to join together in 1899, forming the Société Française de Fabrication des Bébés et Jouets (S.F.B.J.), in an attempt to challenge the market. This well-modelled laughing boy is one of S.F.B.J.'s earliest character dolls. *c.*1910 43cm (17in) high **£850-900**

▲ Popular colours
A Mattel Hot Wheels Hotbird, no.2014. The range (released in 1968) is not as desirable as Dinky and Corgi but there is a collecting base. Pink and purple cars are rare, probably as they were considered 'girly' so fewer were made. Consequently, they are more likely to be valuable. 1978 7.5cm (3in) long **£20-30**

Look for the big names

A famous manufacturer is likely to attract collectors and is often a good indicator of quality, which will further increase value. Bisque doll manufacturers which attract collectors include: Jumeau, Simon & Halbig and Bru. Steiff, Merrythought and Farnell bears are desirable, as are model cars by Dinky and Corgi. Look out for marks on the back of a doll's head or labels on a bear to help with identification.

Fakes are known to exist for many of the most valuable toys, so it may be worth consulting an expert or a specialist auction house, such as Vectis, Christie's South Kensington, Wallis & Wallis or Special Auction Services, if you think you have a toy by one of the top makers. Good provenance can reassure a buyer about a toy's pedigree, help you to identify its age and increase its value. Save photographs of the original owner with their toy. Finally, remember that a bear or doll with an appealing expression will usually find favour.

◄ All in the name
Early bears by the German Steiff factory attract famously high prices, but even later Steiff bears, such as this Zotty bear (*c.*1955), are valuable. Don't confuse it with the rarer Steiff Petsy bear (*c.*1929) or Zotty copies by other manufacturers. Steiff Zotties can be identified by their light-coloured bib. 36cm (14in) high **£150-200**

► Film and television appeal
Toys associated with popular TV programmes and films are often avidly collected by fans. Early Star Wars action figures are extremely valuable, particularly in their original packaging. Some figures, such as this Earlybird Luke Skywalker, are rare and even unboxed examples are valuable. *c.*1978 9.5cm (3¾in) high **£175-250**

TREASURE SPOTTER'S GALLERY
Dinky toys

Originally intended as accessories to Hornby trains, Dinky toys are now avidly collected in their own right and can sell for anything between £10 and £20,000. Value is dependent on the condition of the toy and its box as well as rarity and desirability. If you have a model in good condition from the 1930s – Dinky's 'golden age' – you may be on to a winner.

◄ **Early Trojan van**
The Trojan van was made in various colours and advertising transfers. Most variations were in production for at least two years but the Oxo van was only produced during 1954, making it rare. Collectors might also be drawn to this Oxo van as it was one of the earliest Trojan vans to be released. 1954 **£550-650**

"Dinky toys were popular playthings but, unless you have a rare example, condition is all if you want to sell."

MARC ALLUM BBC *ANTIQUES ROADSHOW* SPECIALIST

▲ **South African model**
During the 1960s, a small number of Dinky toys were shipped to South Africa without being assembled or painted to avoid import duties on luxury goods. They were then finished in unusual colours, such as this mid-green example. South African Dinky models are rare, leading to the high price of this model. 1966 **£400-600**

▲ **Pre-war plane**
Dinky began making large numbers of aeroplanes just before the beginning of World War II. Production tailed off during the 1950s and 1960s, with most models taking the form of commercial airliners. Pre-war models, such as this one, are particularly prone to metal fatigue so examine your example carefully. 1936-1941 **£40-50**

▼ **Damage reduces value**
This Caravan Trailer is in such bad condition that is unlikely to appeal to many collectors. Except for the very rarest variations of pre-war models, any Dinky toys that show metal fatigue or have broken axles or replaced parts are unlikely to be worth large sums. **£25-30**

Would you believe it?

Knowing which Foden trucks are rarer than others can mean the difference between reaping a modest reward and making thousands of pounds. Dinky's Foden Flat Truck was made in several colours. In good condition, the common burgundy version is worth around £100 today while a green version is worth around £1,500. Both of these are respectable sums, but the maroon version is exceptionally rare and almost ten times as valuable as the green truck. Only produced for six months in 1952, the maroon-coloured Foden truck was unpopular with children, perhaps due to its drab colouring, and was expensive at 19 shillings.

▲ **Unpopular toy**
This particular truck was so unpopular it remained unsold in a shop, which means it is in perfect condition and even more likely to fetch a high sum. In fact, it made **£14,000** in 2003 – a substantial increase on its original price.

▲ **Common model**
The Dinky Automatic Morris Mini-Minor was a popular model that was produced for almost a decade. This bright metallic blue colour is not rare and the car has no unusual variations. Despite the very good condition of the car and its box, this example is unlikely to command a high price. 1966-1974 **£40-60**

▶ **Rare model**
Variation is usually more important than date and, in some cases, a later date can indicate a rare model. This Vanwall racing car was issued with a yellow driver and yellow hubs in 1962-1965. As models with green or aluminium hubs had previously been available, fewer yellow-hubbed models were sold, making them rarer today. 1962-1965 **£120-180**

▲ **Thunderbirds are go**
Dinky produced a range of Thunderbirds toys during the late 1960s and early 1970s, all of which are likely to fetch good prices today due to cross-market interest from Dinky and Thunderbirds fans. This model is particularly desirable as it depicts Thunderbird 2, one of the most popular Thunderbirds vehicles. 1967-1973 **£350-450**

▲ **Restoration lowers value**
Beware restoration. The Dinky Heinz Guy Van (featuring an image of ketchup, rather than a baked-bean tin – the latter was produced for longer and is less rare) can fetch more than £1,000. This model has been restored and the transfers are not original, leaving its value at a tenth of that of an unrestored example. **£150-250**

TREASURE SPOTTER'S GALLERY
Teddy bears

In 1902, US president Theodore 'Teddy' Roosevelt refused to shoot a bear cub, inspiring toy-makers to rename their cuddly toys 'teddy' bears. Many early bears are very valuable, particularly those made by the renowned German company Steiff. Other names to look for include Farnell, Chiltern and Merrythought.

◄ Chiltern Hugmee
Chiltern's Hugmee range of bears was introduced in 1923, four years after the British company made its first teddy bear. The range is popular today and many Hugmees consequently fetch good prices. This 1950s example was the largest available in the range, meaning he's likely to be rare (as fewer were sold) and valuable. 66cm (26in) high **£400-600**

▲ Chad Valley
British company Chad Valley produced bears from 1915 and became toy-maker to Queen Elizabeth (later the Queen Mother) in 1938. Chad Valley bears, such as this 1930s example, are charming, but even early examples rarely fetch more than £500. This bear also has replaced paw pads, which decreases its value. 39cm (15½in) high **£150-200**

Judith warns!

The earliest Steiff bears (those made between 1904 and c.1930) are now so valuable that many fakes have been produced, particularly in rare colours, such as dark cinnamon. Beware bears in excellent, clean and unworn condition, as most toys will have suffered some damage in over one hundred years. Clever fakers are aware of this and many artificially age their bears' fur. This is often achieved using a drill with a sanding attachment, so look for worn patches where the fur has been smoothed in a circle. Wear should be all over and look like the result of hugging and stroking. The level of stuffing should also be consistent with the level of wear – years of affection should have softened and redistributed it. The best way to spot a fake is to sniff it, as the smell of an old bear cannot be faked.

◄ Fake Steiff
The heavy wear on this teddy should arouse instant suspicion. With fur this worn, you would also expect the footpads to be damaged but they are intact and apparently original. 43cm (17in) high **£30-40**

◀ **Merrythought Punkinhead**
Established in Shropshire in 1930, Merrythought's most famous bears are Punkinhead and Cheeky. Both have low muzzles and large ears with bells. This Little Patchwork Punkie is from a limited edition of 150 with a certificate, so it may rise in value. Vintage Punkinheads and Cheekies are very collectable – in 2002 a rare Cheeky sold for £2,000. *c.*2009 20cm (8in) high **£65-85**

▶ **Farnell**
Farnell is known as the 'English Steiff' as the bears it produced from 1908 are collectable. This large 1930s bear would have been worth more had it been in better condition, as early Farnell bears are very collectable. 51cm (20in) high **£200-300**

◀ **The first Paddington bear**
Michael Bond's *A Bear Called Paddington* was published in 1958 and the small bear from Peru has been popular ever since. This example, created by British firm Gabrielle Designs in 1972 and designed by Shirley Clarkson, was the first toy version of the famous character, which makes him more valuable than other more recently mass-produced Paddingtons. 1972 45.5cm (18in) high **£40-60**

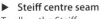

▶ **Steiff centre seam**
To allow the Steiff factory to use mohair most economically, every seventh bear's head was made by joining two smaller pieces of fabric, rather than using one larger piece. Bears with centre seams are consequently six times rarer than bears without, adding to their appeal and value. *c.*1907 51cm (20in) high **£8,000-10,000**

▲ **Schuco miniature novelty bear**
The German company Schuco (previously Schreyer and Co.) is known for the miniature bears it produced during the 1920s-1950s. The range includes clockwork and novelty bears, some of which conceal perfume bottles or, as with this 1920s bear, manicure sets. Rare colours, such as purple, are particularly valuable, while more common gold-coloured bears are still worth more than £350. 12.5cm (5in) high **£2,000-3,000**

TREASURE SPOTTER'S GUIDE
Dolls

The bisque-head doll was introduced in the late 1860s and enjoyed a 'golden age' in the late 19th and early 20th centuries. The best were made in France in the late 19th century and these generally fetch the highest prices today. Large numbers were produced in Germany in the early 20th century.

The most important factor when valuing a bisque doll is the name of the maker. The back of the head may have incised or impressed marks, such as the mould number and the maker's name or motif. Look out for the marks of French makers Jumeau and S.F.B.J. (Société Française de Fabrication des Bébés et Jouets), and German manufacturers Gebrüder Heubach and Simon & Halbig, as these may denote a valuable doll. These should be visible under the wig. You should also consult the reference section (see pages 270-271) for further details.

Next in importance are the age of the doll, which can often be calculated by looking at the style of any original clothing, followed by its size and then its condition. Finally, attractiveness plays a part.

A face with an open mouth with teeth (a feature introduced from c.1890) can add to the appeal of a doll and a pleasant expression certainly will. French manufacturers Jumeau and Bru Jeune & Cie are well-known for producing beautiful and expressive dolls wearing fashionable costumes. The dolls made by boths these factories are avidly collected and achieve high sums.

The head is usually worth about 50 per cent of the overall value of a doll and so it should be examined closely. The bisque should be smooth and clean because any damage, such as cracks and chips, will reduce value considerably even if it does not affect the face. Shining a strong light inside the head will cause cracks to show grey.

Bisque dolls price line

Not all old dolls are valuable
Between 1900 and 1930, the Armand Marseille factory (established 1885 in Thuringia, Germany) produced up to 1,000 doll heads a day using moulds, the most common of which was numbered 390. Unclothed, a 390 doll is likely to fetch less than £50 – this doll is worth more due to her period clothing. 43cm (17in) high **£100-150**

Character will add value
German company J. D. Kestner began making dolls in 1820 and bisque-head dolls in 1880s. Unusually, the company made both the heads and the bodies of its dolls, which are of high quality. This doll is impressed '192' – look out for character dolls impressed '200' as these are desirable and valuable. 1900 23cm (9in) high **£150-250**

Healthy realism in later models
All Simon & Halbig dolls are marked. Look for early dolls from this German maker that do not feature an ampersand in the name as these were made before 1905 and are rarer. This cheerful doll was made c.1920. Her rosy cheeks are typical of Simon & Halbig dolls and reflect the improved health of babies from c.1910. 43cm (17in) high **£350-450**

Barbie

Barbie, the most successful doll ever invented, was launched by American firm Mattel Inc. in 1959 and has since sold several million units. As her popularity grew, she was joined by family and friends, including her boyfriend Ken (1961), and a host of accessories. Barbie's family are not as valuable as Barbie, but they are rare so prices could rise.

The highest prices are reserved for Barbies made before 1972, particularly those from the 'ponytail' era (1959-1966). Red-headed Barbies (introduced in 1961) are rare, which often makes them more valuable than blondes or brunettes.

Other valuable Barbies to look out for include 1960s gift sets, special limited-edition dolls (in editions of less than 35,000), Barbies with bendable legs and 'fashion models' in couture clothes. These clothes must have their original labels to fetch the highest prices. Standard 'pink box' Barbies rarely achieve high sums.

The condition is crucial to the value of any Barbie. A mint condition doll, costume, or accessory in its original box will be worth two to four times more than an example without its box, particularly if the box itself is in good condition and undamaged.

▲ **Ponytail-era Barbie**
This Barbie no.6, 30.5cm (12in) tall, is in good condition and boxed. If she had her red shoes and pearl earrings and her hair was styled she would be worth more. 1962-1966 **£120-180**

Period fashion

An original wig and period clothes are desirable and should always be kept, even if shabby. But period-appropriate, non-original clothing and wigs are accepted as standard by collectors even though they will lower the value. Good-quality period doll clothes and shoes are often valuable, as they can often be used to increase the value of an unclothed doll.

In general, larger dolls are worth more, although some miniatures are very collectable. Also, the more articulated joints a body has, the higher quality it is, and the more likely it is to be valuable.

If you have a doll you think may be worth a significant sum, consult a specialist dealer or auction house, such as Vectis, Christie's South Kensington or Special Auction Services.

Eyes are a feature
This doll by German maker Heubach has a swivel head and sleepy eyes – both of which are good features that add to her value. Although pretty, her face is bland. Heubach is known for its character dolls, which are full of personality and therefore command higher prices. c.1914 57.5cm (22½in) high **£450-550**

All in the mechanism
A complicated internal mechanism is sure to add value. Frenchman Jules Nicholas Steiner was a clock-maker before he began producing walking, talking dolls at his factory in Paris. This doll has a Schilling bisque head, original period clothes and characteristic Steiner tinplate boots. c.1880 32.5cm (12¾in) high **£3,000-4,000**

Collectors pay for character
This doll shows the skilfully formed features and high-quality craftsmanship that Jumeau dolls are prized for – her large 'paperweight' eyes and inquisitive expression appeal to collectors. She also has a jointed papier-mâché body (marked 'Jumeau') and period outfit, which increase her value. c.1900 57.5cm (22½in) high **£5,500-6,500**

REVIVING YOUR FINDS
Caring for dolls and soft toys

Celluloid
Dolls made from some forms of plastic, most notably celluloid, give off fumes when decomposing. The fumes can have a corrosive effect on adjacent plastics, so display plastic dolls in a well-ventilated space and ensure they are not in direct contact with other plastic dolls. For the same reason they should be stored in complete isolation.

Whether they are brand new, old but mint and boxed (in mint condition, in its original box), or playworn, antique and collectable dolls, teddy bears and other animal soft toys can be subject to surprisingly rapid deterioration if they are not properly cared for. At the most basic level this involves, rather sadly, stopping children playing with them. They should then be protected from undue exposure to environmental factors, most notably excessive humidity and damp, and insect attack or infestation.

General rules for handling

- Oils and moisture in fingerprints can not only leave unsightly marks on many of the materials used to make dolls and soft toys, but also attract dust, dirt and even insects. In the worst cases, they can also initiate subtle chemical reactions with the underlying material, resulting in chronic surface degradation. For these reasons, whenever possible wear plain white cotton gloves when handling.
- As an additional precaution when handling, remove sharp-edged items of jewellery, especially rings and bracelets, and avoid wearing items of clothing with overly prominent zips. These may accidently snag or tear soft fabrics, or scratch vulnerable surfaces such as bisque or certain plastics.

General rules for cleaning

- The most effective cleaning technique for preserving antique dolls and animal soft toys is dusting. Hard surfaces should be very gently dusted with a soft-bristled artist's brush. Soft surfaces (clothing and animal 'fur') should be indirectly vacuumed. The technique for vacuuming through an intermediate sheet of nylon monofilament screening in order to avoid snagging or tearing fabrics is described on pages 168-169. However, in this instance use a brush attachment on the vacuum cleaner, rather than a standard nozzle.
- Beyond dusting, the cleaning techniques suitable for dolls' clothing are the same as those recommended for antique textiles. These are described on pages 172-173.

The general rules for cleaning dolls' heads and bodies made of painted wood, composition, glazed earthenware or porcelain are:

- Never attempt to clean flaking, crazed or cracked surfaces. Refer these to a professional restorer.
- Always gently brush off any dust or loose dirt first, using a soft-bristled artist's brush.
- Test for colour-fastness after dusting, especially on areas of painted decoration. If a colour dissolves after contact with a cotton bud dampened with distilled water, do not proceed, or restrict cleaning to unaffected areas.
- Depending on the surface area, gently wipe it with a cotton swab or bud dampened with distilled water. Immediately dry with soft towelling.
- If the surface remains dirty, try cleaning again, this time with a solution of 100 parts distilled water to five parts of a mild, non-conditioning detergent. It is important to re-test this solution for colour fastness before you proceed with cleaning.
- Assuming the solution passes the colour-fast text, apply as with distilled water described above. Immediately rinse by gently wiping or dabbing with a swab or bud moistened with distilled water, then dry as described above.

Making minor repairs

- Any major repairs to valuable antique dolls, teddy bears and other soft toys should be entrusted to a professional restorer. (A list of useful contacts is supplied on pages 280-283.)
- Some minor repairs are within the remit of the amateur, notably resewing loose components. Examples include costume buttons and the eyes of animal soft toys. Resewing frayed seams is also a task suitable for amateurs. Apart from the aesthetic improvement, this helps to prevent the loss of original stuffing materials from soft toys. Such repairs can be carried out with a fine sewing needle and cotton thread or, depending on the age of the piece, polyester thread.

General rules for storing

- To protect against deterioration from exposure to light, heat, moisture and atmospheric pollutants, store in dark, cool, dry, well-ventilated spaces. Cardboard storage (archival) boxes with ventilation holes are excellent for this purpose and, for additional protection, can be used in conjunction with commercial oxygen and chemical scavengers, such as 'activated' charcoal.

The sachets of absorbent agents will need to be renewed at regular intervals as recommended in the manufacturer's instructions.
- For additional protection against dust, or if you are using open shelving rather than storage boxes, dolls and toys can be wrapped individually in acid-free tissue paper, or in pre-washed, unbleached cotton muslin.
- To increase protection against insect infestation and damage during storage, always use a commercial moth inhibitor (traditionally known as 'moth balls'). Do not position them in direct contact with any doll or soft toy.
- If you are storing glove puppets, you can help to maintain their original form by stuffing the hand cavity with acid-free tissue paper or polyester wadding (batting).
- As with all vintage fabrics, always display dolls and animal soft toys in as little light as possible. Prolonged exposure to direct sunlight will cause the dyes in fabric and 'fur' to fade quite rapidly, while strong sunlight or artificial light will degrade heads and bodies made from certain types of plastic, especially celluloid, which is also highly flammable.

Display

Polished wooden surfaces, such as the shelves in some display cabinets, suffer surface degradation from plastic fumes and from direct contact with some plastics. Consequently, always stand or sit a plastic doll on a barrier, such as a small cork mat, rather than placing it directly on a polished wooden surface.

Caring for bisque dolls

Dolls' heads or bodies made of bisque (a low-fired, unglazed porcelain) are particularly prone to accumulating dust and dirt. This is due to the softness and porosity of bisque which, in addition to making it vulnerable to absorbing moisture, also serves to attract dust and dirt. Unlike repairing chips or cracks, which should be entrusted to a professional restorer, cleaning bisque can be tackled at home. The method is described under 'Cleaning unglazed ceramics' on pages 106-107, but should only be adopted with the following precaution: first dab a tiny, unobtrusive area of any painted decoration with a cotton bud moistened with distilled water. If the paint starts to dissolve, restrict cleaning to the initial dusting stage.

▶ A German Kammer & Reinhardt 101 Marie bisque head character doll. c.1909 42cm (16½in) high £2,000-3,000

REVIVING YOUR FINDS
Caring for hard toys

Antique and collectable toys and dolls are made from a wide range of materials, including wood, paper, leather, metals and alloys, plastics and diverse decorative media, notably paints and enamels. These may all deteriorate and reduce the desirability and value of the toys. To stop this happening to pristine toys, and to minimise it on playworn toys, try the preventative and remedial actions outlined below. Some basic recommendations apply to all the materials from which toys are made, while some materials require more specific care and cleaning. All benefit greatly when the toys are retired as playthings for children!

General rules for cleaning

- Regardless of the materials from which they are made, all hard toys benefit from regular dusting, which helps to inhibit a build up of dirt and grime. These can cause permanent surface discolouration or degradation and are notorious for clogging moving parts, such as axles on toy vehicles.
- For most toys, use an artist's brush or a microfibre cloth to remove dust from larger surface areas and a brush to remove it from crevices. A can of photographer's compressed air is useful for removing dust from tight corners.

Beyond dusting, the general rules for cleaning wooden, paper, leather, metal, plastic and painted toys are:
- Never attempt to clean flaking, crazed, cracked or crumbling surfaces. Always entrust these to a professional restorer.
- Never immerse any antique or collectable toy for any length of time in water or other recommended cleaning solutions, regardless of the material from which the toy is made. Prolonged exposure to cleaning agents will cause short or long-term degradation in most materials, including plastics.
- Before applying any cleaning solution, including distilled water, always test it first on an unobtrusive area of the toy. Apply it with the tip of a cotton bud, and if it induces any material changes – such as dissolving colours in painted decoration – do not proceed or restrict cleaning to unaffected areas.

Caring for wooden toys

- Generally, wooden toys are prone to the same problems as wooden furniture, including insect damage such as woodworm, and adverse reactions to humidity fluctuations. The latter can induce wood to alternately shrink and swell, which can crack it and also flake or craze painted decoration.
- For wooden toys with traditional wood finishes such as staining and waxing, caring, cleaning and stain removal techniques are described on pages 62-65. These should not be attempted on valuable wooden toys – repairs to these should be done by a professional toy restorer.
- Refer to 'Cleaning painted decoration' below for caring and cleaning techniques to use on wooden toys with painted or part-painted finishes.

Caring for paper toys

- Paper toys such as origami figures, pop-up books and model planes are vulnerable to strong sunlight (causes fading), insects (especially silver fish and cockroaches), damp and excessive humidity (cause mould growth), and dry atmospheres (cause brittleness).
- Advice on protection and maintenance of paper is given on pages 230-231.

Cleaning plastic
Some plastic toys, especially those made from Celluloid and acrylic sheeting, are easily scratched. When dusting these use a soft artist's hogs'-bristle brush, and flick it over the surface very lightly.

Caring for battery-powered toys

Many toys made since the 1960s use battery power for voice, movement or illumination. To avoid a build up of damaging corrosion on battery terminals, remove batteries when a toy is out of use. Corrosion can often be removed by applying a thick paste of baking soda and water. Wipe it off and dry well.

▶ A Japanese Yoshiya clockwork walking Action Planet Robot.
c.1958 22cm (8¾in) high
£200-300

Caring for leather toys

• Sustained exposure to strong sunlight will fade colour in toys and toy components made of leather. Equally, inadequate ventilation combined with damp or high humidity can provoke the growth of mould. Low temperatures combined with high temperatures will evaporate the natural oils in leather, resulting in major deterioration in its structural fibres. Leather toys should be kept away from heat and light sources.

Caring for metal toys

• Metal-bodied toys, such as trains and cars, deteriorate differently depending on the metal employed. Steel and iron bodies rust. Zinc equivalents do not rust but the metal can become very brittle with age.
• For tips on cleaning and caring for the metals and alloys commonly used in toys, such as aluminium, copper, iron, steel and lead, see pages 144-145. Note that most metal-bodied toys are rarely exclusively metal. They usually also have plastic and rubber elements, such

as car windows and tyres. For care and cleaning of these, refer to the relevant section on this page. Also, many metal-bodied toys are either wholly or partly painted. For these toys, also refer to 'Cleaning painted decoration'.

Caring for plastic toys

• Plastic has been a favoured medium for toy manufacture since the late 19th century, but especially since the 1950s. It presents a number of problems for displaying, storing and cleaning. This is particularly the case with early, unstable plastics such as celluloid.
• Advice on looking after plastics is given on pages 156-157. For information on plastic dolls see pages 216-217.

Cleaning painted decoration

• Apart from lightly dusting, do not attempt to clean a valuable antique or collectable toy with a painted finish that is cracking, flaking or bubbling. Rather, seek professional help and, in the interim, isolate the toy in a sealed container: many old painted finishes were lead-based and, when degraded, are toxic if inhaled or ingested.
• If a painted finish is sound it can, whether applied to wood or metal, be cleaned using the technique for painted wooden dolls on pages 216-217.

General rules for storing

• The basic rules for hard-toy storage are largely the same as for dolls and animal soft toys described on pages 216-217.
• This advice includes the use of commercially available sachets of oxygen and chemical scavengers. These stop or reduce the deterioration of some plastics and rubber. They are particularly useful in helping to preserve rubber tyres on old toy cars.
• Having the original box adds value to your toy. Store the toy in its box, away from sunlight and use a moisture absorber to keep them free from damp.

Leather toys
Leather toys are prey to insect infestation and to atmospheric pollutants such as sulphur dioxide. Combined with high humidity, the latter causes a decomposition known as 'red rot'.

Electronic toys
Consider storing metal toys or toys with electronic components with sachets of silica gel, or a similar desiccant moisture absorber. These are often used by manufacturers in electronic goods packaging to control moisture levels and inhibit corrosion of metal components.

F. SCOTT FITZGERALD
TENDER IS THE NIGHT
TENDER IS THE NIGHT
F. SCOTT FITZGERALD
SCRIBNERS

BOOKS and EPHEMERA

A first edition of a book by an author such as Charles Dickens or Jane Austen will always fetch a high price. But many first editions by 20th-century authors such as J.K. Rowling are prized even higher. These are not the only works on paper that may be worth selling. Posters are highly collectable, particularly those by a well-known artist or from a ground-breaking advertising campaign. Cigarette cards and old postcards generally sell for little, but rock and pop memorabilia can be valuable.

American first editions of the novels of F. Scott Fitzgerald can fetch high prices. This copy of *Tender is the Night* is in very good condition and unusually includes an excellent condition dust jacket. Both of these help to account for its high price. 1934 **£5,500-7,500**

WHAT MAKES PRINT VALUABLE?
Rarity and condition affect value

Many printed items were originally sold for low sums or even given away free. While some exceptional pieces are worth a considerable amount, much ephemera is still worth very little. First editions of 20th-century books in good condition can be more valuable than older volumes.

'Ephemera' is an umbrella term used to describe a range of printed or handwritten objects, usually made from paper or card. Some of the most widely collected examples include programmes, tickets, visiting cards, trade cards, magazines, postcards, and Victorian scraps. Most of these objects were created for a specific (often short-term) purpose after which they would be thrown away. Cigarette cards, on the other hand, were designed to be collected. As a consequence, many ephemeral items are rare today. In some cases, this can make them valuable but most items are worth less than £10.

Specialist subjects

Although there are many collectors who are primarily interested in ephemera, many of the highest prices are driven by other markets. Concert programmes are often bought by music fans, football tickets by football fans, Queen Victoria memorial cards by collectors of Royal memorabilia, and magazines by fans of the person or people depicted on the cover. A link to a major holiday, such as Christmas, is also likely to attract buyers, as is a notable designer name. In general, a link with something that you know to be popular will slightly increase desirability and consequently the value of the item.

An attractive design will usually make an item more appealing to buyers. For example, trade cards featuring complex etchings are more likely to command higher prices than plainer examples. Condition is crucial with all paper items. Tears,

▶ **Popular but not rare**
Fans tend to keep programmes for historic games, such as the 1966 World Cup Final, rather than those for less important games. Although this programme is popular with collectors, values remain relatively low.
£80-120

◀ **Famous tournament**
Memorabilia associated with important golf tournaments is desirable. This ticket for Augusta, the most exclusive tournament on the American tour, is very rare. Signatures by winner Ralph Guldahl, and Sam Snead, increase its value. Memorabilia from British courses, such as St Andrews, is also popular with collectors, especially if it has a link to a player or championship.
1939 **£3,500-4,500**

▲ **Daily life**
Photographic postcards are predominantly worth low sums but those that depict village life can be worth more than landscapes. Postcards showing one-off events, such as the 'Dymock Flower Show of 1910', are likely to be rare as only small numbers would have been produced. 14cm (5½in) wide **£15-25**

creases, missing pieces and crinkled edges will always reduce value and may make more common items almost worthless. Printed paper examples should be stored in an acid-free paper folder and kept away from strong light and damp conditions.

If you have an item of ephemera related to a specific subject, such as sport, it may be best to sell it in a specialist auction dedicated to that market. For example a football programme might be best sold at an auction of sporting memorabilia, such as those held by Graham Budd Auctions or Mullock's. Other pieces of ephemera should be listed on an online auction site, such eBay. Items with aesthetic appeal, such as scraps or postcards, could also be listed on Etsy.com, where they might be of use to crafters.

Condition, rarity, appeal of design and name of author or designer are also major factors that affect the value of books and posters.

▶ **Stylish splendour**
While this 2004 poster, Cherbourg Queen Mary 2 by Razzia (Gerard Courbouleix), is significantly less valuable than the Art Deco examples it invokes, it is worth more than many other recent posters. This is due to the fame of the liner and the stylish design. A similar 1930s poster might be worth thousands of pounds. 447cm (176in) high **£150-200**

◀ **Seasonal greetings**
The Christmas card became extremely popular from around 1870, with large numbers being made and posted every year. Many Victorian cards survive today and most are worth less than £30. This card is in good condition and features movable parts, making it more desirable than most. *c.*1870 12cm (4¾in) high **£40-50**

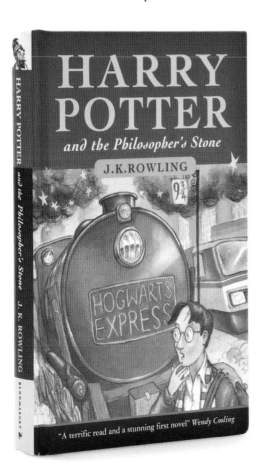

▶ **High fashion**
Vogue magazine launched in 1926. Early editions of the magazine featured sumptuous covers characterised by plain, elegant designs. These can be worth high sums today. Issues from the 1960s can be worth £20-30, while most from the 1980s onwards fetch £2-10. Prices increase for issues featuring celebrities such as the 1960s model Twiggy or Diana, Princess of Wales. 1929 32cm (12½in) high **£100-150**

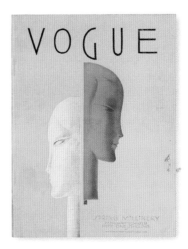

▲ **The boy who lived**
The first edition of *Harry Potter and the Philosopher's Stone* comprised only 500 copies, most of which were sent to libraries and are now in poor condition. Demand for first editions is so high that even extremely battered copies can be worth over £1,000. Good-condition examples, such as this, are worth significantly more. 1997 **£15,000-20,000**

▶ **Designed to be collected**
The value of cigarette cards is usually low, as large numbers were issued to be collected and they were mainly kept in purpose-made books. Some examples can be valuable if they are rare and appeal to more than one group of collectors, but cards that depict landscapes, such as this 1930s *Holidays in Britain* set, are unlikely to generate much interest. 1938 7cm (2¾in) wide **£5-10**

TREASURE SPOTTER'S GUIDE
Books

Old books are not necessarily valuable. Many leather-bound books are bought for around £20, purely to decorate libraries. Conversely, more recent first edition titles by popular authors can fetch five-figure sums or more, especially if they are in good condition and/or signed by the author.

Judith's lucky find

As a student at Edinburgh University in the 1970s, I wrote my dissertation on George Orwell. To do this I needed copies of all his major works, which I bought second-hand at the James Thin bookshop. The copies I bought were unremarkable, I'm afraid, but I remember looking longingly at first editions, one signed personally by 'Eric Blair' (Orwell's given name). Unfortunately, as an impoverished student, there was no way I could afford the asking price of £100 but, judging by the high sums now being paid for Orwell first editions, I should have taken out a loan! In 2010, Gorringes auction house in Lewes, Sussex, sold several excellent condition, first-edition works by Orwell. *The Road to Wigan Pier* (1937) sold for £11,000; *Nineteen Eighty-Four* (1949) sold for £5,000 and a highly important, signed, first edition of Orwell's first book *Down and Out in Paris and London* (1933) sold for £100,000! Clearly the copy I saw in James Thin all those years ago would have been a wise investment.

▶ **Orwell classic**
Keep The Aspidistra Flying was published in 1936, before Orwell became widely known. The first print run comprised 3,000 copies, of which an unknown percentage was remaindered (sold off cheaply). Examples with good-condition dust jackets are extremely rare. The good-condition review wrap makes this example exceptional. 1936 **£13,000-15,000**

▶ **Old but not valuable**
This mid-19th century Bible is a good example of an old book unlikely to fetch a high price. Large numbers of English-language Bibles have been published since the 19th century and most people who might wish to own a Bible have either inherited one or own a newly printed copy. This example is also in poor condition. **£25-35**

Book collectors are primarily interested in what are known as 'true first edition' books: the very first print run of a first edition. Some publishers state that a book is a first edition or use a series of letters or a number '1' in the series of numbers on the copyright page. When books are not marked in this way, first editions can often be identified from a match of the publishing date and copyright date. First editions can have multiple print runs (or impressions) in which errors are corrected, but in most cases these are significantly less valuable. Second, third and all subsequent editions are often worth less (typically much less).

Importance of an author's name

Not all first editions are valuable – they must also be desirable. Works by popular authors are likely to appeal to a large number of collectors, who may compete with each other to own the best examples and consequently drive up prices. Continually popular authors whose books tend to fetch high sums include: Charles Dickens, Arthur Conan Doyle, J.R.R. Tolkien, Ian Fleming, George Orwell and Agatha Christie. The author's signature usually adds value, particularly for 19th-century authors, who are unlikely to have attended large numbers of book signing events. Dedications are of less interest

◄ Rarity and desirability
This is the scarce first edition of the *The Colour of Magic*, the first book of the Discworld series by Terry Pratchett. This copy was bought direct from the publisher, Colin Smythe, Gerrards Cross, at the time of publication – reputedly only 506 copies were printed. Later issues had overlays, or stickers, with book reviews on the flaps; this copy does not. 1983 **£4,000-6,000**

► Sign of the times
Unsigned copies of Nick Hornby's first book *Fever Pitch* are typically worth around £50, while signed copies can be worth as much as £200. If you have a similar modern first edition by a living writer, it may be worth taking it to a book-signing event before you sell it. 1992 **£150-200** signed

than signatures unless the recipient is famous or connected to the author. Classic titles, such as Orwell's *Animal Farm*, are likely to be desirable. However, an author's earlier books might be rarer and more valuable than titles published after they were established and publishers could be sure their work would sell. The early works of authors still writing today, such as J.K. Rowling, Stephen King and Martin Amis, can be worth high sums due to lower print runs for earlier editions.

To fetch the highest prices, books should be complete and undamaged with an undamaged dust jacket. A missing jacket can lower value by up to 50 per cent. If you have a good-condition first edition, you can try selling it in a specialist book sale. The auction house Bloomsbury holds regular sales of books and ephemera and many other large auction houses, including Lyon & Turnbull, have specialist sales several times a year. Unexceptional 18th and 19th-century editions are often sold in general sales by smaller auction houses or can be included on an online auction site. Later editions of books published from 1920 onwards should be listed on Amazon Marketplace or on an online auction site, such as eBay.

Good, Better, Best
James Bond first editions

James Bond, the world's most famous spy, has starred in 12 novels and two collections of short stories by Ian Fleming. The first novel *Casino Royale* was published in 1953 and Bond has since acquired a legion of fans, many of whom are anxious to own first-edition copies of his adventures. Such is the popularity of 007 that even Bond novels by other authors, including John Gardner, can be worth hundreds of pounds, but the highest prices are reserved for early Fleming titles.

Good

By 1964 Bond was extremely popular and 62,000 copies of *You Only Live Twice*, the last Bond novel published in Fleming's lifetime, were pre-ordered. *The Man with the Golden Gun* (1965) and *Octopussy and the Living Daylights* (1966), both fetch around the same amount in excellent condition. Signed copies of *You Only Live Twice* are significantly rarer. 1964 **£250-350**

Better

From Russia, With Love is said to be Fleming's best book and the best Bond movie. This makes copies of the novel highly desirable. An unsigned first edition might be worth £1,000. In 2008, a copy with an inscription to 'Geoffrey Boothroyd… "Armourer" to J. Bond' fetched £15,000. This one is inscribed to a fan. 1957 **£6,500-7,500**

Best

Under 5,000 'true first editions' of Fleming's first Bond novel *Casino Royale* were printed and many were sent to libraries, leaving them in poor condition. Good-condition copies consequently command a premium. Even an unsigned first edition might be worth upwards of £10,000. This record-breaking example features the inscription 'To / the power behind / the publishers' throne! / from / the author / May 1953'. 1953 **£25,000-30,000**

TREASURE SPOTTER'S GUIDE
Posters

Large and striking posters can be valuable, especially if they show a popular brand, film or holiday destination. Key names are also vital – the work of artists such as the Czech-French Alphonse Mucha and Ukranian-French Adolphe Mouron Cassandre realise high prices.

The name of the artist who designed a vintage poster has the biggest influence on value. The next factor which affects price is the style of the design, then the condition, and finally its visual appeal. Bright colours and attractive imagery are keenly collected, as are posters in styles such as Art Deco.

Posters that are large, but easy to display, are popular. Folding, tears and stains will all reduce value, particularly if the image is affected. Conversely, professionally backing a poster on to linen can enhance its appeal. Most vintage posters are bought to be displayed in modern houses. As a consequence, value often increases with a poster's visual appeal. Posters advertising popular

films, classic or cult favourites are likely to attract a large collecting base, which will help to push prices up. An iconic poster design will increase value further. Posters for lesser-known films will appeal to a smaller market but can be worth high sums if they were designed by a famous artist, such as the American Saul Bass. Some film posters are reissued if a film is re-released and many have been reproduced from photographic images of the originals. These later copies are almost always less valuable than the originals.

The value of product posters is dependent on the brand and the item depicted. Posters for popular brands, such as Guinness, invariably fetch more

Poster price line

Recent but valuable
Posters from the 1980s onwards are often less valuable than earlier examples but popular or controversial images can still fetch high sums. This 'United Colors of Benetton' poster was infamous on its release and has since won numerous awards for its striking imagery and controversial decision not to feature the company's product. 1989 79cm (31in) wide **£120-180**

War effort
Most war posters fetch under £200 with values increasing for striking and memorable images designed by notable artists. This 'Salute the Soldier' poster was designed by Englishman Abram Games, who would go on to design the 1951 Festival of Britain logo. The strong primary colours and stark typography are typical of Games' desirable designs. 37cm (14½in) high **£350-450**

Pleasant views
Railway posters are enthusiastically collected by fans of the railways, fans of British graphic art and those with connections to the places depicted. This cross-market interest is likely to increase value. 'The Yorkshire Coast' was painted by Frank Sherwin, who, along with Frank Mason and Charles Shepherd, is one of the most desirable names in railway poster design. 122cm (48in) wide **£1,000-1,500**

than posters for lesser-known brands. As with film posters, a strong design by a notable designer, such as Frenchmen Jean Carlu, Paul Colin or Bernard Villemot, has wide appeal.

The art of travel

Travel posters, which enjoyed a 'golden age' from the 1920s to the 1960s, are also strongly collected. Bright, fresh colours and evocative depictions of popular resorts are likely to appeal to buyers, but the highest prices are paid for Art Deco ocean-liner and railway posters by popular designers such as Cassandre. As well as style and a designer name, a well-known company can also have a strong effect on value. White Star, P&O and Cunard are the biggest names in sea travel; BOAC and Air France in air travel; and the major regional railways, including London and North Eastern Railway (LNER), are sought after in rail travel.

Auction houses, such as Bloomsbury and Onslows, frequently hold specialist poster sales. These are likely to attract large numbers of collectors and consequently generate the highest prices for the best posters. Unappealing posters by unknown designers, or those advertising little-known brands or films, can often be sold in online auctions.

Judith's lucky find

It's always wonderful to be able to tell someone who has visited the BBC *Antiques Roadshow* that something they've brought in is incredibly valuable. One of my favourite moments came a few years ago, when a man visited my table with four posters by French Art Deco artist, Jean Dupas. He'd bought them (as part of a lot of 120) when he was an 11-year-old child for 50p, which represented all his pocket money at the time. I was bowled over. Art Deco designs are highly popular and Jean Dupas is one of the best-known artists in the style. His work is extremely rare and the best examples are worth up to £10,000.

◀ **Advertising power**
This advertisement from 1928, 116cm (45¾in) high, is for the New York department store Arnold Constable. It features mannequins posed as the Three Graces and dressed in past, present and future fashions. It is worth £3,000-4,000.

Sun and snow
The value of skiing posters is largely based on the image. The best examples, such as this poster designed by Sascha Maurer, are highly stylised and suggest speed, glamour and bright sunshine. Further value is added if the poster was designed by a well-known artist and if it advertises a notable resort that many people will have visited. c.1938 106.5cm (42in) high **£3,000-4,000**

Alphonse Mucha
The languid ladies of Czech artist Alphonse Mucha have come to epitomise the Art Nouveau movement. Large, early and rare examples of his work, such as this poster, are likely to fetch the highest prices, but even small and minor works, such as Mucha's posters for Lefèvre-Utile biscuits, can be worth hundreds of pounds. 1897 109cm (43in) high **£8,000-12,000**

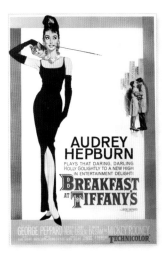

Breakfast at Tiffany's
This poster, designed by American Robert McKinnis, is arguably the most famous in cinematic history. Foreign-language examples can fetch hundreds of pounds but large, English-language examples are significantly more valuable. Posters for this film featuring different artwork are less desirable but can still fetch high sums. 1961 152.5cm (60in) high **£15,000+**

TREASURE SPOTTER'S GALLERY
Rock and pop memorabilia

Items used or owned by the biggest stars can fetch thousands of pounds. Records, tickets, posters and autographs are typically worth less, but can fetch high prices if they are appealing, rare and the artist has a dedicated following. The Beatles and Elvis Presley are among the most sought after. In general, eye-catching memorabilia that shows the stars at their best is likely to have fan-appeal.

◀ **KISS dolls**
American toy manufacturer Mego Corp. held the licences for numerous franchises from 1970 onwards and produced high-quality dolls that are popular with collectors today. These KISS dolls are very rare and sought after, particularly in a full set. Their value would be higher if they retained their original boxes. Single dolls are worth under £100. *c.*1977 33.5cm (13¼in) high **£550-650** the set

▲ **Rolling Stones programme**
Good-condition concert programmes can be valuable if they were produced for a popular artist's early or important concert. Signatures from the artists involved will significantly increase value. This Rolling Stones programme is valuable because it not only features autographs from all the band members, but also soul duo, Inez and Charlie Foxx. 1963 **£700-1,000**

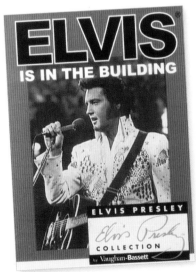

▲ **Elvis poster**
Elvis memorabilia produced during the star's lifetime is highly desirable, although his fans are growing older and prices may soon level out. Later pieces are less likely to fetch high sums, particularly if, like this poster advertising Elvis-inspired furniture, they are only loosely connected to Elvis' music or films. 2002 87.5cm (34½in) high **£35-45**

◀ **Spice Girls clock**
In general, mass-produced memorabilia from the 1990s, such as this Spice Girls clock, are only fetching low prices, even in mint condition. Values could possibly rise as those who supported 1990s artists as teenagers become adults with disposable incomes and begin to collect nostalgically. 1997 30.5cm (12in) high **£20-30**

◄ Madonna picture disc
Vinyl picture discs were made from the 1970s. As sound quality is often poor, value is primarily dependent on the popularity of the recording artist and the visual appeal of the artwork. This Madonna 'Crazy for You' disc is consequently more desirable than many examples. Rare discs by popular artists can be worth more. 1991 28cm (11in) high **£20-40**

► John Lennon's job card
Items of personal ephemera are likely to be valuable, particularly if they relate directly to the star's music career. However, even unrelated pieces, such as John Lennon's

waterworks job card from 1959, can fetch **£7,000-8,000**. In 2011, a letter from Paul McCartney asking an unknown drummer to audition for The Beatles sold for over **£40,000**.

Judith warns!

Many supposed Beatles autographs are actually printed. Look for variations in the lines caused by ink flow and the indentation sometimes left by the pressure of a pen. Once you have established that a signature isn't printed, it must be proved genuine. Unfortunately, autograph books and photos were often signed by roadies or secretaries, or by one or two Beatles on behalf of the whole band. Provenance, such as an eyewitness account, is crucial.

◄ Whose signatures?
This autograph book features the genuine signatures of Paul McCartney and George Harrison. Unfortunately 'Ringo Starr' is also by Harrison and the John Lennon signature is by an unknown hand, which greatly decreases the value. The damage and stains will lower the value further. 1967 11cm (4½in) wide **£500-700**

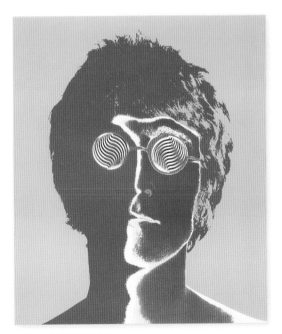

▲ John Lennon poster
Richard Avedon's 'John, Paul, George & Ringo' posters are considered the first major rock star posters. In addition to the Beatles connection, the artwork on these posters is extremely striking and in the desirable Pop Art style, which is likely to attract buyers. This edition has larger dimensions than others, further increasing value. 1967 79cm (31in) high **£2,200-2,800** set

▲ Signed photograph
While autograph books are collected, signed photographs make a more attractive display and prices rise accordingly. This example, which features all four Beatles with the autographs near the appropriate band member, is in exceptional condition. The great provenance – the vendor acquired the signatures following a concert at the Glasgow Odeon in December 1965 – ensures it will be desirable. 20cm (8in) high **£3,000-5,000**

RESTORING YOUR FINDS
Mounting artwork

Before the 1980s, most drawings, watercolours and prints were mounted on card containing acid. When this card deteriorates the acids discolour it, often affecting the artwork. To prevent this from happening, or to minimise damage, the artwork should be re-mounted on acid-free card.

YOU WILL NEED

Craft knife or scalpel

Tweezers

Scissors

Pencil

Cutting board

Mount-cutter kit

Acid-free card/mounting board

Single- and double-sided acid-free adhesive paper tape, 2.5cm (1in) wide

Judith warns!

If the artwork is rare, valuable or fragile, entrust the work to a professional restorer or framer. If any pigment in the artwork has become stuck to glass in a frame, stop and seek professional help.

Mounting artwork

1 Remove the artwork from its frame. You may be able to pull the over-mount and backing mount apart with your fingers. If not, cut through the adhesive strips using a scalpel or craft knife. Use the same method to remove any intermediate mounts. If the artwork is secured to the backing via a triangular envelope at each corner, ease it free. If it is fixed with adhesive corner strips (as in step 3), try gently pulling them off with tweezers. If still stuck, and the strips are discoloured, get professional help. If not discoloured, cut them flush with the edge of the artwork.

2 Using the old mounts as templates, draw the outlines of the new acid-free mounts with a pencil. Then, working on a cutting board, use a mount-cutter kit (available from most craft stores and artists' suppliers) to cut out the new mounts. Instructions on making bevelled edges and how to cut from the rear of the card are supplied with the kit.

3 Hinge the backing mount and over-mount together with 2.5cm (1in) acid-free, single-sided adhesive paper tape, as shown. Then position the artwork on the backing mount, aligned with the aperture in the over-mount and, again, fix the corner with strips of single-sided acid-free tape.

4 Cut small squares of double-sided, adhesive paper tape. Remove the protective film from one side of each square and secure along edges of the reverse and the front of the intermediate mount. Position the intermediate mount over the artwork, remove the protective film from the other side of the tape, and secure on the backing mount.

Caring for books

Books are prone to damage from damp, too much light and attack by moths, mice and silverfish among others. They should be handled with care to prevent the spine from splitting or pages from falling out.

Store or display books in a clean, dry, well-ventilated atmosphere and away from radiators and strong light.

Bookshelves should be deep enough to support the entire underside of all the books placed on them. Do not cram the books onto the shelves or you may damage the spines when you retrieve them.

Dust books regularly with a hog's hair brush. Never open an old or valuable book so that it lies flat at 180 degrees. Always open a book to less than 120 degrees and support the covers with blocks of foam or another soft material – rolled-up hand towels are ideal.

Foxing – the brown spots or speckles that can appear on pages, particularly at the edges – was previously removed using a solution of bleach. The marks are caused by a form of mildew combined with iron (ferrous oxide, from which the condition takes its name) in the paper. It is currently thought that unless the marks obscure the text they are best left alone.

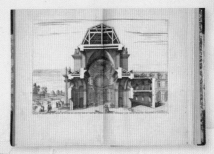

▲ **Architectural drawings**
This book of drawings *c.*1700 by Frenchman Antonie Le Pautre, has stains and foxing. Without them it may be worth twice its value. £550-650

▶ **Complete the mount**
Remove the protective film from the tops of the adhesive paper squares on the upper side of the intermediate mount. Fold the hinged over-mount in position on top of the intermediate mount and artwork, and press down to secure the tape.

REFERENCE

The marks and motifs used to identify items can be useful when researching and valuing items we own today. From the shape of a chair leg to the flower painted on a Chinese vase, knowing what clues to look for can help. The following pages contain the most common features. With a little detective work, you can use them to work out the date and maker of pieces you own.

Top left: chairback shapes See pages 248–251.
Top right: Oriental motifs See pages 258–259.
Centre right: costume jewellery marks See pages 268–269.
Bottom left: ceramic marks See pages 254–257.
Bottom right: glossary See pages 272–277.

Selling your treasures
How do I get the best price?

Once you have identified the treasures in your home and decided to sell them you need to select the sales channel that will give you the best price. But how do you choose the right one? And what do you do next?

Do your research

Before you decide to sell any of your treasures, establish exactly what you have and get a feeling for the market price. Check with a reputable antiques price guide or a collectables handbook and price guide. You can also get a good feel for current prices on the internet, specifically specialist dealers and auction house sites, as well as general markets such as eBay. As to selling, you have many alternatives: at auction, to a dealer, via newspaper advertising, on a stall at a car boot sale or online.

An auction house will sell your item for a fee, known as commission or the seller's premium. It will only accept items, or groups of items, it believes will sell. The seller is paid around 30 days after the sale. A dealer, who may have a shop or sell via a website, will pay you immediately for your pieces. If you sell through an advertisement in your local newspaper, at a car-boot sale or online you will be responsible for the whole process – from advertising and displaying your goods to taking the money and delivering them.

Selling at auction

In an increasingly competitive market, sale by auction could be the best way to achieve the optimum price for your goods. Few other venues attract such a diversity of buyers and bidders across the globe. Most auction houses list their sales online and through 'portal' sites such as www.the-saleroom.com or www.invaluable.com. Buyers can usually bid through the auction house's website or through these portal sites, which host catalogues for hundreds of auction houses and handle bids on auction day.

The staff at your local auction house will be able to advise you on the value of items you wish to sell and whether selling at auction is the best way.

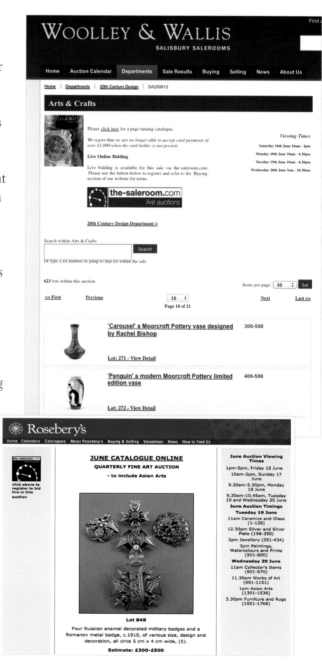

▲ **Selling at auction and online**
Most auction houses post their catalogues online, giving you access to a global audience. Buyers can leave a bid with the auction house or bid by telephone or online if they cannot be in the saleroom when your lot is sold.

Selling at auction

- If you have numerous or particularly large items, the auction house will send a valuer to your home to offer impartial, confidential advice. If you have a few smaller items, it may be worth taking them to the auction house when there is a free valuation day. The valuer will provide free pre-sale estimates.
- Many auction houses have a minimum lot value requirement. If your treasures don't amount to that you will have to sell through a different channel. If they do, you should set a reserve or minimum value below which you are not prepared to part with the object, in consultation with the valuer.
- Most auction houses suggest that the lots are sold at the 'auctioneer's discretion', which gives them a 10 per cent leeway on the lower estimate printed in the catalogue. If you don't agree, ask for a fixed reserve.
- Once the value has been agreed, the valuer will give you a receipt which represents your 'good title' (that you own the objects and have the right to sell them) and your instruction to sell them.
- Prices for selling at auction vary considerably, so you should ask about the commission charges (the average is 10 to 15 per cent plus VAT) and any other fees which may be made for such things as

▲ Selling at auction gives you access to impartial advice
An auctioneer will give you advice to help you to get the best price for your item, as here at Lyon & Turnbull in Edinburgh, but remember that there will be fees to pay.

photography, insurance (often 1.5 per cent of the hammer price plus VAT), transport, lotting fees, internet marketing and advertising fees. When added together these can be considerable.
- Make sure you want to sell before consigning. If you decide to withdraw your lot you will be charged as much as 10 per cent of the mid-estimate, along with any photography charges and VAT.
- Ask the valuer how soon you will receive your money. A good auction house will send you the sales results within 48 hours of the auction. Many will guarantee to pay within 28 days of the sale.

◀ A record price
Expertise at provincial auctioneers Woolley & Wallis in Salisbury, Wiltshire, helped the seller realise a record-breaking £3,900,000 for this extremely rare and large (19cm [7.5in] long) Qianlong period Chinese Imperial white jade carving, depicting a recumbent deer with her young, on a wooden stand.

For more information, see the box above. A number of auction houses are listed on pages 278-281. Look online or in the telephone directory for details of your local auction houses. If possible, look at their websites – this will give you an idea of the sort of goods they sell and you will be able to research the fees they charge to sellers.

If you think you have a specialist item – such as an Oriental vase or Dinky toy – you may want to contact a specialist auction house. While many local auction houses do not have specialist expertise on offer at regional and London venues, you may still get a good price for your items there. If all lots are

listed on their website, antique dealers and collectors will be able to find them and bid on them on the day of the sale by telephone or online by leaving a 'commission' bid (a maximum sum they are willing to pay which the auctioneer will include in the bidding).

Top London houses, such as Christie's, Sotheby's or Bonhams are the best channel for more esoteric items. With the advent of the internet and increased marketing by good provincial rooms, world-record prices are regularly achieved outside of the capital. In May 2011 at Woolley & Wallis in Salisbury, Wiltshire, an Imperial Qianlong white

CAR BOOT SELLING TECHNIQUES

- Make sure your treasures are as clean as possible.
- Label the object and add the price (remember that you will be expected to give a discount).
- Plan to arrive as soon as it opens to set up your stall in a good position – bear in mind that most people will turn right as they enter.
- In winter, take warm clothes and a flask of hot drink; in summer go prepared with sunblock, a hat and plenty of water.
- Remember you will need lots of loose change, a table and your biggest smile.
- Cover your table with a plain, neutral-coloured sheet or tablecloth – fussy fabrics and vibrant colours will compete with your objects.
- Don't put too many treasures on the table – it will look cluttered and hide items from your customers.
- Provide bubble wrap for fragile objects and carrier bags for bulky items.
- Greet visitors and chat to them. Answer as many of their questions as you can.

▲ **Make your best pitch**
If you set out your stock in a tidy and organised way it will help you to sell. If you discover someone is interested in something specific you will be able to find it quickly, and it will show that you mean business and know what your items are worth, helping to discourage 'silly' offers.

jade deer sold for £3,900,000. One month later, Lyon & Turnbull in Edinburgh sold L. S. Lowry's The Hawker's Cart for £667,250. In both cases, it is unlikely a higher price would have been achieved if they had been sold in London. Sometimes, location does matter. Lowestoft porcelain almost invariably does exceptionally well at the specialist Lowestoft Auctions in the Suffolk town.

Most valuers and staff at auction houses are friendly, informative and helpful. If you find someone that is not, simply take your item and try another auction room.

Selling to a dealer

You will have to decide whether to approach a general or specialist dealer. General dealers buy and sell most antiques while specialists deal in one area and are unlikely to be interested in anything else. You will find details of your local antiques shops in the telephone book or online. For specialists contact BADA (The British Antique Dealers' Association www.bada.org) or LAPADA (The Association of Art and Antique Dealers www.lapada.org).

As a rule, it's better to take more valuable objects to a specialist dealer but remember any dealer has to make a profit. They may offer you no more than half the price they will sell for. Dealers have to consider whether the piece needs any restoration, which can be expensive. If you are not happy with the offer, try another dealer.

The good news is that if you do sell to a dealer you will probably be paid in cash immediately. Another option is that the dealer may offer to sell the object on your behalf. They would then take a commission, which you would have to negotiate. You might agree a 20 per cent commission (which is less than many auction houses charge when you add up all the costs). If the object was bought from a particular dealer, it's always a good idea to contact that dealer first as they may be happy to buy it back.

Selling at a car-boot sale

If your treasures include many pieces worth less than £50 it may be best to pay for a pitch at a car-boot sale (prices range from £5–£50 – many are under £10). Your local newspaper will list upcoming events. It may be worth asking friends or neighbours if they can recommend a car-boot sale that is well organised and likely to be well attended. Plan ahead using the tips in the box above and be prepared for a busy – and hopefully profitable – day. Don't accept 'silly' offers (until possibly late in the day when you don't want to pack all your unsold items up and take them home). And watch out for pre-opening 'swoopers'. These are professional traders who'll try to buy your stuff cheap. They can be intimidating – but stand your ground and they soon back off.

If you have lots of more expensive pieces it could be worth applying for a stand at a local collectables fair or market (check prices in local newspapers). How well you do is dependent on how desirable your stock is and how realistic your prices are. Most people will ask for your 'best price', so be prepared to haggle and give at least 10 per cent off.

Advertising in a local newspaper

Most local newspapers take classified advertisements and increasingly include them on their websites. It is extremely important to describe your object correctly and remember that strangers would have to come to your home to view it. You must check that this will not invalidate your household insurance if anything were to go missing, either at the time or subsequently.

Selling online

Selling online is extremely easy. The instructions will take you through the process and offer plenty of help. There are also courses online to assist you.

The first step is to set up an account with a site such as eBay. You have to provide them with details of a valid credit card, debit card or bank account and tell them how you will pay your seller's fees and receive payment. You need an active email account and you will have to become a registered member – providing contact and personal information including your date of birth.

You will be charged a nominal fee for every item you sell. There are various methods of selling in addition to the auction system, such as 'Buy it now' or 'Make me an offer', but you will be charged extra for these services. If you want to use them, make sure they will not reduce your profit too much. Also look out for eBay's occasional 'Free Listing' weekends. If you own a smartphone there is an app you can use to monitor your eBay sales.

Always put the true cost of postage and packing in your listing – not just the cost of the stamps, but the box or envelope and so on. Or you may want to consider offering free delivery as this can generate increased interest in a item. One of the essential secrets of being a good online seller is to use bubble wrap . There is nothing more upsetting to a buyer than that ominous rattle when they pick up a much-anticipated parcel (or to a seller to have to issue

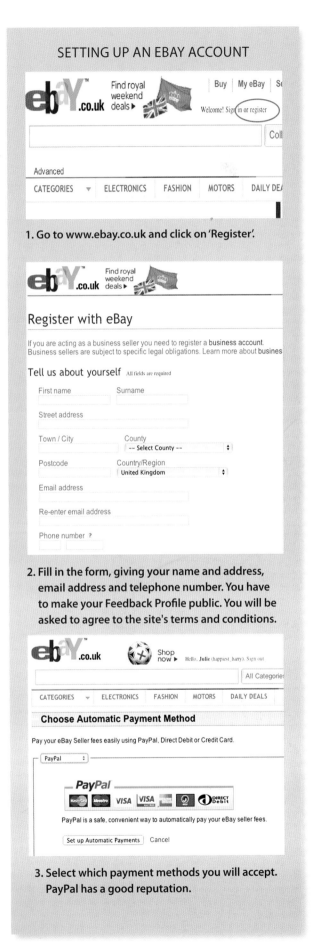

SETTING UP AN EBAY ACCOUNT

1. Go to www.ebay.co.uk and click on 'Register'.

2. Fill in the form, giving your name and address, email address and telephone number. You have to make your Feedback Profile public. You will be asked to agree to the site's terms and conditions.

3. Select which payment methods you will accept. PayPal has a good reputation.

Taking a photograph

- Use diffused natural or artificial lighting, without shadows or harsh reflections.
- Use a background that contrasts with the item. A plain, white backdrop will make your item stand out. For items that are white, use a neutral-coloured backdrop.
- Photograph items at close range and at an angle that provides some noticeable depth.
- Show scale. Place a coin or a ruler next to the item to show its size.
- Photos should be big enough to show details clearly and fill the whole frame if necessary.
- Take multiple pictures of your item so buyers can see as much detail as possible. Include pictures of labels and marks, original packaging and accessories.
- If the item has any flaws, stains, wear and tear, or any other damage, take pictures of those details so buyers know exactly what to expect. Indicate damage with an arrow or a finger.
- Consider using a tripod to produce sharper pictures using indoor lighting without a flash.
- Set the camera to a medium or higher resolution (1024 x 768 pixels or larger) to produce good-quality photos. This allows you to show bigger pictures in your listing and provides better support for photo editing, if needed, before you upload the photos to the site.
- If you are going to sell a large number of items online, it may be worth investing in a diffusing cube, such as BPS photo soft box light tent.

▲ **See things from all angles**
Take as many photographs as you can. Showing your items, with label, packaging and any flaws will help buyers to decide on their bids and minimise the number of questions you receive.

◀ **Put things in perspective**
Use a coin or ruler to show the size of your item. This large teapot dwarfs a 50 pence piece.

SELLING ONLINE

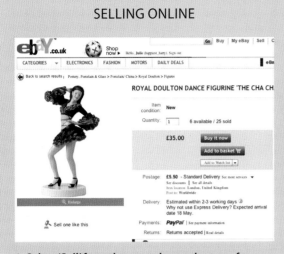

1. Select 'Sell' from the menu bar at the top of any eBay page. This will take you to the Sell page.
2. Type the name of what you are selling in the yellow search box and click 'Sell It'. The website will then guide you through the listing process.
3. Check your account regularly for questions from potential buyers – and answer them promptly.

LISTING

- Before you list any object, do your research so that you can describe it clearly.
- Look at antiques and collectables price guides and objects that have recently sold on eBay to help you select the best category and price.
- Be sure to include key words that buyers will search for and always check your spelling.
- Select a listing duration of one, three, five, seven or ten days. Make sure your selling period includes a weekend, when more buyers have a chance to view – eBay receives the highest number of visitors on a Sunday so you may want to end an auction then as there will be more eyes on screen.
- Examine your item carefully and list any damage.
- Anticipate buyer's questions. What is the item made of? Who made it? When was it made? What condition is it in? Give all dimensions.
- Be prepared to research anything you don't know in response to buyer's questions.
- Include your returns policy and handling time. This is required on every listing.

a refund). Some buyers – and sellers – insist on an insured postal service such as Special Delivery. Even if neither you, nor your customer, think this is necessary, obtain proof of postage from the Post Office. Then, if something does go missing, you can prove when and where you posted it.

Visit eBay's Safety Centre (under the Customer Support tab at the top of every screen) for advice on selling safely and for up-to-date advice on issues such as avoiding scams, rejecting suspicious bids and controlling who can bid on your items. Some sellers choose to reject buyers if they have more than two cases of negative feedback.

If a buyer hasn't paid for an item after three days, it's worth contacting them directly. If payment is still outstanding after a week, you can open an 'unpaid item case' and eBay will pursue the matter for you. Never dispatch anything until you've received payment confirmation from PayPal or through your bank.

You may have to issue a refund if an item has suffered damage due to poor packaging or if a buyer claims their item has not arrived and you have no proof of postage. Always check 'My eBay Messages' to ensure any refund claim comes from the actual buyer and refund the item through the original payment method.

PACKING

◄ **Handle with care**
Wrap your goods carefully before you post them as you will be asked to refund the full cost of an item damaged in transit. Bubble wrap is recommended.

- Use packaging which is appropriate to the item you are sending – most post offices and stationers sell boxes, envelopes and bubble wrap. Scrunched-up newspaper is a cost-effective way to protect fragile items in transit – but wrap your item in bubble wrap or tissue paper first to protect it from the ink.
- To calculate the cost of postage go to the Post Office website (www.postoffice.co.uk), taking into account the size and weight of your package – kitchen or bathroom scales may be helpful. You can even pay and print out your own postage labels for some services (although you will have to take your item to a post box or post office to send it).

IDENTIFYING FEATURES
Understanding the dates of periods and styles

Dates	Monarch	Period	French Period
1558-1603	Elizabeth I	Elizabethan	Renaissance Louis XIII (1610-1643)
1603-1625	James I	Jacobean	
1625-1649	Charles I	Carolean	Louis XIII (1610-1643)
1649-1660	Commonwealth	Cromwellian	Louis XIV (1643-1715)
1660-1685	Charles II	Restoration	
1685-1688	James II	Restoration	
1689-1694	William & Mary	William & Mary	
1694-1702	William III	William III	
1702-1714	Anne	Queen Anne	
1714-1727	George I	Early Georgian	Régence (1715-1723)
1727-1760	George II	Early Georgian	Louis XV (1723-1774)
1760-1811	George III	Late Georgian	Louis XVI (1774-1792) Directoire (1792-1804) First Empire (1804-1814)
1811-1820	George III	Regency	Restauration (1815-1830)
1820-1830	George IV	Regency	
1830-1837	William IV	William IV	Louis Phillipe (1830-1848)
1837-1901	Victoria	Victorian	Second Empire (1848-1870)
1901-1910	Edward VII	Edwardian	Third Republic (1871-1940)
1910-1936	George V		French State (1940-1944) Provisional Government of the French State (1944-1947)
1936-1952	George VI		Fourth Republic (1947-1958)
1952-	Elizabeth II		Fifth Republic (1958-)

German Period	Style	Woods	Dates
Renaissance (to c.1650)	Gothic	Oak (to c.1670)	1558-1603
			1603-1625
	Baroque (c.1620-1700)		1625-1649
Renaissance/ Baroque (c.1650-1700)		Walnut (c.1670-1735)	1649-1660
			1660-1685
			1685-1688
			1689-1694
	Rococo (c.1695-1760)		1694-1702
Baroque (c.1700-1730)		Early mahogany (c.1735-1770)	1702-1714
			1714-1727
Rococo (c.1730-1760)			1727-1760
Neoclassical (c.1760-1800)	Neoclassical (c.1755-1805)	Late mahogany (c.1770-1810)	1760-1811
Empire (c.1800-1815)	Empire (c.1799-1815)		
Biedermeier (c.1815-1848)	Regency (c.1812-1830)	Exotic timbers, calamander, amboyna, ebony (c.1800-1900)	1811-1820
			1820-1830
Revivale (c.1830-1880)	Aesthetic (c.1830-1880)		1830-1837
Historisimus (c.1830-1880)	Arts & Crafts (1880-1900)		1837-1901
Jugendstil (c.1880-1920)	Art Nouveau (c.1890-1915)		1901-1910
	Art Deco (c.1920-1940)	Oak revival, bird's eye maple, rosewood (c.1920-1940)	1910-1936
Weimar Republic (1918-1933)	Moderne (c.1920-1940)		
Third Reich (1933-1945)	Utility (c.1940-1950)	Chrome, tubular steel, bent and moulded plywood (c.1925-)	
Allied military occupation (1945-1949)	Mid-century Modern (c.1945-1980)		1936-1952
Federal and German Democratic Republics (1949-1990)	Minimalism (c.1950-1970)	Aluminium, moulded plastic, fibreglass, teak, Formica (c.1940-)	1952-
	Postmodern (c.1980-1990)		
Reunification (1990)	Contemporary (c.1990-)	MDF, plastic laminates (c.1980-)	

IDENTIFYING FEATURES
Understanding woods

The wood used to make a piece of furniture can help you to date it – essential information if you plan to sell it. These pages show the most common types used to make furniture.

Amboyna   Beech   Birch   Knotted birch

Calamander   Cherry   Chestnut   Coromandel

Ebony   Elm   Burr elm   Kingwood

Mahogany   Fiddle back mahogany   Flame mahogany   Maple

Bird's eye maple   Tiger maple   Oak   Pollard oak

Olive

Pine

Knotted pine

Rosewood

Bazilian rosewood

Satinwood

Sycamore

Walnut

Black walnut

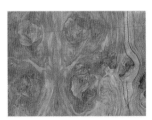

Burr walnut

Yew

Burr yew

DECORATIVE WOOD TECHNIQUES

MARQUETRY

A pictorial mosaic made up of small pieces of different coloured woods and, often, other materials such as mother-of-pearl. These are often enhanced with staining, colouring or engraving. The technique originated in Italy and spread to the Low Countries and Germany in the 16th century. Typical designs include flowers and birds.

PARQUETRY

A form of marquetry that employs geometric designs, rather than figurative or floral motifs. It is usually formed from woods with strong grains, such as kingwood and satinwood. Parquetry was popular during the French Régence and used on Neoclassical furniture.

CROSSBANDING AND STRINGING

Introduced during the Renaissance and used to frame edges. Crossbanding is the practice of laying strips of veneer at right angles to the main veneer. They may be framed with a strip (or string) of contrasting wood or metal.

FEATHER BANDING

Also known as herringbone veneering, feather banding is a refinement of crossbanding and is also used to frame edges. Two strips of straight-grained veneer are cut on the diagonal and laid side by side to form a mirror image of each other. In the early 18th century, it was often used on the finest pieces, particularly case furniture.

IDENTIFYING FEATURES
Understanding pediments

The style of pediment used to decorate the top of a bookcase, bureau, longcase clock or other item of tall furniture can help you to date it – essential information if you are hoping to sell. These pages show the most common pediment shapes in date order.

Mid-17thC protruding foliated cornice, above scrolled acanthus-carved frieze
The Netherlands

Late 17thC moulded cornice above a carved frieze
Wales

Late 17thC moulded cornice, inlaid with foliate reserves
William and Mary, England

Early 18thC stepped cornice
Queen Anne, Britain

Early 18thC swan neck and gilt ball finial pediment
Queen Anne, Britain

Early 18thC double-domed, cavetto-moulded pediment
Queen Anne, Britain

Early 18thC ogee-arched pediment, with large carved central shell
George I, Britain

Early 18thC moulded overhanging pediment
George I, Britain

Early 18thC broken-arch pediment, centred by an urn finial
George I, Britain

Early 18thC bow-shaped moulded pediment
George I, Britain

Early 18thC moulded, broken triangular pediment, centred by a Rococo cartouche
George I, Britain

Mid-18thC broken swan-neck pediment, centred by a coronet finial
George II, Britain

Mid-18thC arch-shaped cornice
Germany

Mid-18thC double-domed pediment
The Netherlands

Mid-18thC moulded, domed pediment
The Netherlands

Mid-18thC dentil-carved broken arched pediment, centred by a Grecian bust
George II, Britain

Mid-18thC broken pediment, centred by urn-shaped finial, leaf-carved frieze
George III, Britain

Mid-18thC moulded cornice, with central carved mythical beasts
The Netherlands

Late 18thC fretwork swan-neck pediment, dentil and drop cornice
George III, Britain

Late 18thC moulded swan-neck broken pediment
George III, Britain

Late 18thC broken triangular pediment, with over-projecting cornice
George III, Britain

Late 18thC arched, cavetto-moulded cornice with a central rosehead
The Netherlands

Late 18thC arched leaf-crested cornice
The Netherlands

Late 18thC moulded pediment, the crest and cornice with dentillated borders
George III, Britain

Early 19thC architectural pediment
George III, Britain

Early 19thC swan-neck pediment, with rosette-carved terminals
Ireland

Early 19thC domed pediment, with a central urn with trailing acanthus
Regency, Britain

Early 19thC astragal beaded pediment, centred by a tablet
Regency, Britain

Early 19thC domed inlaid pediment
Regency, Britain

Mid-19thC triangular open pediment, with carved dentil cornice
Victorian, Britain

Mid-19thC arched and leaf-carved pediment
The Netherlands

Mid-19thC moulded cornice with plain central pediment
Victorian, Britain

Mid-19thC broken pediment, centred by a Grecian urn, above a plain frieze
Victorian, Britain

Mid-19thC arched moulded cornice
Victorian, Britain

Late 19thC broken pediment, centred by a gadrooned, twin-handled urn
Victorian, Britain

Late 19thC stepped cornice, with a scroll-carved pediment
Victorian, Britain

Late 19thC flared, bracketed pediment
Arts and Crafts, Britain

Early 20thC cornice, carved and pierced with whiplash tendril uprights
Art Nouveau, Italy

Early 20thC curved dog-tooth cornice, fretwork pediment, turned vase finials
Edwardian, Britain

IDENTIFYING FEATURES
Understanding furniture handles

The style of handle used on a piece of furniture can help you to date it, which is essential if you are hoping to sell. This page shows the most common handle shapes in date order.

Late 17thC round with drop handle
William III, England

Late 17thC star with split pin
William III, England

Late 17thC ornate with drop
William III, England

Late 17thC round with ring
William III, England

Early 18thC ormolu, swing
Régence, France

Early 18thC bat-wing, swan-neck
George I, Britain

Mid-18thC chinoiserie, fixed
Louis XV, France

Late 18thC circular with drop
George III, Britain

Late 18thC turned pull
George III, Britain

Late 18thC husk and scroll drop
Louis XVI, France

Late 18thC with drop handle
George III, Britain

Late 18thC chinoiserie
The Netherlands

Late 18thC swan-neck
George III, Britain

Late 18thC foliate, shaped drop
Italy

Late 18thC classical, oval
George III, Britain

Late 18thC embossed, drop
George III, Britain

Late 18thC foliate, drop
George III, Britain

Late 18thC ring with backplate
George III, Britain

Early 19thC ormolu foliate
Empire, France

Early 19thC oval, drop
The Netherlands

Early 19thC lion's-head, pendant ring
Regency, Britain

Mid-19thC turned wooden pull
Victorian, Britain

Mid-19thC glass pull
Victorian, Britain

Mid-19thC foliate
Second Empire, France

Late 19thC embossed oval
Victorian, Britain

Late 19thC pierced pull
Victorian, Britain

Late 19thC solid handle
Aesthetic, Britain

Late 19thC heart
Arts & Crafts, Britain

Late 19thC
Arts & Crafts, Britain

Late 19thC hammered,
Arts & Crafts, Britain

Early 20thC
Art Nouveau, Britain

Early 20thC pierced
Art Nouveau, Italy

Early 20thC goose-head pull,
Art Nouveau, France

Early 20thC Bake-lite pull,
Art Deco, Britain

Early 20thC bronze pull
Art Deco, France

Early 20thC chrome gate pull
Art Deco, France

IDENTIFYING FEATURES
Understanding furniture legs and feet

The legs and feet on this page are shown with the dates when the styles were prevalent.
Styles tended to be used for longer in the provinces and revived at later dates.

LEGS

**Cup and cover
leg, block foot**
Charles II, England

**Bobbin-turned
block leg**
Charles II, England

**Barley-twist leg,
flattened bun foot**
Charles II, England

**Turned-inverted
leg, turned foot**
Charles II, England

**Cabriole leg,
pad foot**
George I, Britain

**Shell-carved
cabriole leg**
George II, Britain

**Cabriole leg, hairy
paw and ball foot**
George II, Britain

**Moulded
straight leg**
George III, Britain

**French cabriole
leg, scrolling toes**
George III, Britain

**Turned, tapered
ring-turned leg**
George III, Britain

**Turned, tapering
front leg, pad foot**
George III, Britain

**Reeded, turned,
tapered leg**
George III, Britain

Regency sabre
George III, Britain

**Lobed baluster,
brass cap**
Victorian, Britain

Turned baluster
Victorian, Britain

**Double scroll X-form support,
brass caps**
Victorian, Britain

**Double scroll leg,
hoof foot**
Victorian, Britain

FEET

Block foot
James I-George III

Spanish foot
Charles II-George II

Bun foot
Charles II-George II

Pad foot
George I, Britain

Irish trifid foot
George I, Britain

Claw and ball foot
George II, Britain

Hairy paw foot
George II, Britain

**Shaped bracket
foot**
George II, Britain

Ogee bracket foot
George II, Britain

Spade foot
George III, Britain

Splayed foot
George III, Britain

**Turned toupie
foot**
Victorian, Britain

IDENTIFYING FEATURES
Understanding chairbacks

The style of a chairback – especially the shape and any decoration – can help you to date the chair, which is essential if you are hoping to sell it. These pages show the most common shapes in date order. It may also help to look at the type of wood used (see pages 242-243).

Mid-17thC turned baluster back
Jacobean, England

Mid-17thC carved back-splat
James II, England

Mid-17thC arched and carved top with caned backrest
Charles II, England

Late 17thC carved top rail, double scrolls
William and Mary, England

Early 18thC back with wavy splats framed by scrolls and leaves
William III, England

Early 18thC back with inlaid vase-shaped splat
Queen Anne, Britain

Early 18thC back with moulded top rail and vase-shaped splat
Queen Anne, Britain

Mid-18thC giltwood back, with carved serpentine top rail
Louis XV, France

Mid-18thC giltwood back rail with carved flowers and leaves
Louis XV, France

Mid-18thC back with carved crest rail over pierced waisted splat
George III, Britain

Mid-18thC pierced ladder back
George III, Britain

Mid-18thC back with undulating scrolled top rail and vase splat
George III, Ireland

Late 18thC giltwood back with leaf-and-tongue border
Louis XVI, France

Late 18thC giltwood upholstered back with berry finials
Louis XVI, France

Late 18thC giltwood shaped back with arched top rail
Louis XVI, France

Early 19thC shield-shaped back with foliate and acorn-carved rails
George III, Britain

Early 19thC shield-shaped back, with carved wheat ears and with a pierced splat
George III, Britain

Early 19thC painted shield-shaped back, in the French Hepplewhite style
George III, Britain

Early 19thC Hepplewhite-style arched triple splat shield back
George III, Britain

Early 19thC inlaid shield-shaped back, with heart back and moulded crests
George III, Britain

Early 19thC bar back carved with palmettes
Regency, Britain

Early 19thC back with painted and pierced rails
Regency, Britain

Early 19thC lyre-back, with solid top rail
Regency, Britain

Early 19thC ornamented backrest
Regency, Britain

Early 19thC moulded, tapered square back with scroll supports
Regency, Britain

Early 19thC backrest decorated with a fan motif and floral marquetry
Biedermeier, Germany

Early 19thC shaped back with carved top rail
Empire, Russia

Early 19thC balloon-shaped back with paterae-carved splats
Victorian, Britain

Early 19thC pierced carved back with twisted columns
Gothic Revival, Britain

Early 19thC buttoned blue leather back, with relief-carved thistle cresting
Victorian, Britain

Mid-19thC Venetian shell-shaped back
Italy

Mid-19thC arched scrolling back with shaped vertical splat
Victorian, Britain

Mid-19thC giltwood moulded back with leaf-carved frame
Victorian, Britain

Mid-19thC back elaborately carved with flowers
Victorian, Britain

Mid-19thC back carved with dragons chasing pearls
China

Mid-19thC carved and pierced back with crest
Gothic Revival, Britain

Mid-19thC button-upholstered back
Victorian, Britain

Mid-19thC Anglo-Indian high arched backrest carved in lattice openwork
Victorian, India

Mid-19thC Thonet bentwood scrolling back
Austria

Mid-19thC waisted button back with turned and blocked fluted uprights
Victorian, Britain

Mid-19thC tracery-filled back with castellated top rail
Gothic Revival, Britain

Mid-19thC shaped back with solid top rail
Victorian, Britain

Late 19thC balloon-back
Victorian, Britain

Late 19thC shield-shaped back with vase-shaped splat
Victorian, Britain

Late 19thC papier-mâché back with painted decoration and gilt highlights
Victorian, Britain

Late 19thC lyre back
Victorian, Britain

Late 19thC reeded spindle back with a reeded frame
Victorian, Britain

Late 19thC upholstered back with carved gilt surround
Victorian, Britain

Late 19thC carved Black Forest back with a bear, oak boughs and leaves
Switzerland

Late 19thC back formed from two fallow deer antlers, with cushion
Germany

Late 19thC ladder-back
Arts and Crafts, Britain

Late 19thC tall carved and panelled back
Arts and Crafts, Britain

Late 19thC curved top rail and heart-pierced splat
Arts and Crafts, Britain

Early 20thC ladder-back
Arts and Crafts, Britain

Early 20thC back with waved splats and curved uprights
Art Nouveau, Britain

Early 20thC pierced back with oval crest and central splat inlaid with flowers
Art Nouveau, Britain

Early 20thC triple-splat back
Edwardian, Britain

Early 20thC Jacques-Emile Ruhlmann upholstered oval back
Art Deco, France

Early 20thC stylised acorn back within 'theatre drape curtain' arched frame
Art Deco, France

Early 20thC Thonet upholstered reddish-brown stained beechwood back
Austria

Early 20thC back,
Art Deco, Sweden

Early 20thC Marcel Breuer back, nickel-plated tubular steel and fabric
Bauhaus, Germany

Early 20thC Mies van der Rohe Barcelona back
Germany

Early 20thC Marcel Breuer cantilever back, leather on tubular chrome frame
Germany

Early 20thC René Herbst back, tubular steel with elasticated sprung straps
France

Early 20thC Gerrit Rietveld Zigzag oak back
The Netherlands

Early 20thC Marcel Breuer, birch plywood back
Germany

Mid-20thC Charles and Ray Eames plywood back
USA

Mid-20thC Piero Fornasetti Lyre back, plywood with silk screen print
Italy

Mid-20thC Arne Jacobsen Ant or No 3100 back, moulded plywood
Denmark

Mid-20thC Harry Bertoia Diamond back, chrome wire
USA

Mid-20thC Vernon Panton Cone back
Denmark

Mid-20thC George Nelson Pretzel back, plywood
USA

Mid-20thC Arne Jacobsen Swan back
Denmark

Mid-20thC Eero Aarniro ball back, fibreglass
Finland

IDENTIFYING FEATURES
Understanding registration marks

Marks on the base or back of many items can be helpful with identifying the maker, date and country of manufacture. Here are some of the most common marks and how to decode them.

The Design Registration mark is an aid to dating British pieces. Registration began in 1839 following the Copyright of Design Act. The mark was used from 1842. It also showed what material the item was made from (its class) and how many items were included (bundle or package). The 'Rd' stands for 'registered design'. The system is still in use.

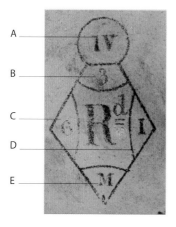

	1842-1867	1868-1883
A	A = class	A = class
B	B = year	B = day
C	C = month	C = bundle
D	D = day	D = year
E	E = bundle	E = month

◀ **A registration mark**
This printed mark on the base of a piece of ceramic shows it was a piece of earthenware made in 1872.

MONTHS

The months from both periods are shown as follows:

A – December	E – May	K – November
B – October	G – February	M – June
C/O – January	H – April	R – August
D – September	I – July	W – March

CLASS

Sometimes the clerks misclassified items, so it is possible to find a bookbinding misfiled as a carpet.

Class 1:	Metal	Class 9 :	Yarn
Class 2:	Wood	Class 10:	Printed Fabrics
Class 3 :	Glass	Class 11:	Furnitures
Class 4:	Earthenware		(printed fabrics)
Class 5 :	Paper Hangings	Class 12 (i):	Other Fabrics
Class 6:	Carpets	Class 12 (ii):	Other Fabrics
Class 7:	Printed Shawls		(Damasks)
Class 8:	Other Shawls	Class 13 :	Lace

YEAR

The letters were not used in sequence but as follows:

1842-1867 (features a number in the right-hand corner of the diamond).

A – 1845	G – 1863	M – 1859	S – 1849	Y – 1853
B – 1858	H – 1843	N – 1864	T – 1867	Z – 1860
C – 1844	I – 1846	O – 1862	U – 1848	
D – 1852	J – 1854	P – 1851	V – 1850	
E – 1855	K – 1857	Q – 1866	W – 1865	
F – 1847	L – 1856	R – 1861	X – 1842	

1868-1883 (letter in the right-hand corner of the diamond).

A – 1871	F – 1873	K – 1883	U – 1874
C – 1870	H – 1869	L – 1882	V – 1876
D – 1878	I – 1872	P – 1877	X – 1868
E – 1881	J – 1880	S – 1875	Y – 1879

The exceptions to these are: from 1-19 September 1857, the letter R was used; in 1860, the letter K was used for December; from 1-6 March 1878, the letter W was used for the year in place of D, and G was used for the month in place of W.

REGISTERED NUMBER

From 1884, designs were each marked with a number, prefixed by Rd or Rd No (Registered or Registered Number). For example, the first registered number in 1887 was 64,520 and the last was 90,482. This guide is an estimate only:

1884	1	1902	385,500
1885	19,754	1903	402,500
1886	40,480	1904	420,000
1887	64,520	1905	447,000
1888	90,483	1906	471,000
1889	116,648	1907	494,000
1890	141,273	1908	519,000
1891	163,767	1909	550,000
1892	185,713	1920	673,750
1893	205,240	1930	751,160
1894	224,720	1940	837,520
1895	246,975	1950	860,854
1896	268,393	1960	895,000
1897	291,241	1970	944,932
1898	311,658	1980	993,012
1899	331,707	1990	2,007,720
1900	351,202	2000	2,089,190
1901	368,154		

Printed marks

The following marks or systems of marking are common to one or more countries.

Country name

In 1890, the American Congress passed legislation requiring a tariff to be paid on all imports of china, glass, leather and metal. As a result, from 1891, all goods which might be imported to America were marked with the country of origin, such as 'France' or 'England'.

Made in…

A royal coat of arms in a mark shows the item was made no earlier than 1800 but it probably denotes a much later date. A country name such as 'England' underneath the mark denotes a date after 1891, while 'Made in …' and the country name usually dates from 1912.

Bone china

The word 'Royal' in a British company's name tends to date from the late 19th or the 20th centuries. 'Bone china' and 'English bone china' are marks that have only been in use since the 20th century.

US patents

American designs may be registered by patent number, design number and/or trademark. The first patent number was issued in 1836. The number recorded on an article shows the date it was registered and not necessarily the date it was made. The design patent and number protect the shape, colour or pattern of an item. The first number was issued in 1843. Trademarks – usually denoted by the symbol ™ – have been used since 1870 and are applied to names, phrases and logos.

Made in occupied Japan

From the end of World War II in 1945 until 1952, items exported from Japan to the US had to be marked to indicate that they came from occupied Japan. Pieces marked 'Occupied Japan' and 'Made in Occupied Japan' were made during this period.

Made in USSR

From c.1925 until 1991, items made in the Union of Soviet Socialist Republics (or Soviet Union) were marked 'Made in USSR'. Since 1991, the names of the individual countries have been used, for example: Russia, Estonia, Latvia, Lithuania, Belarus, Ukraine, Moldova and Georgia.

Made in German zone

From the end of World War II in 1945 until 1949, items made in the US, British, French and Soviet-occupied zones of Germany were marked as such. The marks 'Federal Republic of Germany' (West Germany) or 'German Democratic Republic' (East Germany) date from 1949 to 1990.

Other marks

Pattern numbers don't denote a specific factory. They tend to date from after 1815, usually later.

'Limited' or 'Ltd.' tend to denote a date after 1861 but were more commonly used after 1885.

In the UK, an impressed 'Trademark' can be assumed to be after 1862. For American-made items, it is after 1876.

Items marked 'copyright' date from after 1858 but are usually 20th century. The © symbol was introduced in 1914.

Déposé, the French word for patented, and the equivalent German phrase Gesetzlich Geschützt (Ges. Gesch) were first used in about 1900.

IDENTIFYING FEATURES
Understanding ceramic marks

Many ceramics are marked underneath, so turn your piece over to begin identifying the maker. Here are the most common marks in alphabetical order. Dates refer to the period of use.

Amphora
Czechoslovakia
late 19th-early 20thC

Belleek
Ireland c.1926-1946

Berlin
Germany c.1820-1837

Berlin
Germany c.1820-1832

Berlin
Germany 20thC

Bing & Grøndhal
Denmark
c.1948-1951

Boch Frères
Belgium c.1922-1930

Bristol
Britain c.1770-1781

Capodimonte
Italy c.1771-1781

Caughley
Britain c.1775-1795

Chantilly
France c.1725-1789

Chelsea
Britain Red Anchor
period c.1752-1756

Clarice Cliff, Bizarre
Britain c.1928-1931

Clarice Cliff, Fantasque
Britain c.1929-1934

Coalport
Britain c.1891-1920

Davenport
Britain c.1819-1864

Davenport
Britain c.1815-1830

Derby
Britain c.1782-1800

Derby, Royal Crown
Britain c.1891-1921

PATTERN NUMBERS

Pattern numbers may indicate a particular porcelain factory although few are unique to one factory. Use them, together with other clues, to help to identify a piece of ceramic. For example, from c.1805 Coalport started using these pattern numbers between the following dates:
1-999 were used c.1805 until c.1825;
2/1 – 2/999 were used until c.1832;
3/1 – 3/999 were used c.1832 until 1838;
4/1 – 4/1000 were used c.1838 until 1843;
5/1 – 5/1000 were used c.1843 until 1850.

▲ **Early 20th century large Coalport plate**
This plate was decorated by Frederick H. Chivers. 31cm (12in) diameter **£500-700**

254

DERBY MARKS

From 1882, Royal Crown Derby began using a series of symbols to denote the year.

These symbols can typically be found below the printed mark on the base of a piece.

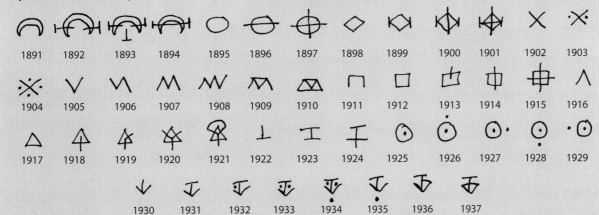

| 1891 | 1892 | 1893 | 1894 | 1895 | 1896 | 1897 | 1898 | 1899 | 1900 | 1901 | 1902 | 1903 |

| 1904 | 1905 | 1906 | 1907 | 1908 | 1909 | 1910 | 1911 | 1912 | 1913 | 1914 | 1915 | 1916 |

| 1917 | 1918 | 1919 | 1920 | 1921 | 1922 | 1923 | 1924 | 1925 | 1926 | 1927 | 1928 | 1929 |

| 1930 | 1931 | 1932 | 1933 | 1934 | 1935 | 1936 | 1937 |

Royal Doulton
Britain c.1922-

Dresden
Germany c.1800-1900

Dresden, Helena Wolfsohn
Germany c.1843-1878

Frankenthal
Germany c.1759-1762

Frankenthal
Germany c.1762-1794

Furstenberg
Germany c.1753-1780

Goldscheider
Austria c.1926-1938

Herend
Hungary c.1935-1948

Höchst
Germany c.1765-1774

Hummel
Germany c.1945-1950

Hutschenreuther
Germany c.1881-1902

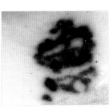

Ludwigsburg
Germany c.1758-1793

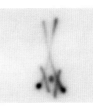

Meissen
Germany Dot period c.1762-1773

Meissen
Germany Marcolini period c.1774-1814

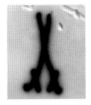

Meissen
Germany 19thC

Minton
Britain c.1863-1872

Judith warns!

Just because a piece has a crossed swords mark, it does not mean it's Meissen. So great was the quality and success of Meissen that there were few 18th and 19th-century factories that did not attempt to pass off their wares as Meissen. This mark is from a mid-18th century Worcester saucer. Even Worcester, one of England's best 18th-century factories, stooped this low.

Minton
Britain
c.1891-1902

Minton
Britain c.1951-

Moorcroft
Britain c.1904-1913

Niderviller
France c.1754-1780

Noritake
Japan c.1908-1930

Nymphenburg
Germany
20thC mark

Paris, Locre factory
France c.1773-1830

Paris, P. L. Dagoty
France c.1810-1822

Paris, Jacob Petit
France c.1830-1860

Pilkington
Britain c.1905-1914

Poole
Britain c.1930-

Rörstrand
Sweden 20thC

Rosenthal
Germany c.1891-1904

Rosenthal
Germany c.1897-1945

Royal Copenhagen
Denmark c.1923-1950

All in the mark

You can tell a lot from a mark if you know how to read it. Always check that it is under the glaze; a mark that sits on top of the glaze is likely to have been faked.

- The interlaced Ls shape signifies the factory: Sèvres.
- The 'KK' is a date mark, signifying the year 1787.
- What looks like a '119' is actually an 'NQ' signalling the painter, Nicquet (1764-1792).
- The gilt 'L' is the gilder's mark for Louis-Francois Lecot.

◀ **Sèvres saucer painted with flowers** The marks painted on the back of the saucer tell the story of its creation and add to its value. 1787 12.75cm (5in) diameter £2,000-2,500

Royal Copenhagen
Denmark c.1889-1922

Royal Dux
Bohemia c.1913-1945

Royal Dux
Czechoslovakia
1947-1990

Sèvres
France c.1845-1848

Sèvres
France c.1780-1793

Spode
Britain c.1784-1800

Spode
Britain c.1790-1833

Spode, Copeland & Garrett
Britain c.1833-1847

Spode, Copeland
Britain
c.1891-1900

St Petersburg
Russia c.1825-1855

St Petersburg
Russia c.1855-1871

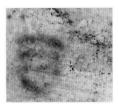

Vienna
Austria c.1749-1810

Vienna
Austria
late 19th-early 20thC

Wedgwood
Britain c.1891-1900

Worcester
Britain c.1755-1790

Worcester
Britain c.1755-1775

**Worcester Barr,
Flight & Barr**
Britain c.1807-1813

**Worcester Barr,
Flight & Barr**
Britain c.1807-1813

**Worcester Flight,
Barr & Barr**
Britain c.1813-1840

**George Grainger & Co,
Worcester**
Britain c.1889-1902

Zolnay Pecs
Hungary c.1863-1891

WEDGWOOD

Wedgwood used an impressed mark from c.1759 onwards. From 1891, 'ENGLAND' was added below it. Where there is a group of three impressed year letters, the third denotes the year.

O – 1860	V – 1867	C – 1874	O – 1886
P – 1861	W – 1868	D – 1875	P – 1887
Q – 1862	X – 1869	E – 1876	Q – 1888
R – 1863	Y – 1870	F – 1877	R – 1889
S – 1864	Z – 1871	G – 1878	S – 1890
T – 1865	A – 1872	H – 1879	T – 1891
U – 1866	B – 1873	I – 1880	U – 1892
		J – 1881	V – 1893
		K – 1882	W – 1894
		L – 1883	X – 1895
		M – 1884	Y – 1896
		N – 1885	Z – 1897

◄ **Wedgwood Jasperware**
A 19th-century cheese bell and stand.
27.5cm (11in) diam **£400-500**

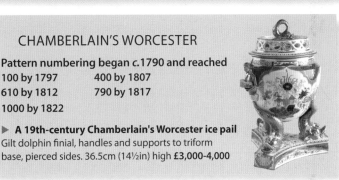

CHAMBERLAIN'S WORCESTER

Pattern numbering began c.1790 and reached

100 by 1797	400 by 1807
610 by 1812	790 by 1817
1000 by 1822	

▶ **A 19th-century Chamberlain's Worcester ice pail**
Gilt dolphin finial, handles and supports to triform base, pierced sides. 36.5cm (14½in) high **£3,000-4,000**

ROYAL WORCESTER

A system of dating a letter per year was used from 1867.

A – 1867	H – 1873	P – 1879	W – 1885
B – 1868	I – 1874	R – 1880	X – 1886
C – 1869	K – 1875	S – 1881	Y – 1887
D – 1870	L – 1876	T – 1882	Z – 1888
E – 1871	M – 1877	U – 1883	O – 1889
G – 1872	N – 1878	V – 1884	a – 1890

▲ **A Royal Worcester jar**
Jar and cover, painted by Horace Price. c.1938 16.5cm (6in) high **£1,500-2,500**

The Royal Worcester England mark was first used in 1891. In 1892, a system of dots was used with the mark, with a dot added for each year from 1892. On this piece there are 15 dots: six either side of the crown and three beneath it, indicating that it was made in 1906.

IDENTIFYING FEATURES
Understanding Oriental marks and motifs

These pages show the most usual depictions of the most common reign marks found on Chinese ceramics, as well as typical motifs found on pieces of Oriental porcelain. The marks will help you to identify and date Chinese items – vital information for selling, especially online. Be aware that many later pieces do bear marks from earlier reigns.

MING

Xuande
1426-1435

Chenghua
1465-1487

Hongzhi
1488-1505

Zhengde
1506-1521

Jiajing
1522-1566

Wanli
1573-1619

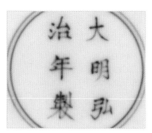

Chongzhen
1628-1643

QING

Kangxi
1662-1722

Yongzheng
1723-1735

Qianlong
1736-1795

Jiaqing
1796-1820

Xianfeng
1851-1861

Tongzhi
1862-1874

Guangxu
1875-1908

Xuantong
1909-1911

REPUBLIC PERIOD

Hongxian (Yuan Shikai)
1915-1916

ORIENTAL SYMBOLISM

Bamboo
Longevity; strength, flexibility
and resilience.

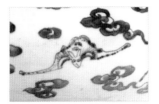

Bat
Happiness. Five bats: the five
blessings: long life, wealth,
health, love of virtue and
peaceful death.

Chrysanthemum
Longevity; the autumn. The
national flower of Japan.

Clouds
Good fortune, particularly in
many colours.

Crane
Longevity; high status.
Flying cranes indicate the wish
to become a high-ranking
official.

Dragon
Cosmic energy; high rank;
power; good fortune. Chasing
a flaming pearl, the quest for
perfection and enlightenment.

Eight Immortals
Together: prosperity, longevity.
Individually: poverty, wealth,
aristocracy, plebeianism, age,
youth, masculinity, femininity.

Eight Auspicious Symbols
Knowledge, thoughts of the
Buddha, protection, triumph of
Buddha's teaching, purity, wealth,
conjugal happiness and harmony.

Fish
Wealth; marriage and children;
also a sign of rank.

Heron
A path; wealth. With the lotus
it stands for 'May your path be
always upward'.

Lotus
Purity. The throne of the
Buddha is often depicted as a
lotus blossom.

Peach
Immortality. The peach is one
of the three abundances.

Peony
Royalty and virtue; wealth
and honour.

Phoenix
Good fortune; the empress.
Shown with the dragon,
it symbolises the perfect
marriage.

Pine tree
Longevity and noble
endurance in the face of
adversity. It is a popular and
auspicious motif.

Plum blossom
Renewal and perseverance. It is
auspicious due to its five petals
(the number five is sacred).

Three Friends of Winter
Pine, bamboo and plum
together represent longevity
and perseverance. Such virtues
are attributed to scholars.

Three Star Gods
God of Fortune carries a young
boy. God of Prosperity holds
a sceptre. God of Longevity
carries a tall staff and a peach.

Tiger
Courage and bravery. It is also
considered a protective charm.

Yin and Yang
The positive and negative forces
of the universe. Yin is unseen
(feminine), Yang seen (masculine).
Together they comprise the Tao.

IDENTIFYING FEATURES
Understanding drinking glass shapes

The style of a drinking glass bowl, stem and knop can help you to date it – invaluable information if you plan to sell. These pages show the most common shapes.

Bowl

Collar

Knop

Stem

Foot

Folded Foot

ANATOMY OF AN 18TH-CENTURY GLASS

Glass with a grey, amber or brown tinge may indicate a 20th-century reproduction. Look for joins between the bowl and the stem and/or the stem and the foot. Examples made from a single piece are 20th-century reproductions. The groups here were compiled by E. Barrington Haynes in his book *Glass Through The Ages*, first published in 1948. They have become the standard. Each represents a type of stem, with sub-groups based on the shape of the bowl or the shape or decorative nature of the stem. The dates represent the dates of popularity of a certain group.

STEM GROUPS

Group I
Baluster
c.1685-c.1725

Group II
Moulded pedestal
c.1715-c.1765

Group III
Balustroid
c.1725-c.1760

Group IV
Light (Newcastle)
c.1735-c.1765

Group V
Composite
c.1745-c.1775

Group VI
Plain straight
c.1740-c.1775

Group VII
Air twist
c.1745-c.1770

Group VIII
Hollow
c.1750-c.1760

Group IX
Incised
c.1750-c.1765

Group X
Opaque white
twist *c.1755-c.1780*

Group XI
Mixed and colour
twist *c.1755-c.1780*

Group XII
Facet cut
c.1760-c.1810

GLASS TYPES

Late 18thC
Jelly

Early 19thC
Ale

Early 19thC
Rummer

Early 19thC
Slice-cut rummer

Late 19thC
Tavern rummer

Late 19thC
Champagne

BOWLS

Bell (joined to stem, here with collar)

Bell with solid base (joined to stem)

Waisted (no join)

Thistle with solid base

Trumpet

Trumpet

Conical

Round funnel

Ovoid

Ogee

Bucket

Saucer or Pan-top

KNOPS

Air-beaded

Inverted baluster

True baluster

Annulated

Blade

Cushioned

Simple knop

Faceted

Annular

Swollen

Angular (here with internal bubble)

Propeller

Bobbin

Opaque twist

STEMS

Multiple spiral air twist

Mercury air twist

Mixed opaque and air twist

Gauze and single ply spiral

Pair of spiral gauzes

Colour twist

IDENTIFYING FEATURES
Understanding silver hallmarks

The complex system of hallmarking used in Britain and Europe dates back to medieval times and yields plenty of clues – all essential information to understand what you may own and what it is worth.

As silver and gold have long been of commercial importance, it became necessary from early times to enforce a standard of purity. A crowned lion's head mark was introduced in England in 1300. Known at the time as a 'leopart', it evolved into the leopard's head used today. It showed that silver was of the required sterling standard of 925 parts per thousand pure silver to 75 parts copper. The crown was removed in around 1821.

In 1327, a charter empowered the Goldsmith's Company at Goldsmith's Hall in London to test and mark – or 'assay' – silver, resulting in the term 'hallmark'. Since then, other assay offices have appeared.

Makers' marks were made compulsory in 1363, with a third mark introduced in 1478 for identifying the warden or assay master responsible for testing

▼ **Hallmarks found on British silver**
These four symbols are typical. They are, from left to right: the maker's mark of the silversmith; the 'lion passant' purity mark; the assay office mark; and the date letter.

LION'S HEAD HALLMARK

The crowned lion's head mark was introduced to guarantee the purity of silver. A leopard's head is used today and is associated with London's assay office.

quality. A fourth mark, known as the 'date' letter, took the form of a letter of the alphabet (using only 20 letters) that changed annually to identify the year the piece was assayed (and probably made).

After the lion passant was introduced for sterling silver in 1544, the leopard's head gradually became recognised as the town mark for London, especially when assay offices, each with its own mark, were opened in several other cities.

From 1784-1890, a tax was imposed on silver and, to prove it had been paid, a fifth mark of the sovereign's head in profile was added. For the first six months of 1785, this was intaglio (fully indented), but after this period, it became cameo (raised), like other silver marks. The mark was last used in 1890, when the tax was finally abolished.

Use a comprehensive guide book to help you to interpret a set of hallmarks.

OTHER MARKS

From 1697-1720, the silver standard was raised and 'Britannia' and lion's head marks were used (1 and 6). Other marks showing a sovereign's head indicate years of production: Elizabeth II's silver jubilee in 1977 (2); George V's silver jubilee in 1935 (3); and Elizabeth II's coronation in 1953 (4). From 1976, some assay offices in certain countries used a common control mark that became legally acceptable internationally (5).

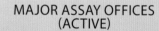

| 1 | 2 | 3 | 4 | 5 | 6 |

MAJOR ASSAY OFFICES (ACTIVE)

London
1478-1821

London
1822-present

Birmingham
1773-present

Sheffield
1773-present

Edinburgh
1485-present

Edinburgh
1759-1974

Edinburgh
1975-present

Dublin
1637-present

Dublin
1731-present

MAJOR ASSAY OFFICES (INACTIVE)

Chester
1686-1962

Exeter
1701-1882

Glasgow
1536-1964

Newcastle
1423-1884

Norwich
17thC

Norwich
1423-1697

York
1423-1700

York
1701-1856

SILVER IMPORTED INTO BRITAIN

From 1904, all items made from silver imported into the UK had to be marked to show the purity of the metal, eg '.925'. The decimal point was removed from this mark in 1973. In addition, a date letter was applied to the silver, and each UK assay office had its own mark (London is shown below) which was used.

FRENCH HALLMARKS

Marks were used as early as 1272, but the system was inconsistent. In general, before the French Revolution in 1789, up to four marks were used. These comprise a maker's mark, a community or 'juranada' mark, a city charge mark and sometimes a related city discharge mark (see below).

FRENCH CITY CHARGE MARKS (PARIS)

Charge mark
1744-50

Discharge mark
1744-50

Discharge mark
1744-50

SOME FRENCH POST-REVOLUTIONARY MARKS

Head
1793-97

Cockerel
1798-1819

Head
1809-19

Old Man
1819-38

Old Man
1819-38

Old Man
1819-38

Minerva
1879 onwards

Minerva
1879 onwards

SOME GERMAN CITY MARKS

Berlin
18thC

Berlin
19thC

Dresden
19thC

Frankfurt
17th-18thC

Hamburg
18thC

Munich
18thC

Nuremberg
19thC

Stuttgart
19thC

OTHER EUROPEAN SILVER MARKS

In general, marking systems used by European countries were inconsistent, if they existed at all. Many marks are of little use but city or country marks may be more reliable. Some of the many examples are shown below.

Florence
17th-18thC

Milan
c.1810

Rome
late 17thC

Turin
18th-19thC

Italy
after 1934

Italy
after 1934

Amsterdam
assay mark

The Hague
assay mark

Rotterdam
assay mark

Netherlands
after 1953

Netherlands
after 1953

Moscow
c.1880

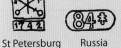
St Petersburg
dated 1742

Russia
1882 onwards

Russia
1896-1908

Moscow
dated 1782

Russia
1908-17

USSR
1927-58

Barcelona
18thC

Madrid
late 18thC

Spain
after 1881

Spain
after 1881

Stockholm
18th-19thC

Zurich
18thC

Geneva
19thC

Switzerland
1882-1934

Switzerland
1882-1934

IDENTIFYING FEATURES
Understanding gold and platinum marks

Here, the system ued for marking gold and platinum in Britain is explained. These marks will help you to identify and date a piece of gold or platinum. Many buyers will ask for this information, especially for online purchases.

BRITISH GOLD MARKS

Like silver marks, gold marks were introduced in 1300, with the earliest being a leopard's head (see page 262). A maker's mark was also required from 1363 and a date letter from 1578. From 1544, the leopard's head was replaced with a lion passant (or walking lion). In 1477, the standard was reduced from 191/5 to 18 carats and lasted until 1575, when it was superseded by the current 22-carat standard. In 1798, the lower 18-carat standard was reintroduced. It was indicated by a crown mark and remained until 1844. The crown was then used for both standards. In 1854, three more standards were introduced: 9, 12, and 15 carat. The standard was indicated by both a figure and a percentage. These were used until 1932, when the 12 and 15-carat standards were replaced by the 14-carat standard.

22 carat
to 1974

18 carat
to 1974

14 carat
to 1974

9 carat
to 1974

22 carat
1975-present

...

14 carat
1975-present

9 carat
1975-present

22 carat
Foreign imports

18 carat
Foreign imports

14 carat
Foreign imports

9 carat
Foreign imports

Edinburgh
(replaces crown)

Glasgow
(replaces crown)

Glasgow
(replaces crown)

GOLD AND PLATINUM ASSAY OFFICE MARKS

Birmingham

Chester

Dublin

Edinburgh

Exeter

Glasgow

London

Newcastle

Sheffield

York

INTERNATIONAL GOLD MARKS

As with silver marks, few countries have adopted a reliable, consistent policy of marking gold wares. In general the mark '750' should indicate 18-carat gold, '585' 14-carat gold, and '375' 9-carat gold. Marks on pieces made in the US may read '14KT' for 14-carat gold. But '14KR' indicates 14-carat rolled (or plated) gold. Always consult a specialist book to ensure accuracy.

IMPORTED FOREIGN PIECES

From 1842, pieces were hallmarked. From 1876, an 'F' was included. From 1904, each assay office used its own mark.

Birmingham

Chester

Edinburgh

Glasgow

London

Sheffield

PLATINUM MARKS

Platinum came under the hallmarking law in 1973. From 1975, all UK platinum wares are marked with orb, date and assay office marks.

Birmingham

Date letter

Imported

London

Orb

Sheffield

IDENTIFYING FEATURES
Understanding candlestick shapes

The shape and proportions of a candlestick can help you to date it, which will help you to achieve a good price. This page shows the most common styles in date order.

Late 16thC brass 'capstan'
Elizabethan, England

Late 17thC silver fluted column
William III, England

Late 17thC brass knopped stem
William III, England.

Mid-18thC silver knopped stem
George II, Britain

Mid-18thC silver baluster
George II, Britain

Mid-18thC silver caryatid
George II, Britain

Mid-18thC silver baluster
George III, Britain

Mid-18thC silver ionic capitals
George III, Britain

Late 18thC silver fluted capitals
George III, Britain

Late 18thC brass stop-fluted
George III, Britain

Late 18thC silver fluted capital
George III, Britain

Late 18thC silver flared octagonal
George III, Britain

Early 19thC silver Neoclassical
George III, Britain

Early 19thC silver tapered
George III, Britain

Early 19thC silver short, tapered
George III, Britain

Early 19thC silver Rococo baluster
George III, Britain

Early 19thC silver foliate base
George III, Britain

Mid-19thC silver circular, draped
Biedermeier, Germany

Late 19thC silver swagged column
Victorian, Britain

Late 19thC silver shell and scroll
Victorian, Britain

Late 19thC silver Corinthian capital
Victorian, Britain

Late 19thC silver tapering
Victorian, Britain

Early 20thC silver-plate pierced
Art Nouveau, Britain

IDENTIFYING FEATURES
Understanding silver shapes

The shape of a piece of silver can help you to date it and get a fair price for it. These pages show the most common teapot, coffee pot, mug and sauceboat shapes in date order.

TEAPOTS

Early 18thC pear
Queen Anne, Britain

Early 18thC octagonal
George I, Britain

Early 18thC apple
George I, Britain

Mid-18thC globular
George III, Britain

Mid-18thC ovoid
George III, Britain

Late 18thC reverse-pear
George III, Britain

Late 18thC oval
George III, Britain

Late 18thC oval
George III, Britain

Late 18thC faceted tapering oval
George III, Britain

Late 18thC oval panelled tapering
George III, Britain

Late 18thC fluted oval
George III, Britain

Early 19thC rounded rectangular
Regency, Britain

Early 19thC circular part fluted
Regency, Britain

Mid-19thC shaped oval straight-sided
Victorian, Britain

Mid-19thC baluster
Victorian, Britain

Late 19thC baluster
Victorian, Britain

Late 19thC partly-fluted circular
Victorian, Britain

Early 20thC compressed circular
Edwardian, Britain

Early 20thC tapering circular
Art Deco, Britain

Early 20thC shaped oval
Art Deco, Britain

COFFEE POTS

Early 18thC tapering cylinder
George II, Britain

Mid-18thC straight-tapered
George II, Britain

Mid-18thC pyriform
George III, Britain

Mid-18thC plain baluster
George III, Britain

Mid-18thC baluster
George III, Britain

Late 18thC vase, reeded girdles
George III, Britain

**Late 18thC
embossed pedestal**
George III, Britain

**Early 19thC
Classical vase**
George III, Britain

**Early 19thC
ovoid pedestal**
George III, Britain

**Early 19thC
cylindrical**
Regency, Britain

**Mid-19thC
lobed baluster**
Victorian, Britain

**Mid-19thC
baluster**
Victorian, Britain

Mid-19thC ovoid
Victorian, Britain

**Late 19thC
tapering circular**
Victorian, Britain

**Late 19thC
chased cylindrical**
Victorian, Britain

**Late 19thC spiral
baluster**
Victorian, Britain

**Late 19thC rounded
rectangular**
Victorian, Britain

**Early 20thC
straight tapered**
Art Deco, Britain

MUGS

**Early 18thC
plain tapered**
George I, Britain

**Mid-18thC
embossed baluster**
George II, Britain

Mid-18thC baluster
George II, Britain

**Early 19thC
embossed baluster**
George III, Britain

Early 19thC straight
George IV, Britain

**Early 19thC
demi-fluted baluster**
George IV, Britain

**Mid-19thC
embossed campana**
Victorian, Britain

**Mid-19thC
embossed baluster**
Victorian, Britain

**Late 19thC
baluster pedestal**
Art Nouveau, Britain

**Early 20thC
embossed circular**
Britain

SAUCEBOATS

**Mid-18thC chased
oval**
George II, Britain

Mid-18thC fluted oval
George II, Britain

**Mid-18thC low-bellied
oval**
George III, Britain

**Mid-18thC
quilted-girdle oval**
George III, Britain

**Late 18thC
boat-shaped**
George III, Britain

**Late 18thC
tripod helmet**
George III, Britain

**Late 18thC
beaded oval**
George III, Britain

**Late 18thC
embossed oval**
George III, Britain

**Late 18thC
inverted helmet**
George III, Britain

**Late 19thC
embossed oval**
Victorian, Britain

IDENTIFYING FEATURES
Understanding costume jewellery marks

The marks on a piece of costume jewellery can help you to identify the maker and even the date it was made – which will help you to make an accurate sale, especially online. These pages show the most common 20th-century company marks in alphabetical order.

Art
American, used 1940s
until the late 1960s

Beaujewel
American, used 1950s
until the 1970s

Boucher
American, used 1950s
until the 1970s

BSK
American, used 1948
until the 1980s

Butler & Wilson
British, used c.1970
until the present

Hattie Carnegie
American, used c.1950
until 1979

Alice Caviness
American, used 1945
until c.2000

Chanel Novelty Co.
American, used early
1930s until the 1940s

Chanel
French, used 1925 until
the present

Ciner
American, used 1931
until the present

Coro
American, used 1938
until 1979

DeMario
American, used 1945
until 1965

Christian Dior
French, mark with date
for 1958

Eisenberg Original
American, used
1935 until 1945

Eugene
American, used
1952 until 1962

Florenza
American, used
1950 until 1981

Grosse
German, dated 1953

Stanley Hagler
American, used
1983 until 1996

Har
American, used 1950s
until the 1960s

Miriam Haskell
American, used 1940s
until the 1960s

Hobe
American, used
1958 until 1983

Hollycraft
American, used 1948
until 1988

Jomaz
American, used 1950
until 1965

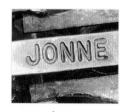

Jonne
American, used c.1950
until 1960

Joseff of Hollywood
American, used 1938
until the present

Joseff of Hollywood
American, used 1938 until the present

Kramer
American, used 1943 until 1980

KTF
American, used 1935 until the 1940s

Christian Lacroix
French, used from c.1980 until the present

Kenneth Jay Lane
American, used 1963 until the present

Leru
American, used c.1950 until the 1960s

Lisner
American, used 1938 until c.1985

Marboux
American, used 1937 until the 1960s

Marvella
American, used 1911 until the present

Matisse
American, used 1952 until 1964

Napier
American, used 1922 until 1999

Pennino
American, used 1927 until 1961

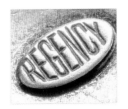

Rebajes
American, used 1932 until 1967

Regency
American, used c.1950 until 1970

Réja
American, used 1940 until 1954

Renoir
American, used 1946 until 1964

Robert
American, used 1942 until 1979

Yves St Laurent
French, used 1960s to the present

Schreiner
American, used 1939 until 1977

Schiaparelli
American, used from 1949 until the 1960s

COPYRIGHT MARKS

Before the mid-1950s, many costume jewellery companies imitated each other's designs. In 1952, Trifari took Coro to court over design copyright infringement. Two years later Trifari won the case, establishing copyright for costume jewellery designs as works of art. From 1955 onwards, Trifari and many other companies included a copyright mark.

▲ **Trifari crown mark**
American, used 1937 until the present.

Selini
American, used 1955 until the 1960s

Sphinx
American, used 1950 until the present

Vendôme
American, used 1944 until 1979

Weiss
American, used 1942 until 1971

Westwood
British, used c.2000

Whiting & Davis
American, used in the 1950s

IDENTIFYING FEATURES
Understanding dolls and teddy bears

Dolls, teddy bears and other soft toys are often marked with the maker's name, making identification simple. Unmarked dolls can be assessed by looking at the materials they are made from, the hairstyle, the clothes they are wearing and overall quality.

DOLL TYPES

Wooden dolls
Made for the wealthy in the 16th and 17th centuries. Many were homemade or made on lathes by chair-makers.

Cloth dolls
Made for as long as wooden dolls but many were thrown away or have not survived. Mass production began c.1830.

Papier-mâché dolls
Made from c.1550. Early 19th-century shoulder-heads were exported by the German maker Friedrich Müller.

'China' dolls
Heads made of glazed, hard-paste porcelain were first made in Thuringia, Germany; popular c.1830 to 1880.

Bisque dolls
Unglazed porcelain heads common c.1840-1930s. French dolls pre-eminent until German dolls were introduced in 1890s.

Wax dolls
Small numbers of carved, pressed-wax dolls were made until c.1840, when British makers began to make poured-wax dolls.

Composition dolls
Wood and paper pulp with other ingredients was a cheap alternative to bisque and china in 18th and 19th centuries.

Celluloid dolls
Fragile material used for dolls' heads from c.1870 until the 1950s, mostly by German, French and American makers.

Hard plastic dolls
Inexpensive and durable. Used from 1945 until the 1950s. British makers include Rosebud and Pedigree.

Soft plastic (vinyl) dolls
Hard plastic superseded by soft plastic in the 1950s. The Barbie doll was launched by US firm Mattel in 1959.

DOLL MARKS

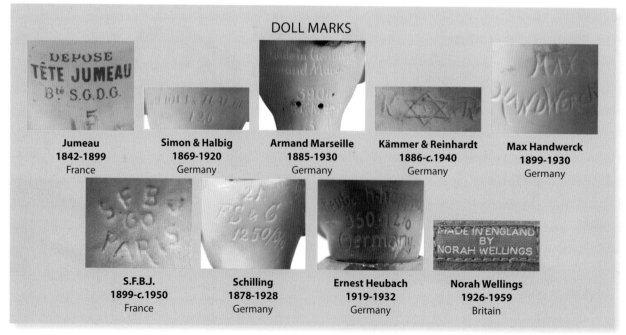

Jumeau
1842-1899
France

Simon & Halbig
1869-1920
Germany

Armand Marseille
1885-1930
Germany

Kämmer & Reinhardt
1886-c.1940
Germany

Max Handwerck
1899-1930
Germany

S.F.B.J.
1899-c.1950
France

Schilling
1878-1928
Germany

Ernest Heubach
1919-1932
Germany

Norah Wellings
1926-1959
Britain

STEIFF TEDDY BEAR LABELS

Steiff patented its 'button-in-the-ear' trademark (attached to the left ear with two prongs) in 1905. The design of the button has changed many times over the years. Knowing the styles used can help you to date your Steiff bear.

Elephant button
1904-1905

Blank button
1905-1909

Steiff with underscored 'F'
1905-1950s

Steiff script
1952-1970

Steiff script with label
1952-1970

Chrome button with Steiff
script 1965

Brass button, Steiff in script
and label 2012

OTHER TEDDY BEAR LABELS

Chad Valley 1920s-1930s

Chad Valley 1930s

Chad Valley 1938-1953

Chiltern 1950s onwards

Dean's Rag Book 1930s

Dean's Rag Book 1956-1980s

Farnell 1925-c.1945

Merrythought 1930-1945

Merrythought 1945-1956

Merythought 1957-1991

Pixie Toy 1940s

Glossary

Acid marks Signature applied to glass using etching acid on a rubber stamp.

Applied Denotes a separate part that has been added to an object, such as a handle or decoration to a ceramic body.

Apron Lower front edge of a piece of furniture.

Aurora Borealis stone An iridescent coating on rhinestones giving a metallic sheen reminiscent of the shimmering green and blue Northern Lights. The effect was developed in the 1950s by the Austrian firm Swarovski with French designer Christian Dior.

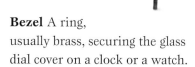

Backstamp The mark printed on the base of a ceramic object that identifies the manufacturer, the model name and/or number and sometimes the designer.

Bakelite A strong and heavy type of plastic, made of phenolic resin and formaldehyde, patented by Dr Leo Baekeland in 1907 and used widely in the 1920s and 1930s. It can be brightly coloured but mottled brown and black are the most common colours.

Base metal Any non-precious metal such as brass, bronze, iron and steel or an alloy. It may be coated with a precious metal, such as gold or silver.

Bauhaus The term describing an artistic style of the 20th century was coined by the German architect Walter Gropius, who became director of the Weimar school of Arts and Crafts in 1919 and renamed it the Bauhaus.

Bentwood Solid or laminated wood steamed and bent into a curvilinear shape. The process was developed by Austrian Michael Thonet in the early 19th century.

Bezel A ring, usually brass, securing the glass dial cover on a clock or a watch.

Bisque An unglazed porcelain used to make dolls' heads from around 1860 to around 1925.

Boulle A decorative inlay, named after French cabinet-maker André-Charles Boulle, usually using tortoiseshell and brass, pewter, ivory and mother-of-pearl. The technique was revived in Britain between 1815 and 1840 and known as Buhl marquetry.

Bright cutting A type of engraving or cutting used on metal, gems or glass where the surface is cut at an angle to form facets that reflect the light.

Cabochon A smooth, domed gemstone, either oval or round.

Cameo A stone, shell, gem or glass object with a design carved in relief, usually contrasting with the background. Designs include portraiture and Classical imagery.

Cane A length of glass made by fusing together a bundle of glass rods. The rods may be coloured to create a multi-coloured cane.

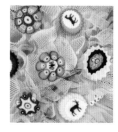

Carded A term used when referring to toy figures and other merchandise which is still in the original packaging, comprising a card backing with a plastic cover that allows the enclosed objects to be seen. 'Loose' refers to an object no longer in its packaging.

Cartouche A framed ornamental panel, often in the shape of a paper scroll or shield, which can be inscribed. Popular in the Rococo period, it is often found on furniture or small boxes.

Carved in the round Often considered the most complex type of carving, this technique creates three-dimensional objects that can be viewed from any angle.

Carver A dining chair with arms.

Cartel clock Type of ornate, spring-driven wall-hung clock, produced mainly in France during the 18th century.

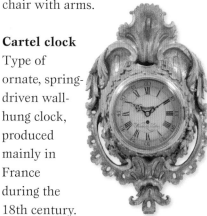

Catalin A type of brightly coloured plastic made of cast phenolic. It was used from around 1938 to around 1946 to produce radio cabinets, costume jewellery and other small, simply shaped items.

Celluloid An early form of plastic created in the late 19th century. A new non-flammable form was developed in 1926.

Chinoiserie A style popular in late 17th and 18th century Europe, in which Oriental-style figures and motifs were used to decorate western-style wares.

Chronograph A precision watch that can measure time accurately to the nearest second or fraction of a second, often to determine time in sporting events.

Chryselephantine The term used to describe items made from a combination of bronze and ivory.

Cloisonné A type of enamelling where a fine metal wire is attached to a body to form connecting compartments or cells; these are filled with coloured enamel paste before the object is fired in a kiln to harden the enamel. See *Enamel*.

Cold-painted bronze Bronze items painted with coloured enamel paints after casting.

Composition A substance similar to plaster, used to make dolls and other toys. It is usually made from a mixture of whiting (chalk), resin and size (glue).

Creamware Cream-coloured, durable earthenware with a transparent lead glaze. First developed by Josiah Wedgwood in around 1765, who referred to it as Queen's ware after Queen Charlotte had visited the factory.

Cut steel Jewellery made from faceted steel studs imitating precious stones. A popular substitute for more expensive diamond jewellery.

Diamanté A faceted glass gem or artificial crystal that is highly reflective and sparkling, also called rhinestone. See *Rhinestone*.

Die-cast An inexpensive method of casting metal alloys in a reusable mould. It was used to make toy cars or figures.

Doucai Meaning 'contrasting colours', this type of ceramic decoration, introduced in 15th-century China, uses overglaze enamels (red, yellow, purple and green) within an underglaze-blue outline.

Embossed A method of creating a large-scale relief design on metal or leather by hammering or pressing on the reverse; other techniques using hammers and punches are then used to add the fine detail.

Enamel A form of decoration involving the application of metal oxides to metal, glass or ceramic objects. These are usually then fired to produce a hard decorative or protective coating.

Engine-turned Textured patterns, created by turning metal on a machine-driven lathe.

Escapement A device regulating the delivery of power to the movement of a clock or watch and also determining the speed at which the hands rotate. The verge escapement was developed first but it was superceded by the cylinder escapement in the 19th century. The lever escapement has dominated since the 1830s.

Famille jaune A palette used on Chinese porcelain. A variation of the *famille verte* palette, using a yellow ground.

Famille noire A palette used on Chinese porcelain. A variation of the *famille verte* palette, using a black ground.

Famille rose A palette used on Chinese porcelain from the 18th century onwards, which includes a dominant opaque pink; also copied in Europe on ceramics from the 18th century onwards.

Famille verte A palette used from the 17th century on Chinese porcelain, distinguished by a dominant, bright apple green.

Fazzoletto A handkerchief-shaped vase, made by Murano glass-makers, particularly the Venini factory, from the 1950s and widely emulated.

Figuring The pattern made by the natural grain of wood.

Filigree Decorative openwork panels of fine gold or silver wire or plate.

Finial A decorative knob on a lid or used as the terminal of a piece, such as the decorative shape at the end of a handle on a spoon or the lid of a teapot.

Fluting A pattern of parallel grooves repeated in vertical lines, running along a surface to form concave columns.

Foliate Leaf-and-vine decoration.

Frieze The horizontal band found below the cornice on a piece of furniture such as a cabinet or bookcase. A frieze rail is the wooden support found below the surface of a table or desk.

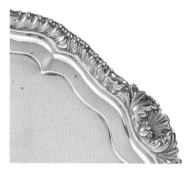

Gadrooning A continuous pattern of vertical or spiralling curves in a convex profile, found on silver, ceramics and furniture.

Gesso A plaster-like substance applied to an inexpensive secondary timber in thick layers before being carved and gilded or painted.

Gilt A gold finish applied to a silver or electroplated object or to a ceramic, wood or glass item. There are several gilding techniques.

Girandole Mirror for suspending on a wall, the earliest type from the mid-17th century, usually with a highly ornate frame.

Glaze A smooth, shiny, decorative and protective surface on ceramics. Tin and celadon glazes are opaque, a lead glaze is transparent.

Ground The background or base colour of an object. Decoration is often applied on top of it.

Gu An ancient Chinese bronze wine vessel, or object of that shape, that tapers to a slim centre section.

Hallmark The series of marks usually found on a British silver or gold item, attesting to its purity and typically identifying its maker, date of manufacture and the city in which it was assayed or tested for quality.

Hardstone A term describing any semi-precious stone, such as malachite or agate.

Highboy The American term for a chest-on-stand.

Hollow-casting A method of casting metal figures involving pouring molten metal alloy into a mould. As soon as the outer layer has set, the molten metal in the interior is poured out.

Impressed marks Marks made in the surface of a ceramic, glass or metal body, usually on the base of a piece. They may provide information of the manufacturer, designer, pattern or range.

Incised decoration A pattern or inscription scratched into a ceramic, glass or metal body by using a sharp tool such as a metal point.

Intaglio Incised decoration where the design is cut into the surface of glass, ceramic, metal or hardstone, creating a recessed pattern.

Knees (of a chair) Curved section of leg under the apron. See *Apron*.

Knop A rounded, bulbous part on the stem of a drinking glass or a similar shaped handle on a lid.

Lacquer Oriental objects carved in wood and coated with successive layers of the sap of the lacquer tree, which turns hard and black on exposure to sunlight and air. It can be carved and polished. The sap can also be coloured with various dyes and inlaid with powders, shell etc.

Ladder back A country chair with a series of horizontal back-rails.

Lampwork A method of producing decorative glassware by manipulating rods or tubes of glass over a flame. First used in 15th-century Venice.

Lowboy Name now given to a small dressing table, usually with either a single frieze drawer or a small central shallow drawer flanked on either side by a deep drawer.

Lucite A transparent plastic first produced commercially in the 1930s. Also known as Plexiglass (and later Perspex), it sometimes yellows and cracks with age.

Lustre ware The term describes ceramics with an iridescent, metallic sheen which is produced by adding or applying one of several metal oxides to the glaze.

Maki-e Japanese for 'sprinkled illustration'. This decorative technique, applied to lacquerwork (See *Lacquer*), involves sprinkling gold or coloured dust on to wet black, gold or red lacquer to form a design. It can be found on boxes and inro (small containers that hung from a belt and were often used to carry seals).

Marriage An item of furniture that has been made up from two or more associated pieces, usually from the same period.

Martelé A French term for silverware with a fine, hammered decorative surface.

Millefiori A glass-making technique where coloured glass canes are cut into sections to reveal the patterns they contain and then embedded into clear glass. Together the canes can form larger designs. From the Italian term for 'a thousand flowers', the technique is closely associated with paperweights.

Mint condition The term describing an item in pristine, and complete condition, showing no signs of age, wear and tear or any other damage. This can enhance value considerably.

Moulding Strips of wood, metal or other material applied to a surface to form a decorative profile. Designs are often based on architectural features and used to hide joints.

Murrine A type of Murano glassware where short lengths or slices of coloured glass canes (murrine), are used to form a mosaic pattern on the surface of an object.

Parian porcelain Fine, matt, white porcelain, sometimes lightly glazed, resembling fine Parian marble, developed mid-19th century by Copeland. Used mainly for miniature copies of Classical statuary.

Parure A matching set of jewellery, usually comprising a necklace, brooch, bracelet and earrings. A demi-parure comprises matching earrings and brooch.

Paste A hard glass compound that is extremely versatile, having many of the properties of gemstones when certain minerals and oxides are added to it. Pastes have been used to make jewellery in a wide range of colours since the 18th century.

Pâte de verre A type of translucent glass produced by making a paste of powdered glass mixed with paint or enamels, from the French meaning 'glass paste'. The technique was used by French glassmakers in the 19th century to create small, elaborate objects.

Pier glass A tall, narrow mirror intended to hang between the windows of a drawing room.

Pillar-cutting A method of cutting glass that leaves a pattern of deeply cut vertical flutes.

Pinchbeck An alloy of copper and zinc, invented *c*.1720 as a substitute for gold. Widely used for jewellery in the 19th century.

Planishing A technique of producing a smooth finish on metalwork by gently hammering or rolling the surface.

Plate Originally, domestic items made of gold or silver. Now used to describe articles made of base metal and covered with silver, such as or electroplate.

Plique à jour An unbacked translucent enamel reminiscent of stained-glass windows when light shines through

them. It was popular for Art Nouveau jewellery.

Relief decoration Mould-made, stamped or carved ornamentation which is raised above the surface.

Repeating mechanism A mechanism in clocks and watches that repeats the strike of the previous hour – and sometimes quarter hour and last five minutes – when a cord is pulled or a button is pressed. It is also known as a repeater.

Repoussé French for 'pushed out', a method of embossing silver or other metals by hammering them into a mould from the reverse side.

Resist An area on a ceramic body that is covered with wax or paper to resist, or block, a lustre solution applied to the rest of the piece. When the solution has been applied, the resist is removed.

Reticulated A pattern in the form of a network or web, either open or filled in (blind reticulation).

Rhinestone Originally, this term referred to a type of clear quartz used in costume jewellery. Now it describes any colourless paste or rock crystal used to imitate diamond in costume jewellery. See *Diamanté*.

Sabot French term for the gilt-bronze 'shoe' at the bottom of furniture legs.

Salt glaze A type of glaze which is applied to stoneware.

The process involves throwing salt into the kiln during firing. The salt vaporises leaving behind a thin, clear glaze.

Sancai Meaning three-coloured, and used to describe Chinese Tang period wares made as funerary goods and decorated with viscous lead glazes.

Sang-de-boeuf A bright plum-red glaze used to decorate ceramics, from the French meaning 'bull's blood'. It was developed in China in the 16th century.

Sans travers decoration Decoration which covers the whole front of a piece of furniture.

Seed pearl A small, imperfectly formed pearl.

Self-winding In clocks and watches, a mechanism that uses the constant movement of the hands to wind the instrument automatically.

Sgraffito A form of ceramic decoration created by scratching or scoring a design through unfired, coloured slip to reveal the ground beneath.

Silvered brass Brass that is coloured silver by the application of a silvering compound.

Sleeping eyes Dolls' eyes that are weighted internally so they are open when the doll is upright and closed when the doll is lying down.

Slip A smooth, diluted clay, which is often coloured and used for decorating ceramics. Slip is also used to bond two pieces of ceramic together.

Slip-moulding The manufacture of thin-bodied ceramics by pouring slip into a mould.

Sommerso A glass-making technique in which one or more layers of differently coloured glass is encased in a thick layer of clear glass. Up to four layers of coloured glass can be used under the clear layer. From the Italian for 'submerged'.

Squab cushion A removable stuffed cushion for a chair or stool. They were a popular feature of chairs and stools from the 17th to the 19th centuries. The term occasionally refers to a large padded seat.

Spleter Zinc alloy used in the production of figures as an inexpensive alternative to bronze.

Standee A self-standing display promoting a product or event, typically made of cardboard.

Stuffover Thick seat pad enclosing most or all of the rails on the sides of a piece of furniture. The cover is tacked under the frame or fixed to the face of the rails.

Tallboy A tall chest-of-drawers mounted on another, slightly larger chest. Also known as a chest-on-chest.

Tessera An individual tile used to make a mosaic.

Tessuto A glass-making technique originating in Italy, in which finely striped canes decorate the body in a criss-crossing pattern to resemble woven fabric.

Tin plate A tin alloy coating is applied to steel then hand-painted or decorated with a transfer. Tin plate was used for toys from the mid 19th to the mid-20th century.

Top rail The highest horizontal bar on the back of a chair.

Trompe l'oeil A type of decoration that imitates another surface or texture, such as wood or marbling or a realistic scene. From the French meaning 'trick the eye'.

Tube lining Thick slip is trailed or piped on to the surface of a ceramic piece to decorate it.

Tunbridgeware Souvenir wooden boxes and small household goods with inlaid decoration made in Tunbridge Wells in Kent.

Vermeil Silver that has been plated, or covered, in a thin layer, or 'wash', of gold. The term is derived from the French word for 'rosy'.

Vignette A carved ornament with a continuous design of grapevines, leaves and tendrils. The word also refers to a photograph or a drawing in which the edges fade away.

Vinaigrette A small hinged box to hold a sponge soaked in vinegar or perfume to combat offensive odours.

Wheel engraving A technique using a small rotating wheel, fitted with a stone or copper disc and abrasive paste to incise decoration on glass.

Wucai Meaning 'five coloured', this is a type of ceramic decoration developed in 16th-century China using the same palette as *doucai* but within overglaze black or red outlines, instead of underglaze-blue.

Yang cai The shades of pink and red used in *famille rose* decoration. The term means 'foreign colours' as they were introduced to China from Europe in around 1685.

Resources

AUCTION HOUSES

ANDERSON & GARLAND
Anderson House, Crispin Court,
Newbiggin Lane, Westerhope,
Newcastle upon Tyne
NE5 1BF
Tel: 0191 430 3000
www.andersonandgarland.com

ANTIQUORUM
595 Madison Ave., Fifth Floor,
New York, NY 10022, USA
Tel: 001 212 750 1103
www.antiquorum.com

BAINBRIDGES
The Auction Room,
Ickenham Road, West Ruislip,
Middlesex HA4 7DL
Tel: 01895 621991
www.bainbridgesauctions.
co.uk

BEARNES HAMPTON & LITTLEWOOD
St Edmund's Court,
Okehampton Street,
Exeter, Devon EX4 1DU
Tel: 01392 413100
www.bhandl.co.uk

BLOOMSBURY AUCTIONS
24 Maddox Street,
London W1S 1PP
Tel: 020 7495 9494
www.bloomsburyauctions.com

BONHAMS
101 New Bond Street,
London W1S 1SR
Tel: 020 7447 74447
Montpelier Street,
Knightsbridge,
London SW7 1HH
Tel: 020 7393 3900
www.bonhams.com

GRAHAM BUDD AUCTIONS LTD
P.O. Box 47519
London N14 6XD
Tel: 020 8366 2525
www.grahambuddauctions.co.uk

CAPES DUNN
The Auction Galleries,
38 Charles Street,
Manchester M1 7DB
Tel: 0161 273 1911
www.capesdunn.com

CHARTERHOUSE
The Long Street Salerooms,
Sherborne, Dorset DT9 3BS
Tel: 01935 812 277
www.charterhouse-auction.com

CHEFFINS
Clifton House,
1 & 2 Clifton Road,
Cambridge CB1 7EA
Tel: 01223 213 343
www.cheffins.co.uk

CHRISTIE'S
8 King Street,
London SW1Y 6QT
Tel: 020 7839 9060
85 Old Brompton Road,
London SW7 3LD
Tel: 020 7581 7611
www.christies.com

DEE, ATKINSON & HARRISON
The Exchange Saleroom,
Driffield, East Yorkshire
YO25 6LD
Tel: 01377 253 151
www.dahauctions.com

DREWEATTS
Donnington Priory,
Donnington, Newbury,
Berkshire RG14 2JE
Tel: 01635 553 553
www.dnfa.com

DUKE'S
The Dorchester Fine Art
Saleroom, Weymouth Avenue,
Dorchester, Dorset DT1 1QS
Tel: 01305 265 080
www.dukes-auctions.com

EWBANK CLARKE GAMMON WELLERS
Burnt Common Auction
Rooms, London Road, Send,
Woking, Surrey GU23 7LN
Tel: 01483 223 101
www.ewbankauctions.co.uk

FIELDING'S
Mill Race Lane, Stourbridge,
West Midlands DY8 1JN
Tel: 01384 444 140
www.fieldings
auctioneers.co.uk

GARDINER HOULGATE
9 Leafield Way, Corsham,
Bath, Avon SN13 9SW
Tel: 01225 812 912
www.gardinerhoulgate.co.uk

T. W. GAZE
Auction Rooms, Roydon Road,
Diss, Norfolk IP22 4LN
Tel: 01379 650 306
www.twgaze.com

GORRINGES
15 North Street, Lewes,
East Sussex, BN7 2PD
Tel: 01273 472 503
www.gorringes.co.uk

ANDREW HARTLEY
Victoria Hall Salerooms,
Little Lane, Ilkley,
West Yorkshire LS29 8EA
Tel: 01943 816 363
www.andrewhartleyfinearts.
co.uk

HISTORICAL & COLLECTABLE
Kennetholme, Midgham,
Reading, Berkshire, RG7 5UX
Tel: 0118 9712420
www.historicalandcollectable.com

LAWRENCES
Norfolk House, High Street,
Bletchingley, Surrey, RH1 4PA
Tel: 01883 743 323
www.lawrencesbletchingley.
co.uk

LYON & TURNBULL LTD
33 Broughton Place,
Edinburgh EH1 3RR
Tel: 0131 557 8844
www.lyonandturnbull.com

MAXWELLS
133A Woodford Road,
Woodford, Cheshire SK7 1QD
Tel: 0161 439 5182
www.maxwells-auctioneers.co.uk

MORPHETS
6 Albert Street, Harrogate
North Yorkshire HG1 1JL
Tel: 01423 530 030
www.morphets.co.uk

MULLOCK'S LTD
The Old Shippon
Wall under Heywood
Church Stretton
Shropshire SY6 7DS
Tel: 01694 771771
www.mullocksauctions.co.uk

JOHN NICHOLSONS
The Auction Rooms,
Longfield, Midhurst Road,
Fernhurst, Haslemere,
Surrey GU27 3HA
Tel: 01428 653 727
www.johnnicholsons.com

ONSLOWS
The Coach House,
Manor Road, Stourpaine,
Dorset DT11 8TQ
Tel: 01258 488 838
www.onslows.co.uk

W & H PEACOCK
26 Newnham Street,
Bedford, Bedfordshire
MK40 3JR
Tel: 01234 266 366
www.peacockauction.co.uk

POTTERIES SPECIALIST AUCTIONS
271 Waterloo Road,
Cobridge, Stoke On Trent
ST6 3HR
Tel: 01782 286 622
www.potteriesauctions.com

ROSEBERY'S
74-76 Knights Hill,
West Norwood SE27 0JD
Tel: 020 8761 2522
www.roseberys.co.uk

SOTHEBY'S
34-35 New Bond Street,
London, W1A 2AA
Tel: 020 7293 5000
www.sothebys.com

SPECIAL AUCTION SERVICES

81 New Greenham Park,
Newbury, Berkshire
RG19 6HW
Tel: 01635 580 595
www.specialauctionservices.
com

SWORDERS

Cambridge Road,
Stansted Mountfitchet, Essex
CM24 8GE
Tel: 01279 817 778
www.sworder.co.uk

KERRY TAYLOR AUCTIONS

249-253 Long Lane,
Bermondsey, London SE1 4PR
Tel: 020 8676 4600
www.kerrytaylorauctions.com

TENNANTS

The Auction Centre,
Leyburn, North Yorkshire
DL8 5SG
Tel: 01969 623 780
www.tennants.co.uk

TRING MARKET AUCTIONS

Brook Street, Tring
Hertfordshire HP23 5EF
Tel: 01442 826 446
www.tringmarket
auctions.co.uk

VECTIS AUCTIONS LTD

Fleck Way, Thornaby,
Stockton on Tees TS17 9JZ
Tel: 01642 750 616
www.vectis.co.uk

WALLIS & WALLIS

West Street Auction Galleries,
Lewes, East Sussex BN7 2NJ
Tel: 01273 480 208
www.wallisandwallis.co.uk

WOOLLEY & WALLIS

51-61 Castle Street,
Salisbury, Wiltshire SP1 3SU
Tel: 01722 424 500
www.woolleyandwallis.co.uk

DEALERS

Decorative Arts

ART DECO ETC.

73 Upper Gloucester Road,
Brighton, Sussex
BN1 3LQ
Tel: 01273 202 937
johnclark@artdecoetc.co.uk

THE DESIGN GALLERY

5 The Green, Westerham,
Kent TN16 1AS
Tel: 01959 561 234
www.designgallery.co.uk

GALLERY 1930

18 Church Street,
Marylebone,
London NW8 8EP
Tel: 020 7723 1555
gallery1930@aol.com

JAZZY ART DECO

Tel: 020 8451 3062
www.jazzyartdeco.co.uk

TITUS OMEGA

Tel: 020 7688 1295
www.titusomega.com

Carpets and Rugs

GALLERY YACOU

127 Fulham Road,
London SW3 6RT
Tel: 020 7584 2929
www.galleryyacou.com

WADSWORTH'S

Marehill, Pullborough,
West Sussex RH20 2DY
Tel: 01798 873 555
www.wadsworthsrugs.com

Ceramics

BETH ADAMS

Alfies Antique Market,
13-25 Church Street,
London NW8 8DT
Tel: 07776 136 003
www.alfiesantiques.com

ALBERT AMOR

37 Bury Street,
London SW1Y 6AU
Tel: 020 7930 2444
www.albertamor.co.uk

ANDREW DANDO

34 Market Street,
Bradford-on-Avon,
Wiltshire BA15 1LL
Tel: 01225 865 444
www.andrewdando.co.uk

KEN GRANT

Alfies Antique Market,
13-25 Church Street,
London NW8 8DT
Tel: 020 7723 1370
www.alfiesantiques.com

ADRIAN GRATER

Tel: 020 8579 0357
adriangrater@tiscali.co.uk

JOHN HOWARD AT HERITAGE

6 Market Place, Woodstock,
Oxfordshire OX20 1TA
Tel: 01993 812580
www.antiquepottery.co.uk

KCS CERAMICS

Tel: 020 8384 8981
www.kcsceramics-
international.co.uk

R & G MCPHERSON ANTIQUES

www.orientalceramics.com

ROGERS DE RIN

76 Royal Hospital Road,
Paradise Walk, Chelsea,
London SW3 4HN
Tel: 020 7352 9007
www.rogersderin.co.uk

STEPPES HILL FARM ANTIQUES

Steppes Hill Farm,
Stockbury, Sittingbourne,
Kent, ME9 7RB
Tel: 01795 842 205
www.steppeshillfarm
antiques.com

STOCKSPRING ANTIQUES

114 Kensington Church Street,
London W8 4BH
Tel: 020 7727 7995
www.antique-porcelain.co.uk

W.W. WARNER ANTIQUES

The Green, High Street,
Brasted, Westerham,
Kent TN16 1JL
Tel: 01959 563698

Clocks

RICHARD PRICE & ASSOCIATES

Bullpits House, Bourton,
Dorset SP8 5AX
Tel: 01747 840084
www.antiqueclocks.tv

DEREK ROBERTS

25 Shipbourne Road,
Tonbridge, Kent TN10 3DN
Tel: 01732 358986
www.qualityantiqueclocks.
com

Costume Jewellery and Accessories

LINDA BEE

Stand L18-21, Grays Antique
Market, 1-7 Davies Mews,
London W1K 2LP
Tel: 020 7629 5921
www.graysantiques.com

CRISTOBAL

26 Church Street,
Marylebone,
London NW8 8EP
Tel: 020 7724 7230
www.cristobal.co.uk

RICHARD GIBBON

neljeweluk@aol.com

MARIE ANTIQUES

Tel: 07956 128 698
www.marieantiques.co.uk

PAOLA & IAIA

Stand S057,
Alfies Antiques Market,
13-25 Church Street,
London NW8 8DT
Tel: 07751 084 135
www.alfiesantiques.com

Fashion

CANDY SAYS

Tel: 01277 212 134
www.candysays.co.uk

THE GIRL CAN'T HELP IT!
www.thegirlcanthelpit.com

SARA HUGHES
sara@sneak.freeserve.co.uk

IT'S VINTAGE DARLING
Tel: 01778 344 949
www.itsvintagedarling.com

MARY & GEOFF TURVIL
www.glitzguru.com

VINTAGE TO VOGUE
28 Milsom Street, Bath,
Avon BA1 1DG
Tel: 01225 337 323
www.vintagetovoguebath.
co.uk

BASIA ZARZYCKA
52 Sloane Square,
London W1W 8AX
Tel: 020 7730 1660
www.basia-zarzycka.com

Fountain Pens

BATTERSEA PEN HOME
P.O. Box 6128,
Epping CM16 4GG
Tel: 01992 578 885
www.penhome.co.uk

Furniture

BAGGOT CHURCH STREET LTD
Church Street,
Stow-on-the-Wold,
Gloucestershire GL54 1BB
Tel: 01451 831392
www.baggottantiques.com

BLANCHARD LTD
86/88 Pimlico Road,
London SW1W 8PL
Tel: 020 7823 6310
www.jwblanchard.com

JOHN BLY
Woburn Abbey Antiques,
Woburn, Bedfordshire
MK17 9WA
www.johnbly.com

CHRISTOPHER BUCK ANTIQUES
56-60 Sandgate High Street,
Sandgate, Folkestone,
Kent CT20 3AP
Tel: 01303 221229
chrisbuck@throwley.freeserve.
co.uk

PETER BUNTING
Harthill Hall, Alport,
Bakewell, Derbyshire
DE45 1LH
Tel: 01629 636203
www.countryoak.co.uk

CARLTON ANTIQUES
43 Worcester Road,
Malvern, Worcestershire,
WR14 4RB
Tel: 01684 573 092
www.carlton-antiques.com

LENNOX CATO
1 The Square, Church Street,
Edenbridge, Kent TN8 5BD
Tel: 01732 865 988
www.lennoxcato.com

ELAINE PHILLIPS ANTIQUES LTD
1 & 2 Royal Parade, Harrogate,
North Yorkshire HG1 2SZ
Tel: 01423 569745
www.elainephillipsantiques.
co.uk

GEORGIAN ANTIQUES
10 Pattison Street, Leith Links,
Edinburgh EH6 7HF
Tel: 0131 553 7286
www.georgianantiques.net

MAC HUMBLE ANTIQUES
7-9 Woolley Street, Bradford-
on-Avon, Wiltshire BA15 1AD
Tel: 01225 866329

REINDEER ANTIQUES
81 Kensington Church Street,
London W8 4BG
Tel: 020 7937 3754
43 Watling Street, Potterspury,
Northamptonshire NN12 7QD
Tel: 01908 542407
www.reindeerantiques.co.uk

ROBERT YOUNG ANTIQUES
68 Battersea Bridge Road,
London SW11 3AG
Tel: 020 7228 7847
www.robertyoungantiques.
com

WAKELIN & LINFIELD
PO Box 48, Billingshurst,
West Sussex RH14 0YZ
Tel: 01403 700004

WITNEY ANTIQUES
96-100 Corn Street, Witney,
Oxfordshire OX28 6BU
Tel: 01993 703902
www.witneyantiques.com

Glass

JEANETTE HAYHURST FINE GLASS
Long Street Antiques,
14 Long Street, Tetbury,
Gloucestershire GL8 8AQ
Tel: 07831 209814
www.antiqueglass-london.com

THE LALIQUE MASCOT COLLECTORS' CLUB
The White Lion Garage,
Clarendon Place,
Brighton BN2 1JA
Tel: 01273 622 722
www.carsofbrighton.co.uk

ANDREW LINEHAM FINE GLASS
P.O. Box 465, Chichester,
PO18 8WZ
Tel: 01243 576 241
www.antiquecolouredglass.com

M & D MOIR
www.manddmoir.co.uk

Jewellery

N. BLOOM & SON
PO Box 54807,
London SW1Y 6WZ
Tel: 07973 149 363
www.nbloom.com

CHARLOTTE SAYERS
Shop 313, Grays Antiques
Market, 58 Davies Street,
London W1K 5LP
www.charlottesayers.co.uk

Posters

VINMAGCO
39/43 Brewer Street,
London, W1R 9UD
Tel: 020 7439 8525
www.vinmag.com

Sculpture

BURSTOW & HEWETT
Lower Lake, Battle,
East Sussex TN33 0AT
Tel: 01424 772 374
www.burstowandhewett.co.uk

Silver

DIDIER ANTIQUES
58-60 Kensington Church
Street, London W8 4DB
Tel: 020 7938 2537
www.didierantiques.com

DANIEL BEXFIELD ANTIQUES
26 Burlington Arcade,
London W1J 0PU
Tel: 020 7491 1720
www.bexfield.co.uk

ALASTAIR DICKENSON
90 Jermyn Street, London
SW1Y 6JD
www.alastairdickenson.co.uk

GOODWINS ANTIQUES LTD
15 & 16 Queensferry Street,
Edinburgh EH2 4QW
Tel: 0131 225 4717
www.goodwinsantiques.com

SHAPIRO & COMPANY
380 Grays Antiques Markets,
58 Davies Street, London
W1K 5LP
Tel: 020 7491 2710
www.graysantiques.com

STEPPES HILL FARM ANTIQUES
Steppes Hill Farm,
Stockbury, Sittingbourne,
Kent, ME9 7RB
Tel: 01795 842 205
www.steppeshillfarm
antiques.com

Toys and Dolls

BÉBÉS ET JOUETS
Tel: 01289 304 802
bebesetjouets@tiscali.co.uk

VICTORIANA DOLLS
101 Portobello Rd,
London, W11 2BQ
Tel: 01737 249 525
heather.bond@totalserve.co.uk

KARL FLAHERTY COLLECTABLES
193 Hipswell Highway,
Wyken, Coventry,
West Midlands, CV2 5FN
Tel: 02476 445 627
Kfckarl@aol.com

THE MAGIC TOYBOX
210 Havant Road, Drayton,
Portsmouth PO6 2EH
Tel: 02392 221 307
www.magictoybox.co.uk

**TEDDY BEARS OF
WITNEY**
99 High Street, Witney,
Oxfordshire, OX28 6HY
Tel: 01993 706 616
www.teddybears.co.uk

Twentieth-Century Design

FRAGILE DESIGN
14/15 The Custard Factory,
Digbeth,
Birmingham B9 4AA
Tel: 0121 224 7378
www.fragiledesign.com

GARY GRANT
18 Arlington Way,
London EC1R 1UY
Tel: 020 7713 1122
garygrant@btopenworld.com

MANIC ATTIC
Alfies Antiques Market,
13-25 Church Street,
London NW8 8DT
Tel: 020 7723 6066
ianbroughton@hotmail.com

RENNIES
47 The Old High Street,
Folkestone, Kent
CT20 1RN
Tel: 01303 242 427
www.rennart.co.uk

GEOFFREY ROBINSON
Alfies Antiques Market,
13-25 Church Street,
London, NW8 8DT
Tel: 020 7723 0449
www.alfiwesantiques.co.uk

VENTESIMO
Alfies Antique Market,
13-25 Church Street,
Marylebone, London NW8
8DT
Tel: 07767 498 766
www.alfiwesantiques.co.uk

Watches

KLEANTHOUS ANTIQUES
144 Portobello Road, London
W11 2DZ
Tel: 020 7727 3649
www.kleanthous.com

THE WATCH GALLERY
129 Fulham Road, London
SW3 6RT
Tel: 020 7581 3239
www.thewatchgallery.co.uk

FABRIC SUPPLIERS

LAURA ASHLEY
PO Box 19, Newtown,
Powys SY16 1DZ
www.lauraashley.com

DESIGNER'S GUILD
267-277 Kings Road,
London SW3 5EN
www.designersguild.com

**GAINSBOROUGH SILK
WEAVING COMPANY**
Alexandra Road, Sudbury,
Suffolk CO1O 2XH
www.gainsborough.co.uk

HARLEQUIN
Ground Floor, Centre Dome,
G12, Design Centre,
Chelsea Harbour, Lots Road,
London SW10 0XE
www.harlequin.uk.com

LEE JOFA
19 Design Centre, Chelsea
Harbour, London SW10 0XE
www.leejofa.com

WILLIAM MORRIS & CO
Chalfont House, Oxford Road,
Denham UB9 4DX
www.william-morris.co.uk

OSBORNE & LITTLE
Riverside House,
26 Osiers Road,
London, SW18 1NH
www.osborneandlittle.com

SANDERSON
Design Centre,
Chelsea Harbour, Lots Road,
London SW10 0XE
www.sanderson-uk.com

TIMOROUS BEASTIES
384 Great Western Road,
Glasgow G4 9HT
www.timorousbeasties.com/
contact

**WATTS OF
WESTMINSTER**
3/12 Third Floor,
Centre Dome, Design Centre,
Chelsea Harbour,
London SW10 0XE
www.watts1874.co.uk

ZOFFANY
Design Centre Chelsea
Harbour, Lots Road,
London SW10 0XE
www.zoffany.com

USEFUL MATERIALS

The materials for the restoration projects in this book can be purchased from the following stores:

Furniture restoration and upholsterers' suppliers: French chalk, French polish, French polish, gimp pins, gold metallic powder, hessian, liquid gold size, magnetic upholsterer's hammer, oil of spike lavender, panel pins, ripping chisel, tack lifter, teak oil, upholsterer's needle, upholsterer's tacks, varnishing brush, whiting powder.

Artists' supply shops: acid-free adhesive paper tape, acid-free card/mounting board, artist's powder pigments, artist's brushes, artist's oil paint, boiled linseed oil, clear lacquer, cold-cure lacquer, craft knife, cutting board, dusting brush, linseed oil, mount cutter kit, modelling clay, scalpel, steel ruler, titanium dioxide.

DIY stores: carpenter's wooden mallet, distilled water, clear lacquer fabric adhesive, face mask, fine sand, furniture wax, grain filler, liquid metal polish, methylated spirits, plastic goggles, needle files, paint stripper, paraffin, pliers, spray adhesive, silicon-carbide paper, white spirit, wood stain, white PVA adhesive.

Craft and hobby stores: French wire, jeweller's rouge, silk thread, two-part epoxy-resin adhesive, two-part epoxy putty.

Chemists and supermarkets: acetone, ammonia, beeswax furniture polish, borax, glycerine, microcrystalline wax, potato flour, potato starch, wax furniture polish.

Many can also be bought online from websites such as www.amazon.co.uk.

For information about furniture restoration contact the British Antique Furniture Restorers' Association www.bafra.org.uk.

For information about upholstery contact the Association of Master Upholsterers & Soft Furnishers www.upholsterers.co.uk

Acknowledgements

The publisher would like to thank the following people for their help with the creation of this book: Jane Birch, Geoff Fennell, Daniel Goode, Giulia Hetherington, Jennifer Veal and Ginny Zeal.

The publisher would like to thank the following for permission to use their images in this book.

Key: **TL** top left, **TC** top centre, **TR** top right, **ML** middle left, **C** centre, **MR** middle right, **B** bottom, **BL** bottom left, **BC** bottom centre, **BR** bottom right.

Beth Adams
www.alfiesantiques.com 83 TR.
Albert Amor
www.albertamor.co.uk 105 BL.
Anderson & Garland
www.andersonandgarland.com 89 T, 91 MR, 91 BR, 148 BR, 277 TC
Antiquités Bonneton
www.antiquites-bonneton.com 35 L
Antiquorum
www.antiquorum.com 200 BR, 201 BL, 201 BR, 202 TL, 202 BR, 203 R
Art Deco Etc.
73 Upper Gloucester Road, Brighton, BN1 3LQ 85 BL, 140 TL
Atlantique City
www.atlantiquecity.com 157 BL
At The Movies
www.atthemovies.co.uk 227 BR
Battersea Pen Home
www.penhome.co.uk 188 L, 188 C, 189 TC
Bearnes Hampton & Littlewood
www.bhandl.co.uk 12 TL, 58 BL, 193 BL, 193 BC
Bébés et Jouets
bebesetjouets@tiscali.co.uk 209 ML
Linda Bee
www.graysantiques.com 185 BR
Bertoia Auctions
www.bertoiaauctions.com 219
Block Glass Ltd.
www.blockglass.com 124 BL
N. Bloom & Son 1912 Ltd
www.nbloom.com 193 TL
Bloomsbury Auctions
www.bloomsburyauctions.com 189 TR, 189 BR, 220, 223 L, 225 all, 229 BL
Bonhams
www.bonhams.com 9 BR, 208 BL, 217

Roger Bradbury
www.trocadero.com/rogerbradbury/ 100 BC
Bucks County Antique Center
Route 202, 8 Skyline Drive, Lahaska PA 18914 USA 155 TC
Bukowskis
www.bukowskis.se 122 BL © DACS 2012
John Bull Silver
www.jbsilverware.co.uk 133 C R
Burstow & Hewett
www.burstowandhewett.co.uk 95 BR
Calderwood Gallery
www.calderwoodgallery.com 27 BR
The Calico Teddy
www.calicoteddy.com 213 BL
Candy Says
www.candysays.co.uk 160, 163 C, 168 BL, 170 TR, 177 BL, 178 BL, 181 TL
Capes Dunn
www.capesdunn.com 86 BL, 222 M
Carlton Antiques
www.carlton-antiques.com 222 BR, 223 BR
Lennox Cato
www.lennoxcato.com 25 TL
I. M. Chait
www.chait.com 97 TC
Charterhouse
www.charterhouse-auction.com 150 C, 200 BL, 210 BL
Cheffins
www.cheffins.co.uk 83 BL, 114 M, 131 T
Chisholm Larsson
www.chisholm-poster.com 226 BL
Cristobal
www.cristobal.co.uk 7, 178 BC, 196 BR, 197 BL, 198 TR, 198 BC, 199 ML, 199 MR, 268 all, 269 all
Deco Jewels
131 Thompson Street, New York, 10012 NY USA 179 BC
Decodame.com
www.decodame.com 197 BC
Dee, Atkinson & Harrison
www.dahauctions.com 54 BR, 83 TL
Delorme et Collin du Bocage
parisencheres@orange.fr 9 BL
The Design Gallery
www.designgallery.co.uk 146, 182 BR, 197 TL
Designer's Guild
www.designersguild.com 29 TL, TR, BR; 31 CBR
Dr. Fischer
www.auctions-fischer.de 15 T

Dorotheum
www.dorotheum.com 11 TL, 11 TR, 12 BL, 13 BL, 20, 38 TR, 39 BR, 48 BL © ADAGP, Paris and DACS, London 2012, 71 ML, 108, 121 BR, 124 T, 272 TL
Dreweatts
www.dnfa.com 10 BR, 15 BL, 16 BL, 22 BR, 26 BL, 26 BC, 27 BC, 34 BL, 40 TL, 40 BL, 40 R, 41 TL, 47 BR, 50 BL, 50 BR, 59 TL, 60 TR, 61 TR, 81 CB, 82 T, 82 M, 91 TL, 91 TR, 104 L, 118 M, 136 TR, 137 ML, 141 MR, 143 TL, 149 ML, 150 BL, 153 TR, 155 BC, 162 BL, 165 BL, 187 BL, 189 BL, 193 BR, 201 BC
Duke's
www.dukes-auctions.com 49 TR
The Dunlop Collection
dunloppaperweights@mac.com 124 TL, 125 MR
The End of History
548 1/2 Hudson Street, NYC 10014 USA 122 TC
Ewbank Clarke Gammon Wellers
www.ewbankauctions.co.uk 80 BL
Fielding's
www.fieldingsauctioneers.co.uk 17 BL, 85 C, 93 BR, 124 BR, 276 BR
Karl Flaherty Collectables
www.kfcollectables.com 209 BR
Fragile Design
www.fragiledesign.com 18 BR
Freeman's
www.freemansauction.com 10 BL, 18 BL, 25 BL, 48 TL © ARS, NY and DACS, London 2012, 57 BL, 61 BL, 79 C, 81 BL, 99 BL, 103 TL, 103 MR, 117 TR, 136 BR, 152 BC, 153 ML, 164 TL, 171 BL, TR, 181 C
Gainsborough Silk Weaving Company
www.gainsborough.co.uk 29 BC; 31 TC, TR, TR, BL
Galerie Koller
www.galeriekoller.ch 13 MR
Gallery 1930
18 Church Street, London NW8 8EP 84 TL
Gardiner Houlgate
www.gardinerhoulgate.co.uk 200 BC
T. W. Gaze
www.twgaze.com 49 BR, 120 BL, 186 BL, 212 B, 228 BL, 229 TL
Richard Gibbon
neljeweluk@aol.com 138 B, 178 BR, 179 BR
The Girl Can't Help It!
www.thegirlcanthelpit.com 177 TL, 180 C, 180 BL

Goodwins Antiques Ltd
www.goodwinsantiques.com 137 TR
Gorringes
www.gorringes.co.uk 8 BL, 8 BC, 8 BR, 17 TR, 23 TR, 47 TR, 79 CT, 93 TR, 102 TL, 103 TR, 148 BL, 152 L, 159 BL, 163 MR, 163 BR, 214 BL, 224 L, 228 MR, 275 M
Graham Cooley Collection
118 L, 118 R, 119 TR 119 C, BR, 120 BC, 123 BL, 140 BL, 141 BR
Gary Grant
garygrant@btopenworld.com 88 BL
Ken Grant
www.alfiesantiques.com 150 BR
Adrian Grater
adriangrater@tiscali.co.uk 88 R
Andrea Hall Levy
www.loftyvintage.com 179 BL
Harlequin
www.harlequin.uk.com 31 TR
Andrew Hartley
www.andrewhartleyfinearts.co.uk 46 BL, 83 ML, 226 BR
Jeanette Hayhurst Fine Glass
www.antiqueglass-london.com 111 R, 115 L, 115 R, 122 BR, 123 TL
Leslie Hindman Auctioneers
www.lesliehindman.com 14 BR, 16 TR, 23 BL, 79 BL, 110 BR, 128, 143 TR, 143 BR, 168 BC, 176 L, 176 C, 190, 199 TR, 274 TR
Sara Hughes
sara@sneak.freeserve.co.uk, 183 TL
It's Vintage Darling
www.itsvintagedarling.com 181 TR
Ivey Selkirk Auctioneers
www.iveyselkirk.com 55 ML, 130
James D Julia Inc
www.jamesdjulia.com 125 BR, 159 R, 18 4 BR
Jazzy Art Deco
www.jazzyartdeco.co.uk 51 BR
Auktionshaus Kaupp
www.kaupp.de 78 BL, 110 T, 215 BL
KCS Ceramics
www.kcsceramics-international.co.uk 89 MR
The Lalique Mascot Collectors' Club
www.carsofbrighton.co.uk 187 TR
Laura Ashley
www.lauraashley.com 31 BR
Lawrences
www.lawrencesbletchingley.co.uk 96 TR

Andrew Lineham
www.antiquecolouredglass.com
114 R, 184 TL

Lucy's Hat
shak06@aol.com 177 BR

Lyon & Turnbull Ltd
www.lyonandturnbull.com
1, 9 BC, 10 TR, 17 TR, 22 TL, 23 TL,
26 BR, 34 R, 46 BR, 50 TL, 51 TC,
51 TR, 51 BL, 54 BL, 56 TL, 61 BR,
85 TR, 87 BR, 97 BL, 99 CR, 103
ML, 111 TL, 111 C, 119 TL, 121
BL, 131 BR, 132 TR, BR, 134 BR,
135 BR, 137 BR, 138 ML, 138 TR,
139 BL, 139 BC, 139 BR © ADAGP,
Paris and DACS, London 2012,
154 B, 163 TR, 164 BR, 183 BR,
188 B, 192 TL, 192 C,195 BR, 222
BL, 229 BR, 235 TR

Macklowe Gallery
www.macklowegallery.com
35 BR, 116 BL, 139 T

The Magic Toybox
www.magictoybox.co.uk 215
TR, BC

Manic Attic
www.alfiesantiques.com 19 TR

Marie Antiques
www.marieantiques.co.uk 192 B

Mark of Time
lecoultre@verizon.net 186 BR,
201 TR, 202 BL

Maxwells
www.maxwells-auctioneers.
co.uk 25 BR

R & G McPherson Antiques
www.orientalceramics.com 100
BL, 100 BR, 101 BL, 101 BC, 101 BR

Auktionshaus Metz
www.Metz-Auktion.de 78 TL

Morphets
www.morphets.co.uk 224 BR

William Morris & Co
www.william-morris.co.uk 31 BC

Alan Moss
436 Lafayette Street, New York,
NY 10003, USA 41 BL

Nagel Auktionen
www.auction.de 71 TL

Lillian Nassau
www.lilliannassau.com 123 BR

Neet-O-Rama
www.neetstuff.com 183 BL,
228 TL

John Nicholsons
www.johnnicholsons.com
48 BR, 49 ML

Norman Adams Ltd
www.normanadams.com 34 BL

Onslows
www.onslows.co.uk 226 BC

Osborne & Little
www.osborneandlittle.com
29 TL

Holly Palmer/Alamy
236 TR

Paola & Iaia
www.alfiesantiques.com 149 TR

W & H Peacock
www.peacockauction.co.uk 23
BR, 90 BL, 91 BC, 92 all, 93 TR, 93
BL, 159 T

Pook & Pook
www.pookandpook.com 34 TL,
154 ML

Potteries Specialist Auctions
www.potteriesauctions.com 91 BC

Quittenbaum Kunstauktionen
www.quittenbaum.de 18 TL, 27
BL, 57 TL, 86 BR, 116 BR, 120 T,
120 BR, 121 T, 121 BC

David Rago Auctions
www.ragoarts.com 38 B, 41 BR,
48 TR, 49 TL, 49 BL, 56 BR, 57
TR, 57 BR, 59 BR, 116 T, 117 L ©
ADAGP, Paris and DACS, London
2012, 164 BL, 165 TL, 185 TL, 185
TC, 185 TR, 185 BL, 277 CB

Rennies
www.rennart.co.uk 88 TL

Ritchies
www.ritchies.com 165 CL

Derek Roberts Clocks
www.qualityantiqueclocks.com
272 BR

Geoffrey Robinson
www.alfiesantiques.com 141 BL

Rosebery's
www.roseberys.co.uk 17 BR, 60
TL, 90 TL, 93 TL, 158 BR

Sanderson,
www.sanderson-uk.com, 30 BR,
31 CTL, CTC, CTR

**Charlotte Sayers Antique
Jewellery**
www.charlottesayers.co.uk 273 CB

Sign of the Tymes
www.millantiques.com 209 BL

Skinner inc.
www.skinnerinc.com 13 TR, 55
BL, 55 BR, 87 T, 215 BR

Terry Smith Rex Features
9 TR

Sotheby's
www.sothebys.com 7, 54 TR, 55
T, 94 BR, 142 TL, 165 BR, 203 BL

Special Auction Services
www.specialauctionservices.
com 187 TL, 187 BR, 209 TL, 210
BR, 211 ML

Steppes Hill Farm Antiques
www.steppeshillfarmantiques.
com 71 BL

Swann Galleries
www.swanngalleries.com 227
TR, 227 BL, 227 BC

Sworders
www.sworder.co.uk 59 BL, 60 BL,
81 T, 82 B, 151 MR, 276 CL

Kerry Taylor Auctions
www.kerrytaylorauctions.com
162 T, 169 BC, BR, 171 BC, BR

Tecta
www.tecta.de 56 BC

Teddy Bears of Witney
www.teddybears.co.uk 213 TL

Tennants
www.tennants.co.uk 14 TR, 39
TL, 39 BL, 39 TR, 41 MR, 54 TL,
58 TR, 60 TL, 81 BR, 123 TR, 132
T, 134 BL, 135 M, 137 TL, 137 BL,
151 TR, 183 MR, 187 ML, 203 ML,
238 TR, 273 CT, 274 T, 275 CR,
276 C, 277 CL, 277 TR

Timorous Beasties
www.timorousbeasties.com 30
BL, 31 TL, TR, TC, CL

Titus Omega
www.titusomega.com 15 BR

Tring Market Auctions
www.tringmarketauctions.co.uk
60 BR, 272 C, 276 BL

Mary and Geoff Turvil
Forest.Antiques@virgin.net 157
BR, 182 BL, 183 TR

Van Sabben
www.vansabbenauctions.nl
223 TR

Vectis Auctions Ltd
www.vectis.co.uk 208 BR, 210 TL,
211 TR, 211 MR, 211 BR, 214 MB

Ventesimo
www.alfiesantiques.com 211 BL

Victoriana Dolls
heather.bond@totalserve.co.uk
214 BR, 215 BC

VinMagCo
www.vinmag.com 223 MR

Vintage Eyewear of NYC inc.
Tel: 001 646 319 9222 176 R

Vintage to Vogue
www.vintagetovoguebath.co.uk
170 TL

**Von Zezschwitz Kunst und
Design**
www.von-zezschwitz.de
274 TL

Wallis & Wallis
www.wallisandwallis.co.uk 210
TR

Watts of Westminster
www.watts1874.co.uk, 31 BC,
BL, BC

Woolley & Wallis
www.woolleyandwallis.co.uk 9
BML, 14 BL, BR, 19 BL, 19 BR, 22
BL, 35 TR, 39 MR, 41 TR, 46 TR, 47
L, 51 TL, 53 BR, 68, 78 BR, 79 TR, 79
BR, 80 BC, 80 BR, 84 M, 84 BR, 85
MR, 85 BR, 87 BC, 87 BR, 90 TR, 94
L, 94 TR, 95 TL, 95 TR, 95 C, 95 BL,
96 BL, 97 TL, 97 TR, 97 BR, 98 all,
99 TL, TR, CR, 102 BR, 104 TR, 104
BR, 123 MR © DACS 2012, 125 TL,
125 TR, 127, 132 BL, 133 CL, BL,
134 TL, 136 left, 142 BR, 143 BL,
150 TL, 151 BL, 152 TC, 154 TL, 186
T, 203 TL, 234 BL, 272 TL, 273 BR,
274 CL, 275 BL, 275 TL

Basia Zarzycka
www.basia-zarzycka.com 180
TL, 180 TR

Zoffany
www.zoffany.com 30 BL

We would like to thank the
following for their help in
compiling the understanding
furniture, ceramics, silver
and glass information on
pages 242-267: Albert Amor,
Alderfer, Alfies Antiques
Market, Anderson & Garland,
Antique Glass @ Frank Dux
Antiques, Auktionshaus
Kaupp, Bearnes, Hampton
& Littlewood, Bellmans,
Bergmann, Bonhams, Brunk
Auctions, Calderwood Gallery,
Capes Dunn, Charterhouse,
Cheffins, Clevedon Auction
Rooms, The Country Seat,
Daniel Bexfield Antiques,
David Lowe, Dee Atkinson &
Harrison, DeLorenzo Gallery,
Dorotheum, Dreweatts, Dukes,
DuMouchelles, Eileen Lane,
Elaine Phillips Antiques,
Fieldings, Freeman's, Galerie
Girard, Galerie Hélène
Fournier Guérin, Gillian Neale,
Gorringes, Hartley's, IM Chait, J
Clarke, Jazzy Art Deco, Jeanette
Hayhurst, John Howard, John
Nicholson, Law Fine Art,
Lawrences, Lennox Cato, Leslie
Hindman, Lyon & Turnbull,
Mallets, Moderne Gallery,
Northeast Auctions, P Weiss,
Pantry and Hearth, Partridges,
Pook & Pook, Puritan Values,
Quittenbaum Kuntsauktionen,
R&G McPhearson, David Rago
Auctions, Richard Gardner
Antiques, Ritches, Roseberys,
Sue Brewer, Skinner Inc,
Somervale Antiques, Sothebys,
Steppes Hill Antiques,
Stockspring Antiques,
Sworders, Tecta, Tennants,
Tooveys, Tring Auction Rooms,
Von Zezschwitz, W&H Peacock,
Wiener Kunst Auktionen -
Palais Kinsky, William Walters,
Woolley & Wallis.

For their help with compiling
the understanding dolls and
teddy bears information on
pages 270-271: Bergmann,
Bertoia Auctions, Black Horse
Antique Showcase, Dawson &
Nye Auctioneers & Appraisers,
Fellows & Sons, Kathy Martin,
Kunst-Auktionshaus Martin
Wendl, Leander Harwood,
Magic Toy Box, Skinner
Inc, Teddy Bears of Witney,
Victoriana Dolls.

All other images property of
Miller's/Octopus Publishing
Group Ltd.

Index